# Computing Essentials

## Making IT work for you

**INTRODUCTORY 2014**

# • The O'Leary Series

## Computing Concepts

- *Computing Essentials 2012* Introductory & Complete Editions
- *Computing Essentials 2013* Introductory & Complete Editions
- *Computing Essentials 2014* Introductory & Complete Editions

## Microsoft Office Applications

- *Microsoft® Office 2010: A Case Approach*
- *Microsoft® Office Word 2010: A Case Approach* Introductory & Complete Editions
- *Microsoft® Office Excel 2010: A Case Approach* Introductory & Complete Editions
- *Microsoft® Office Access 2010: A Case Approach* Introductory & Complete Editions
- *Microsoft® Office PowerPoint 2010: A Case Approach* Introductory & Complete Editions
- *Microsoft® Windows 7: A Case Approach*
- *Microsoft® Office 2013: A Case Approach*
- *Microsoft® Office Word 2013: A Case Approach* Introductory Edition
- *Microsoft® Office Excel 2013: A Case Approach* Introductory Edition
- *Microsoft® Office Access 2013: A Case Approach* Introductory Edition
- *Microsoft® Office PowerPoint 2013: A Case Approach* Introductory Edition

# Computing Essentials

## Making IT work for you

### INTRODUCTORY 2014

**Timothy J. O'Leary**

*Professor Emeritus*
*Arizona State University*

**Linda I. O'Leary**

McGraw Hill

*Connect*
*Learn*
*Succeed*™

COMPUTING ESSENTIALS 2014 INTRODUCTORY EDITION: MAKING IT WORK FOR YOU
Published by McGraw-Hill, a business unit of The McGraw-Hill Companies, Inc., 1221 Avenue of the Americas, New York, NY, 10020. Copyright © 2014 by The McGraw-Hill Companies, Inc. All rights reserved. Printed in the United States of America. No part of this publication may be reproduced or distributed in any form or by any means, or stored in a database or retrieval system, without the prior written consent of The McGraw-Hill Companies, Inc., including, but not limited to, in any network or other electronic storage or transmission, or broadcast for distance learning.

Some ancillaries, including electronic and print components, may not be available to customers outside the United States.

This book is printed on acid-free paper.

2 3 4 5 6 7 8 9 0 QVS/QVS 1 0 9 8 7 6 5 4 3

ISBN      978-0-07-779153-7
MHID      0-07-779153-3
ISSN      2159-6336

Senior Vice President, Products & Markets: *Kurt L. Strand*
Vice President, General Manager, Products & Markets: *Brent Gordon*
Vice President, Content Production & Technology Services: *Kimberly Meriwether David*
Director: *Scott Davidson*
Senior Brand Manager: *Wyatt Morris*
Executive Director of Development: *Ann Torbert*
Development Editor: *Alan Palmer*
Digital Development Editor: *Kevin White*
Marketing Manager: *Tiffany Russell*
Project Manager: *Marlena Pechan*
Senior Buyer: *Michael R. McCormick*
Senior Designer: *Srdjan Savanovic*
Cover Design: *George Kokkonas*
Cover Image: *©Leigh Prather/Veer*
Senior Content Licensing Specialist: *Jeremy Cheshareck*
Photo Researcher: *Colleen Miller*
Media Project Manager: *Brent dela Cruz*
Media Project Manager: *Cathy L. Tepper*
Typeface: *10/12 Palatino LT*
Compositor: *Laserwords Private Limited*
Printer: *Quad/Graphics*

All credits appearing at the end of the book are considered to be an extension of the copyright page.

The Internet addresses listed in the text were accurate at the time of publication. The inclusion of a website does not indicate an endorsement by the authors or McGraw-Hill, and McGraw-Hill does not guarantee the accuracy of the information presented at these sites.

www.mhhe.com

# Dedication

We dedicate this edition to Dan, Nicole, and Katie—our inspiration.

# Brief Contents

# Contents

# New to Computing Essentials 2014

Every Making IT Work for You, Ethics, Environment, and Exploration has been carefully reevaluated, enhanced, and/or replaced. Additionally, this in-chapter content has been carefully coordinated with a new end-of-chapter section titled Discussion that provides thought-provoking questions designed for in-class discussion or homework assignments. More specific new coverage includes the following.

| | |
|---|---|
| Chapter 1 | Expansion of the traditional five-part information system to formally include connectivity |
| | Expanded coverage of Windows 8, tablets, and servers. |
| | New Making IT Work: Installing a Free Antivirus |
| Chapter 2 | Expanded coverage of cascading style sheets (CSS), JavaScript, AJAX, applets, Apple's Mail, and Microsoft's Outlook |
| | New Making IT Work for You: Online Entertainment |
| | New Look to the Future: Your Car's Dashboard as a Powerful, Internet-Connected Computing Device |
| Chapter 3 | Combined last year's Chapter 3, "Basic Application Software," and Chapter 4, "Specialized Application Software," into a single chapter titled "Application Software" |
| | Focused discussion of word processors, spreadsheets, database management systems, and presentation programs on essential concepts |
| | New Making IT Work for You: Image Editing |
| | New Look to the Future: Next-Generation User Interfaces |
| Chapter 4 | Expanded coverage of gesture controls, mobile operating systems, Microsoft's Windows 8, and Apple's Mountain Lion |
| | New Making IT Work for You: Windows Task Manager |
| Chapter 5 | Expanded coverage comparing smartphone, tablet, notebook, and desktop components |
| | New Making IT Work for You: Keeping Your Computer Cool |
| | New Look to the Future: Chips inside Your Brain |
| Chapter 6 | Expanded comparison of traditional, notebook, virtual, and thumb keyboards |
| | Added coverage of game controllers, motion-sensing devices, robotics, and ergonomics |
| | New Making IT Work for You: Skype |
| | New Look to the Future: Augmented Reality Displays |
| Chapter 7 | Expanded coverage of Blu-ray discs |
| | Added coverage of a new IT Career: Disaster recovery specialist |
| | New Look to the Future: Next-Generation Storage |
| Chapter 8 | Expanded coverage of Bluetooth, Wi-Fi, infrared, and routers |
| | Added graphics for ring, tree, and mesh networks |
| | New Making IT Work for You: Mobile Internet |
| | New Making IT Work for You: Remote Access |
| Chapter 9 | Expanded coverage of http cookies, flash cookies, cybercrimes, and wireless networks |
| | New Making IT Work for You: Security Suites |
| | New Making IT Work for You: Cloud-Based Backup |
| | Added coverage of a new IT Career: IT security analysts |
| | New Look to the Future: The End of Anonymity |

The 20th century brought us the dawn of the digital information age and unprecedented changes in information technology. There is no indication that this rapid rate of change will be slowing—it may even be increasing. As we begin the 21st century, computer literacy is undoubtedly becoming a prerequisite in whatever career you choose.

The goal of *Computing Essentials* is to provide you with the basis for understanding the concepts necessary for success. *Computing Essentials* also endeavors to instill an appreciation for the effect of information technology on people and our environment and to give you a basis for building the necessary skill set to succeed in the 21st century.

Times are changing, technology is changing, and this text is changing too. As students of today, you are different from those of yesterday. You put much effort toward the things that interest you and the things that are relevant to you. Your efforts directed at learning application programs and exploring the web seem, at times, limitless. On the other hand, it is sometimes difficult to engage in other equally important topics such as personal privacy and technological advances.

In this text, we present practical tips related to key concepts through the demonstration of interesting applications that are relevant to your lives. Topics presented focus first on outputs rather than processes. Then, we discuss the concepts and processes.

Motivation and relevance are the keys. This text has several features specifically designed to engage and demonstrate the relevance of technology in your lives. These elements are combined with a thorough coverage of the concepts and sound pedagogical devices.

# Visual Learning

## VISUAL CHAPTER OPENERS

Each chapter begins with a list of chapter competencies or objectives and provides a brief introduction to what will be covered in the chapter. Additionally, the "Why Should I Read This?" feature provides relevance through a brief discussion of the content's historical context.

## VISUAL SUMMARIES

Visual summaries appear at the end of every chapter and summarize major concepts covered throughout the chapter. Like the chapter openers, these summaries use graphics to reinforce key concepts in an engaging and meaningful way.

# Learning Tools: The CE 2014 App

Download the free *Computing Essentials 2014* App for:

## • Key term flash cards

## • Quizzes

## • Game, *Over the Edge*

# Hands-On

## MAKING IT WORK FOR YOU

Special-interest topics are presented in the Making IT Work for You section found within nearly every chapter. These topics include Online Entertainment, Image Editing, Google Docs, Skype, and Cloud Storage.

# Reinforcing Key Concepts

## CONCEPT CHECKS

Located at points throughout each chapter, the Concept Check cues you to note which topics have been covered and to self-test your understanding of the material already discussed.

### ☑ concept check

Define data. List four common types of files.

Define connectivity and the wireless revolution.

What is a network? Describe the Internet, web, and cloud computing.

## KEY TERMS

### KEY TERMS

active display area (163)
active-matrix organic light-emitting diode (AMOLED) (163)
artificial intelligence (AI) (169)
aspect ratio (163)
bar code (159)
bar code reader (159)
bar code scanner (159)
card reader (159)
carpal tunnel syndrome (173)
cathode-ray tube (CRT) (165)
clarity (162)
cloud printer (167)
combination key (155)
contrast ratio (163)
cordless mouse (156)
dance pad (157)
digital camera (160)
digital media player (168)
digital video camera (160)
digital whiteboard (165)
display screen (162)
document scanner (159)
dot pitch (163)
dots per inch (dpi) (166)
duplex printing (166)
e-book reader (163)
e-books (163)
e-ink (163)
e-reader (163)
electronic books (163)
ergonomics (172)
flat-panel monitor (163)
flatbed scanner (159)
game controller (157)
gamepads (157)
gloves (172)
Google Cloud Print (167)
grayscale (166)
handwriting recognition software (157)
hard copy (165)
headgear (172)
headsets (168)

high-definition television (HDTV) (165)
household robot (169)
immersive experience (172)
industrial robot (169)
inkjet printer (166)
input (154)
input device (154)
interactive whiteboard (165)
Internet telephone (169)
Internet telephony (169)
IP telephony (169)
joystick (157)
keyboard (154)
laser printer (167)
liquid crystal display (LCD) (163)
magnetic card reader (159)
magnetic-ink character recognition (MICR) (160)
mobile digital television (168)
mobile DTV (168)
mobile robot (169)
monitor (162)
motion-sensing device (157)
mouse (156)
mouse pointer (156)
multifunctional device (MFD) (169)
multitouch screen (157)
notebook keyboard (155)
optical-character recognition (OCR) (160)
optical-mark recognition (OMR) (160)
optical mouse (156)
optical scanner (158)
output (162)
output device (162)
perception system
robot (169)
personal laser printer (167)
photo printer (161)

picture element (162)
pixel (162)
pixel pitch (163)
platform scanner (159)
plotter (167)
pointing device (156)
pointing stick (157)
portable media player (168)
portable scanner (159)
printer (165)
repetitive strain injury (RSI) (173)
resolution (162, 166)
RFID reader (160)
RFID (radio-frequency identification) tag (159)
robot (169)
robotics (169)
scanner (158)
scanning devices (158)
shared laser printer (167)
Skype (169)
soft copy (162)
speakers (168)
stylus (157)
technical writer (174)
telephony (169)
thermal printer (167)
thin-film transistor liquid crystal (TFT-LC) (163)
thumb keyboard (155)
toggle key (155)
touch pad (157)
touch screen (157)
trackball (156)
traditional keyboard (155)
Universal Product Code (UPC) (159)
virtual keyboard (155)
virtual reality (VR) (172)
voice over IP (VoIP) (169)
voice recognition system (161)
wand reader (159)
webcam (161)
wheel button (156)
wireless mouse (156)

## KEY TERMS

Throughout the text, the most important terms are presented in bold and are defined within the text. You will also find a list of key terms at the end of each chapter and in the glossary at the end of the book.

## CHAPTER REVIEW

Following the Visual Summary, the chapter review includes material designed to review and reinforce chapter content. It includes a Key Terms list that reiterates the terms presented in the chapter, Multiple-Choice questions to help test your understanding of information presented in the chapter, Matching exercises to test your recall of terminology presented in the chapter, and Open-Ended questions or statements to help review your understanding of the key concepts presented in the chapter.

### MULTIPLE CHOICE

Circle the letter of the correct answer.

1. The keyboard, mouse, monitor, and system unit are:
   - a. hardware
   - b. output devices
   - c. storage devices
   - d. software

2. Programs that coordinate computer resources, provide an interface, and run applications are known as:
   - a. application programs
   - b. operating systems
   - c. storage systems
   - d. utility programs

3. A browser is an example of a:
   - a. general-purpose application
   - b. specialized program
   - c. system application
   - d. utility program

4. Although not as powerful as a supercomputer, this type of computer is capable of great processing speeds and data storage.
   - a. mainframe
   - b. midrange
   - c. notebook
   - d. tablet

5. The smallest type of microcomputer:
   - a. handheld
   - b. notebook
   - c. midrange
   - d. tablet

6. RAM is a type of:
   - a. computer
   - b. memory
   - c. network
   - d. secondary storage

7. Unlike memory, this type of storage holds data and programs even after electric power to the computer system has been turned off.
   - a. primary
   - b. RAM
   - c. ROM
   - d. secondary

8. The type of file created by word processors to save, for example, memos, term papers, and letters.
   - a. database
   - b. document
   - c. presentation
   - d. worksheet

9. Uses the Internet and the web to shift many computer activities from a user's computer to computers on the Internet.
   - a. cloud computing
   - b. high definition
   - c. network
   - d. USB

10. The largest network in the world is [the]:
    - a. Facebook
    - b. Internet
    - c. web
    - d. USB

For an interactive multiple-choice practice test, visit our website at www.computing2014.com and enter the keyword multiple1. You can also access quizzes using the *Computing Essentials 2014* app.

# The Future of Information Technology

## CAREERS IN IT

Some of the fastest-growing career opportunities are in information technology. Each chapter highlights one of the most promising careers in IT by presenting job titles, responsibilities, educational requirements, and salary ranges. Among the careers covered are webmaster, software engineer, and database administrator. You will learn how the material you are studying relates directly to a potential career path.

## A LOOK TO THE FUTURE

Each chapter concludes with a brief discussion of a recent technological advancement related to the chapter material, reinforcing the importance of staying informed.

# Unique End-of-Chapter Discussion Materials

## MAKING IT WORK FOR YOU

Making IT Work for You discussion questions are carefully integrated with the chapter's Making IT Work for You topics. The questions facilitate in-class discussion or written assignments focusing on applying specific technologies into a student's day-to-day life. They are designed to expand a student's awareness of technology applications.

## EXPLORATIONS

Explorations discussion questions are carefully integrated with the chapter's marginal Explorations boxes. The questions facilitate in-class discussion or written assignments focusing on locating and learning more in-depth content on specific topics. They are designed to encourage independent investigation and learning.

### DISCUSSION

Respond to each of the following questions.

**1 Making IT Work for You: ONLINE ENTERTAINMENT**

Are you one of the millions of people who regularly use streaming technology to watch favorite television programs, movies, and other video content? Review the Making IT Work for You: Online Entertainment on pages 30 and 31 and then respond to the following: (a) Do you currently have a subscription to Netflix, Hulu Plus, or another service that allows you to stream movies and TV shows? If so, which ones? If not, do you plan on using one in the future? Why or why not? (b) Name at least three TV shows that you currently watch or are interested in watching. Next, list a few services that include these shows as part of a subscription. If none does, list a few online stores where you can purchase and stream these episodes. (c) What device do you use most often to watch video content from the web? Would you consider purchasing a dedicated streaming device such as the Roku? Why or why not? (d) Could ever see yourself canceling or "cutting the cord" from your current cable or satellite service? Why or why not?

**2 Making IT Work for You: TWITTER**

Did you know that Twitter can be used to follow friends, businesses, and celebrities, as well as discover breaking news and emerging trends? Review the Making IT Work for You: Twitter on pages 40 and 41 and create a Twitter account if you do not already have one. Then respond to the following: (a) In your opinion, what are the primary benefits of Twitter? (b) List five users that you currently follow or would like to follow in the future. Why did you select those individuals or organizations? (c) If you have already posted your own tweets, briefly explain the type of content you typically post. If you have not posted anything, do you feel that you will in the future? Why or why not?

**3 Explorations: INTERNET HISTORY**

How much do you know about the history of the Internet and the web? Review the Explorations box on page 28 and then respond to the following: (a) What was the original Internet known as? In what year was it activated? How many locations did it connect? (b) In what year was TCP/IP created? Why was this development so important? (c) Who created the World Wide Web? In what year was it introduced to the public? What were some of the factors that allowed it to succeed? (d) What was the first graphical web browser? Who created it? Why was the browser so revolutionary?

**4 Explorations: DIGITAL WALLETS**

Did you know that your smartphone could be used to hold all your credit cards, coupons, and gift cards? Review the Explorations box on page 45 and then respond to the following: (a) What is the name of the digital wallet product? Which mobile operating systems is it compatible with? Does your smartphone need to have a specific technology to complete in-person transactions? If so, what? (b) How does this product work? Provide details on both the setup and use of the product. (c) Is this technology safe and secure? Support your answer with details. (d) Find three stores in your area that accept payments with this technology. If none exists in your area, list three online stores. (e) Would you use a digital wallet? Why or why not?

---

**5 Ethics: BLOGS**

Almost half a million people are paid to create blogs, and many of those are being paid to write favorable reviews of products and services. Review the Ethics box on page 38 and respond to the following: (a) Do you think it is unethical for bloggers to write positive reviews for the companies that pay them? Why or why not? (b) Should there be disclaimers on paid blog posts? If so, how can such a policy be enforced? Explain your answer. (c) If you found out that a particular company paid bloggers for favorable reviews, would you continue to buy its products? Why or why not? (d) If you were to use a blog for product information, what could you do to determine whether the content is unbiased?

**6 Ethics: FILTERING AND MONITORING**

Parents can use content filters and monitoring software to restrict or monitor their child's Internet behavior. Review the Ethics box on page 49 and respond to the following: (a) Is it ethical for parents to filter Internet content that they deem to be unsafe or inappropriate for their children? Does your answer depend on the age of the child? Defend your position. (b) Is it ethical for parents to monitor the Internet activity of their children? What if the monitoring software captures more than just web pages? What if it records instant messages, incoming e-mail, and even passwords? Explain your position. (c) Should parents inform their children that Internet activity is being filtered or monitored? Why or why not? (d) Do you feel that filtering or monitoring software is the best way to protect children? Do you feel that it hurts the trust between a parent and child? In your responses, be sure to include your opinion as to whether or not you would ever use such software.

**7 Environment: E-MAIL**

Did you know that using e-mail and managing your bills on the web are good for the environment? Review the Environment box on page 35 and then respond to the following: (a) When it comes to sending letters, holiday cards, and invitations to friends and family, do you mostly use e-mail or postal mail? What are your reasons for choosing one over the other? (b) Are there any situations where you feel that using e-mail would not be advantageous? (c) Have you signed up for paperless billing from your financial institutions and utility companies? Why or why not? (d) Go through all the paper mail you have received in the last week or two. Is there anything there that you could receive via e-mail or view on the web? List a few examples.

**8 Environment: CLOUD COMPUTING**

Did you know that the move to cloud computing could benefit the environment? Review the Environment box on page 46 and then use a search engine to find a cloud computing company that claims to offer energy-saving benefits. Respond to the following questions about your research: (a) How does this company's cloud services benefit the environment? (b) What steps has the cloud company taken to reduce their carbon emissions? (c) Do you believe that cloud computing is more energy efficient than having many companies running their own servers? Why or why not? (d) Is it possible that the expansion of cloud computing could actually increase the overall energy consumption of the planet? Explain your answer.

## ETHICS

Ethics discussion questions are carefully integrated with the chapter's marginal Ethics boxes. The questions facilitate in-class discussion or written assignments focusing on ethical issues relating to technology. They are designed to develop a student's ability to think critically and communicate effectively.

## ENVIRONMENT

Environment discussion questions are carefully integrated with the chapter's marginal Environment boxes. The questions facilitate in-class discussion or written assignments focusing on environmental issues relating to technology. They are designed to develop a student's ability to think critically and communicate effectively.

# Support Materials

The Instructor's Manual offers lecture outlines with teaching notes and figure references. It provides definitions of key terms and solutions to the end-of-chapter material, including multiple-choice, matching, and open-ended questions.

The PowerPoint slides are designed to provide instructors with a comprehensive resource for lecture use. The slides include a review of key terms and topics, as well as artwork taken from the text to further explain concepts covered in each chapter.

The testbank contains over 2,200 questions categorized by level of learning (definition, concept, and application). This is the same learning scheme that is introduced in the text to provide a valuable testing and reinforcement tool. Text page references have been provided for all questions, including a level-of-difficulty rating. The testbank is offered in Word files, as well as in EZ Test format.

The instructor support materials can be downloaded at www.mhhe.com/ce2014.

# The O'Leary Website

The O'Leary website can be found at www.computing2014.com. Students can find a host of additional resources on the website, including animations of key concepts and in-depth coverage of select topics.

## O'LEARY SERIES

The O'Leary Application Series for Microsoft® Office is available separately or packaged with *Computing Essentials*. The O'Leary Application Series offers a step-by-step approach to learning computer applications and is available in both complete and introductory versions.

## SIMNET ONLINE TRAINING AND ASSESSMENT FOR OFFICE APPLICATIONS

SIMnet™ Online provides a way for you to test students' software skills in a simulated environment. SIMnet provides flexibility for you in your applications course by offering:

- Pretesting options
- Posttesting options
- Course placement testing
- Diagnostic capabilities to reinforce skills
- Web delivery of tests
- Learning verification reports

For more information on skills assessment software, please contact your local sales representative, or visit us at www.simnetkeepitsimple.com.

# Acknowledgments

A special thank-you goes to Ralph De Arazoza of Miami Dade College and to Lyn Belisle of Trinity University for their outstanding contributions. Professor Belisle reviewed, edited, and developed content and questions for the Ethics feature that appears throughout the text. Professor De Arazoza's contributions spanned the entire text. His consultation on content and his contributions to the Making IT Work for You, Explorations, Ethics, Environment, and The Computer Buyer's Guide features were invaluable. We would also like to extend our thanks to the professors who took time out of their busy schedules to provide us with the feedback necessary to develop the 2014 edition of this text. The following professors offered valuable suggestions on revising the text:

**Diane Stark**
*Phoenix College*

**Fred Bartlett Jr.**
*The Community College of Baltimore County, Catonsville*

**Brenda Killingsworth**
*East Carolina University*

**Beverly Bohn**
*Park University*

**Jane Liefert**
*Middlesex County College*

**Mary Ann Zlotow**
*College of DuPage*

**Debra Geoghan**
*Bucks County Community College*

**Ruth Kurlandsky**
*SUNY College of Environmental Science and Forestry*

**Gabriele Meiselwitz**
*Towson University*

**Phil Feinberg**
*Palomar College*

**Hak Joon Kim**
*Southern Connecticut State University*

**James Gordon Patterson**
*Paradise Valley Community College*

**Matthew Zullo**
*Wake Technical Community College*

**Karen Crisonino**
*County College of Morris*

**Laura Ringer**
*Piedmont Technical College*

**Laura Hunt**
*Tulsa Community College*

**Marianne Murphy**
*North Carolina Central University*

**Michael W. Scroggins**
*Missouri State University*

**Harry Reif**
*James Madison University*

**Walter Pistone**
*Palomar College*

**Syed Raza**
*Talladega College*

**David H. Trimble**
*Park University, Fort Bliss Campus*

**Janine Tiffany**
*Reading Area Community College*

**Patti Hammerle**
*IUPUI Kelley School of Business*

**Bahram Zartoshty**
*California State University, Northridge*

**Cindy Herbert**
*Metropolitan Community College, Longview*

**Paul Benjamin**
*Pace University*

**Sandy Weber**
*Gateway Technical College*

**Katherine Herbert-Berger**
*Montclair State University*

**Lynne Lyon**
*Durham College, Oshawa Campus*

**Morris Pondfield**
*Towson University*

**Irene Joos**
*La Roche College*

**Maureen J. Dunn**
*Penn State University*

**Bala R. Subramanian**
*Kean University*

**William E. Spangler**
*Duquesne University*

**Charles R. Whealton**
*Delaware Technical & Community College*

**Diane Lending**
*James Madison University*

**Brenda Nielsen**
*Mesa Community College, Red Mountain Campus*

**Arthur Schneider**
*Portland Community College*

**Bonita Volker**
*Tidewater Community College, Norfolk Campus*

**Kim Hopkins**
*Weatherford College*

**Jeffrey S. Childs**
*Clarion University of Pennsylvania*

**Shannon Scanlon**
*Henry Ford Community College*

**Antoon W. Rufi**
*ECPI University*

**Cindi Smatt**
*Texas A&M University*

**Ram Raghuraman**
*Joliet Junior College*

**Rachel Hinton**
*Broome Community College*

**Ted Ahlberg**
*Our Lady of the Lake University*

**Diane Kosharek**
*Madison Area Technical College*

**Cliff Brozo**
*Monroe College*

**Norma E. Hall**
*Manor College*

**Hollis Davis**
*Fisher College*

**Barbara Buckner**
*Lee University*

**Dr. Don Southwell**
*Delta College*

**Hal P. Kingsley**
*Trocaire College*

**Emily Holliday**
*Campbell University*

**Gerald Hensel**
*University of Central Florida*

**Shaunda Roach**
*Oakwood University*

**Linda Johnsonius**
*Murray State University*

**Mary Carole Hollingsworth**
*Georgia Perimeter College*

**Gerald Sampson**
*Walla Walla Community College*

**Barbara Neequaye**
*Central Piedmont Community College*

**Dave Evans**
*Pasadena City College*

**Farha Ali**
*Lander University*

**James Chaffee**
*University of Iowa*

**David Barnes**
*Penn State University Altoona*

**Astrid Hoy Todd**
*Guilford Technical Community College*

**Joyce Thompson**
*Lehigh Carbon Community College*

**Susan Mahon**
*Collin College*

**Debra Chapman**
*University of South Alabama*

**Carson Haury**
*Central Oregon Community College*

**Michael Taylor**
*Seattle Central Community College*

**Mike Jochen**
*East Stroudsburg University*

**Kate Burkes**
*Northwest Arkansas Community College*

**Terri Holly**
*Indian River State College*

**David Largent**
*Ball State University*

**Glenna Stites**
*Johnson County Community College*

**Timothy Holston**
*Mississippi Valley State University*

**Anthony Nowakowski**
*Buffalo State College*

**Wilma Andrews**
*Virginia Commonwealth University*

**Bettye J. Parham**
*Daytona State College*

**Charles DeSassure**
*Tarrant County College, Southeast Campus*

**Asela M. Thomason**
*California State University, Long Beach*

**Stefan Robila**
*Montclair State University*

**Irene Bruno**
*George Mason University*

**Richard A. Flores**
*Citrus College*

**Kristi Smith**
*Allegany College of Maryland*

**Sue Bajt**
*Harper College*

**Yolanda Pritchard**
*Wayne Community College*

**Anita Laird**
*Schoolcraft College*

**Debbie Franklin**
*Bryant & Stratton College*

**Stephen Cheskiewicz**
*Keystone College*

**Gina Bowers-Miller**
*Harrisburg Area Community College*

**Deb Fells**
*Mesa Community College*

**John P. Panzica**
*Community College of Rhode Island*

**John Mensing**
*Brookdale Community College*

**Ramona R. Santa Maria**
*Buffalo State College*

**Owen Herman**
*Metropolitan State College of Denver*

**Eloise Newsome**
*Northern Virginia Community College*

**Jennifer Ivey**
*Central Carolina Community College*

**John Jemison**
*Dallas Baptist University*

**Mike Michaelson**
*Palomar College*

**Andrew Hardin**
*University of Nevada, Las Vegas*

**Karen Arlien**
*Bismarck State College*

**Casey Wilhelm**
*North Idaho College*

**Sophia Wilberscheid**
*Indian River State College*

**Beverly Amer**
*Northern Arizona University*

**Emanuel Emanouilidis**
*Kean University*

**Patricia Partyka**
*Schoolcraft College*

**Diane Santurri**
*Johnson & Wales University*

**Janet Pickard**
*Chattanooga State Community College*

**Gary L. Shelton**
*Southern Crescent Technical College*

**Michelle Vlaich-Lee**
*Greenville Technical College*

**Vicky Seehusen**
*Metropolitan State College Denver*

**Terri Holly**
*Indian River State College*

**Kate LeGrand**
*Broward College, South Campus*

**Steve St. John**
*Tulsa Community College*

**Eric Bothur**
*Midlands Technical College*

**Penny Cypert**
*Tarrant County College, Northeast Campus*

**Susan Fuschetto**
*Cerritos College*

**Sue Van Boven**
*Paradise Valley Community*

Our sincere thanks also go to Gary Sibbitts at Saint Louis Community College at Meramec for authoring the learning outcomes for LearnSmart; to Laurie Zouharis at Suffolk College for authoring probes for LearnSmart, for revising the Instructor's Manual, test bank, and online/app quizzes; and to Rachelle Hall at Glendale Community College for revising the PowerPoint presentations to accompany this text.

Tim and Linda O'Leary live in the American South-west and spend much of their time engaging instructors and students in conversation about learning. In fact, they have been talking about learning for over 25 years. Something in those early conversations convinced them to write a book, to bring their interest in the learning process to the printed page. Today, they are as concerned as ever about learning, about technology, and about the challenges of presenting material in new ways, in terms of both content and method of delivery.

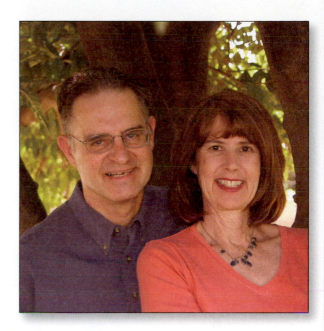

A powerful and creative team, Tim combines his 25 years of classroom teaching experience with Linda's background as a consultant and corporate trainer. Tim has taught courses at Stark Technical College in Canton, Ohio, and at Rochester Institute of Technology in upstate New York, and is currently a professor emeritus at Arizona State University in Tempe, Arizona. Linda offered her expertise at ASU for several years as an academic advisor. She also presented and developed materials for major corporations such as Motorola, Intel, Honeywell, and AT&T, as well as various community colleges in the Phoenix area.

Tim and Linda have talked to and taught numerous students, all of them with a desire to learn something about computers and applications that make their lives easier, more interesting, and more productive.

Each new edition of an O'Leary text, supplement, or learning aid has benefited from these students and their instructors who daily stand in front of them (or over their shoulders). *Computing Essentials* is no exception.

# Computing Essentials

## Making IT work for you

**INTRODUCTORY 2014**

# Information Technology, the Internet, and You

▲ Download the free *Computing Essentials 2014* app for videos, key term flashcards, quizzes, and the game, *Over the Edge!*

## Competencies

**After you have read this chapter, you should be able to:**

**1** Explain the parts of an information system: people, procedures, software, hardware, data, and connectivity.

**2** Distinguish between system software and application software.

**3** Discuss the three kinds of system software programs.

**4** Define and compare general purpose, specialized, and mobile applications.

**5** Identify the four types of computers and the four types of microcomputers.

**6** Describe the different types of computer hardware, including the system unit, input, output, storage, and communication devices.

**7** Define data and describe document, worksheet, database, and presentation files.

**8** Explain computer connectivity, the wireless revolution, the Internet, and cloud computing.

## Why should I read this chapter?

When microcomputers were first introduced, they were used by relatively few people to create simple documents and analyze data. These computers were expensive, slow, and difficult to use. Now, microcomputers are used widely throughout the world. Every day billons of people use microcomputers and the Internet socially and professionally. Today's microcomputers are inexpensive, very powerful, and easy to use.

This chapter provides a very concise overview of computing and the organization of this text. It presents the various features of the text including boxes presenting environmental and ethical issues and special coverage of how you can make your computer work efficiently and effectively for you. Additionally, an overview of hardware, software, and data is presented. Finally, the concept of connectivity is introduced along with the Internet, web, the wireless revolution, and cloud computing. To effectively start to use this text, you need to understand these things.

## chapter .1

# Introduction

**Welcome to *Computing Essentials*. I'm Alan and I work in information technology. On the following pages, we'll be discussing some of the most exciting new developments in computer technology including smartphones, tablet computers, and cloud computing. Let me begin in this chapter by giving you an overview of the book and showing you some of its special features.**

The purpose of this book is to help you become competent with computer technology. **Computer competency** refers to acquiring computer-related skills—indispensable tools for today. They include how to effectively use popular application packages and the Internet.

In this chapter, we present an overview of an information system: people, procedures, software, hardware, data, and connectivity. It is essential to understand these basic parts and how connectivity through the Internet and the web expands the role of information technology in our lives. Later, we describe these parts of an information system in detail.

Twenty years ago, most people had little to do with computers, at least directly. Of course, they filled out computerized forms, took computerized tests, and paid computerized bills. But the real work was handled by specialists. Then microcomputers came along and changed everything. Today it is easy for nearly everybody to use a computer.

- Microcomputers are common tools in all areas of life. Writers write, artists draw, engineers and scientists calculate—all on microcomputers. Students and businesspeople do all this and more.

- New forms of learning have developed. People who are homebound, who work odd hours, or who travel frequently may take online courses. A college course need not fit within a quarter or a semester.

**People**
are end users who use computers to make themselves more productive.

**Software**
provides step-by-step instructions for computer hardware.

**Procedures**
specify rules or guidelines for computer operations.

**Figure 1-1 Parts of an information system**

- New ways to communicate, to find people with similar interests, and to buy goods are available. People use electronic mail, electronic commerce, and the Internet to meet and to share ideas and products.

To be competent with computer technology, you need to know the parts of an information system: people, procedures, software, hardware, data, and connectivity. You also need to understand the wireless revolution, the Internet, and the web and to recognize the role of information technology in your personal life as well as your professional life.

# Information Systems

When you think of a microcomputer, perhaps you think of just the equipment itself. That is, you think of the monitor or the keyboard. Yet, there is more to it than that. The way to think about a microcomputer is as part of an information system. An **information system** has several parts: *people, procedures, software, hardware, data,* and *connectivity*. (See Figure 1-1.)

- **People:** It is easy to overlook people as one of the parts of an information system. Yet this is what microcomputers are all about—making **people**, **end users** like you, more productive.
- **Procedures:** The rules or guidelines for people to follow when using software, hardware, and data are **procedures**. These procedures are typically

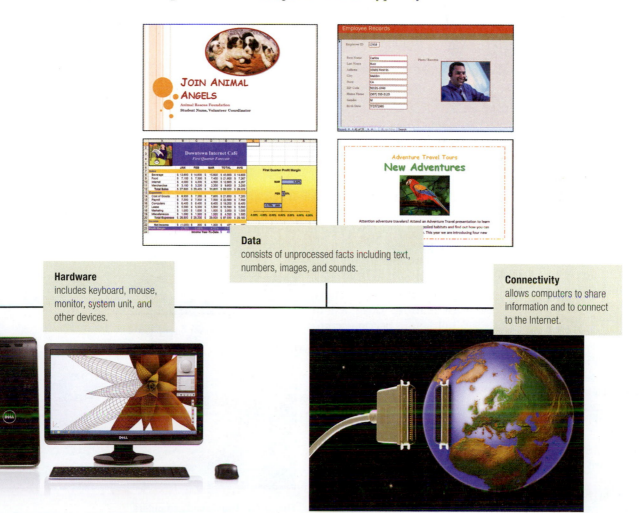

**Data** consists of unprocessed facts including text, numbers, images, and sounds.

**Hardware** includes keyboard, mouse, monitor, system unit, and other devices.

**Connectivity** allows computers to share information and to connect to the Internet.

documented in manuals written by computer specialists. Software and hardware manufacturers provide manuals with their products. These manuals are provided in either printed or electronic (web link) form.

- **Software:** A **program** consists of the step-by-step instructions that tell the computer how to do its work. **Software** is another name for a program or programs. The purpose of software is to convert **data** (unprocessed facts) into **information** (processed facts). For example, a payroll program would instruct the computer to take the number of hours you worked in a week (data) and multiply it by your pay rate (data) to determine how much you are paid for the week (information).

- **Hardware:** The equipment that processes the data to create information is called **hardware**. It includes the keyboard, mouse, monitor, system unit, and other devices. Hardware is controlled by software.

- **Data:** The raw, unprocessed facts, including text, numbers, images, and sounds, are called data. Processed data yields information. Using the previous example of a payroll program, the data (number of hours worked and pay rate) is processed (multiplied) to yield information (weekly pay).

- **Connectivity:** Almost all of today's computer systems add an additional part to the information system. This part, called **connectivity**, typically uses the Internet and allows users to greatly expand the capability and usefulness of their information systems.

## concept check

What are the parts of an information system?

What is a program?

What is the difference between data and information?

# People

People are surely the most important part of any information system. Our lives are touched every day by computers and information systems. Many times the contact is direct and obvious, such as when we create documents using a word processing program or when we connect to the Internet. Other times, the contact is not as obvious. (See Figure 1-2.)

Throughout this book you will find a variety of features designed to help you become computer competent and knowledgeable. These features include Making IT Work for You, Explorations, Environment, Ethics, Tips, Careers in IT, and the Computing Essentials website.

- **Making IT Work for You.** Throughout this book you will find

**Figure 1-2 People and computers**

| Application | Description |
| --- | --- |
| Online Entertainment | Use your computer to watch your favorite television programs, movies, and other video content. See page 30. |
| Image Editing | Manage and fix the problems with your photos with a free image editing program. See page 75. |
| Google Docs | Create, collaborate, and access documents from almost anywhere with a free online office suite. See page 83. |
| SKYPE | Visit face to face with friends and family located almost anywhere at little or no cost. See page 170. |
| Cloud Storage | Send large files using a free tool and the cloud. See page 198. |

To see additional applications, visit our website at www.computing2014.com and enter the keyword MIW.

**Figure 1-3 Making IT Work for You applications**

Making IT Work for You features that present numerous interesting and practical IT applications. For just a few of the Making IT Work for You topics, see Figure 1-3. For a complete list, visit our website at www.computing2014.com.

- **Tips.** We all can benefit from a few tips or suggestions. Throughout this book you will find numerous Tips to make your computing safer, more efficient, and more effective. These tips range from the basics of keeping your computer system running smoothly to how to protect your privacy while surfing the web. For a partial list of the Tips presented in the following chapters, see Figure 1-4. For a complete list, visit our website at www.computing2014.com.

Are you getting the most out of your computer? Here are just a few of the tips to make your computing safer, more efficient, and more effective.

1. **Low battery.** Do you find that your laptop's battery keeps its charge for less time than it used to? Here some ways to make your battery last longer. See page 139.

2. **Compressed files.** Have you ever received a compressed file that you could not open? If so, follow these steps to acquire a free program that can open most compressed files. See page 191.

3. **Lost files.** Have you ever accidentally deleted or lost important files from your flash drive? Here are a few suggestions that might help. See page 195.

4. **Identity theft.** Identity theft is a growing problem that can be financially devastating. Some steps to help protect your identity are on page 245.

5. **Wireless networks.** Do you use your laptop to connect to wireless networks at school, coffee shops, airports, or hotels? If so, it is important to use caution to protect your computer and your privacy. A few suggestions are on page 223.

To see additional tips, visit our website at www.computing2014.com and enter the keyword tips.

**Figure 1-4 Selected tips**

- **Explorations.** The informational content of the web is limitless; the challenge is to locate the information you are looking for. In this chapter and the ones that follow, you will find Explorations boxes in the margin that direct you to relevant web information locations.

- **Ethics.** Most people agree that we should behave ethically. That is, we should follow a system of moral principles that direct our everyday lives. However, for any given circumstance, people often do not agree on the ethics of the situation. Throughout this book you will find numerous Ethics boxes posing a variety of different ethical/unethical situations for your consideration.

- **Environment.** Today it is more important than ever that we be aware of our impact on the environment. In this chapter and the following ones, you will find Environment boxes in the margin that present important relevant environmental information.

- **Careers in IT.** One of the most important decisions of your life is to decide upon your life's work or career. Perhaps you are planning to be a writer, an artist, or an engineer. Or you might become a professional in **information technology (IT)**. Each of the following chapters highlights a specific career in information technology. This feature provides job descriptions, projected employment demands, educational requirements, current salary ranges, and advancement opportunities.
- **Computing Essentials Website.** Throughout the text you will find numerous text references to the Computing Essentials website at www.computing2014 .com. This site is carefully integrated with the textbook. At the site, you'll find animations, career information, tips, test review materials, and much more.

## ☑ concept check

Which part of an information system is the most important?

Describe the Making IT Work for You, Tips, Explorations, and Ethics features.

Describe the Environment, the Careers in IT, and the Computing Essentials website features.

# Software

Software, as we mentioned, is another name for programs. Programs are the instructions that tell the computer how to process data into the form you want. In most cases, the words *software* and *programs* are interchangeable. There are two major kinds of software: *system software* and *application software.* You can think of application software as the kind you use. Think of system software as the kind the computer uses.

## System Software

The user interacts primarily with application software. **System software** enables the application software to interact with the computer hardware. System software is "background" software that helps the computer manage its own internal resources.

System software is not a single program. Rather it is a collection of programs, including the following:

- **Operating systems** are programs that coordinate computer resources, provide an interface between users and the computer, and run applications. Microsoft's Windows 8 and Apple's Mac OS X are two of the best-known operating systems for today's microcomputer users. (See Figures 1-5 and 1-6.)
- **Utilities** perform specific tasks related to managing computer resources. One of the most essential utility programs that every computer system should have is an antivirus program. These programs protect your computer system from **viruses** or malicious programs that are all too often deposited onto your computer from the Internet. These programs can damage software and hardware, as well as compromise the security and privacy of your personal data. If your computer does not have an antivirus program installed on it, you need to get one. To see how you can install a free antivirus program on your computer, see Making IT Work for You: Installing a Free Antivirus Program on page 10.

**Figure 1-5 Windows 8**

**Figure 1-6 Mac OS X**

- **Device drivers** are specialized programs designed to allow particular input or output devices to communicate with the rest of the computer system.

### Application Software

**Application software** might be described as end user software. Three types of application software are *general-purpose*, *specialized*, and *mobile apps*.

**General-purpose applications** are widely used in nearly all career areas. They are the kinds of programs you have to know to be considered computer competent. One of these general-purpose applications is a browser to navigate, explore, and find information on the Internet. The three most widely used browsers are Mozilla's Firefox, Microsoft's Internet Explorer, and Google's Chrome.

**Specialized applications** include thousands of other programs that are more narrowly focused on specific disciplines and occupations. Two of the best known are graphics and web authoring programs.

**Mobile apps**, or **mobile applications**, are small programs designed for mobile devices such as smartphones, tablet computers, and other mobile devices. There are over half a million apps. The most popular mobile apps are for text messaging, Internet browsing, and connecting to social networks.

### ☑ concept check

Describe the two major kinds of software.

Describe three types of system software programs.

Define and compare general-purpose, specialized, and mobile applications.

## Hardware

Computers are electronic devices that can follow instructions to accept input, process that input, and produce information. This book focuses principally on microcomputers. However, it is almost certain that you will come in contact, at least indirectly, with other types of computers.

# INSTALLING A FREE ANTIVIRUS PROGRAM

Have you or someone you know had a slower computing experience due to a spyware infection? Even worse, perhaps a malicious piece of software stole crucial, personal information or caused a total system failure. Most of these problems can be averted by having an up-to-date antivirus program running in your computer's memory at all times. This exercise shows you how to download and install a free antivirus program if your computer does not yet have one.

**Getting Started**   First, make sure your computer does not have an antivirus or security suite running. If it does, be sure to completely uninstall that program, even if the subscription is expired. Now, follow these steps to install AVG, a popular, free antivirus program:

**1** Visit http://free.avg.com and click the *Download* button. You will be asked to confirm that you want the free edition and then redirected to a download site.

**2** Run the installation file and follow the prompts.

**3** Select *basic protection* if you are asked which product you would like to install.

**4** Choose *Express Install* and wait for files to be downloaded and installed.

**Using AVG**   Generally speaking, your antivirus program watches your system for malware and updates itself automatically. However, you can always download updates manually, set a schedule for full-system scans, and change basic settings for various components of the software.

**1** After installation, verify that the software is downloading updates by clicking *Update now* on the left side. Wait for all updates to be downloaded.

**2** Click *Scan now* to run a full scan on your computer.

**3** Just below that, click *Scan options* if you want to set a schedule for automated scans.

**4** Click *Overview* to reach the main screen, where you can click various elements of the program to configure them. For example, clicking *Anti-Virus* will allow you turn on a feature that detects cookies that may be used to track your online activity.

The web is continually changing, and some of the specifics presented in this Making IT Work for You may have changed.

**To learn about other ways to make information technology work for you, visit our website at www.computing2014.com and enter the keyword miw.**

**Figure 1-7** Supercomputer

## Types of Computers

There are four types of computers: supercomputers, mainframe computers, mid-range computers, and microcomputers.

- **Supercomputers** are the most powerful type of computer. These machines are special high-capacity computers used by very large organizations. IBM's Blue Gene supercomputer is one of the fastest computers in the world. (See Figure 1-7.)

- **Mainframe computers** occupy specially wired, air-conditioned rooms. Although not nearly as powerful as supercomputers, mainframe computers are capable of great processing speeds and data storage. For example, insurance companies use mainframes to process information about millions of policyholders.

- **Midrange computers**, also referred to as **servers**, are computers with processing capabilities less powerful than a mainframe computer yet more powerful than a microcomputer. Originally used by medium-size companies or departments of large companies to support their processing needs, today midrange computers are most widely used to support or serve end users for such specific needs as retrieving data from a database or supplying access to application software.

- **Microcomputers** are the least powerful, yet the most widely used and fastest-growing type of computer. There are four types of microcomputers: *desktop, notebook, tablet,* and *handheld computers.* (See Figure 1-8.) **Desktop computers** are small enough to fit on top of or alongside a desk yet are too big to carry around. **Notebook computers**, also known as **laptop computers**, are portable and lightweight and fit into most briefcases. **Tablets**, also known as **tablet computers**, are the newest type of computer. They are smaller, lighter, and generally less powerful than notebooks. Like a notebook, tablets have a flat screen but typically do not have a standard keyboard. Instead tablets typically use a virtual keyboard that appears on the screen and is touch-sensitive. The best known tablet is Apple's iPad. **Handheld computers** are the smallest and are designed to fit into the palm of one hand. These systems contain an entire computer system, including the electronic

**Desktop**

**Notebook**

**Tablet**

**Handheld**

**Figure 1-8** Microcomputers

components, secondary storage, and input and output devices. **Personal digital assistants (PDAs)** and **smartphones** are the most widely used handheld computers. Smartphones are cell phones with wireless connections to the Internet and processing capabilities. Their growth has been explosive in the past few years.

### Microcomputer Hardware

Hardware for a microcomputer system consists of a variety of different devices. See Figure 1-9 for a typical desktop system. This physical equipment falls into four basic categories: system unit, input/output, secondary storage, and communication. Because we discuss hardware in detail later in this book, here we will present just a quick overview of the four basic categories.

- **System unit:** The **system unit** is a container that houses most of the electronic components that make up a computer system. Two important components of the system unit are the *microprocessor* and *memory*. (See Figure 1-10.) The **microprocessor** controls and manipulates data to produce information. **Memory** is a holding area for data, instructions, and information. One type, **random-access memory (RAM)**, holds the program and data that is currently being processed. This type of memory is sometimes referred to as *temporary storage* because its contents will typically be lost if the electric power to the computer is disrupted.

- **Input/output:** **Input devices** translate data and programs that humans can understand into a form that the computer can process. The most common input devices are the **keyboard** and the **mouse**. **Output devices** translate the processed information from the computer into a form that humans can understand. The most common output devices are **monitors** (see Figure 1-11) and **printers**.

System unit to house electronic components

Monitor to display information

Keyboard to input instructions

Mouse to select items

**Figure 1-9 Microcomputer system**

- **Secondary storage:** Unlike memory, **secondary storage** holds data and programs even after electric power to the computer system has been turned off. The most important kinds of secondary media are *hard disks, solid-state storage,* and *optical discs*. **Hard disks** are typically used to store programs and very large data files. Using rigid metallic platters and read/write heads that move across the platters, data and information are stored using magnetic charges on

Microprocessor

Memory

**Figure 1-10 System unit**

Figure 1-11 Monitor

Figure 1-12 Optical disc

the disk's surface. In contrast, **solid-state storage** does not have any moving parts, is more reliable, and requires less power. It saves data and information electronically similar to RAM except that it is not volatile. Three types are **solid-state drives (SSDs)** that are used much the same way as an internal hard disk, **flash memory cards** that are widely used in portable devices, and **USB drives** that are a widely used compact storage medium for transporting data and information between computers and a variety of specialty devices. **Optical discs** use laser technology to store data and programs. (See Figure 1-12.) Three types of optical discs are **compact discs ( CDs)**, **digital versatile** (or **video**) **discs (DVDs)**, and **Blu-ray discs**.

- **Communication:** At one time, it was uncommon for a microcomputer system to communicate with other computer systems. Now, using **communication devices**, a microcomputer can communicate with other computer systems located as near as the next office or as far away as halfway around the world, using the Internet. A **modem** is a widely used communication device that modifies audio, video, and other types of data communications into a form that can be processed by a computer. Modems also modify computer output into a form that can be transmitted across standard cable and telephone lines.

## concept check

What are the four types of computers?

Describe the four types of microcomputers.

Describe the four basic categories of microcomputer hardware.

# Data

Data is raw, unprocessed facts, including text, numbers, images, and sounds. As we mentioned earlier, processed data becomes information. When stored electronically in files, data can be used directly as input for the system unit.

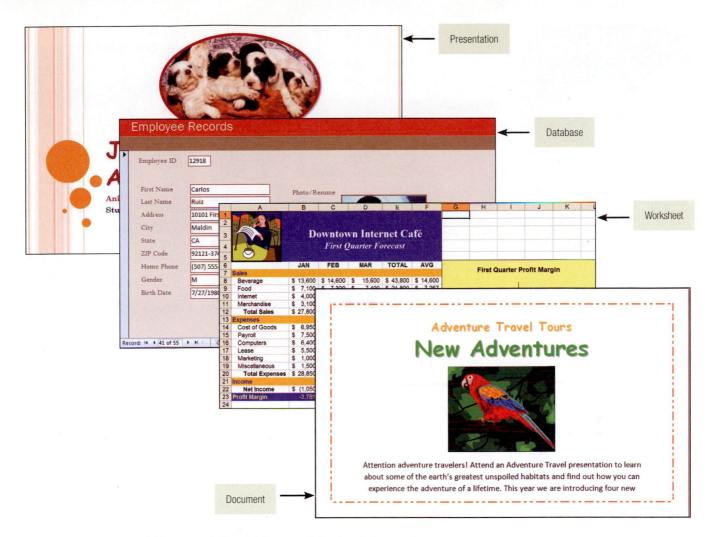

**Figure 1-13** Four types of files: presentation, database, worksheet, and document

Four common types of files (see Figure 1-13) are

- **Document files**, created by word processors to save documents such as memos, term papers, and letters.
- **Worksheet files**, created by electronic spreadsheets to analyze things like budgets and to predict sales.
- **Database files**, typically created by database management programs to contain highly structured and organized data. For example, an employee database file might contain all the workers' names, Social Security numbers, job titles, and other related pieces of information.
- **Presentation files**, created by presentation graphics programs to save presentation materials. For example, a file might contain audience handouts, speaker notes, and electronic slides.

# Connectivity

**Connectivity** is the capability of your microcomputer to share information with other computers. The two most dramatic changes in connectivity in the past five years have been the widespread use of mobile or wireless communication devices

**Figure 1-14** Wireless communication devices

and cloud computing. For just a few of these mobile devices, see Figure 1-14. Many experts predict that these wireless applications are just the beginning of the **wireless revolution**, a revolution that will dramatically affect the way we communicate and use computer technology.

Central to the concept of connectivity is the **network**. A network is a communications system connecting two or more computers. The largest network in the world is the **Internet**. It is like a giant highway that connects you to millions of other people and organizations located throughout the world. The **web** provides a multimedia interface to the numerous resources available on the Internet. **Cloud computing** uses the Internet and the web to shift many computer activities from a user's computer to computers on the Internet. The wireless revolution and cloud computing promise the potential to dramatically affect the entire computer industry and how you and I will interact with computers. Each will be discussed in detail in the following chapters.

# Careers in IT

As mentioned previously, each of the following chapters highlights a specific career in information technology. Each provides specific job descriptions, salary ranges, advancement opportunities, and more. For a partial list of these careers, see Figure 1-15. For a complete list, visit our website at www.computing2014.com and enter the keyword careers.

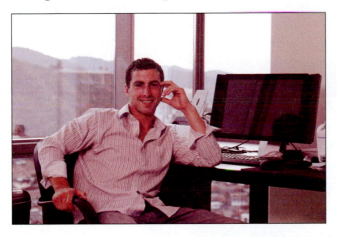

**Now that you know the basic outline and important features of this book, I'd like to talk about some of the most exciting and well-paid careers in information technology.**

| Career | Description |
|--------|-------------|
| Webmaster | Develops and maintains websites and web resources. See page 51. |
| Software engineer | Analyzes users' needs and creates application software. See page 82. |
| Computer support specialist | Provides technical support to customers and other users. See page 112. |
| Computer technician | Repairs and installs computer components and systems. See page 141. |
| Technical writer | Prepares instruction manuals, technical reports, and other scientific or technical documents. See page 174. |
| Network administrator | Creates and maintains computer networks. See page 229. |

**Figure 1-15  Careers in information technology**

# A LOOK TO THE FUTURE

## Using and Understanding Information Technology Means Being Computer Competent

The purpose of this book is to help you use and understand information technology. We want to help you become computer competent in today's world and to provide you with a foundation of knowledge so that you can understand how technology is being used today and anticipate how technology will be used in the future. This will enable you to benefit from six important information technology developments.

### The Internet and the Web

The Internet and the web are considered by most to be the two most important technologies for the 21st century. Understanding how to efficiently and effectively use the Internet to browse, communicate, and locate information are essential skills. These issues are presented in Chapter 2, The Internet, the Web, and Electronic Commerce.

### Powerful Software

The software that is now available can do an extraordinary number of tasks and help you in an endless number of ways. You can create professional-looking documents, analyze massive amounts of data, create dynamic multimedia web pages, and much more. Today's employers are expecting the people they hire to be able to effectively and efficiently use a variety of different types of software. General-purpose, specialized, and mobile applications are presented in Chapter 3. System software is presented in Chapter 4.

### Powerful Hardware

Microcomputers are now much more powerful than they used to be. Smartphones, tablets, and communication technologies such as wireless networks are dramatically changing the ways to connect to other computers, networks, and the Internet. However, despite the rapid change of specific equipment, their essential features remain unchanged. Thus, the competent end user should focus on these features. Chapters 5 through 8

explain what you need to know about hardware. For those considering the purchase of a computer, an appendix—The Buyer's Guide: What Type of Computer to Purchase—is provided at the end of this book. This guide provides a very concise comparison of desktops, notebooks, tablets, and smartphones.

### Security and Privacy

What about people? Experts agree that we as a society must be careful about the potential of technology to negatively impact our personal privacy and security. Additionally, we need to be aware of potential physical and mental health risks associated with using technology. Finally, we need to be aware of negative effects on our environment caused by the manufacture of computer-related products. Thus, Chapter 9 explores each of these critical issues in detail.

### Organizations

Almost all organizations rely on the quality and flexibility of their information systems to stay competitive. As a member or employee of an organization, you will undoubtedly be involved in these information systems. In order to use, develop, modify, and maintain these systems, you need to understand the basic concepts of information systems and know how to safely, efficiently, and effectively use computers. These concepts are covered throughout this book.

### Changing Times

Are the times changing any faster now than they ever have? Almost everyone thinks so. Whatever the answer, it is clear we live in a fast-paced age. The Evolution of the Computer Age section presented at the end of this book tracks the major developments since computers were first introduced.

After reading this book, you will be in a very favorable position compared with many other people in industry today. You will learn not only the basics of hardware, software, connectivity, the Internet, and the web but also the most current technology. You will be able to use these tools to your advantage.

## INFORMATION SYSTEMS

The way to think about a microcomputer is to realize that it is one part of an **information system**. There are several parts of an information system:

- **People** are an essential part of the system. The purpose of information systems is to make people, or **end users** like you, more productive.
- **Procedures** are rules or guidelines to follow when using software, hardware, and data. They are typically documented in manuals written by computer professionals.
- **Software (programs)** provides step-by-step instructions to control the computer to convert **data** into **information**.
- **Hardware** consists of the physical equipment. It is controlled by software and processes data to create information.
- **Data** consists of unprocessed facts including text, numbers, images, and sound. **Information** is data that has been processed by the computer.
- **Connectivity** allows computers to connect and share information.

To be computer competent, end users need to understand **information technology (IT)**, including software, hardware, data, and connectivity.

## PEOPLE

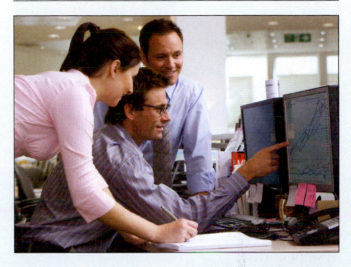

People are the most important part of an information system. This book contains several features to demonstrate how people just like you use computers. These features include the following:

- **Making IT Work for You** presents several interesting and practical applications. Topics include using digital video editing and locating job opportunities.
- **Tips** offer a variety of suggestions on such practical matters as how to improve slow computer performance and how to protect your privacy while on the web.
- **Explorations** direct you to important information and websites that relate to computers and technology.
- **Ethics** boxes pose a variety of different ethical/unethical situations for your consideration.
- **Environment** discusses important and relevant environmental issues. The impact of computers and other technologies is more critical today than ever before.
- **Careers in IT** presents job descriptions, employment demands, educational requirements, salary ranges, and advancement opportunities.
- **Computing Essentials website** integrates the textbook with information on the web, including animations, career information, tips, test review materials, and much more.

To prepare for your future as a competent end user, you need to understand the basic parts of an information system: people, procedures, software, hardware, data, and connectivity. Also you need to understand the Internet and the web and to recognize the role of technology in your professional and personal life.

## SOFTWARE

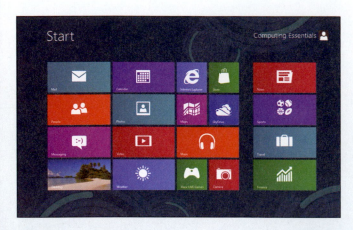

Software, or programs, consists of system and application software.

### System Software

System software enables application software to interact with computer hardware.

- **Operating systems** coordinate resources, provide an interface, and run applications.
- **Utilities** perform specific tasks to manage computer resources.
- **Device drivers** are specialized programs to allow input and output devices to communicate with the rest of the computer system.

### Application Software

Application software includes general-purpose, specialized, and mobile applications.

- **General purpose**—widely used in nearly all career areas; programs include browsers, word processors, spreadsheets, database management systems, and presentation graphics.
- **Specialized**—focus more on specific disciplines and occupations; programs include graphics and web authoring.
- **Mobile apps**—designed for mobile devices; most popular are for text messaging, Internet browsing, and connecting to social networks.

## HARDWARE

Hardware consists of electronic devices that can follow instructions to accept input, process the input, and produce information.

### Types of Computers

Supercomputer, mainframe, midrange (server), and microcomputer are four types of computers. Microcomputers can be desktop, notebook (laptop computer), tablet, or handheld (PDAs and smartphones are the most widely used handheld microcomputers).

### Microcomputer Hardware

There are four basic categories of hardware devices.

- **System unit** contains electronic circuitry, including the **microprocessor** and **memory**. **Random-access memory (RAM)** holds the program and data currently being processed.
- **Input/output devices** are translators between humans and computers. **Input devices** include the **keyboard** and **mouse**. **Output devices** include **monitors** and **printers**.
- **Secondary storage** holds data and programs. Typical media include **hard disks, solid-state storage (solid-state drives, flash memory cards,** and **USB drives),** and **optical discs (CD, DVD,** and **Blu-ray).**
- **Communication devices** allow microcomputers to communicate with other computer systems. **Modems** modify audio, video, and other types of data for transmission and processing.

## DATA

Data is the raw unprocessed facts about something. Common file types include

- **Document files** created by word processors.

- **Worksheet files** created by spreadsheet programs.

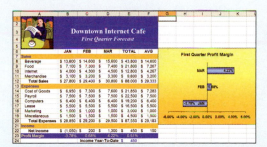

- **Database files** created by database management programs.

- **Presentation files** created by presentation graphics programs.

## CONNECTIVITY

### Connectivity

**Connectivity** describes the ability of end users to use resources well beyond their desktops.

### The Wireless Revolution

The **wireless revolution** is the widespread and increasing use of mobile (wireless) communication devices.

### Internet

The **Internet** is the world's largest computer **network**. The **web** provides a multimedia interface to resources available on the Internet.

### Cloud Computing

**Cloud computing** uses the Internet and the web to shift many activities from users' computers to computers on the Internet.

## CAREERS IN IT

| Career | Description |
|---|---|
| Webmaster | Develops and maintains websites and web resources. See page 51. |
| Software engineer | Analyzes users' needs and creates application software. See page 82. |
| Computer support specialist | Provides technical support to customers and other users. See page 112. |
| Computer technician | Repairs and installs computer components and systems. See page 141. |
| Technical writer | Prepares instruction manuals, technical reports, and other scientific or technical documents. See page 174. |
| Network administrator | Creates and maintains computer networks. See page 229. |

# KEY TERMS

application software   (9)
Blu-ray disc   (14)
cloud computing   (16)
communication device   (14)
compact disc (CD)   (14)
computer competency   (4)
connectivity   (6, 15)
data   (6)
database file   (15)
desktop computer   (11)
device driver   (9)
digital versatile disc (DVD)   (14)
digital video disc (DVD)   (14)
document file   (15)
end user   (5)
flash memory card   (14)
general-purpose application   (9)
handheld computer   (11)
hard disk   (13)
hardware   (6)
information   (6)
information system   (5)
information technology (IT)   (8)
input device   (12)
Internet   (16)
keyboard   (12)
laptop computer   (11)
mainframe computer   (11)
memory   (12)
microcomputer   (11)
microprocessor   (12)
midrange computer   (11)
mobile app (application)   (9)

modem   (14)
monitor   (12)
mouse   (12)
network   (16)
notebook computer   (11)
operating system   (8)
optical disc   (14)
output device   (12)
people   (5)
personal digital assistant (PDA)   (12)
presentation file   (15)
printer   (12)
procedures   (5)
program   (6)
random-access memory (RAM)   (12)
secondary storage   (13)
server   (11)
smartphone   (12)
software   (6)
solid-state drive (SSD)   (14)
solid-state storage   (14)
specialized application   (9)
supercomputer   (11)
system software   (8)
system unit   (12)
tablet   (11)
tablet computer   (11)
USB drive   (14)
utility   (8)
virus   (8)
web   (16)
wireless revolution   (16)
worksheet file   (15)

To test your knowledge of these key terms with animated flash cards, visit our website at www.computing2014.com and enter the keyword terms1. You can also access flash cards using the *Computing Essentials 2014* app.

# MULTIPLE CHOICE

Circle the letter of the correct answer.

1. The keyboard, mouse, monitor, and system unit are:
   - a. hardware
   - b. output devices
   - c. storage devices
   - d. software

2. Programs that coordinate computer resources, provide an interface, and run applications are known as:
   - a. application programs
   - b. operating systems
   - c. storage systems
   - d. utility programs

3. A browser is an example of a:
   - a. general-purpose application
   - b. specialized program
   - c. system application
   - d. utility program

4. Although not as powerful as a supercomputer, this type of computer is capable of great processing speeds and data storage.
   - a. mainframe
   - b. midrange
   - c. notebook
   - d. tablet

5. The smallest type of microcomputer:
   - a. handheld
   - b. notebook
   - c. midrange
   - d. tablet

6. RAM is a type of:
   - a. computer
   - b. memory
   - c. network
   - d. secondary storage

7. Unlike memory, this type of storage holds data and programs even after electric power to the computer system has been turned off.
   - a. primary
   - b. RAM
   - c. ROM
   - d. secondary

8. The type of file created by word processors to save, for example, memos, term papers, and letters.
   - a. database
   - b. document
   - c. presentation
   - d. worksheet

9. Uses the Internet and the web to shift many computer activities from a user's computer to computers on the Internet.
   - a. cloud computing
   - b. high definition
   - c. network
   - d. USB

10. The largest network in the world is [the]:
    - a. Facebook
    - b. Internet
    - c. web
    - d. USB

For an interactive multiple-choice practice test, visit our website at www.computing2014
.com and enter the keyword multiple1. You can also access quizzes using the *Computing Essentials 2014* app.

# MATCHING

Match each numbered item with the most closely related lettered item. Write your answers in the spaces provided.

a. desktop
b. modem
c. network
d. output
e. presentation
f. program
g. software
h. solid-state
i. system software
j. system unit

____ 1. Consists of the step-by-step instructions that tell the computer how to do its work.

____ 2. Another name for a program.

____ 3. Enables the application software to interact with the computer hardware.

____ 4. Type of computer that is small enough to fit on top of or alongside a desk yet is too big to carry around.

____ 5. A container that houses most of the electronic components that make up a computer system.

____ 6. Devices that translate the processed information from the computer into a form that humans can understand.

____ 7. Unlike hard disks, this type of storage does not have any moving parts, is more reliable, and requires less power.

____ 8. The most widely used communication device.

____ 9. A type of a file that might contain, for example, audience handouts, speaker notes, and electronic slides.

____10. A communications system connecting two or more computers.

For an interactive matching practice test, visit our website at www.computing2014.com and enter the keyword matching1. You can also access quizzes using the *Computing Essentials 2014* app.

# OPEN-ENDED

On a separate sheet of paper, respond to each question or statement.

1. Explain the parts of an information system. What part do people play in this system?

2. What is system software? What kinds of programs are included in system software?

3. Define and compare general-purpose, specialized, and mobile application software. Describe some different types of general-purpose applications. Describe some types of specialized applications.

4. Describe the different types of computers. What is the most common type? What are the types of microcomputers?

5. What is connectivity? What are wireless devices and the wireless revolution? What is a computer network? What are the Internet and the web? What is cloud computing?

# DISCUSSION

Respond to each of the following questions.

## ① Making IT Work for You

Making it a habit of keeping current with technology applications can be a key to your success. Numerous full-page spreads identified as *Making IT Work for You* are presented in the following chapters. These sections address some of today's most interesting and useful applications. They include online entertainment in Chapter 2, Skype in Chapter 6, cloud storage in Chapter 7, and remote access in Chapter 8. Select one that you find the most interesting and then respond to the following: (a) Why did you select this application? (b) Have you used this application? If so when and how? If not, do you plan to in the near future? (c) Go to the chapter containing your selected application and locate the application's Making IT Work for You coverage. Review and briefly describe its contents. (d) Did you find the coverage useful? Why or why not?

## ② Explorations

Expanding your knowledge of select technology topics beyond this textbook can be very valuable to you. Numerous Explorations boxes appear in the margins of the upcoming chapters. These boxes direct you to information sources for a variety of topics. These topics include Linux in Chapter 4, robots in Chapter 6, BitTorrent in Chapter 8, and privacy organizations in Chapter 9. Select one topic that you find the most interesting and then respond to the following: (a) Why did you select this topic? (b) Do you have knowledge or experience with the topic? If so, describe your knowledge or experience. If not, do you anticipate using knowledge of the topic in the near future? (c) Go to the chapter containing your selected topic and locate the Explorations box. Then connect to the information source and briefly describe its contents. (d) Did you find the coverage useful? Why or why not?

## ③ Ethics

Computer ethics are guidelines for the morally acceptable use of computers in our society. Numerous Ethics boxes appear in the margins of the upcoming chapters presenting a variety of ethical issues. These issues include job loss due to technology in Chapter 3, unauthorized use of webcams in Chapter 6, and unauthorized monitoring of Internet activity in Chapter 8. Select one issue that you find the most interesting and then respond to the following: (a) Why did you select this issue? (b) Do you have knowledge or experience with the issue? If so, describe your knowledge or experience. If not, do you consider the issue critical for individuals or organizations? (c) Go to the chapter containing your selected issue, locate the Ethics box, then read it and describe its contents. (d) Did you find the coverage thought-provoking? Why or why not?

## ④ Environment

Almost everyone agrees that protecting our environment today is more important than ever before. Numerous Environment boxes appear in the margins of the upcoming chapters. These boxes present a variety of environmental topics including cloud computing benefits in Chapter 2, operating systems reducing energy consumption in Chapter 4, recycling in Chapter 5, and robots and pollution in Chapter 6. Select one that you find the most interesting and then respond to the following: (a) Why did you select this topic? (b) Do you have knowledge or experience with the topic? If so, describe your knowledge or experience. If not, do you consider the topic to be important for protecting the environment? (c) Go to the chapter containing your selected topic, locate the Environment box, read it, and describe its contents. (d) Did you find the coverage thought-provoking? Why or why not?

# The Internet, the Web, and Electronic Commerce

▲ Download the free *Computing Essentials 2014* app for videos, key term flashcards, quizzes, and the game, *Over the Edge!*

## Competencies

**After you have read this chapter, you should be able to:**

1 Discuss the origins of the Internet and the web.

2 Describe how to access the web using providers and browsers.

3 Discuss Internet communications, including e-mail, text messaging, instant messaging, social networking, blogs, microblogs, webcasts, podcasts, and wikis.

4 Describe search tools, including search engines and specialized search engines.

5 Evaluate the accuracy of information presented on the web.

6 Discuss electronic commerce, including B2C, C2C, B2B, and security issues.

7 Describe cloud computing, including the three-way interaction of clients, Internet, and service providers.

8 Describe web utilities including plug-ins, filters, file transfer utilities, and Internet security suites.

## Why should I read this chapter?

The beginning of the Internet can be traced to 1969 when mainframe computers located in different parts of the United States were linked to one another. It was used exclusively to facilitate communication between researchers and was limited to text. That was then and this is now. Now, emerging Internet technologies are changing the way the world works and the way you interact with the world.

This chapter discusses these technologies including the web; wireless Internet access; and social networking including Facebook, Google+, and LinkedIn. Additionally, you'll learn about webcasts, streaming technology, podcasts, Twitter, cloud computing, and much more. To be competent and to be competitive in today's professional workplace, you need to know and understand these things.

# Introduction

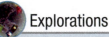 **Explorations**

Many individuals and institutions played a part in the development of the Internet and the web.

**To learn more about the history of the Internet and web, visit our site at www .computing2014.com and enter the keyword history.**

Want to communicate with a friend across town, in another state, or even in another country? Looking for a long-lost friend? Looking for travel or entertainment information? Perhaps you're researching a term paper or exploring different career paths. Where do you start? For these and other information-related activities, most people use the Internet and the web.

The Internet is often referred to as the Information Superhighway. In a sense, it is like a highway that connects you to millions of other people and organizations. Unlike typical highways that move people and things from one location to another, the Internet moves ideas and information. The web provides an easy-to-use interface to Internet resources. It has become an everyday tool for all of us to use.

Competent end users need to be aware of the resources available on the Internet and the web. Additionally, they need to know how to access these resources, to effectively communicate electronically, to efficiently locate information, to understand electronic commerce, and to use web utilities.

# The Internet and the Web

As mentioned earlier, the **Internet** was launched in 1969 when the United States funded a project that developed a national computer network called **Advanced Research Project Agency Network (ARPANET)**. The Internet is a large network that connects together smaller networks all over the globe. The **web** was introduced in 1991 at the **Center for European Nuclear Research (CERN)** in Switzerland. Prior to the web, the Internet was all text—no graphics, animations, sound, or video. The web made it possible to include these elements. It provided a multimedia interface to resources available on the Internet.

The first generation of the web, known as **Web 1.0**, focused on linking existing information. In 2001, the second generation, **Web 2.0**, evolved to support more dynamic content creation and social interaction. Facebook is one of the best-known Web 2.0 applications. Some suggest that we have entered into the next generation, **Web 3.0**. It focuses on computer-generated information requiring less human interaction to locate and to integrate information.

It is easy to get the Internet and the web confused, but they are not the same thing. The Internet is the actual network. It is made up of wires, cables, satellites, and rules for exchanging information between computers connected to the network. Being connected to this network is often described as being **online**. The Internet connects millions of computers and resources throughout the world. The web is a multimedia interface to the resources available on the Internet. Every day over a billion users from nearly every country in the world use the Internet and the web. What are they doing? The most common uses are the following:

- **Communicating** is by far the most popular Internet activity. You can exchange e-mail, photos, and videos with your family and friends from

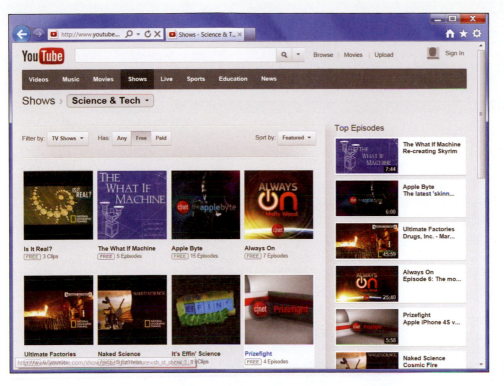

Figure 2-1 Entertainment site

almost anywhere in the world. You can locate old friends and make new friends. You can join and listen to discussions and debates on a wide variety of special-interest topics.

- **Shopping** is one of the fastest-growing Internet applications. You can window shop, look for the latest fashions, search for bargains, and make purchases.
- **Searching** for information has never been more convenient. You can access some of the world's largest libraries directly from your home computer. You can find the latest local, national, and international news.
- **Education** or **e-learning** is another rapidly emerging web application. You can take classes on almost any subject. There are courses just for fun, and there are courses for high school, college, and graduate school credit. Some cost nothing to take and others cost a lot.
- **Entertainment** options are nearly endless. You can find music, movies, magazines, and computer games. You will find live concerts, movie previews, book clubs, and interactive live games. (See Figure 2-1.) To learn more about online entertainment, see Making IT Work for You: Online Entertainment on pages 30 and 31.

The first step to using the Internet and the web is to get connected, or to gain access to the Internet.

## concept check

Describe how the Internet and the web started. What are the three web generations?

What is the difference between the Internet and the web?

List and describe five of the most common uses of the Internet and the web.

## ONLINE ENTERTAINMENT

Are you one of the millions of people who regularly use their computers to watch their favorite television programs, movies, and other video content? Many have "cut the cord" from their cable or satellite TV providers and have turned to online content. It's easy and convenient. Typically, the content is provided by a subscription or a pay-as-you-go service. Users watch the content on their TVs or their computers (including tablets and smartphones).

**Subscription Services**  These services provide access to their library of videos for a fee. You can select and view as many of these videos as you want. Three of the most popular subscription services are Netflix, Hulu Plus, and Amazon Prime.

**1** ● **Netflix offers the largest library of movies and TV programs for a low monthly fee. Additionally, it offers DVD/Blu-ray disc rental plans with postal delivery.**

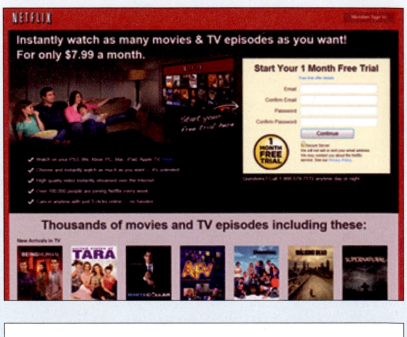

**2** ● **Hulu Plus focuses on current TV programs. Although it does use limited advertising, Hulu Plus's low monthly subscription and current content makes it attractive.**

**3** ● Amazon Prime is a newer service with annual billing. Like Netflix, it offers a variety of online content, albeit with a more limited library. However, the plan comes with additional benefits such as free two-day shipping throughout the store.

**Watch Anywhere**

In the living room ...          ... online ...          ... or on the go.

amazon instant video is available on

kindle fire HD    kindle fire    PS3    XBOX 360.

ROKU    SONY    TiVo    Panasonic    Logitech    SAMSUNG    LG

* Prime eligible instant videos are not currently available on TiVo devices

**Pay-As-You-Go Services** These services provide online access to specific titles in their libraries for a charge. Amazon, iTunes, and Vudu are just a few of the companies that let you rent or purchase movies and TV programs. Movie rentals cost only a few dollars and can be viewed several times over a 24-hour period. The price can increase by one or two dollars for HD quality.

**Viewing Video Content** Many people own Internet-ready TVs that will directly accept content from the Internet. Most Blu-ray disc players and many gaming consoles also provide this access. You can also purchase specialized devices like Roku, which will connect TVs to many of the services listed above.

Many viewers use their computer and a browser to display the video content. Also, many services provide apps for tablet and smartphone viewing.

To learn about other ways to make information technology work for you, visit our website at www.computing2014.com and enter the keyword miw.

# Access

The Internet and the telephone system are similar—you can connect a computer to the Internet much like you connect a phone to the telephone system. Once you are on the Internet, your computer becomes an extension of what seems like a giant computer—a computer that branches all over the world. When provided with a connection to the Internet, you can use a browser program to search the web.

## Providers

The most common way to access the Internet is through an **Internet service provider (ISP)**. The providers are already connected to the Internet and provide a path or connection for individuals to access the Internet. Your college or university most likely provides you with free access to the Internet while you are on campus.

The most widely used commercial Internet service providers use telephone lines, cable, and/or wireless connections. Some of the best-known providers are AT&T, Comcast, Sprint, T-Mobile, and Verizon.

As we will discuss in Chapter 8, users connect to ISPs using one of a variety of connection technologies including **DSL, cable,** and **wireless modems**.

## Browsers

**Browsers** are programs that provide access to web resources. This software connects you to remote computers; opens and transfers files; displays text, images, and multimedia; and provides in one tool an uncomplicated interface to the Internet and web documents. Browsers allow you to explore, or to **surf**, the web by easily moving from one website to another. Four well-known browsers are Apple Safari, Google Chrome, Microsoft Internet Explorer, and Mozilla Firefox. (See Figure 2-2.)

For browsers to connect to resources, the **location** or **address** of the resources must be specified. These addresses are called **uniform resource locators (URLs)**. All URLs have at least two basic parts. (See Figure 2-3.)

- The first part presents the protocol used to connect to the resource. As we will discuss in Chapter 8, **protocols** are rules for exchanging data between computers. The protocol *http* is used for web traffic and is the most widely used Internet protocol.

- The second part presents the **domain name**. It indicates the specific address where the resource is located. In Figure 2-3 the domain is identified as www.mtv.com. (Many URLs have additional parts specifying directory paths, file names, and pointers.) The last part of the domain name following the dot (.) is the **top-level domain (TLD)**. Also known as the **web suffix**, it typically identifies the type of organization. For example, *.com* indicates a commercial site. (See Figure 2-4.)

Once the browser has connected to the website, a document file is sent back to your computer. This document typically contains **Hypertext Markup Language (HTML)**, a markup language for

## tips

**Are you getting the most out of your web browser? Here are a few suggestions to make you faster and more efficient.**

**1** **Bookmarks/Favorites Bar:** Most browsers have a bookmarks or favorites bar just below the address bar. Add your top 5 or 10 most often visited websites here. The next time you want to visit one of these sites, select it from the bookmarks/favorites list rather than entering the site's URL.

**2** **Shortcuts:** Keyboard shortcuts are often faster than using a mouse. Use the following: F5 (refresh); Alt+left arrow (back); Ctrl+T (new tab); Ctrl+W (close tab); Ctrl+Enter (adds "www" and ".com" to any domain name you type in the address bar).

**3** **Extensions/Add-Ons:** Many browsers, such as Chrome and Firefox, allow users to install small, third-party programs that extend, or add to, the capabilities of the browser. These programs can perform a variety of tasks, from providing easy access to your cloud services to making it easier to capture information on a web page.

**4** **Configure Settings:** All browsers have a settings or options page that provide many time-saving options. For example, you can set all the web pages that should open when you start your browser, or you can configure autocomplete options that help you to quickly fill out web forms.

To see other tips, visit our website at www.computing2014.com and enter the keyword tips.

**Figure 2-2** Browser

displaying web pages. The browser interprets the HTML formatting instructions and displays the document as a **web page**. For example, when your browser first connects to the Internet, it opens up to a web page specified in the browser settings. Web pages present information about the site along with references and **hyperlinks** or **links** that connect to other documents containing related information—text files, graphic images, audio, and video clips. (See Figure 2-5.)

**Figure 2-3** Basic parts of a URL

There are various technologies used to provide highly interactive and animated websites. These technologies include

- **Cascading style sheets (CSS)** are separate files referenced by or lines inserted into an HTML document that control the appearance of a web page, including layout, colors, and fonts. CSS help ensure that related web pages have a consistent presentation or look.

- **JavaScript** is a language often used within HTML documents to trigger interactive features, such as opening new browser windows and checking information entered in online forms.

- **AJAX**, an advanced use of JavaScript, is used to create interactive websites that respond quickly.

- **Applets** are programs that can be downloaded quickly and run by most browsers. They are used to present animation, display graphics, provide interactive games, and much more.

Today it is common to access the Internet from a variety of mobile devices like smartphones and tablets. Special browsers called **mobile browsers** are designed to run on these portable devices. Unlike a traditional web browser that is typically displayed on a large screen, a mobile browser is displayed on a very small screen and special navigational tools are required to conveniently view web content. The Apple iPhone, for example, enables you to "pinch" or "stretch" the screen with two fingers to zoom web content in and out. (See Figure 2-6.)

To learn more about browsers, visit our website at www.computing2014.com and enter the keyword **browsers**.

| Domain | Type |
|--------|------|
| .com | Commercial |
| .edu | Educational |
| .gov | Government |
| .mil | U.S. military |
| .net | Network |
| .org | Organization |

**Figure 2-4** Traditional top-level domains

Figure 2-5 Web page

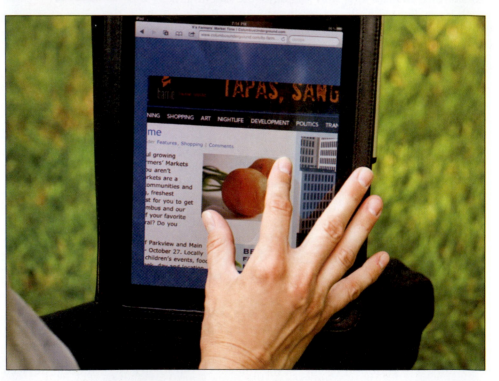

Figure 2-6 Zoom web content

## ☑ concept check

What is the function of an ISP? Describe two types of ISPs.

What is the function of a browser? What is the function of a mobile browser?

What are URLs, HTML, web pages, hyperlinks, CSS, JavaScript, AJAX, and applets?

# Communication

As previously mentioned, communication is the most popular Internet activity, and its impact cannot be overestimated. At a personal level, friends and family can stay in contact with one another even when separated by thousands of miles. At a business level, electronic communication has become a standard, and many times preferred, way to stay in touch with suppliers, employees, and customers. Some popular types of Internet communication are e-mail, messaging, social networking, blogs, microblogs, webcasts, podcasts, and wikis.

## E-mail

**E-mail** or **electronic mail** is the transmission of electronic messages over the Internet. There are two basic types of e-mail accounts: client-based and web-based.

- **Client-based e-mail accounts** require a special program known as an **e-mail client** to be installed on your computer. Before you can begin e-mailing, you need to run the e-mail client from your computer, which communicates with the e-mail service provider. Two of the most widely used e-mail clients are Apple's Mail and Microsoft's Outlook.

- **Web-based e-mail accounts** do not require an e-mail program to be installed on your computer. Once your computer's browser connects to an e-mail service provider, a special program called a **webmail client** is run on the e-mail provider's computer and then you can begin e-mailing. This is known as **webmail**. Most Internet service providers offer webmail services. Three free webmail service providers are Google's Gmail, Microsoft's Hotmail, and Yahoo!'s Yahoo!Mail.

For individual use, webmail is more widely used because it frees the user from installing and maintaining an e-mail client on every computer used to access e-mail. With webmail, you can access your e-mail from any computer anywhere that has Internet access.

A typical e-mail message has three basic elements: header, message, and signature. (See Figure 2-7.) The **header** appears first and typically includes the following information:

- **Addresses:** E-mail messages typically display the addresses of the person or persons to whom the e-mail is sent. The e-mail message in Figure 2-7 is to dcoats@usc.edu, with a copy sent to aboyd@wsu.edu. Additionally, there may be copies sent to others. These are blind copies, meaning that their addresses do not appear on any other copies of the e-mail. E-mail addresses have two basic parts. (See Figure 2-8.) The first part is the user's name and the second part is the domain name, which includes the top-level domain. In our example e-mail, *dcoats* is Dan's user name. The server providing e-mail service for Dan is *usc.edu*. The top-level domain indicates that the provider is an educational institution.

- **Subject:** A one-line description, used to present the topic of the message. Subject lines typically are displayed when a person checks his or her mailbox.

- **Attachments:** Many e-mail programs allow you to attach files such as documents and images. If a message has an attachment, the file name typically appears on the attachment line.

The letter or **message** comes next. Finally, the **signature** provides additional information about the sender. This information may include the sender's name, address, and telephone number.

E-mail can be a valuable asset in your personal and professional life. However, like many other valuable technologies, there are drawbacks too. Americans receive billions of unwanted and unsolicited e-mails every year. This unwelcome

## environment

Did you know that using e-mail is good for the environment? Writing letters and attaching files using e-mail reduce the amount of paper sent via postal mail. In addition, managing your financial and utilities accounts on the web is also healthy for the environment as it reduces the amount of paper bills you receive at home. To see more environmental facts, visit our website at www.computing2014 .com and enter the keyword environment.

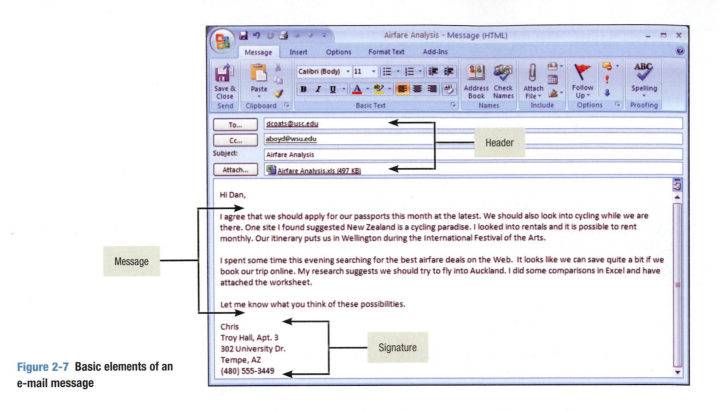

**Figure 2-7** Basic elements of an e-mail message

**Figure 2-8** Two parts of an e-mail address

mail is called **spam**. While spam is indeed a distraction and nuisance, it also can be dangerous. For example, computer **viruses** or destructive programs are often attached to unsolicited e-mail. Computer viruses and ways to protect against them will be discussed in Chapter 4.

In an attempt to control spam, antispam laws have been added to our legal system. For example, CAN-SPAM requires that every marketing-related e-mail provide an opt-out option. When the option is selected, the recipient's e-mail address is to be removed from future mailing lists. Failure to do so results in heavy fines. This approach, however, has had minimal impact since over 50 percent of all spam originates from servers outside the United States. A more effective approach to controlling spam has been the development and use of **spam blockers**, also known as **spam filters**. Most e-mail programs provide limited spam-blocking capabilities. Additionally, powerful specialized spam-blocking programs are available. Many of these programs are free, including SPAMfighter and Intego Personal Antispam for Mac.

## Messaging

While e-mail was one of the first and is one of the most popular electronic messaging systems, other messaging systems have followed. Two of the best known are text messaging and instant messaging.

- **Text messaging**, also known as **texting**, is the process of sending a short electronic message, typically less than 160 characters, using a wireless network to another person who views the message on a mobile device such as a smartphone. Today, billions of people send text messages every day. It has become one of the most widely used ways to send very short messages from one individual to another. A great deal of attention has been directed

### tips

**Are you tired of sorting through an inbox full of spam? Here are a few spam-reducing suggestions:**

1 **Keep a low profile.** Many spammers collect e-mail addresses from personal web pages, social networking sites, and message boards. Be cautious when posting your address.

2 **Use caution when giving out your address.** Many companies collect and sell e-mail addresses to spammers. Be sure to read the privacy policy of a site before providing your address.

3 **Don't ever respond to spam.** Many are a trick to validate active e-mail addresses. These addresses are worth more to spammers, who then sell the addresses to other spammers.

4 **Use antispam and filter options.** Most e-mail programs and web-based e-mail services have antispam and filter options that can be configured. Use them.

To see other tips, visit our website at www.computing2014 .com and enter the keyword tips.

toward texting while driving. A study by *Car and Driver* concluded that texting while driving had a greater negative impact on driver safety than being drunk. Several states have passed laws prohibiting texting while driving.

- **Instant messaging (IM)** allows two or more people to contact each other via direct, live communication. To use instant messaging, you register with an instant messaging server and then specify a list of **friends**. Whenever you connect to the Internet, special software informs your messaging server that you are online. In response, the server will notify you if any of your friends are online. At the same time, it notifies your friends that you are online. You can then send messages directly back and forth to one another. Most instant messaging programs also include video conferencing features, file sharing, and remote assistance. Many businesses routinely use these instant messaging features. To see how instant messaging works, visit our website at www.computing2014.com and enter the keyword **im**.

## Social Networking

**Social networking** is one of the fastest-growing and most significant Web 2.0 applications. Social networking sites focus on connecting people and organizations that share a common interest or activity. These sites typically provide a wide array of tools that facilitate meeting, communicating, and sharing. There are hundreds of social networking sites. Three of the best known are Facebook, Google+, and LinkedIn.

- **Facebook** was initially launched by a student at Harvard University for college students in 2004. By 2008 it was the most widely used social networking site. It now has a billion users worldwide. Facebook provides a wide array of features and applications including instant messaging, photo and video sharing, games, and much more.

  There are three basic categories of Facebook users: individuals, businesses, and communities. Individuals create **Facebook Profiles**, which may include photos, lists of personal interests, contact information, and other personal information. (See Figure 2-9.)

  In general, these profiles are available to friends, family members, and others who may be searching for old friends, lost relatives, or people who share a common interest. Businesses create **Facebook Pages** to promote products and services. Public figures such as politicians and entertainers frequently use Facebook Pages to connect to their constituents and fans. Communities of individuals who share a common interest create **Facebook groups** to share information. Typically, groups are organized around topics, events, or ideas. Groups allow a number of people to come together online to share information and discuss specific subjects.

- Google Inc. launched **Google+**, also known as **Google Plus**, in 2011. It is a combination of some of Google Inc.'s previously existing services with some new services. These new services include **Circles** for grouping individuals according to common interests or other criteria, **Hangouts** for communicating with up to 10 people at a time, and **Sparks**, which automatically provides news on selected topics of interest and facilitates sharing this information with others to *spark* further discussion.

**Figure 2-9  Facebook Profile**

| Organization | Site |
|---|---|
| Facebook | www.facebook.com |
| Google+ | plus.google.com |
| LinkedIn | www.linkedin.com |

**Figure 2-10  Social networking sites**

Google+ and Facebook offer similar services. Facebook, however, has been around longer and has many more users. Google+, however, is growing very fast and has over 100 million users. Some project that Google+ will to continue to grow and their number of users will approach Facebook's.

- **LinkedIn** started in 2003 and has become the premier business-oriented social networking site. Although not nearly as large as Facebook or Google+, it is the largest social networking site focusing on business professionals. It has well over 100 million users. LinkedIn provides tools to maintain business contacts, develop extended business networks, research individual businesses, search for job opportunities, and more.

For a list of some of the most popular social networking sites, see Figure 2-10.

### Blogs, Microblogs, Webcasts, Podcasts, and Wikis

In addition to social networking sites, there are other Web 2.0 applications that help ordinary people communicate across the web including blogs, microblogs, webcasts, podcasts, and wikis.

Many individuals create personal websites, called **blogs** or **web logs**, to keep in touch with friends and family. Blog postings are time-stamped and arranged with the newest item first. Often, readers of these sites are allowed to comment. Some blogs are like online diaries with personal information; others focus on information about a hobby or theme, such as knitting, electronic devices, or good books. Although most are written by individual bloggers, there are also group blogs with multiple contributors. Some businesses and newspapers also have started blogging as a quick publishing method. Several sites provide tools to create blogs. Two of the most widely used are Blogger and WordPress. (See Figure 2-11.)

A **microblog** publishes short sentences that only take a few seconds to write, rather than long stories or posts like a traditional blog. Microblogs are designed

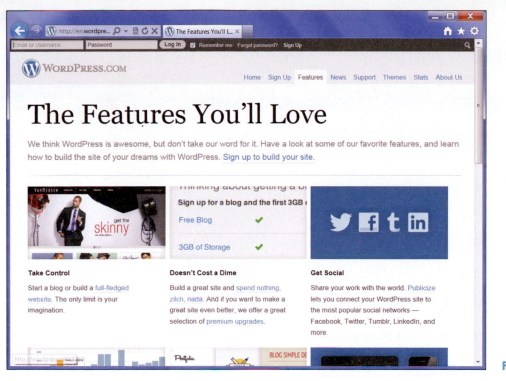

Figure 2-11 **Blog creation site**

to keep friends and other contacts up to date on your interests and activities. The most popular microblogging site, **Twitter**, enables you to add new content from your browser, instant messaging application, or even a mobile phone. To learn more about Twitter, see Making IT Work for You: Twitter on pages 40 and 41.

Both webcasts and podcasts deliver media content such as music and movies over the Internet to your computer. **Webcasts** use **streaming** technology in which audio and video files are continuously downloaded to your computer while you are listening to and/or viewing the file content. After a webcast has been completed, there are no files remaining on your computer. Webcasts typically broadcast live events. For example, the popular website YouTube.com as well as other sites routinely webcast live movie premiers and sporting events.

**Podcasts** do not use streaming technology. Before a podcast can be run, the media files have to be downloaded and saved to your computer. Once downloaded, the files can be run to listen to music or watch a movie as often as you would like. The media files can also be transferred from your computer to a media player such as an iPod. Podcasts are widely used to download music, tutorials, and educational training.

A **wiki** is a website specially designed to allow visitors to use their browser to add, edit, or delete the site's content. "Wiki" comes from the Hawaiian word for *fast*, which describes the simplicity of editing and publishing through wiki software. Wikis support collaborative writing in which there isn't a single expert author, but rather a community of interested people that builds knowledge over time. Perhaps the most famous example is **Wikipedia**, an online encyclopedia, written and edited by anyone who wants to contribute, that has millions of entries in over 20 languages. (See Figure 2-12.)

Creating blogs and wikis are examples of web authoring. We will discuss web authoring software in detail in Chapter 3. To learn more about creating your own personal website, visit us at www.computing2014.com and enter the keyword blog.

# Making IT work for you

## TWITTER

Have you used Twitter? Did you know that you can follow friends, businesses, and celebrities, as well as discover breaking news and emerging trends? It's an easy and powerful application.

**Sign Up**   To create a new Twitter account:

**1** ● Visit http://twitter.com/signup.

**2** ● Follow the on-screen instructions to create an account.

**3** ● Complete the brief tutorial from which you will choose a few users to follow.

The user name you choose will be a unique identifier for your Twitter account. For example, if your user name is "computing2014," then you will be referred to as *@computing2014* and your tweets can be viewed at *http://twitter.com/computing2014*.

**Reading Tweets**   Your Twitter home page will contain posts from everyone you follow (those whose tweets, or messages, you would like to read regularly), starting with the newest. For each tweet you can do the following:

**1** ● Move your mouse over a specific tweet to see several options.

**2** ● Click *Reply* to post a public reply to this tweet.

**3** ● Click *Retweet* if you want to share this post with your followers.

**4** ● Click *Favorite* to save this tweet to your favorites list.

**5** ● Click *Expand* to see more information about this tweet.

Some tweets have links to web pages, photos, and videos, while others have links to topics (#) or other Twitter members (@).

**Composing a Tweet**   To create a new message:

**1** ● Click the *Compose new Tweet* box.

**2** ● Type a message, noting the 140-character limit (abbreviations are encouraged). You may add a photo and/or your current location by clicking the related icons.

**3** ● Click the *Tweet* button to post the message.

Normally, only your followers will be reading your tweets on a regular basis, as the tweets will appear in their home pages or on their smartphones. However, unless you have set your account to private, keep in mind that all your tweets can be viewed by anyone on the web. Therefore, be mindful what you write.

**Following Others**   Twitter members can be people or organizations. There are several ways to find members to follow:

**1** ● If you know the name of the member, just type it in the *Search* box at the top.

**2** ● In the results area, click the *Follow* button next to the member you were looking for.

Search box

Follow button

Alternatively, you can click any *mention* (@) link in a Tweet to bring up that member's profile, or you can use the # *Discover* area discussed below.

**Trends and Stories**   One of the most powerful features of Twitter is its ability to inform us of trending topics and stories. It analyzes what members are posting about most often and which topics are creating the most buzz at the moment. To discover these trends and stories:

**1** ● Click the # *Discover* button at the top of the page. Top stories appear on the right.

**2** ● Click any of the trends on the left side to view all tweets that include that topic (this area also appears on your home page).

The web is continually changing, and some of the specifics presented in this Making IT Work for You may have changed. **To learn about other ways to make information technology work for you, visit our website at www.computing2014.com and enter the keyword** miw.

Figure 2-12 Wikipedia

## concept check

Define e-mail. What is the difference between client- and web-based e-mail accounts? What is webmail?

What is text messaging? What is instant messaging?

What is social networking? Describe three well-known sites.

Describe the differences between blogs, microblogs, webcasts, podcasts, and wikis.

# Search Tools

The web can be an incredible resource, providing information on nearly any topic imaginable. Are you planning a trip? Writing an economics paper? Looking for a movie review? Trying to locate a long-lost friend? Information sources related to these questions, and much, much more, are available on the web.

With over 20 billion pages and more being added daily, the web is a massive collection of interrelated pages. With so much available information, locating the precise information you need can be difficult. Fortunately, a number of organizations called **search services** operate websites that can help you locate the information you need. They maintain huge databases relating to information provided on the web and the Internet. The information stored at these databases includes addresses, content descriptions or classifications, and keywords appearing on web pages and other Internet informational resources. Special programs called **spiders** continually look for new information and update the search services' databases. Additionally, search services provide

**Figure 2-13** Google search engine

special programs called *search engines* that you can use to locate specific information on the web.

## Search Engines

**Search engines** are specialized programs that assist you in locating information on the web and the Internet. To find information, you go to a search service's website and use its search engine. For example, see Figure 2-13 for Google's search engine.

To use a search website, you enter a keyword or phrase reflecting the information you want. The search engine compares your entry against its database and returns a list of **hits**, or sites that contain the keywords. Each hit includes a link to the referenced web page (or other resource) along with a brief discussion of the information contained at that location. Many searches result in a large number of hits. For example, if you were to enter the keyword *music,* you would get billions of hits. Search engines order the hits according to those sites that most likely contain the information requested and present the list to you in that order, usually in groups of 10. See Figure 2-14 for a list of commonly used search engines.

Since each search service maintains its own database, the hits returned by one search engine will not necessarily be the same hits returned by another search engine. Therefore, when researching a topic, it is best to use more than one search engine.

| Search Service | Site |
| --- | --- |
| Ask | www.ask.com |
| Bing | www.bing.com |
| Google | www.google.com |
| Yahoo! | www.yahoo.com |

**Figure 2-14** Search engines

## Specialized Search Engines

**Specialized search engines** focus on subject-specific websites. Specialized sites can potentially save you time by narrowing your search. For a list of just a few selected specialized search engines, see Figure 2-15. For example, let's say you are researching a paper about the fashion industry. You could begin with a general search engine like Yahoo! Or you could go to a search engine that specializes specifically in fashion, such as www.shopstyle.com.

| Topic | Site |
| --- | --- |
| Environment | www.ecoearth.info |
| Fashion | www.shopstyle.com |
| History | www.historynet.com |
| Law | www.findlaw.com |
| Medicine | www.webmd.com |

**Figure 2-15** Select specialized search engines

To locate other specialized search engines, use a search service and enter the topic area followed by *specialized search engine*. For example, entering *sports specialized search engine* will return several search engines dedicated specifically to sports information.

### Content Evaluation

Search engines are excellent tools to locate information on the web. Be careful, however, how you use the information you find. Unlike most published material found in newspapers, journals, and textbooks, not all the information you find on the web has been subjected to strict guidelines to ensure accuracy. In fact, anyone can publish content on the web. Many sites, such as Wikipedia.org, allow anyone to post new material, sometimes anonymously and without critical evaluation. To learn how you can publish on the web, visit our website at www.computing2014.com and enter the keyword blog.

To evaluate the accuracy of information you find on the web, consider the following:

- **Authority.** Is the author an expert in the subject area? Is the site an official site for the information presented, or is the site an individual's personal website?

- **Accuracy.** Has the information been critically reviewed for correctness prior to posting on the web? Does the website provide a method to report inaccurate information to the author?

- **Objectivity.** Is the information factually reported or does the author have a bias? Does the author appear to have a personal agenda aimed at convincing or changing the reader's opinion?

- **Currency.** Is the information up to date? Does the site specify the date when the site was updated? Are the site's links operational? If not, the site is most likely not being actively maintained.

## concept check

What are search services, spiders, and search engines?

Compare search engines and specialized search engines.

What are the four considerations for evaluating website content?

# Electronic Commerce

**Electronic commerce**, also known as **e-commerce**, is the buying and selling of goods over the Internet. Electronic commerce is fast-growing and widely used in part because it provides incentives for both buyers and sellers. From the buyer's perspective, goods and services can be purchased at any time of day or night from any location that has an Internet connection. From the seller's perspective, the costs associated with owning and operating a retail outlet can be eliminated. Another advantage is reduced inventory. Traditional stores maintain an inventory of goods in their stores and periodically replenish this inventory from warehouses. With e-commerce, there is no in-store inventory and products are shipped directly from warehouses.

While there are numerous advantages to e-commerce, there are disadvantages as well. Some of these disadvantages include the inability to provide immediate delivery of goods, the inability to "try on" prospective purchases, and questions relating to the security of online payments. Although these issues are being addressed, very few observers suggest that e-commerce will replace bricks-and-mortar businesses entirely. It is clear that both will coexist and that e-commerce will continue to grow.

Just like any other type of commerce, electronic commerce involves two parties: businesses and consumers. There are three basic types of electronic commerce:

- **Business-to-consumer (B2C)** commerce involves the sale of a product or service to the general public or end users. It is the fastest-growing type of e-commerce. Whether large or small, nearly every existing corporation in the United States provides some type of B2C support as another means to connect to customers. Because extensive investments are not required to create traditional retail outlets and to maintain large marketing and sales staffs, e-commerce allows start-up companies to compete with larger established firms. The three most widely used B2C applications are for *online banking*, financial trading, and shopping. Amazon.com is one of the most widely used B2C sites.

- **Consumer-to-consumer (C2C)** commerce involves individuals selling to individuals. C2C often takes the form of an electronic version of the classified ads or an auction. **Web auctions** are similar to traditional auctions except that buyers and sellers seldom, if ever, meet face to face. Sellers post descriptions of products at a website, and buyers submit bids electronically. Like traditional auctions, sometimes the bidding becomes highly competitive and enthusiastic. One of the most widely used auction sites is eBay.com. For a list of some of the most popular web auction sites, see Figure 2-16.

| Organization | Site |
|---|---|
| eBid | www.ebid.net |
| QuiBids | www.quibids.com |
| eBay | www.ebay.com |
| uBid | www.ubid.com |

**Figure 2-16 Auction sites**

- **Business-to-business (B2B)** commerce involves the sale of a product or service from one business to another. This is typically a manufacturer-supplier relationship. For example, a furniture manufacturer requires raw materials such as wood, paint, and varnish.

## Security

The two greatest challenges for e-commerce are (1) developing fast, secure, and reliable payment methods for purchased goods and (2) providing convenient ways to submit required information such as mailing addresses and credit card information.

The two basic payment options are by credit card and by digital cash:

- Credit card purchases are faster and more convenient than check purchases. Credit card fraud, however, is a major concern for both buyers and sellers. We will discuss this and other privacy and security issues related to the Internet in Chapter 9.

- **Digital cash** is the Internet's equivalent to traditional cash. Buyers purchase digital cash from a third party (a bank that specializes in electronic currency) and use it to purchase goods. (See Figure 2-17.) Sellers convert the digital cash to traditional currency through the third party. Although not as convenient as credit card purchases, digital cash is more secure. For a list of digital cash providers, see Figure 2-18.

Explorations

Some companies have developed payment systems known as digital wallets that store your credit cards, coupons, and gift cards on your smartphone.

**To learn more about these new digital wallets, visit our website at www.computing2014.com and enter the keyword wallet.**

**Figure 2-17** PayPal offers digital cash

| Organization | Site |
|---|---|
| Amazon | payments.amazon.com |
| Google | wallet.google.com |
| Serve | www.serve.com |
| PayPal | www.paypal.com |

**Figure 2-18** Digital cash providers

☑ **concept check**

What is electronic commerce?

What are the three basic types of e-commerce?

What are the two basic payment options?

## environment

Did you know that the move to cloud computing could benefit the environment? Large computers, such as servers and mainframes, use a significant amount of energy for both their operation and their cooling. Using large cloud computing data centers, which are shared by many companies, can be more energy efficient than having the individual companies using their own servers. To see more environmental facts, visit our website at www.computing2014.com and enter the keyword environment.

# Cloud Computing

Typically, application programs are owned by individuals or organizations and stored on their computer system's hard disks. As discussed in Chapter 1, **cloud computing** uses the Internet and the web to shift many of these computer activities from the user's computer to other computers on the Internet.

While some suggest that *cloud computing* is merely a marketing term designed to promote new products, many others see cloud computing as a new model for computing that frees users from owning, maintaining, and storing software and data. It provides access to these services from anywhere through an Internet connection. Several prominent firms are aggressively pursuing this new concept. These firms include Google, IBM, Intel, and Microsoft to name just a few.

The basic components to cloud computing are clients, the Internet, and service providers. (See Figure 2-19.)

• Clients are corporations and end users who want access to data, programs, and storage. This access is to be available anywhere and anytime that a connection to the Internet is available. End users do not need to buy, install, and maintain application programs and data.

**Figure 2-19 Cloud computing**

- The Internet provides the connection between the clients and the providers. Two of the most critical factors determining the efficiency of cloud computing are (1) the speed and reliability of the user's access to the Internet and (2) the Internet's capability to provide safe and reliable transmission of data and programs.

- Service providers are organizations with computers connected to the Internet that are willing to provide access to software, data, and storage. These providers may charge a fee or may be free. For example, Google Apps provides free access to programs with capabilities similar to Microsoft's Word, Excel, and PowerPoint. (See Figure 2-20.)

**Figure 2-20 Web-based service (Google Apps)**

In the following chapters, you will learn more about the services provided through cloud computing. You will also learn about security and privacy challenges associated with cloud computing.

## concept check

What is cloud computing?

What are the three basic components of cloud computing?

What are the two most critical factors that determine the efficiency of cloud computing?

# Web Utilities

Utilities are programs that make computing easier. **Web utilities** are specialized utility programs that make using the Internet and the web easier and safer. Some of these utilities are browser-related programs that either become part of your browser or are executed from your browser. Others are designed to protect children from dangerous and inappropriate website material. File transfer utilities allow you to efficiently copy files to and from your computer across the Internet.

## Plug-ins

**Plug-ins** are programs that are automatically started and operate as a part of your browser. Many websites require you to have one or more plug-ins to fully experience their content. Some widely used plug-ins include

- Acrobat Reader from Adobe—for viewing and printing a variety of standard forms and other documents saved in a special format called PDF.
- Flash Player from Adobe—for viewing videos, animations, and other media.
- QuickTime from Apple—for playing audio and video files. (See Figure 2-21.)
- Windows Media Player from Microsoft—for playing audio files, video files, and much more.
- RealPlayer from RealNetworks—for playing audio and video files.

**Figure 2-21 QuickTime movie at Apple.com**

Some of these utilities are included in many of today's browsers and operating systems. Others must be installed before they can be used by your browser. To learn more about plug-ins and how to download them, visit some of the sites listed in Figure 2-22.

| Plug-in | Source |
|---------|--------|
| Reader | get.adobe.com/reader |
| Flash Player | get.adobe.com/flashplayer |
| QuickTime | www.apple.com/quicktime |
| Silverlight | www.microsoft.com/silverlight |

**Figure 2-22 Plug-in sites**

### Filters

**Filters** block access to selected sites. The Internet is an interesting and multifaceted arena. But one of those facets is a dark and undesirable one. Parents, in particular, are concerned about children roaming unrestricted across the Internet. Filter programs allow parents as well as organizations to block out selected sites and set time limits. (See Figure 2-23.) Additionally, these programs can monitor use and generate reports detailing the total time spent on the Internet and the time spent at individual websites. For a list of some of the best-known filters, see Figure 2-24.

### File Transfer Utilities

Using file transfer utility software, you can copy files to your computer from specially configured servers. This is called **downloading**. You also can use file transfer utility software to copy files from your computer to another computer on the Internet. This is called **uploading**. Three popular types of file transfer are FTP, web-based, and BitTorrent.

**Figure 2-23 Net Nanny is a web filter**

| Filter | Site |
|---|---|
| CyberPatrol | www.cyberpatrol.com |
| Pearl Echo | www.pearlsw.com |
| Norton Online Family | onlinefamily.norton.com |
| Net Nanny | www.netnanny.com |
| Symantec Web Gateway | symantec.com/web-gateway |

**Figure 2-24** Filters

- **File transfer protocol (FTP)** and **secure file transfer protocol (SFTP)** allow you to efficiently copy files to and from your computer across the Internet, and are frequently used for uploading changes to a website hosted by an Internet service provider. FTP has been used for decades and still remains one of the most popular methods of file transfer.

- **Web-based file transfer services** make use of a web browser to upload and download files. This eliminates the need for any custom software to be installed. A popular web-based file transfer service is Dropbox.com.

- **BitTorrent** distributes file transfers across many different computers for more efficient downloads, unlike other transfer technologies where a file is copied from one computer on the Internet to another. A single file might be located on dozens of individual computers. When you download the file, each computer sends you a tiny piece of the larger file, making Bit-Torrent well-suited for transferring very large files. Unfortunately, BitTorrent technology often has been used for distributing unauthorized copies of copyrighted music and video.

### Internet Security Suites

An **Internet security suite** is a collection of utility programs designed to maintain your security and privacy while you are on the web. These programs control spam, protect against computer viruses, provide filters, and much more. You could buy each program separately; however, the cost of the suite is typically much less. Two of the best-known Internet security suites are McAfee's Internet Security and Symantec's Norton Internet Security. (See Figure 2-25.)

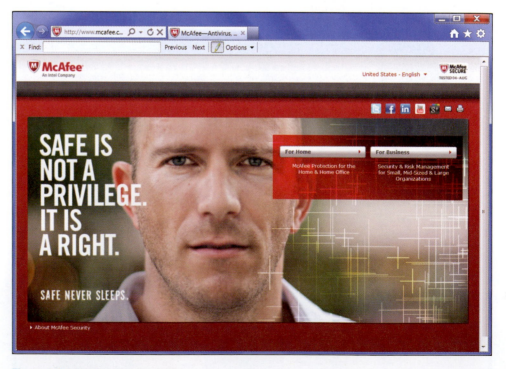

**Figure 2-25** McAfee security suite

# Careers in IT

**Webmasters** develop and maintain websites and resources. The job may include backup of the company website, updating resources, or development of new resources. Webmasters are often involved in the design and development of the website. Some webmasters monitor traffic on the site and take steps to encourage users to visit the site. Webmasters also may work with marketing personnel to increase site traffic and may be involved in development of web promotions.

Employers look for candidates with a bachelor's or associate's degree in computer science or information systems and knowledge of common programming languages and web development software. Knowledge of HTML and CSS is considered essential. Those with experience using web authoring software and programs like Adobe Illustrator and Adobe Flash are often preferred. Good communication and organizational skills are vital in this position.

Webmasters can expect to earn an annual salary of $56,000 to $80,000. This position is relatively new in many corporations and tends to have fluid responsibilities. With technological advances and increasing corporate emphasis on a web presence, experience in this field could lead to managerial opportunities. To learn about other careers in IT, visit us at www.computing2014.com and enter the keyword careers.

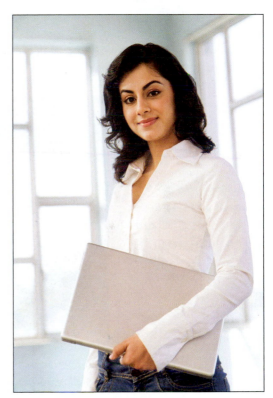

Now that you've learned about the Internet, the web, and electronic commerce, I'd like to tell you about my career as a webmaster.

# A LOOK TO THE FUTURE

## Your Car's Dashboard as a Powerful, Internet-Connected Computing Device

Do you often wish that your car could provide information as quickly and easily as your computer? Today, many of your car's functions are already governed by a computer located within the vehicle. That computer is responsible for various safety and diagnostic features. However, compared to activities and conveniences that you enjoy on your notebooks, tablets, and smartphones, cars have fallen way behind. Even fancy $2000 navigation systems that many manufacturers offer are limited in comparison to modern computing devices.

Imagine if Apple or Google created a partnership with automobile manufacturers to place iPad or Android devices into the center of the main console. Cars could connect to Wi-Fi access points or 4G networks to reach the Internet as the modern smartphone does. These developments would allow your vehicle to provide many services that normally require a smartphone but in a safer and more integrated manner.

One of the immediate benefits involves quick access to information. Drivers would get real-time traffic data, weather, store hours, and much more. Next is the access to all the apps that you expect to have. One example is the Pandora service, which allows you to stream free, ad-supported music from stations you create yourself. Why pay for satellite radio or listen to stations that you don't enjoy when you can access your favorite online music services right from your dashboard? Another benefit is the entertainment of your passengers or children. Some vehicles include screens that face the back seats, allowing parents to play DVDs for their children. Since many individuals already pay for an online streaming video service, wouldn't it be more convenient to give your children access to this enormous library of cartoons and movies instead of sliding DVDs in and out each time you enter the vehicle? In fact, with a tabletlike interface, your child could choose from a preset selection of movies or educational games, depending on their mood.

Now, such a tool at your fingertips has the risk of becoming a distraction while you're driving. There is no question that safety features must be built in to prevent accidents from occurring. Luckily, there is already a piece of technology that will prevent the driver from ever having to touch the dashboard: voice recognition.

In the same way that Apple's "Siri" has revolutionized the way individuals interact with their iPhones, a similar system could be installed in the new dashboards. Drivers will simply speak their commands to get the information they need and to use the vehicle's controls. Furthermore, this computer system could use existing technologies that recognize and speak English to the user. This will allow the driver to hear e-mail messages, social network updates, and today's news and weather while driving to work.

Some companies have already taken a step in implementing this future technology. Ford uses voice recognition in some of its vehicles with a feature called Sync with MyFord Touch. Audi has added 3G connectivity in its new A7 model. However, the real breakthrough will come when your car's dashboard becomes as useful and versatile as an iPad or Android tablet and the vehicle itself can reliably connect to Wi-Fi and 4G networks. According to *Car and Driver* magazine, this may happen within the next five years. When it does, do you see yourself paying for this upgrade in your next car? Are you willing to pay for it if it requires another monthly data plan from a wireless provider?

## INTERNET AND WEB

### Internet

Launched in 1969 with **ARPANET**, the **Internet** consists of the actual physical network.

### Web

Introduced in 1991 at **CERN**, the **web** provides a multimedia interface to Internet resources. Three generations: **Web 1.0** (existing information), **Web 2.0** (content creation and social interaction), **Web 3.0** (computer-generated information).

### Common Uses

The most common uses of the Internet and the web include

- Communication—the most popular Internet activity.
- Shopping—one of the fastest-growing Internet activities.
- Searching—access libraries and local, national, and international news.
- Education—**e-learning** or taking online courses.
- Entertainment—music, movies, magazines, and computer games.

## ACCESS

Once connected to the Internet, your computer seemingly becomes an extension of a giant computer that branches all over the world.

### Providers

**Internet service providers** are connected to the Internet, providing a path for individuals to access the Internet. Connection technologies include **DSL**, **cable**, and **wireless modems**.

### Browsers

**Browsers** access the web allowing you to **surf** or explore. Some related terms are

- **URLs**—**locations** or **addresses** to web resources; two parts are **protocol** and **domain name**; **top-level domain (TLD)** or **web suffix** identifies type of organization.
- **HTML**—commands to display **web pages**; **hyperlinks (links)** are connections.

Technologies providing interactive, animated websites include **cascading style sheets**, or **CSS** (to control the appearance of web pages); **JavaScript** (to trigger interactive features); **AJAX** (to create quick response interactive websites; and **applets** (to present animation, display graphics, provide interactive games, and more).

**Mobile browsers** run on portable devices.

To be a competent end user, you need to be aware of resources available on the Internet and web, to be able to access these resources, to effectively communicate electronically, to efficiently locate information, to understand electronic commerce, and to use web utilities.

## COMMUNICATION

### E-mail

**E-mail (electronic mail)** is the transmission of electronic messages. There are two basic types of e-mail accounts:

- **Client-based e-mail accounts** use **e-mail clients** installed on your computer.
- **Web-based e-mail accounts** use **webmail clients** located on the e-mail provider's computer. This is known as **webmail**.

A typical e-mail has three basic elements: **header** (including **address**, **subject**, and perhaps **attachment**), **message**, and **signature**.

**Spam** is unwanted and unsolicited e-mail that may include a *computer* **virus** or destructive programs often attached to unsolicited e-mail. **Spam blockers**, also known as **spam filters**, are programs that identify and eliminate spam.

### Messaging

While e-mail is the most widely used, two other messaging systems are

- **Text messaging**—sending short electronic messages between mobile devices.
- **Instant messaging (IM)**—supports live communication between friends.

## COMMUNICATION

### Social Networking

**Social networks** connect individuals to one another. Many sites support a variety of different activites. Three of the best known are **Facebook** (provides access to **Facebook Profiles**, **Facebook Pages**, and **Facebook groups**), **Google+** (provides access to **Circles**, **Hangouts**, and **Sparks**), and **LinkedIn**.

### Blogs, Webcasts, and Wikis

Other sites that help individuals communicate across the web are blogs, microblogs, webcasts, podcasts, and wikis.

- **Blogs (web logs)** and **microblogs** are online journals that support chronological postings. Unlike blogs that often contain detailed postings, microblogs publish short, concise sentences. **Twitter** is the most popular microblogging site.
- **Webcasts** and **podcasts** deliver audio, video, and other media content over the Internet. Unlike podcasts, webcasts use **streaming** technology.
- A **wiki** is a website designed to allow visitors to use their browsers to add, edit, or delete the site's content. Wikis are often used to support collaborative writing in which there is a community of interested contributors. **Wikipedia** is one of the most popular wikis.

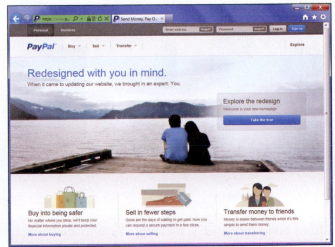

**Search services** maintain huge databases relating to website content. **Spiders** are programs that update these databases.

### Search Engines

**Search engines** are specialized programs to help locate information. To use, enter a keyword or phrase and a list of **hits** or links to references is displayed.

### Specialized Search Engines

**Specialized search engines** focus on subject-specific websites.

### Content Evaluation

To evaluate the accuracy of information found on the web, consider the following:

* Authority. It the author an expert? Is the site official or does it present one individual's or organization's opinion.
* Accuracy. Has the information been critically reviewed? Does the site provide a method to report inaccurate information?
* Objectivity. Is the information factual or does the author have a bias? Does the author appear to have a personal agenda to convince or form a reader's opinion?
* Currency. Is the information up to date? Does the site specify when information is updated? Are the site's links operational?

| Topic | Site |
|-------|------|
| Environment | www.ecoearth.info |
| Fashion | www.shopstyle.com |
| History | www.historynet.com |
| Law | www.findlaw.com |
| Medicine | www.webmd.com |

**Electronic commerce**, or **e-commerce**, is the buying and selling of goods over the Internet. Three basic types of e-commerce are **business-to-consumer, consumer-to-consumer**, and **business-to-business**.

* **Business-to-consumer (B2C)** commerce involves sales from business to the general public. It is the fastest-growing type. Three of the most widely used applications are online banking, financial trading, and shopping.
* **Consumer-to-consumer (C2C)** commerce involves sales between individuals, often as the electronic version of classified ads or an auction. **Web auctions** are similar to traditional auctions except buyers and sellers rarely, if ever, meet face to face.
* **Business-to-business (B2B)** commerce involves sales from one business to another, typically a manufacturer-supplier relationship.

### Security

The two greatest challenges for e-commerce are the development of

* Safe, secure payment methods. Two types are **credit cards** and **digital cash** (third party sells digital cash to buyers and redeems for sellers).
* Convenient ways to provide required information such as mailing addresses and credit card information.

| Organization | Site |
|--------------|------|
| eBid | www.ebid.net |
| QuiBids | www.quibids.com |
| eBay | www.ebay.com |
| uBid | www.ubid.com |

# CLOUD COMPUTING

Cloud computing uses the Internet and the web to shift many computer activities from the user's computer to other computers on the Internet.

## Components

There are three basic components to cloud computing:

- Clients are corporations and end users who want access to data, programs, and storage.
- The Internet provides the connection between the clients and providers. Two critical factors are the speed and reliability of the user's access and the Internet's capability to provide safe and reliable access.
- Service providers are organizations with computers connected to the Internet that are willing to provide access to software, data, and storage.

# WEB UTILITIES

| Plug-in | Source |
| --- | --- |
| Reader | get.adobe.com/reader |
| Flash Player | get.adobe.com/flashplayer |
| QuickTime | www.apple.com/quicktime |
| Silverlight | www.microsoft.com/silverlight |

Web utilities are specialized utility programs that make using the Internet and the web easier and safer.

## Plug-ins

Plug-ins are automatically loaded and operate as part of a browser. Many websites require specific plug-ins to fully experience their content. Some plug-ins are included in many of today's browsers; others must be installed.

## Filters

Filters are used by parents and organizations to block certain sites and to monitor use of the Internet and the web.

## File Transfer Utilities

File transfer utilities copy files to (**downloading**) and from (**uploading**) your computer. Three types are

- **File transfer protocol (FTP)** and **secure file transfer protocol (SFTP)** allow you to efficiently copy files across the Internet.
- **Web-based file transfer services** make use of a web browser to upload and download files.
- **BitTorrent** distributes file transfers across many different computers.

## Internet Security Suite

An **Internet security suite** is a collection of utility programs designed to protect your privacy and security on the Internet.

# CAREERS IN IT

**Webmasters** develop and maintain websites and web resources. Bachelor's or associate's degree in computer science or information systems and knowledge of common programming languages and web development software are required. Salary range is $56,000 to $80,000.

# KEY TERMS

address   (32, 35)
Advanced Research
Project Agency Network
(ARPANET)   (28)
AJAX   (33)
applets   (33)
attachment   (35)
BitTorrent   (50)
blog   (38)
browser   (32)
business-to-business
(B2B)   (45)
business-to-consumer
(B2C)   (45)
cable   (32)
cascading style sheets
(CSS)   (33)
Center for European
Nuclear Research
(CERN)   (28)
Circles   (37)
client-based e-mail
account   (35)
cloud computing   (46)
consumer-to-consumer
(C2C)   (45)
digital cash   (45)
domain name   (32)
downloading   (49)
DSL   (32)
e-commerce   (44)
e-learning   (29)
electronic
commerce   (44)
electronic mail   (35)
e-mail   (35)
e-mail client   (35)
Facebook   (37)
Facebook groups   (37)

Facebook Pages   (37)
Facebook Profile   (37)
file transfer protocol
(FTP)   (50)
filter   (49)
friend   (37)
Google Plus   (37)
Google+   (37)
Hangouts   (37)
header   (35)
hit   (43)
hyperlink   (33)
Hypertext Markup
Language (HTML)   (32)
instant messaging
(IM)   (37)
Internet   (28)
Internet security
suite   (50)
Internet service provider
(ISP)   (32)
JavaScript   (33)
link   (33)
LinkedIn   (38)
location   (32)
message   (35)
microblog   (38)
mobile browser   (33)
online   (28)
plug-in   (48)
podcast   (39)
protocol   (32)
search engine   (43)
search service   (42)
secure file transfer
protocol (SFTP)   (50)
signature   (35)
social networking   (37)
spam   (36)

spam blocker   (36)
spam filter   (36)
Sparks   (37)
specialized search
engine   (43)
spider   (42)
streaming   (39)
subject   (35)
surf   (32)
texting   (36)
text messaging   (36)
top-level domain
(TLD)   (32)
Twitter   (39)
uniform resource
locator (URL)   (32)
uploading   (49)
virus   (36)
web   (28)
Web 1.0   (28)
Web 2.0   (28)
Web 3.0   (28)
web auction   (45)
web-based e-mail
account   (35)
web-based file transfer
services   (50)
webcasts   (39)
web log   (38)
webmail   (35)
webmail client   (35)
webmaster   (51)
web page   (33)
web suffix   (32)
web utility   (48)
wiki   (39)
Wikipedia   (39)
wireless modem   (32)

To test your knowledge of these key terms with animated flash cards, visit our website at www.computing2014.com and enter the keyword terms2. Or use the free *Computing Essentials 2014* app.

# MULTIPLE CHOICE

Circle the correct answer.

1. The network that connects computers all over the world.
   - **a.** CERN
   - **b.** Internet
   - **c.** LAN
   - **d.** web

2. The rules for exchanging data between computers.
   - **a.** DSL
   - **b.** protocols
   - **c.** web
   - **d.** WWW

3. Client-based e-mail accounts require this special program to be installed on your computer.
   - **a.** e-mail client
   - **b.** hyperlink
   - **c.** JavaScript
   - **d.** utility

4. Communities of individuals who share a common interest typically create Facebook:
   - **a.** clients
   - **b.** groups
   - **c.** Pages
   - **d.** Profiles

5. E-mail that does not require an e-mail program installed on a user's computer is known as:
   - **a.** a blog
   - **b.** a podcast
   - **c.** webmail
   - **d.** a utility

6. A very well-known microblog.
   - **a.** LinkedIn
   - **b.** Google+
   - **c.** Twitter
   - **d.** Wikipedia

7. These programs continually look for new information and update search services' database programs.
   - **a.** filters
   - **b.** IM
   - **c.** spiders
   - **d.** wikis

8. Using a keyword, a search engine returns a list of related sites known as:
   - **a.** blogs
   - **b.** hits
   - **c.** podcasts
   - **d.** strikes

9. This is the Internet's equivalent to traditional cash.
   - **a.** digital cash
   - **b.** e-commerce
   - **c.** icash
   - **d.** Internet dollars

10. Using file transfer utility software, you can copy files to your computer from specially configured servers on the Internet. This is called:
    - **a.** downloading
    - **b.** filtering
    - **c.** blogging
    - **d.** uploading

For an interactive multiple-choice practice test, visit our website at www.computing2014.com and enter the keyword multiple2. Or use the free *Computing Essentials 2014* app.

# MATCHING

Match each numbered item with the most closely related lettered item. Write your answers in the spaces provided.

a. communicating
b. C2C
c. e-mail
d. Internet
e. ISP
f. LinkedIn
g. microblog
h. search services
i. universal
j. web log

_____ 1. The most popular Internet activity.

_____ 2. The most common way to access the Internet is through a(n) _____.

_____ 3. Transmission of electronic messages over the Internet.

_____ 4. Type of instant messaging service that supports a variety of different IM services.

_____ 5. The premier business-oriented social networking site.

_____ 6. Another name for a blog.

_____ 7. Publishes short sentences that only take a few seconds to write.

_____ 8. Maintain huge databases relating to information provided on the web and the Internet.

_____ 9. Electronic commerce involving individuals selling to individuals.

_____10. The basic components of cloud computing are clients, service providers, and the _____.

For an interactive matching practice test, visit our website at www.computing2014.com and enter the keyword matching2. Or use the free *Computing Essentials 2014* app.

# OPEN-ENDED

On a separate sheet of paper, respond to each question or statement.

1. Discuss the Internet, including its origins, the three generations of the web, and the most common uses.

2. Describe how to access the Internet. What are providers? Define browsers and discuss URLs, HTML, CSS, JavaScript, AJAX, applets, and mobile browsers.

3. Discuss Internet communications including client-based and web-based e-mail, instant and text messaging, social networking, blogs, microblogs, webcasts, podcasts, and wikis.

4. Define search tools including search services. Discuss search engines and specialized search engines. Describe how to evaluate the content of a website.

5. Describe electronic commerce including business-to-consumer, consumer-to-consumer, and business-to-business e-commerce, and security.

6. What is cloud computing? Describe the three basic components of cloud computing.

7. What are web utilities? Discuss plug-ins, filters, file transfer utilities, and Internet security suites.

# DISCUSSION

Respond to each of the following questions.

### 1 Making IT Work for You: ONLINE ENTERTAINMENT

Are you one of the millions of people who regularly use streaming technology to watch favorite television programs, movies, and other video content? Review the Making IT Work for You: Online Entertainment on pages 30 and 31 and then respond to the following: (a) Do you currently have a subscription to Netflix, Hulu Plus, or another service that allows you to stream movies and TV shows? If so, which ones? If not, do you plan on using one in the future? Why or why not? (b) Name at least three TV shows that you currently watch or are interested in watching. Next, list a few services that include these shows as part of a subscription. If none does, list a few online stores where you can purchase and stream these episodes. (c) What device do you use most often to watch video content from the web? Would you consider purchasing a dedicated streaming device such as the Roku? Why or why not? (d) Could ever see yourself canceling or "cutting the cord" from your current cable or satellite service? Why or why not?

### 2 Making IT Work for You: TWITTER

Did you know that Twitter can be used to follow friends, businesses, and celebrities, as well as discover breaking news and emerging trends? Review the Making IT Work for You: Twitter on pages 40 and 41 and create a Twitter account if you do not already have one. Then respond to the following: (a) In your opinion, what are the primary benefits of Twitter? (b) List five users that you currently follow or would like to follow in the future. Why did you select those individuals or organizations? (c) If you have already posted your own tweets, briefly explain the type of content you typically post. If you have not posted anything, do you feel that you will in the future? Why or why not?

### 3 Explorations: INTERNET HISTORY

How much do you know about the history of the Internet and the web? Review the Explorations box on page 28 and then respond to the following: (a) What was the original Internet known as? In what year was it activated? How many locations did it connect? (b) In what year was TCP/IP created? Why was this development so important? (c) Who created the World Wide Web? In what year was it introduced to the public? What were some of the factors that allowed it to succeed? (d) What was the first graphical web browser? Who created it? Why was the browser so revolutionary?

### 4 Explorations: DIGITAL WALLETS

Did you know that your smartphone could be used to hold all your credit cards, coupons, and gift cards? Review the Explorations box on page 45 and then respond to the following: (a) What is the name of the digital wallet product? Which mobile operating systems is it compatible with? Does your smartphone need to have a specific technology to complete in-person transactions? If so, what? (b) How does this product work? Provide details on both the setup and use of the product. (c) Is this technology safe and secure? Support your answer with details. (d) Find three stores in your area that accept payments with this technology. If none exists in your area, list three online stores. (e) Would you use a digital wallet? Why or why not?

## 5 · Ethics: BLOGS

Almost half a million people are paid to create blogs, and many of those are being paid to write favorable reviews of products and services. Review the Ethics box on page 38 and respond to the following: (a) Do you think it is unethical for bloggers to write positive reviews for the companies that pay them? Why or why not? (b) Should there be disclaimers on paid blog posts? If so, how can such a policy be enforced? Explain your answer. (c) If you found out that a particular company paid bloggers for favorable reviews, would you continue to buy its products? Why or why not? (d) If you were to use a blog for product information, what could you do to determine whether the content is unbiased?

## 6 · Ethics: FILTERING AND MONITORING

Parents can use content filters and monitoring software to restrict or monitor their child's Internet behavior. Review the Ethics box on page 49 and respond to the following: (a) Is it ethical for parents to filter Internet content that they deem to be unsafe or inappropriate for their children? Does your answer depend on the age of the child? Defend your position. (b) Is it ethical for parents to monitor the Internet activity of their children? What if the monitoring software captures more than just web pages? What if it records instant messages, incoming e-mail, and even passwords? Explain your position. (c) Should parents inform their children that Internet activity is being filtered or monitored? Why or why not? (d) Do you feel that filtering or monitoring software is the best way to protect children? Do you feel that it hurts the trust between a parent and child? In your responses, be sure to include your opinion as to whether or not you would ever use such software.

## 7 · Environment: E-MAIL

Did you know that using e-mail and managing your bills on the web are good for the environment? Review the Environment box on page 35 and then respond to the following: (a) When it comes to sending letters, holiday cards, and invitations to friends and family, do you mostly use e-mail or postal mail? What are your reasons for choosing one over the other? (b) Are there any situations where you feel that using e-mail would not be advantageous? (c) Have you signed up for paperless billing from your financial institutions and utility companies? Why or why not? (d) Go through all the paper mail you have received in the last week or two. Is there anything there that you could receive via e-mail or view on the web? List a few examples.

## 8 · Environment: CLOUD COMPUTING

Did you know that the move to cloud computing could benefit the environment? Review the Environment box on page 46 and then use a search engine to find a cloud computing company that claims to offer energy-saving benefits. Respond to the following questions about your research: (a) How does this company's cloud services benefit the environment? (b) What steps has the cloud company taken to reduce their carbon emissions? (c) Do you believe that cloud computing is more energy efficient than having many companies running their own servers? Why or why not? (d) Is it possible that the expansion of cloud computing could actually increase the overall energy consumption of the planet? Explain your answer.

# Application Software

## Competencies

### After you have read this chapter, you should be able to:

1 Discuss general-purpose applications.

2 Describe word processors, spreadsheets, database management systems, and presentation programs.

3 Discuss specialized applications.

4 Describe graphics programs, web authoring programs, and other specialized professional applications.

5 Describe mobile apps and app stores.

6 Discuss software suites.

7 Describe office suites, cloud suites, specialized suites, and utility suites.

## Why should I read this chapter?

At one time all document preparation was a manual process performed by clerical staff. That was then and this is now. Now, a required skill for nearly every profession is the ability to create documents, to analyze data, to develop presentations, and to store and retrieve information. Professionals need to know how to use software applications on their desktops or from the cloud to perform these activities.

This chapter discusses these applications including word processors, spreadsheets, database management systems, and presentation graphics. Additionally, you'll learn about cloud computing applications, integrated packages, and software suites. To be competent and to be competitive in today's professional workplace, you need to know and to understand these things.

## chapter 3

# Introduction

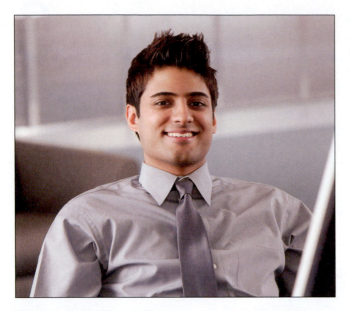

Not long ago, trained specialists were required to perform many of the operations you can now do with a microcomputer. Market analysts used calculators to project sales. Graphic artists created designs by hand. Data processing clerks created electronic files to be stored on large computers. Now you can do all these tasks—and many others—with a microcomputer and the appropriate application software.

Think of the microcomputer as an electronic tool. You may not consider yourself very good at typing, calculating, organizing, presenting, or managing information. However, a microcomputer can help you do all these things and much more. All it takes is the right kinds of software.

Competent end users need to understand the capabilities of general-purpose application software, which includes word processors, spreadsheets, database management systems, and presentation programs. They need to know about integrated packages and software suites.

Hi, I'm James, and I'm a software engineer. I'd like to talk with you about application software . . . programs that we all need to know. I'd also like to talk with you about how to access and use these traditional programs using cloud computing.

# Application Software

As we discussed in Chapter 1, there are two kinds of software. **System software** works with end users, application software, and computer hardware to handle the majority of technical details. **Application software** can be described as end-user software and is used to accomplish a variety of tasks.

Application software can be divided into three categories. One category, **general-purpose applications**, includes word processing programs, spreadsheets, database management systems, and presentation graphics. Another category, **specialized applications**, includes thousands of other programs that tend to be more narrowly focused and used in specific disciplines and occupations. The third category, **mobile apps**, are add-on features or programs designed for a variety of mobile devices including smartphones and tablets.

## User Interface

A **user interface** is the portion of the application that allows you to control and to interact with the program. Almost all applications use a **graphical user interface (GUI)** that displays graphical elements called **icons** to represent familiar objects and a mouse. The mouse controls a **pointer** on the screen that is used to select items such as icons. Another feature is the use of windows to display information. A **window** is simply a rectangular area that can contain a document, program, or message. (Do not confuse the term *window* with the various versions of Microsoft's Windows operating systems, which are programs.) More than one window can be opened and displayed on the computer screen at one time.

Traditionally, most software programs use a system of menus, toolbars, and dialog boxes. (See Figure 3-1.)

- **Menus** present commands that are typically displayed in a **menu bar** at the top of the screen.
- **Toolbars** typically appear below the menu bar and include small graphic elements called **buttons** that provide shortcuts for quick access to commonly used commands.
- **Dialog boxes** provide additional information and request user input.

Figure 3-1 **Traditional graphical user interface**

Many Microsoft and other applications use an interface known as the **Ribbon GUI** to make it easier to find and use all the features of an application; this GUI uses a system of ribbons, tabs, and galleries. (See Figure 3-2.)

- **Ribbons** replace menus and toolbars by organizing commonly used commands into a set of tabs. These tabs display command buttons that are the most relevant to the tasks being performed by the user.
- **Tabs** are used to divide the ribbon into major activity areas. Each tab is then organized into **groups** that contain related items. Some tabs, called **contextual tabs**, only appear when they are needed and anticipate the next operations to be performed by the user.
- **Galleries** simplify the process of making a selection from a list of alternatives. This is accomplished by graphically displaying the effect of alternatives before being selected.

Figure 3-2 **Ribbon GUI**

### Common Features

Most applications provide a variety of features to make entering/presenting, editing, and formatting documents easy. Some of the most common features include:

- Spell checkers—look for misspelled words
- Alignment—either centers, right-aligns, or left-aligns numbers and characters
- Font and font sizes (perhaps use character effects)—specifies the size and style of entered numbers and text
- Tables—presents numbers and text in table format
- Reports—provides a variety of different types and styles to report information

---

## ✔ concept check

List three categories of application software.

What is a graphical user interface? What are windows, menus, toolbars, and dialog boxes?

What is the Ribbon GUI? What are ribbons, tabs, and galleries?

Discuss some of the most common features in application programs.

---

# General-Purpose Applications

As mentioned previously, general-purpose applications include word processors, spreadsheets, database management systems, and presentation graphics.

### Word Processors

**Word processors** create text-based **documents** and are one of the most flexible and widely used software tools. All types of people and organizations use word processors to create memos, letters, and faxes. Organizations create newsletters, manuals, and brochures to provide information to their customers. Students and researchers use word processors to create reports. Word processors can even be used to create personalized web pages.

Microsoft Word is the most widely used word processor. Other popular word processors include Corel WordPerfect, Apple Pages, OpenOffice Writer, and Google Docs.

Assume that you have accepted a job as an advertising coordinator for Adventure Travel Tours, a travel agency specializing in active adventure vacations. Your primary responsibilities are to create and coordinate the company's promotional materials, including flyers and travel reports. To see how you could use Microsoft Word as the advertising coordinator for the Adventure Travel Tours, see Figures 3-3 and 3-4.

---

## tips

Did you know that Microsoft provides thousands of free templates on its website? Here's how to quickly access a variety of templates ranging from party invitations and exercise planners to professional communications.

**1** Connect to office.microsoft.com.

**2** Click the *Templates* menu option at the top.

**3** Use the search feature or browse through a variety of categories.

**4** Once you find a template you want to use, download it and then open it in the appropriate MS Office program.

To see other tips, visit our website at www.computing2014.com and enter the keyword tips.

## Creating a Flyer

You have been asked to create a promotional advertising flyer. After discussing the flyer's contents and basic structure with your supervisor, you start to enter the flyer's text. As you enter the text, the spelling checker and grammar checker catch some spelling and grammatical errors. Once the text has been entered, you proofread the text and then focus your attention on enhancing the visual aspects of the flyer. You add a photograph and experiment with different character and paragraph formats, including fonts, font sizes, colors, and alignments. ●

**Spelling Checker**
Correcting spelling and typing errors identified by the **spelling checker** creates an error-free and professional-looking document.

**Fonts and Font Size**
Using interesting **fonts** and a large **font size** in the flyer's title grabs the reader's attention.

**Center-Aligning**
**Center-aligning** all of the text in the flyer creates a comfortable, balanced appearance.

Adventure Travel Tours
New Adventures

Attention adventure travelers! Attend an Adventure presentation to learn about some of the earth's greatest unspoiled habitats and find out how you can experience the adventure of a lifetime. This year we are offering four new tours:

- India Wildlife Adventure
- Inca Trail to Machu Picchu
- Safari in Tanzania
- Costa Rica Rivers and Rainforests

Call Student Name at 1-800-555-0004 for presentation locations, full color brochures, itinerary information, costs, and trip dates.

**Character Effects**
Adding **character effects** such as bold and color makes important information stand out and makes the flyer more visually interesting.

**Grammar Checker**
Incomplete sentences, awkward wording, and incorrect punctuation are identified and corrections are offered by the **grammar checker**.

**Figure 3-3 Flyer**

## Creating a Report

Your next assignment is to create a report on Tanzania and Peru. After conducting your research, you start writing your paper. As you enter the text for the report, you notice that the AutoCorrect feature automatically corrects some grammar and punctuation errors. Your report includes several figures and tables. You use the captions feature to keep track of figure and table numbers, to enter the caption text, and to position the captions. You use the footnote feature to assist in adding notes to further explain or comment on information in the report.

Finally, you prepare the report for printing by adding header and footer information. ●

**AutoCorrect**
As you enter text, you occasionally forget to capitalize the first word in a sentence. Fortunately, **Auto-Correct** recognizes the error and automatically capitalizes the word.

**Captions**
Identifying figures with **captions** in a report makes the report easier to read and more professional.

**Header or Footer**
Page numbers and other document-related information can be included in a **header** or **footer**.

**Footnote**
To include a note about Mt. Kilimanjaro, you use the footnote feature. This feature inserts the **footnote** superscript number and automatically formats the bottom of the page to contain the footnote text.

---

# Tanzania & Peru

## Tanzania

### Geography and Climate

"In the midst of a great wilderness, full of wild beasts...I fancied I saw a summit...covered with a dazzlingly white cloud (qtd. in Cole 56). This is how Johann Krapf, the first outsider to witness the splendor of Africa's highest mountain, described Kilimanjaro. The peak was real, though the white clouds he "fancied" he saw were the dense layer of snow that coats the mountain.[1]

FIGURE1 GIRAFFE IN SERENGETI

Tanzania is primarily a plateau that slopes gently downward into the country's five hundred miles of Indian Ocean coastline. Nearly three-quarters of Tanzania is dry savannah, so much so that the Swahili word for the central plateau is *nyika*, meaning "wasteland." Winding through these flatlands is the Great Rift Valley, which forms narrow and shallow lakes in its long path. Several of these great lakes form a belt-like oasis of green vegetation. Contrasting with the severity of the plains are the coastal areas, which are lush with ample rainfall. In the north the plateau slopes dramatically into Mt. Kilimanjaro.

### Ngorongoro Conservation Area

Some of Tanzania's most distinguishing geographical features are found in the Ngorongoro Conservation Area.[2] The park is composed of many craters and gorges, as well as lakes, forest, and plains. Among these features is the area's namesake, the Ngorongoro Crater. The Crater is a huge expanse, covering more than one hundred square miles. On the Crater's floor, grasslands blend into swamps, lakes, rivers, and woodland. Also within the Conservation Area's perimeter is the Olduvai Gorge, commonly referred to as the "Cradle of Mankind," where in 1931 the stone

[1] Mt. Kilimanjaro is 19,340 feet high, making it the fourth tallest mountain in the world.

[2] The Conservation Area is a national preserve spanning 3,196 square miles.

Tanzania & Peru |

2

**Figure 3-4** Report

## Spreadsheets

**Spreadsheets** organize, analyze, and graph numeric data such as budgets and financial reports. Once used exclusively by accountants, spreadsheets are widely used by nearly every profession. Marketing professionals analyze sales trends. Financial analysts evaluate and graph stock market trends. Students and teachers record grades and calculate grade point averages.

The most widely used spreadsheet program is Microsoft Excel. Other spreadsheet applications include Apple Numbers and OpenOffice Calc.

Assume that you have just accepted a job as manager of the Downtown Internet Café. This café provides a variety of flavored coffees as well as Internet access. One of your responsibilities is to create a financial plan for the next year. To see how you could use Microsoft Excel, as the manager for the Downtown Internet Café, see Figures 3-5 and 3-6.

### Creating a Sales Forecast

Your first project is to develop a first-quarter sales forecast for the café. You begin by studying sales data and talking with several managers. After obtaining sales and expense estimates, you are ready to create the first-quarter forecast. You start structuring the worksheet by inserting descriptive text entries for the row and column headings. Next, you insert numeric entries, including formulas and functions to perform calculations. To test the accuracy of the worksheet, you change the values in some cells and compare the recalculated spreadsheet results with hand calculations. ●

**Worksheets**
**Worksheets** are used for a wide range of different applications. One of the most common uses is to create, analyze, and forecast budgets.

**Text Entries**
**Text entries** provide meaning to the values in the worksheet. The rows are labeled to identify the various sales and expense items. The columns are labeled to specify the months.

**Functions**
One advantage of using **functions** rather than entering formulas is that they are easier to enter. In this case, cell C20 (Total Expenses for February) contains the function SUM(C14:C19) rather than the formula = C14+C15 +C16+C17+C18+C19.

**Cells**
**Cells** can contain labels, numbers, formulas, and functions. A cell's content is indicated by the row and column labels. For example, cell D15 contains a number for the Payroll expense expected for March.

**Formulas**
**Formulas** provide a way to perform calculations in the worksheet. In this case, cell C22 has the formula = C12 (Total Sales for February) – C20 (Total Expenses for February) that contains a number for the Net Income for February.

| | A | B | C | D | E | F |
|---|---|---|---|---|---|---|
| | | | | | | |
| | | **Downtown Internet Café** | | | | |
| | | *First Quarter Forecast* | | | | |
| | | | | | | |
| 6 | | JAN | FEB | MAR | TOTAL | AVG |
| 7 | **Sales** | | | | | |
| 8 | Beverage | $ 13,600 | $ 14,600 | $ 15,600 | $ 43,800 | $ 14,600 |
| 9 | Food | $ 7,100 | $ 7,300 | $ 7,400 | $ 21,800 | $ 7,267 |
| 10 | Internet | $ 4,000 | $ 4,300 | $ 4,500 | $ 12, | |
| 11 | Merchandise | $ 3,100 | $ 3,200 | $ 3,300 | $ 9, | |
| 12 | Total Sales | $ 27,800 | $ 29,400 | $ 30,800 | $ 88, | |
| 13 | **Expenses** | | | | | |
| 14 | Cost of Goods | $ 6,950 | $ 7,300 | $ 7,600 | $ 21, | |
| 15 | Payroll | $ 7,500 | $ 7,500 | $ 7,500 | 22, | |
| 16 | Computers | $ 6,400 | $ 6,400 | $ 6,400 | $ 19, | |
| 17 | Lease | $ 5,500 | $ 5,500 | $ 5,500 | $ 16, | |
| 18 | Marketing | $ 1,000 | $ 1,000 | $ 1,000 | $ 3,000 | $ 1,000 |
| 19 | Miscellaneous | $ 1,500 | $ 1,500 | $ 1,500 | $ 4,500 | $ 1,500 |
| 20 | Total Expenses | $ 28,850 | $ 29,200 | $ 29,500 | $ 87,550 | $ 29,183 |
| 21 | **Income** | | | | | |
| 22 | Net Income | $ (1,050) | $ 200 | 1,300 | 450 | 150 |
| 23 | **Profit Margin** | -3.78% | 0.68% | 4.22% | 0.51% | |
| 24 | | | Income Year-To-Date | | $ 450 | |

**Figure 3-5** First-quarter forecast

## Analyzing Your Data

After presenting the First-Quarter Forecast to the owner, you revise the format and expand the workbook to include worksheets for each quarter and an annual forecast summary. You give each worksheet a descriptive sheet name. At the request of the owner, you perform a what-if analysis to test the effect of different estimates for payroll, and you use a chart to visualize the effect. ●

**Workbook**
The first worksheet in a **workbook** is often a summary of the following worksheets. In this case, the first worksheet presents the entire year's forecast. The subsequent worksheets provide the details.

### Downtown Internet Café
#### Annual Forecast

| | JAN | FEB | MAR | APR | MAY | JUN | JUL | AUG | SEP |
|---|---|---|---|---|---|---|---|---|---|
| **Sales** | | | | | | | | | |
| Beverage | $18,000 | $ 17,500 | $ 17,200 | $18,039 | $ 17,940 | $19,074 | $10,993 | $ 9,099 | $12,909 |
| Food | $ 8,500 | $ 8,200 | $ 8,000 | $ 8,123 | $ 9,231 | $ 7,001 | $ 6,912 | $ 5,500 | $ 8,700 |
| Internet | $ 5,700 | $ 7,400 | $ 7,200 | $ 8,021 | $ 6,751 | $ 5,781 | $ 4,510 | $ 8,233 | $ 7,811 |
| Merchandise | $ 3,600 | $ 3,500 | $ 3,300 | $ 2,390 | $ 1,290 | $ 1,592 | $ 1,677 | $ 3,008 | $ 2,987 |
| **Total Sales** | $35,800 | $ 36,600 | $ 35,700 | $36,573 | $ 35,212 | $33,448 | $24,092 | $25,840 | $32,407 |
| **Expenses** | | | | | | | | | |
| Cost of Goods | $ 8,750 | $ 8,475 | $ 8,300 | $ 8,750 | $ 8,475 | $ 8,300 | $ 8,750 | $ 8,475 | $ 8,300 |
| Payroll | $ 9,398 | $ 8,700 | $ 8,100 | $ 9,398 | $ 8,700 | $ 8,100 | $ 9,398 | $ 8,700 | $ 8,100 |
| Computers | $ 6,400 | $ 6,400 | $ 6,400 | $ 6,400 | $ 6,400 | $ 6,400 | $ 6,400 | $ 6,400 | $ 6,400 |
| Lease | $ 6,000 | $ 6,000 | $ 6,000 | $ 6,000 | $ 6,000 | $ 6,000 | $ 6,000 | $ 6,000 | $ 6,000 |
| Advertising | $ 1,000 | $ 1,000 | $ 1,000 | $ 1,000 | $ 1,000 | $ 1,000 | $ 1,000 | $ 1,000 | $ 1,000 |
| Miscellaneous | $ 1,500 | $ 1,500 | $ 1,500 | $ 1,500 | $ 1,500 | $ 1,500 | $ 1,500 | $ 1,500 | $ 1,500 |
| **Total Expenses** | $33,048 | $ 32,075 | $ 31,300 | $33,048 | $ 32,075 | $31,300 | $33,048 | $32,075 | $31,300 |
| **Income** | | | | | | | | | |
| **Net Income** | $ 2,752 | $ 4,525 | $ 4,400 | $ 2,752 | $ 4,525 | $ 4,400 | $ 2,752 | $ 4,525 | $ 4,400 |
| **Profit Margin** | 7.69% | 12.36% | 12.32% | 7.69% | 12.36% | 12.32% | 7.69% | 12.36% | 12.32% |
| Quarter Profit Margin | | | 10.80% | | | 10.80% | | | 10.80% |
| Income Year-To-Date | | | $ 11,677 | | | $ 23,353 | | | $ 35,030 |

Year / First Quarter / Second Quarter / Third Quarter / Fourth Quarter / Scenario Summary / D

**Sheet Name**
Each worksheet has a unique **sheet name**. To make the workbook easy to navigate, it is a good practice to always use simple yet descriptive names for each worksheet.

**What-If Analysis**
**What-if analysis** is a very powerful and simple tool to test the effects of different assumptions in a spreadsheet.

E10 = =E22/E12

### Downtown Internet Café
#### First Quarter Forecast

| | JAN | FEB | MAR | TOTAL | AVG |
|---|---|---|---|---|---|
| **Sales** | | | | | |
| Beverage | $ 18,000 | $ 17,500 | $ 17,200 | $ 52,700 | $ 17,567 |
| Food | $ 8,500 | $ 8,200 | $ 8,000 | $ 24,700 | $ 8,233 |
| Internet | $ 5,700 | $ 7,400 | $ 7,200 | $ 20,300 | $ 6,767 |
| Merchandise | $ 3,600 | $ 3,500 | $ 3,300 | $ 10,400 | $ 3,467 |
| **Total Sales** | $ 35,800 | $ 36,600 | $ 35,700 | $ 108,100 | $ 36,033 |
| **Expenses** | | | | | |
| Cost of Goods | $ 8,750 | $ 8,475 | $ 8,300 | $ 25,525 | $ 8,508 |
| Payroll | $ 9,398 | $ 8,700 | $ 8,100 | $ 26,198 | $ 8,733 |
| Computers | $ 6,400 | $ 6,400 | $ 6,400 | $ 19,200 | $ 6,400 |
| Lease | $ 6,000 | $ 6,000 | $ 6,000 | $ 18,000 | $ 6,000 |
| Marketing | $ 1,000 | $ 1,000 | $ 1,000 | $ 3,000 | $ 1,000 |
| Miscellaneous | $ 1,500 | $ 1,500 | $ 1,500 | $ 4,500 | $ 1,500 |
| **Total Expenses** | $ 33,048 | $ 32,075 | $ 31,300 | $ 96,423 | $ 32,141 |
| **Income** | | | | | |
| **Net Income** | $ 2,752 | $ 4,525 | $ 4,400 | $ 11,677 | $ 3,892 |
| **Profit Margin** | 7.69% | 12.36% | 12.32% | 10.80% | |
| | | Income Year-To-Date | | $ 11,677 | |

**First Quarter Profit Margin**

MAR — 12.32%
FEB — 12.36%
JAN — 7.69%

0.00%  5.00%  10.00%  15.00%

**Goal Seek**
Set cell: E23
To value: 15
By changing cell: $E$10
OK    Cancel

Year / First Quarter / Second Quarter / Third Quarter / Fourth Quarter / Scenario Summary / D

**Chart**
Once data is in the worksheet, it is very easy to **chart** the data. All you need to do is to select the data to chart, select the chart type, and add some descriptive text.

**Figure 3-6** Anual forecast and analysis

## Database Management Systems

A **database** is a collection of related data. It is the electronic equivalent of a file cabinet. A **database management system (DBMS)** or **database manager** is a program that sets up, or structures, a database. It also provides tools to enter, edit, and retrieve data from the database. All kinds of individuals use databases, from hospital administrators recording patient information to police officers checking criminal histories. Colleges and universities use databases to keep records on their students, instructors, and courses. Organizations of all types maintain employee databases.

Two widely used database management systems designed for microcomputers are Microsoft Access and OpenOffice Base.

Assume that you have accepted a job as an employment administrator for the Lifestyle Fitness Club. To see how you could use Microsoft Access, see Figure 3-7.

## Presentation Graphics

Research shows that people learn better when information is presented visually. **Presentation graphics** are programs that combine a variety of visual objects to create attractive, visually interesting presentations. They are excellent tools to communicate a message and to persuade people.

**tips**

Are you getting ready for a classroom or a boardroom presentation and need some help? Did you know that both Apple and Microsoft provide expert guidance on creating professional-looking presentations? Here's how to access that guidance.

1 For Apple, connect to www.apple.com/iwork/keynote/#easy and play the videos Choose a theme, Add and edit graphics with ease, Add stunning effects, 3D charts and chart animations, and Benefit from helpful tools.

2 For Microsoft, connect to www.microsoft.com/atwork/skills and select 3 Ways to simplify your PowerPoint presentations.

To see other tips, visit our website at www.computing2014.com and enter the keyword tips.

People in a variety of settings and situations use presentation graphics programs to make their presentations. For example, marketing managers use presentation graphics to present proposed marketing strategies to their superiors. Salespeople use these programs to demonstrate products and encourage customers to make purchases. Students use presentation graphics programs to create high-quality class presentations.

Three of the most widely used presentation graphics programs are Microsoft PowerPoint, OpenOffice Impress, and Apple Keynote.

Assume that you have volunteered for the Animal Rescue Foundation, a local animal rescue agency. You have been asked to create a powerful and persuasive presentation to encourage other members from your community to volunteer. To see how you could use Microsoft PowerPoint, see Figure 3-8.

## concept check

What are word processors? What are they used for?

What are spreadsheets? What are they used for?

What are database management systems? What are they used for?

What are presentation graphics programs? What are they used for?

## Creating a Database

You have been asked to create an employee database to replace the club's manual system for recording employee data. The first step in creating the database management system is to plan. You study the existing manual system focusing on how and what data is collected and how it is used. Next, using Microsfot Access, one of the most widely used DBMS programs, you design the basic structure or organization of the new database system to include a table that will make entering data and using the database more efficient. You create the table structure by specifying the fields and primary key field. To make the process faster and more accurate, you create a form and enter the data for each employee as a record in the table. •

**Primary Key**
The **primary key** is the unique employee identification number. You considered using the last name field as the primary key but realized that more than one employee could have the same last name. Primary keys are often used to link tables.

**Fields**
**Fields** are given field names that are displayed at the top of each table. You select the field names to describe their contents.

**Table**
**Tables** make up the basic structure of a relational database with columns containing field data and rows containing record information. This table records basic information about each employee, including name, address, and telephone number.

**Record**
Each **record** contains information about one employee. A record often includes a combination of numeric, text, and object data types.

| Employee ID | Last Name | First Name | Address | City | State | ZIP Code | Home Phone | Gender | Birth Date | |
|---|---|---|---|---|---|---|---|---|---|---|
| 12920 | Larson | | | | | 92121-3740 | (941) 555-7717 | F | 6/21/1983 | (0) |
| 13416 | Lembi | | | | | 92120-3741 | (941) 555-4747 | M | 9/12/1979 | (0) |
| 11747 | Lettow | Ryan | 358 Maple Dr. | Maldin | CA | 92121-3740 | (507) 555-2805 | M | 11/15/1981 | (0) |
| 22085 | Lindau | Kristina | 1947 E. Watson | Landis | CA | 92120-3741 | (941) 555-6363 | F | 2/24/1977 | (0) |
| 03406 | Lopez | Mina | 4290 E. Alameda Dr. | Maldin | CA | 92121-3740 | (507) 555-5050 | F | 2/25/1977 | (0) |
| 04731 | Marchant | Roberta | 564 Palm Avenue | Landis | CA | 92120-3741 | (507) 555-6707 | F | 5/13/1980 | (2) |
| 13543 | Martinez | Julie | 1920 First Ave. | Maldin | CA | 92121-3740 | (941) 555-1044 | F | 12/10/1982 | (0) |
| 13635 | Martinez | Juan | 7115 E Roosevelt Dr. | Maldin | CA | 92121-3740 | (507) 555-2935 | M | 12/10/1983 | (0) |
| 22407 | Mazeau | Rebecca | 7383 Oak Dr. | Landis | CA | 92120-3741 | (941) 555-1093 | F | 9/23/1979 | (0) |
| 03225 | Morgan | Dan | 564 S. Lemon Dr. | Maldin | CA | 92121 | (507) 555-5567 | M | 3/5/1975 | (0) |
| 99999 | Name | Student | 1234 N. Fifth St. | Chesterfield | CA | 92122-1268 | (507) 555-1234 | F | 4/1/1982 | (0) |
| 00617 | Nichols | Cathy | 75 Brooklea Dr. | Landis | CA | 92120-3741 | (507) 555-0001 | F | 5/19/1965 | (0) |
| 00907 | Pennington | Mark | 23 Mill Ave. | Landis | CA | 92120-3741 | (507) 555-3333 | M | 7/7/1969 | (0) |
| 12194 | Polonsky | Mitch | 8701 E. Sheridan | Maldin | CA | 92121-3740 | (507) 555-1018 | M | 3/13/1980 | (0) |
| 12247 | Rath | Kathy | 87 E. Aurora Ave. | Chesterfield | CA | 92122-1268 | (507) 555-9797 | F | 5/30/1978 | (0) |
| 12594 | Reddie | Mark | 900 W. Campus Dr. | Maldin | CA | 92121 | (507) 555-1139 | M | 11/5/1983 | (0) |
| 12230 | Reddie | Suzanne | 932 E. Parkway Dr. | Landis | CA | 92120-3741 | (507) 555-1191 | F | 7/14/1978 | (0) |
| 13005 | Reilly | Emily | 125 N. Marigold St. | Maldin | CA | 92121-3740 | (941) 555-6532 | F | 5/21/1985 | (0) |
| 12612 | Richards | Melissa | 5522 W. Marin Lane | River Mist | CA | 92123 | (507) 555-7789 | F | 9/30/1978 | (0) |
| 06000 | Robertson | Kirk | 832 S. William Ave. | Maldin | CA | 92121 | (507) 555-3730 | M | 4/5/1974 | (0) |
| 22297 | Rogondino | Patricia | 7583 Turquoise | Chesterfield | CA | 92122-1268 | (941) 555-7539 | F | 8/30/1977 | (0) |
| 07287 | Roman | Anita | 2348 S. Bala Dr. | Maldin | CA | 92121-3740 | (507) 555-9870 | F | 3/15/1981 | (0) |
| 12918 | Ruiz | Carlos | 10101 First St. | Maldin | CA | 92121-3740 | (507) 555-5125 | M | 7/27/1992 | (1) |
| 08391 | Ruiz | Enrique | 35 Palm St. | Chesterfield | CA | 92122-1268 | (507) 555-0091 | M | 12/10/1973 | (0) |
| 04321 | Sabin | Greg | 90 E. Rawhide Av | | | | | | | |
| 00212 | Schiff | Chad | 235 N. Cactus Dr. | | | | | | | |
| 22114 | Schneider | Paul | 1731 Jackson | | | | | | | |
| 01421 | Spehr | Timothy | 90 Royal Dr. | | | | | | | |
| 12366 | Stacey | David | 737 S. College Rd | | | | | | | |
| 13497 | Steele | Jeff | 1011 E. Holly Ln. | | | | | | | |
| 12668 | Stueland | Valerie | 34 University Dr. | | | | | | | |
| 12583 | | | | | | | | | | |
| 12867 | | | | | | | | | | |
| 03890 | | | | | | | | | | |
| 22304 | | | | | | | | | | |
| 22100 | | | | | | | | | | |

**Form**
Like printed paper forms, electronic **forms** should be designed to be easy to read and use. This form makes it easy to enter and view all employees' data, including their photographs.

**Employee Records**

| | |
|---|---|
| Employee ID | 12918 |
| First Name | Carlos |
| Last Name | Ruiz |
| Address | 10101 First St. |
| City | Maldin |
| State | CA |
| ZIP Code | 92121-3740 |
| Home Phone | (507) 555-5125 |
| Gender | M |
| Birth Date | 7/27/1992 |

Photo/Resume

Record: 41 of 55    No Filter    Search

**Figure 3-7** Database

You have been asked to create a powerful and persuasive presentation for the director of the foundation designed to encourage other members from your community to volunteer. The first step is to meet with the director of the foundation to determine the content of the presentation. Then using PowerPoint, you begin creating the presentation by selecting a presentation template and document theme. After entering the content, you add interest to the presentation by adding animation to selected objects and using slide transition effects.

**Document Theme**
To make your presentation more professional and eye-catching, you select a **document theme**, built-in sets of colors, fonts, and effects that can be quickly applied to your entire presentation.

**How Does The Foundation Help?**
- Provide temporary homes
- Provide obedience training
- Provide veterinary care
- Find loving permanent home

**Who Is An Anim**
- Believes unwanted pets deserve a home
- Believes you can teach an
- Believes you can retrain a

**Templates**
**Templates** provide an excellent way to quickly create a presentation by providing predesigned styles and layouts as well as suggested content based on the type of template you select.

**Animation**
To provide additional emphasis to items or show the information on a slide in phases, you add **animation** to text and objects. Finally, you use slide **transition** effects to animate the transition from one slide to the next.

Join Animal Angels

Animal Rescue Foundation

**Figure 3-8 Presentation**

# Specialized Applications

While general-purpose applications are widely used in nearly every profession, specialized applications are widely used within specific professions. These programs include graphics programs and web authoring programs.

## Graphics

Graphics are widely used by professionals in the graphic arts profession. They use desktop publishing programs, image editing programs, illustration programs, and image galleries.

- **Desktop publishing programs**, or **page layout programs**, allow you to mix text and graphics to create publications of professional quality. While word processors focus on creating text and have the ability to combine text and graphics, desktop publishers focus on page design and layout and provide greater flexibility. Professional graphic artists use desktop publishing programs to create documents such as brochures, newsletters, newspapers, and textbooks.

  Popular desktop publishing programs include Adobe InDesign, Microsoft Publisher, and QuarkXPress. While these programs provide the capability to create text and graphics, typically graphic artists import these elements from other sources, including word processors, digital cameras, scanners, image editors, illustration programs, and image galleries.

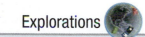

**Explorations**

Adobe is one of the leaders in specialized applications, particularly in the graphics, publishing, and web authoring fields.

**To learn more about these specialized applications, visit our website at www .computing2014.com and enter the keyword** adobe**.**

Letter A

Expanded view

**Figure 3-9** Bitmap image

- **Image editors**, also known as **photo editors**, are specialized graphics programs for editing or modifying digital photographs. They are often used to touch up photographs to remove scratches and other imperfections. The photographs consist of thousands of dots or **pixels** that form images often referred to as **bitmap** or **raster** images. One limitation of bitmap images, however, is that when they are expanded, the images can become pixelated, or jagged on the edges. For example, when the letter *A* in Figure 3-9 is expanded, the borders of the letter appear jagged, as indicated by the expanded view.

  Popular image editors include Adobe Photoshop, Corel Paint Shop Pro, GIMP (GNU Image Manipulation Program), and Windows Live Photo Gallery. To learn more about using one of the most popular free image editing programs, see Making IT Work for You: Image Editing on pages 75 and 76.

- **Illustration programs**, also known as **drawing programs**, are used to create and edit vector images. While bitmap images use pixels to represent images, **vector images**, also known as **vector illustrations**, use geometric shapes or objects. (See Figure 3-10.) These objects are created by connecting lines and curves. Because these objects can be defined by mathematical equations, they can be rapidly and easily resized, colored, textured, and manipulated. An image is a combination of several objects.

  Illustration programs are often used for graphic design, page layout, and creating sharp artistic images. Popular illustration programs include Adobe Illustrator, CorelDRAW, and Inkscape. (See Figure 3-11.)

- **Image galleries** are libraries of electronic images. These images are used for a wide variety of applications from illustrating textbooks to providing visual interest to presentations.

**Figure 3-10** Vector image

**Figure 3-11** Adobe Illustrator

# IMAGE EDITING

Would you like a simple way to fix problems in your photos? Do you need a tool that can manage your images locally and on the cloud? Windows Live Photo Gallery is a free, easy-to-use photo editing and management program. Besides powerful photo-repairing features, it allows you to identify or "tag" people and places for easy searching in the future. In addition, it includes 7 GB of free online storage/backup using the Microsoft SkyDrive service.

**Installing the Software** Windows Live Photo Gallery is a free download for Windows users. Some Windows users will find that they have it already. If not, follow these steps to install it:

**1** Go to http://windows.microsoft.com, and type "photo gallery" in the search box. Click the first search result.

**2** Click the *Download Now* button.

**3** Follow the instructions to complete the installation.

Once installed, the software will scan your Pictures library (including My Pictures and Public Pictures folders) for photos.

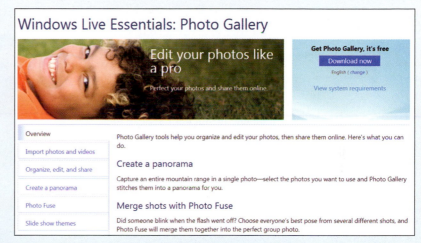

**Basic Photo Editing** You should now see many of your photos in the center of the interface. Here are some of the most common fixes your photos might need:

**1** Double-click the photo that needs editing. The *Edit* tab of the ribbon is now active.

**2** Click the *Rotate left* or *Rotate right* buttons to change the orientation of the photo.

**3** Click the *Crop* button to remove an unwanted section of the photo. When the *Crop* window appears on top of your photo, move it around and resize it to include the section of the photo you want to keep. Press the Enter key to complete the crop.

**4** Click the *Red eye* button to fix red eye problems in photos. Simply drag the mouse pointer to surround the entire red section of the person's eye, and it is instantly fixed.

**5** Click the *Retouch* button to activate a very powerful feature that can remove a blemish or discoloration on a photo. It does this by using the surrounding area as a sample of what it should look like. Simply drag the mouse pointer to surround the problem area, and Photo Gallery will attempt to remove the blemish.

**Tag and Caption** Photo Gallery has the ability to detect faces in photos so that you can tag those individuals with a name. You are also encouraged to add a brief caption to each of your photos. Once these are done, you will be able to search your computer for photos by using a person's name or any text in the caption.

**1** From the *Home* tab, click the *Batch people tag* button. Photo Gallery may display some faces that you can start tagging. Otherwise, click the *Tag them* link in the center of the window.

**2** Select a detected face, and click the *Tag as* button on the ribbon.

**3** Type a name in the box that appears, and press Enter. The face will immediately disappear because this individual is now tagged. This face will appear in your Home ribbon (for quick searches), and the name will be remembered for future tagging.

**4** Click the *Close* button on the ribbon once you have finished tagging all the detected faces.

**5** Double-click a photo in your collection. You are now in the *Edit* tab. Make sure the *Tag and caption* button is selected on the ribbon.

**6** Click the *Add caption* box, and type a very brief title for the photo. Press Enter to finish.

**Sharing/Uploading Photos** You can share any of the photos and videos on your computer with your friends by using such popular services as Facebook and YouTube. Most noteworthy is Microsoft's free SkyDrive service, which you can sign up for by using a Microsoft account. Follow these steps to upload all your photos to SkyDrive:

**1** Click the *Create* tab of the ribbon.

**2** Select all the photos you wish you upload (Ctrl + A selects all photos).

**3** Click the *SkyDrive* button in the Publish group of the ribbon and then sign in.

**4** Select the *Large (1600px)* option, and type the name for this new album. Click *Publish*.

The web is continually changing, and some of the specifics presented in this Making IT Work for You may have changed.

**To learn about other ways to make information technology work for you, visit our website at www.computing2014.com and enter the keyword miw.**

| Organization | Site |
|---|---|
| Classroom Clipart | www.classroomclipart.com |
| MS Office clip art | office.microsoft.com/clipart |
| iStockphoto | istockphoto.com |
| Flickr Creative Commons | www.flickr.com/creativecommons |

**Figure 3-12 Select web image galleries**

There are two basic types of electronic images in these galleries: stock photographs and clip art. **Stock photographs** are photographs on a variety of subject material from people to landscapes. **Clip art** are graphic illustrations representing a wide range of topics. Most applications provide access to a limited selection of free clip art. For example, in Microsoft Word, you can gain access to clip art by issuing the command Insert>Clip Art.

There are numerous web image galleries. (See Figure 3-12.) Some of these sites offer free images and clip art, while others charge a fee.

### Web Authoring Programs

There are over a billion websites on the Internet, and more are being added every day. Corporations use the web to reach new customers and to promote their products. (See Figure 3-13.) Individuals create online diaries or commentaries, called **blogs**. Creating a site is called **web authoring**. It begins with site design followed by creation of a document file that displays the website's content.

A website is an interactive multimedia form of communication. Designing a website begins with determining the site's overall content. The content is then broken down into a series of related pieces of information. The overall site design is commonly represented in a **graphical site map**.

Notice that in the graphical site map shown in Figure 3-14, each block in the map represents a web page. Lines joining the blocks represent links to related

**Figure 3-13 Flora Photographs website**

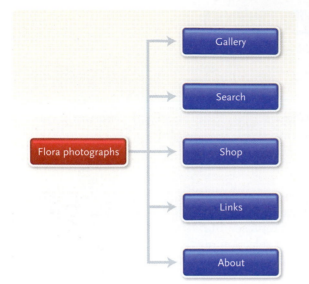

**Figure 3-14 Partial graphical site map for the Flora Photographs website**

pages of information that make up the website. The first page, or main page, typically serves as an introduction and supplies a table of contents. The following pages present the specific pieces or blocks of information.

Multimedia elements are added to individual pages to enhance interest and interactivity. One multimedia element found on many websites is moving graphics called **animations**. These animations can be simple moving text or complicated interactive features. There are many specialized programs available to aid in the creation of animation. One type of interactive animation is produced using software called Adobe **Flash**. Flash movies can be inserted as a part of the page or to encompass the entire screen.

As we mentioned in Chapter 2, web pages are typically HTML (Hypertext Markup Language) and CSS (cascading style sheets) documents. With knowledge of HTML and a simple text editor, you can create web pages. Even without knowledge of HTML, you can create simple web pages using a word processing package like Microsoft Word.

More specialized and powerful programs, called **web authoring programs**, are typically used to create sophisticated commercial sites. Also known as **web page editors** and **HTML editors**, these programs provide support for website design and HTML coding. Some web authoring programs are **WYSIWYG (what you see is what you get) editors**, which means you can build a page without interacting directly with HTML code. WYSIWYG editors preview the page described by HTML code. Widely used web authoring programs include Adobe Dreamweaver and Microsoft Expression Web. The website depicted in Figure 3-13 was created using Adobe Dreamweaver. (See Figure 3-15.)

### Other Professional Specialized Applications

There are numerous other specialized applications including accounting, personal finance, and project management applications. Accounting applications help companies record and report their financial operations. Personal financial applications help individuals track their personal finances and investments. Project management software is widely used in business to help coordinate and plan complicated projects.

## concept check

Discuss desktop publishing programs, image editors, and illustration programs.

What are image galleries? Stock photos? Clip art?

What are blogs? What is web authoring? What are animations? What is Flash?

What are web authoring programs, web page editors, HTML editors, and WYSIWYG editors?

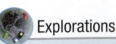
# Mobile Apps

**Mobile apps** or **mobile applications** are add-on programs for a variety of mobile devices including smartphones and tablets. Sometimes referred to simply as **apps**, mobile apps have been widely used for years. The traditional applications include address books, to-do lists, alarms, and message lists. With the introduction of

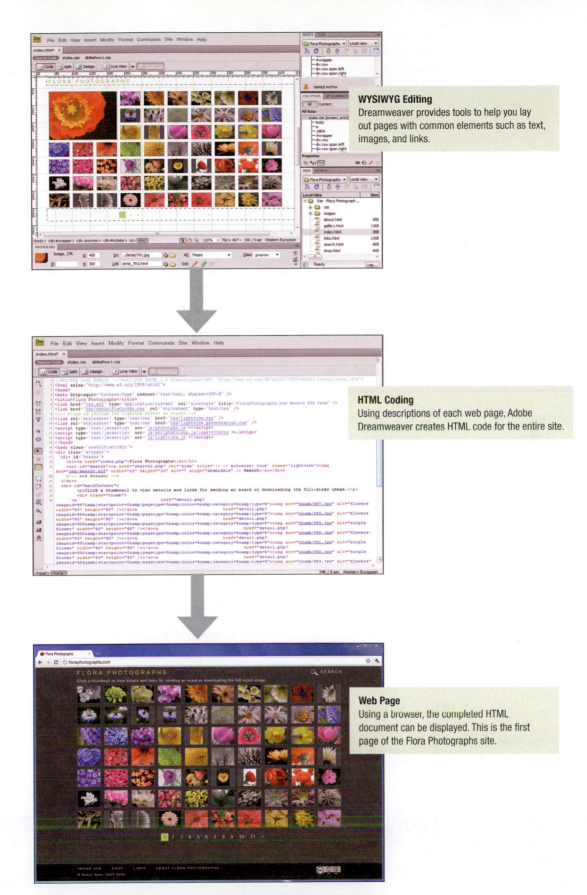

**WYSIWYG Editing**
Dreamweaver provides tools to help you lay out pages with common elements such as text, images, and links.

**HTML Coding**
Using descriptions of each web page, Adobe Dreamweaver creates HTML code for the entire site.

**Web Page**
Using a browser, the completed HTML document can be displayed. This is the first page of the Flora Photographs site.

**Figure 3-15 Adobe Dreamweaver and the Flora Photographs website**

| App | Description | Site |
|---|---|---|
| Facebook | Connects to Facebook | www.facebook.com/appcenter |
| Documents To Go | Edits MS Offfice documents | www.rim.com |
| Instagram | Photo effects and sharing | www.instagram.com |

Figure 3-16  Specialized apps

smartphones, tablets, and wireless connections to the Internet, mobile capabilities have exploded. Now, any number of applications are available.

## Apps

The breadth and scope of available mobile applications for smartphones and other mobile devices are ever expanding. There are over 500,000 apps just for Apple's iPhone alone. Some of the most widely used are social networking, messaging, web browsing, e-mail, photo sharing, and games. See Figure 3-16 for a list of some specialized apps.

One of the fastest-growing apps is **QR code readers**. These readers allow mobile devices to use their digital cameras to scan QR codes. **QR codes**, also known as **quick response codes**, are graphics that typically appear as black and white boxes that automatically link mobile devices to a variety of different content including games, text, videos, and websites. You likely have seen QR codes in magazines, newspapers, and even in books. See Figure 3-17.

Many apps are written for a particular type of mobile device and will not run on other types. For example, app designed for Apple's iPhone may not work with Google's Android.

## App Stores

An **app store** is typically a website that provides access to specific mobile apps that can be downloaded either for a nominal fee or free of charge. Three of the best-known stores are Apple's App Store, Google Play, and Windows Phone Marketplace. (See Figure 3-18.) Although most of the best-known app stores

Figure 3-17  QR Code

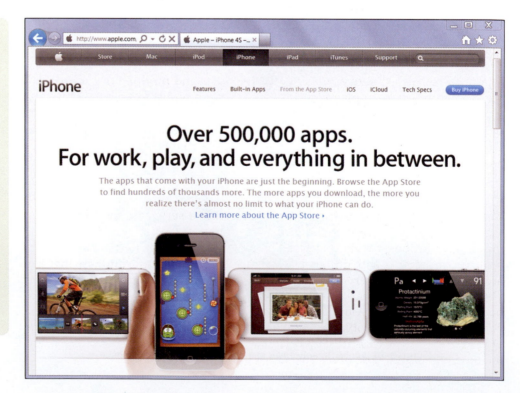

Figure 3-18  Apple's App Store

| App | Focus | Site |
|---|---|---|
| Apple App Store | iOS devices | www.appstore.com |
| Google Play | Android devices | play.google.com |
| BlackBerry App World | BlackBerry products | appworld.blackberry.com |
| Windows Phone Marketplace | Windows phones | windowsphone.com/marketplace |

Figure 3-19  App stores

specialize in applications for a particular line of mobile device, other less well-known stores provide apps for a wide variety of mobile devices. For a list of some more widely used app stores, see Figure 3-19.

## concept check

What are mobile apps?

What are some of the most common applications? What are QR codes and QR code readers?

What are app stores?

# Software Suites

A **software suite** is a collection of separate application programs bundled together and made available as a group. While the applications function exactly the same whether purchased in a suite or separately, it is significantly less expensive to buy a suite of applications than to buy each application separately. Four types of suites are office suites, cloud suites, specialized suites, and utility suites.

### Office Suites

**Office suites**, also known as **office software suites** and **productivity suites**, contain general-purpose application programs that are typically used in a business situation. Productivity suites commonly include a word processor, spreadsheet, database manager, and a presentation application. The best known is Microsoft Office. (See Figure 3-20.) Other well-known productivity suites are Apple iWork and OpenOffice.

Figure 3-20  Microsoft Office

### Cloud Computing

**Cloud suites** or **online office suites** are stored at a server on the Internet and are available anywhere you can access the Internet. Documents created using online applications can also be stored online, making it easy to share and collaborate on documents with others. One downside to cloud applications is that you are dependent on the server providing the application to be available whenever you need it. For this reason, when using online applications, it is important to have backup copies of your documents on your computer and to have a desktop office application available to use. Popular online office suites include Google Docs, Zoho, and Microsoft Office Web Apps. To learn more about one of the most widely used online office suites, see Making IT Work for You: Google Docs on page 83.

### Specialized and Utility Suites

Two other types of suites that are more narrowly focused are specialized suites and utility suites.

- **Specialized suites** focus on specific applications. These include graphics suites, financial planning suites, and many others.
- **Utility suites** include a variety of programs designed to make computing easier and safer. Two of the best known are Norton SystemWorks and Norton Internet Security Suite. (Utility suites will be discussed in detail in Chapter 4.)

## concept check

What is a software suite? What are the advantages of purchasing a suite?

What is the difference between a traditional office suite and a cloud or online suite?

What is a specialized suite?

What is a utility suite?

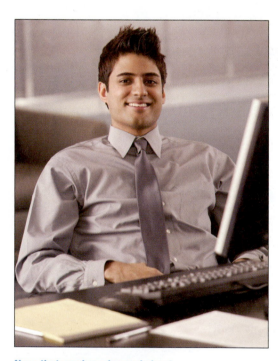

Now, that you have learned about application software, I'd like to tell you about my career as a software engineer.

# Careers in IT

**Software engineers** analyze users' needs and create application software. Software engineers typically have experience in programming but focus on the design and development of programs using the principles of mathematics and engineering.

A bachelor's or an advanced specialized associate's degree in computer science or information systems and an extensive knowledge of computers and technology are required by most employers. Internships may provide students with the kinds of experience employers look for in a software engineer. Those with specific experience with web applications may have an advantage over other applicants. Employers typically look for software engineers with good communication and analytical skills.

Software engineers can expect to earn an annual salary in the range of $53,000 to $97,000. Starting salary is dependent on both experience and the type of software being developed. Experienced software engineers are candidates for many other advanced careers in IT. To learn about other careers in information technology, visit us at www.computing2014.com and enter the keyword careers.

# GOOGLE DOCS

Do you need to create and collaborate with others on a document, presentation, or spreadsheet? Do you need access from different computers in different locations? If so, an online office suite, such as Google Docs, might be just what you need.

**Creating a Document**    You must have a free Google account in order to start creating and sharing documents. To get started:

**1** ● Go to www.google.com. If you are not currently signed in or you do not have a Google account, click the *Sign in* button and follow the appropriate instructions.

**2** ● Once you are signed in, click *Documents* at the top of the page. If the Google Drive screen appears, click the *Get star*ted button to continue.

**3** ● Click the *Create* button; then select *Document*.

**4** ● Start typing in the blank document. You will notice many familiar buttons in the toolbar above the document area.

**5** ● Click the *Untitled document* area at the top left, and you will be prompted to enter a name for the document.

**6** ● Close the browser tab (or window) in order to close the document.

You may have noticed that there is no save option. This is because your document is automatically being saved as you work on it.

**Sharing a Document**    Any document that you create can be shared with one or more individuals. Those individuals can be granted read-only access, or they could be allowed to edit the document, even at the same time that you are working on it. To share a document:

**1** ● With the document open, click the *Share* button at the top right.

**2** ● Type in the e-mail addresses of those with whom you wish you share the document.

**3** ● To the right of this text box, select the permission these individuals will have for the document.

**4** ● Click the *Share & save* button to finish.

The web is continually changing, and some of the specifics presented in this Making IT Work for You may have changed.

**To learn about other ways to make information technology work for you, visit our website at www.computing2014.com and enter the keyword miw.**

## Next-Generation User Interfaces

How will you be interacting with computers in the future? Will you continue using a mouse and keyboard for your desktop, or will touch screen and voice recognition replace them? Will a new type of interface emerge? One thing is for sure: We humans interact with the world around us in many ways, ranging from using our fingers to manipulate objects to making verbal requests. The goal of any future user interface is to bring that same level of interaction to a computer.

There are several challenges with designing interfaces. First is the simple fact that individuals have varying preferences. Some might prefer to interact with a friend through text messages, while others prefer voice communication. Therefore, it is doubtful that a single interface will become dominant. The second challenge is ergonomic in nature; that is, it must be comfortable to use.

Since tablets and smartphones have touch-screen interfaces, many people believe that all home and business computers will eventually have them too. In futuristic movies individuals use both hands to interact with a large screen. Such a setup allows a person to interact with multiple objects at the same time. The only problem with a multitouch, multigesture screen is that it is not comfortable to extend our arms for prolonged periods. Knowing this, many companies are looking toward large, interactive surfaces that perform the same function while lying flat on a desk. Microsoft has already developed a product called "Surface" that acts like a large, interactive table. It responds to both human interactions and objects that are placed on top of it. Although costs prevent it from replacing the desktop of today, the strain on a person's neck from looking down could prevent it from being used for long periods of time. The ideal use of Surface appears to be activities involving collaboration and teamwork.

Voice recognition is another form of input that is already available, but much improvement is needed. Computers are becoming better at following specific voice commands, but they cannot engage in everyday conversation or follow complex requests. Researchers in the field of artificial intelligence are working to improve natural language processing to help computers understand our writing and speech. When that is fully developed, you will be able to speak to your computer in the same way you would speak to another person.

The field of interactivity generating the most buzz involves using the entire body. Both cameras and software are becoming sophisticated enough to observe and interpret our movements and gestures. The "Kinect" system for the Xbox 360 is enjoying success for its ability to use body movements to interact with various games and fitness programs. Researchers at MIT are also working with cameras that can observe our gestures and the physical objects we interact with in order to communicate with a computer. In the future, computers could become so attuned to our emotions and expressions that they will be able to see our frustration with the current operation and take various corrective actions to relieve that frustration.

Which type of interface do you currently enjoy using the most? Do you think that touch-screen interfaces will replace keyboards? Do you believe that a computer can ever understand your speech as well as another human does?

## APPLICATION SOFTWARE

The three categories of application software are **general purpose**, **specialized**, and **mobile**.

### User Interface

You control and interact with a program using a **user interface**. A **graphical user interface (GUI)** uses **icons** selected by a mouse-controlled **pointer**. A **window** contains a document, program, or message. Software programs with a traditional GUI have:

- **Menus**—present commands listed on the **menu bar**.
- **Toolbars**—contain **buttons** for quick access to commonly used commands.
- **Dialog box**—provides additional information or requests user input.

Software programs with a **Ribbon GUI** have:

- **Ribbons**—replace menus and toolbars.
- **Tabs**—divide ribbons into **groups. Contextual tabs** automatically appear when needed.
- **Galleries**—graphically display alternatives before they are selected.

### Common Features

Common features include spell checkers, alignment, fonts and font sizes, tables, and reports.

## GENERAL-PURPOSE APPLICATIONS

**General-purpose applications** include word processors, spreadsheets, database management systems, and presentation graphics.

### Word Processors

**Word processors** create text-based documents. Individuals and organizations use word processors to create memos, letters, and faxes. Organizations also create newsletters, manuals, and brochures to provide information to their customers. Microsoft Word is the most widely used word processor. Others include Corel WordPerfect, Apple Pages, OpenOffice Writer, and Google Docs.

### Spreadsheets

**Spreadsheets** organize, analyze, and graph numeric data such as budgets and financial reports. They are widely used by nearly every profession. Microsoft Excel is the most widely used spreadsheet program. Others include Apple Numbers and OpenOffice Calc.

To be a competent end user, you need to understand the capabilities of general-purpose and specialized application software. Additionally, you need to know about mobile applications and software suites.

## GENERAL-PURPOSE APPLICATIONS

### Database Management Systems

A **database** is a collection of related data. A **database management system (DBMS)** or **database manager** is a program that structures a database. It provides tools to enter, edit, and retrieve data from the database. Organizations use databases for many purposes including maintaining employee records. Two widely used database management systems designed for microcomputers are Microsoft Access and OpenOffice Base.

### Presentation Graphics

**Presentation graphics** are programs that combine a variety of visual objects to create attractive, visually interesting presentations. They are excellent tools to communicate a message and to persuade people. People in a variety of settings and situations use presentation graphics programs to make their presentations more interesting and professional. Three of the most widely used presentation graphics programs are Microsoft PowerPoint, OpenOffice Impress, and Apple Keynote.

## SPECIALIZED APPLICATIONS

Specialized applications are widely used within specific professions. They include graphics programs and web authoring programs.

### Graphics Programs

**Graphics programs** are used by graphic arts professionals.

- **Desktop publishing programs (page layout programs)** mix text and graphics to create professional-quality publications.
- **Image editors (photo editors)** edit digital photographs consisting of thousands of dots or **pixels** that form **bitmap** or **raster** images.
- **Illustration programs (drawing programs)** create and edit vector images. **Vector images (vector illustrations)** use geometric shapes.
- **Image galleries** are libraries of electronic images. Two basic types are **stock photographs** and **clip art**.

### Web Authoring Programs

**Web authoring** is the process of creating a website. Individuals create online diaries called **blogs**. Many sites have **animations** (moving graphics) and **Flash** movies (interactive animation). Website design is represented by a **graphical site map**.

Web authoring programs (**web page editors, HTML editors**) create sophisticated commercial websites. Some are **WYSIWYG (what you see is what you get)** editors.

# MOBILE APPS

Mobile apps (mobile applications, apps) are add-on programs for a variety of mobile devices. Traditional applications include address books, to-do lists, alarms, and message lists. Recently mobile capabilities have exploded.

## Apps

One of the fastest-growing apps is **QR code readers**. These readers allow mobile devices to use their digital cameras to scan QR codes. **QR codes (quick response codes)** are graphics that automatically link mobile devices to content, including games, text, videos, and websites.

## App Stores

An **app store** is typically a website that provides access to specific mobile apps that can be downloaded either for a nominal fee or free of charge. Two of the best-known stores are Apple's App Store and Google Play.

| App | Focus | Site |
|---|---|---|
| Apple App Store | iOS devices | www.appstore.com |
| Google Play | Android devices | play.google.com |
| BlackBerry App World | BlackBerry products | appworld.blackberry.com |
| Windows Phone Marketplace | Windows phones | windowsphone.com/ marketplace |

# SOFTWARE SUITES

A **software suite** is a collection of individual application packages sold together.

- **Office suites (office software suites** or **productivity suites)** contain professional-grade application programs.
- **Cloud suites (online office suites)** are stored on servers and available through the Internet.
- **Specialized suites** focus on specific applications such as graphics.
- **Utility suites** include a variety of programs designed to make computing easier and safer.

# CAREERS IN IT

**Software engineers** analyze users' needs and create application software. Bachelor's or advanced specialized associate's degree in computer science or information systems and extensive knowledge of computers and technology are required. Salary range is $53,000 to $97,000.

# KEY TERMS

animation   (78)
app   (78)
application software   (64)
app store   (80)
bitmap   (74)
blog   (77)
button   (64)
clip art   (77)
cloud suite   (81)
contextual tab   (65)
database   (71)
database management system
(DBMS)   (71)
database manager   (71)
desktop publishing program   (73)
dialog box   (64)
document   (66)
drawing program   (74)
Flash   (78)
gallery   (65)
general-purpose application   (64)
graphical site map   (77)
graphical user interface (GUI)   (64)
group   (65)
HTML editor   (78)
icon   (64)
illustration program   (74)
image editor   (74)
image gallery   (74)
menu   (64)
menu bar   (64)
mobile app   (64, 78)
mobile application   (78)
office software suite   (81)

office suite   (81)
online office suite   (81)
page layout program   (73)
photo editor   (74)
pixel   (74)
pointer   (64)
presentation graphics   (71)
productivity suite   (81)
QR code   (80)
QR code reader   (80)
quick response code   (80)
raster   (74)
ribbon   (65)
Ribbon GUI   (65)
software engineer   (82)
software suite   (81)
specialized application   (64)
specialized suite   (82)
spreadsheet   (69)
stock photograph   (77)
system software   (64)
tab   (65)
toolbar   (64)
user interface   (64)
utility suite   (82)
vector illustration   (74)
vector image   (74)
web authoring   (77)
web authoring program   (78)
web page editor   (78)
window   (64)
word processor   (66)
WYSIWYG (what you see is what
you get) editor   (78)

To test your knowledge of these key terms with animated flash cards, visit our website at www.computing2014.com and enter the keyword terms3. Or use the free *Computing Essentials 2014* app.

# MULTIPLE CHOICE

Circle the correct answer.

1. This type of software works with end users, application software, and computer hardware to handle the majority of technical details.

   a. application
   b. general purpose
   c. system
   d. utility

2. A rectangular area that can contain a document, program, or message.

   a. dialog box
   b. form
   c. frame
   d. window

3. Programs that create text-based documents.

   a. DBMS
   b. suites
   c. spreadsheets
   d. word processors

4. Programs that organize, analyze, and graph numerical data such as budgets and financial reports.

   a. DBMS
   b. suites
   c. spreadsheets
   d. word processors

5. Program that allows you to mix text and graphics to create publications of professional quality.

   a. database
   b. desktop publishing
   c. presentation
   d. productivity

6. The type of image that consists of geometric shapes.

   a. bitmap
   b. raster
   c. ribbon
   d. vector

7. An online diary or commentary.

   a. bitmap
   b. blog
   c. HTML
   d. vector

8. Programs that combine a variety of visual objects to create attractive, visually interesting presentations.

   a. DBMS
   b. presentation graphics
   c. spreadsheet
   d. word processor

9. Graphics that typically appear as black and white boxes that automatically link mobile devices to various content.

   a. Flash
   b. animation
   c. vector
   d. QR codes

10. Also known as an online suite.

    a. cloud
    b. integrated
    c. office
    d. utility

For an interactive multiple-choice practice test, visit our website at www.computing2014 .com and enter the keyword multiple3. Or use the free *Computing Essentials 2014* app.

# MATCHING

Match each numbered item with the most closely related lettered item. Write your answers in the spaces provided.

a. buttons
b. cloud
c. database
d. galleries
e. image editor
f. map
g. spreadsheet
h. store
i. utility
j. word processor

____ 1. Toolbars typically appear below the menu bar and include small graphic elements called _____.

____ 2. Simplifies the process of making a selection from a list of alternatives by graphically displaying the effect of alternatives before being selected.

____ 3. A general-purpose program that creates text-based documents.

____ 4. Program that organizes, analyzes, and graphs numerical data.

____ 5. A collection of related data.

____ 6. Also known as a photo editor, this specialized graphics program edits or modifies digital photographs.

____ 7. The overall site design for a website is commonly represented in a graphical site _____.

____ 8. A website that provides access to specific mobile apps is known as an app _____.

____ 9. A type of suite that is stored at a server on the Internet and is available anywhere you can access the Internet.

____ 10. A type of specialized suite that includes a variety of programs designed to make computing easier and safer.

For an interactive matching practice test, visit our website at www.computing2014.com and enter the keyword matching3. Or use the free *Computing Essentials 2014* app.

# OPEN-ENDED

On a separate sheet of paper, respond to each question or statement.

1. Explain the difference between general-purpose and specialized applications. Also discuss the common features of application programs, including those with traditional and ribbon graphical user interfaces.

2. Discuss general-purpose applications, including word processors, spreadsheets, database management systems, and presentation graphics.

3. Discuss specialized applications, including graphics programs, web authoring programs, and other professional specialized applications.

4. Describe mobile apps, including QR code readers and app stores.

5. Describe software suites, including office suites, cloud suites, specialized suites, and utility suites.

# DISCUSSION

Respond to each of the following questions.

## 1  Making IT Work for You: IMAGE EDITORS

Would you like a simple way to fix problems in your photos? Review the Making IT Work for You: Image Editors on pages 75 and 76 and then respond to the following: (a) What software do you currently use to edit your photos? Why did you choose this particular one? If you do not use photo editing software, would you consider installing Windows Live Photo Gallery? Why or why not? (b) List and briefly describe three features of photo editing software.

(c) Do you normally tag your friends and family in photos, either with your software or on a social networking site? Why or why not? (d) Other than on your computer, where else do you store your photos? Do you have all your important folders backed up? If so, where? Would you consider using a cloud service, such as SkyDrive, to store your photos in the future? Why or why not?

## 2  Making IT Work for You: GOOGLE DOCS

Would you like to try free alternatives to traditional office software suites? Review the Making IT Work for You: Google Docs on page 83 and then respond to the following: (a) Do you currently use Google Docs? If so, what types of documents do you typically create? If not, then list some possible benefits Google Docs could provide. (b) Do you share documents and/or collaborate with others? How do you do it? If you have used Google Docs, describe how you would share documents. (c) Using a search engine or your own research, list a few differences between Google Docs and Microsoft Office Web Apps. Which one do you prefer? Why?

## 3  Explorations: ADOBE

Did you know that Adobe is one of the leaders in developing software for the graphics, publishing, and web authoring industries? Review the Explorations box on page 73 and then respond to the following: (a) What is the difference between Adobe Reader and Adobe Acrobat? What are some of the benefits of using Acrobat to create and edit PDF files? (b) Which Adobe product is used for professional video editing? What are some key features of video editing software? (c) Briefly describe an Adobe software suite that contains several related products. What are the benefits of purchasing such a suite? (d) What is the Adobe Creative Cloud? Would you use this service instead of purchasing the software? Why or why not?

### 4  Exploration: MICROSOFT OFFICE APP

Did you know that there are several apps that allow you to create and edit Microsoft Office files? Review the Explorations box on page 78 and then respond to the following: (a) Which mobile operating systems will work with this app? (b) Which types of Microsoft Office files can be created and edited? When these files are viewed on this app, do they retain their formatting and layout? If so, how does the app accomplish this? (c) Does this app offer file synchronization with your desktop or notebook computer? How about the cloud? If so, what are the supported services? (d) Would you purchase this app? Why or why not?

### 5  Ethics: IMAGE EDITING

Various image and video editing applications have made it easy for both professionals and amateurs to alter photographs and videos. Some of these edits raise ethical concerns when they are used inappropriately. Review the Ethics box on page 77. Research examples of digital photo or video editing that have resulted in controversy and then respond to the following: (a) Do you see any ethical issues related to altering photographs or videos? (b) What do you consider the boundary to be between acceptable editing and deceptive or misleading practices? (c) How does such editing affect courtrooms where visual evidence is often presented? (d) Do you feel the old saying "seeing is believing" needs to be reconsidered for the digital age? Defend your answers.

### 6  Ethics: AUTOMATION AND APPLICATION SOFTWARE

Modern application software has become easy to use, and many are able to automate many manual processes. This raises an ethical concern about automation reducing the need for human workers in many types of businesses. Review the Ethics box on page 78 and respond to the following: (a) What kind of jobs do you feel are at risk from such software? (b) What are the benefits of businesses using this software? Do customers also benefit? Why or why not? (c) Are there any professions that could enjoy an increase in demand from automation? Explain your answer. (d) How do you feel about automation? Should we regulate the types of programs they develop? How about businesses that use software that replaces human workers? Defend your position.

## 7    Environment: DOWNLOADING SOFTWARE

Did you know that downloading software can actually generate energy savings? Review the Environment box on page 65 and then respond to the following: (a) Why does purchasing software as a digital download benefit the environment? (b) List a few examples of software that you have purchased and downloaded in the past. If you have never done so, find three examples of application software that you can purchase using this technique. (c) Do you feel that there are any disadvantages to purchasing software online? Explain your answer.

## 8    Environment: APPS

Did you know that using mobile devices and apps can benefit the environment? Review the Environment box on page 80 and then respond to the following: (a) In what ways are mobile devices helping the environment? (b) Do you currently read any books on mobile devices? If so, list a few of your most recent ones. If you do not, name three of your traditional textbooks that are available as e-books. (c) List and briefly describe three apps that allow you to take notes on your mobile device. If you do not own a mobile device, research these apps for any mobile operating system. (d) Is it possible that mobile devices could actually be worse for the environment? Discuss your response.

# System Software

▲ Download the free *Computing Essentials 2014* app for videos, key term flashcards, quizzes, and the game, *Over the Edge!*

## Competencies

**After you have read this chapter, you should be able to:**

1 Describe the differences between system software and application software.

2 Discuss the four types of system software programs.

3 Discuss the basic functions, features, and categories of operating systems.

4 Discuss mobile operating systems, including BlackBerry OS, iOS, Android, Windows Phone, and WebOS.

5 Describe desktop operating systems, including Windows, Mac OS, UNIX, Linux, and virtualization.

6 Describe the purpose of utilities and utility suites.

7 Identify the four most essential utilities.

8 Discuss Windows utility programs.

9 Describe device drivers, including Windows' Add a Device Wizard and Update.

## Why should I read this chapter?

Many years ago, microcomputers were very limited in what they could do. A major limitation was their operating systems, which often required computer specialists to keep them running. That was then and this is now. Now, the possibilities seem limitless with the powerful operating systems of today. These programs make it easy and safe for any of us to use computers, the Internet, and the web.

This chapter discusses a variety of operating systems for desktop computers including Windows 7 and 8 and Mac OS X. Additionally, you'll learn about mobile operating systems including Apple's iOS, Android, and Windows Phone. You also will learn about how to use programs that recognize and correct computer problems and use programs that guard your computer against viruses. To be competent and to be competitive in today's professional workplace, you need to know and to understand these things.

## chapter .4

# Introduction

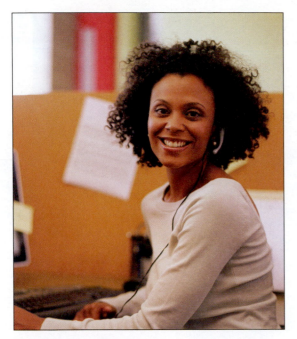

When most people think about computers, they think about surfing the web, creating reports, analyzing data, storing information, making presentations, and any number of other valuable applications. We typically think about applications and application software. Computers and computer applications have become a part of the fabric of our everyday lives. Most of us agree that they are great . . . as long as they are working.

We usually do not think about the more mundane and behind-the-scenes computer activities: loading and running programs, coordinating networks that share resources, organizing files, protecting our computers from viruses, performing periodic maintenance to avoid problems, and controlling hardware devices so that they can communicate with one another. Typically, these activities go on behind the scenes without our help.

That is the way it should be, and the way it is, as long as everything is working perfectly. But what if new application programs are not compatible and will not run on our current computer system? What if we get a computer virus? What if our hard disk fails? What if we buy a new digital video camera and can't store and edit the images on our computer system? What if our computer starts to run slower and slower?

**Hi, I'm Ann, and I'm a computer support specialist. I'd like to talk with you about system software, programs that do a lot of the work behind the scenes so that you can run applications and surf the web. I'd also like to talk about the mobile operating systems that control smartphones and other small portable computers.**

These issues may seem mundane, but they are critical. This chapter covers the vital activities that go on behind the scenes. A little knowledge about these activities can go a long way to making your computing life easier. To effectively use computers, competent end users need to understand the functionality of system software, including operating systems, utility programs, and device drivers.

# System Software

End users use application software to accomplish specific tasks. For example, we use word processing programs to create letters, documents, and reports. However, end users also use system software. **System software** works with end users, application software, and computer hardware to handle the majority of technical details. For example, system software controls where a word processing program is stored in memory, how commands are converted so that the system unit can process them, and where a completed document or file is saved. See Figure 4-1.

System software is not a single program. Rather it is a collection or a system of programs that handle hundreds of technical details with little or no user intervention. System software consists of four types of programs:

- **Operating systems** coordinate computer resources, provide an interface between users and the computer, and run applications.
- **Utilities** perform specific tasks related to managing computer resources.
- **Device drivers** are specialized programs that allow particular input or output devices to communicate with the rest of the computer system.
- **Language translators** convert the programming instructions written by programmers into a language that computers understand and process.

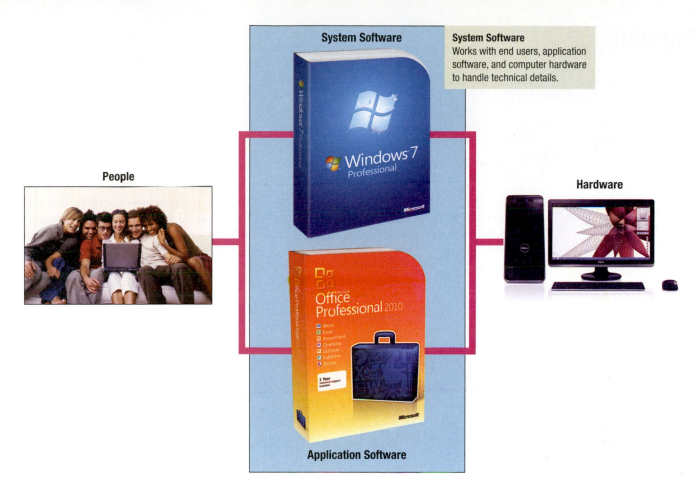

People

System Software

**System Software**
Works with end users, application software, and computer hardware to handle technical details.

Hardware

Application Software

**Figure 4-1** System software handles technical details

# Operating Systems

An **operating system** is a collection of programs that handle many of the technical details related to using a computer. In many ways, an operating system is the most important type of computer program. Without a functioning operating system, your computer would be useless.

## Functions

Every computer has an operating system and every operating system performs a variety of functions. These functions can be classified into three groups:

- **Managing resources:** Operating systems coordinate all the computer's resources including memory, processing, storage, and devices such as printers and monitors. They also monitor system performance, schedule tasks, provide security, and start up the computer.

- **Providing user interface:** Operating systems allow users to interact with application programs and computer hardware through a **user interface**. Many older operating systems used a character-based interface in which users communicated with the operating system through written commands such as "Copy A: assign.doc C:". Almost all newer operating systems use a **graphical user interface (GUI)**. As we discussed in Chapter 3, a graphical user interface uses graphical elements such as icons and windows.

- **Running applications:** Operating systems load and run applications such as word processors and spreadsheets. Most operating systems support **multitasking**, or the ability to switch between different applications stored in memory. With multitasking, you could have Word and Excel running at the same time and switch easily between the two applications. The program that you are currently working on is described as running in the **foreground**. The other program or programs are running in the **background**.

## Features

Starting or restarting a computer is called **booting** the system. There are two ways to boot a computer: a warm boot and a cold boot. A **warm boot** occurs when the computer is already on and you restart it without turning off the power. A warm boot can be accomplished in several ways. For many computer systems, they can be restarted by simply pressing a sequence of keys. Starting a computer that has been turned off is called a **cold boot**. To learn more about booting your computer system and POST (power on self-test), visit our website at www.computing2014.com and enter the keyword boot.

You typically interact with the operating system through the graphical user interface. Most provide a place, called the **desktop**, that provides access to computer resources. (See Figure 4-2.) Operating systems have several features in common with application programs, including

- **Icons**—graphic representations for a program, type of file, or function.
- **Pointer**—controlled by a mouse, trackpad, or touch screen, the pointer changes shape depending on its current function. For example, when shaped like an arrow, the pointer can be used to select items such as an icon.

**Figure 4-2 Desktop**

- **Windows**—rectangular areas for displaying information and running programs.
- **Menus**—provide a list of options or commands.
- **Tabs**—divide menus into major activity areas.
- **Dialog boxes**—provide information or request input.
- **Help**—provides online assistance for operating system functions and procedures.
- **Gesture control**—ability to control operations with finger movements, such as swiping, sliding, and pinching.

Most operating systems store data and programs in a system of files and folders. **Files** are used to store data and programs. Related files are stored within a **folder**, and, for organizational purposes, a folder can contain other folders. For example, you might organize your electronic files in the *Documents* folder on your hard disk. This folder could contain other folders, each named to indicate its contents. One might be "Computer Class" and could contain all the files you have created (or will create) for this course.

**Figure 4-3 Handheld devices have embedded operating systems**

### Categories

While there are hundreds of different operating systems, there are only three basic categories: embedded, network, or stand-alone.

- **Embedded operating systems** are used for handheld devices such as smartphones, cable and satellite television tuner boxes, video game systems, and other small electronics. (See Figure 4-3.) The entire operating system is stored within or embedded in the device.
- **Network operating systems (NOS)** are used to control and coordinate computers that are networked or linked together. Many networks are small and connect only a limited number of microcomputers. Other networks, like those at colleges and universities, are very large and complex. These networks may include other smaller networks and typically connect a variety of different types of computers.

  Network operating systems are typically located on one of the connected computers' hard disks. Called the **network server**, this computer coordinates all communication between the other computers. Popular network operating systems include Linux, Windows Server, and UNIX.

- **Stand-alone operating systems**, also called **desktop operating systems**, control a single desktop or notebook computer. (See Figure 4-4.) These operating systems are located on the computer's hard disk. Often desktop computers and notebooks are part of a network. In these cases, the desktop operating system works with the network's NOS to share and coordinate resources. In these situations, the desktop operating system is referred to as the *client operating system*.

The operating system is often referred to as the **software environment** or **software platform**. Almost all application programs are designed to run with a specific platform. For example, Apple's iMovie software is

**Figure 4-4 Stand-alone operating system**

designed to run with the Mac OS environment. Many applications, however, have different versions, each designed to operate with a particular platform. For example, one version of Microsoft Office is designed to operate with Windows. Another version is designed to operate with Mac OS.

## concept check

What is system software? What are the four kinds of system software programs?

What is an operating system? Discuss operating system functions and features.

Describe each of the three categories of operating systems.

# Mobile Operating Systems

**Mobile operating systems**, also known as **mobile OS**, are a type of embedded operating system. Just like other computer systems, mobile computers including smartphones and tablets require an operating system. These mobile operating systems are less complicated and more specialized for wireless communication.

While there are numerous mobile operating systems, some of the best known are Android, BlackBerry OS, iOS, WebOS, and Windows Phone.

- **Android** was introduced in 2007. It was originally developed by Android Inc. and later purchased by Google. Android is widely used in many of today's smartphones.
- **BlackBerry OS**, also known as **RIM OS**, was first introduced in 1999 by a small Canadian firm called Research In Motion. Originally designed as the platform for the BlackBerry handheld computer, it has evolved into a powerful mobile operating system.
- **iOS**, formerly known as **iPhone OS**, was originally developed in 2007 by Apple. It is based on Mac OS and is used as the platform for Apple's iPhone, iPod Touch, and iPad. See Figure 4-5.
- **WebOS** was originally developed in 2009 by Palm, Inc. and later purchased by the Hewlett-Packard Company. Originally developed for Palm's handheld computers, it has evolved to support Hewlett-Packard's smartphones and tablet computers.
- **Windows Phone 8** was introduced in 2012 by Microsoft to support a variety of mobile devices, including smartphones. It has the ability to run many powerful programs designed for desktop and laptop computers.

In the last chapter, we discussed that not all mobile applications will run on all smartphones. That is because an app is designed to run on a particular software platform or operating system. Before downloading an app, be sure that it is designed to run with the mobile operating system on your mobile device.

**Figure 4-5** **Apple iPhone**

# Desktop Operating Systems

Every microcomputer has an operating system controlling its operations. The most widely used desktop operating systems are Windows, Mac OS, Unix, and Linux.

### Windows

Microsoft's **Windows** is the most widely used microcomputer operating system. Because its market share is so large, more application programs are developed to run under Windows than any other operating system. Windows comes in a variety of different versions and is designed to run with a variety of different microprocessors.

There are many versions of Windows. The two recent versions are Windows 7 and Windows 8.

- **Windows 7** was released in 2009 and has a traditional user interface similar to previous versions of Windows. (See Figure 4-6.) It provided enhanced features, including improved handwriting recognition and advanced searching capabilities for finding files and other content on a computer.
- **Windows 8** was released in 2012 and was created to better integrate Microsoft's desktop operating systems with its mobile operating systems. (See Figure 4-7.) It provided support for gestures, cloud integration, and apps. Windows 8 also introduced a new interface. This interface is very similar to the interface for Microsoft's mobile operating system, Windows Phone, and is a dramatic shift from the traditional Windows interface. Windows 8 offers a **start screen** consisting of tiles. Each **tile** displays active content linked to an application. A desktop similar to the traditional Windows desktop can be accessed various ways. **Windows RT** is a version of Windows 8 designed to run with tablets using a particular microprocessor from ARM.

**Figure 4-6** Windows 7

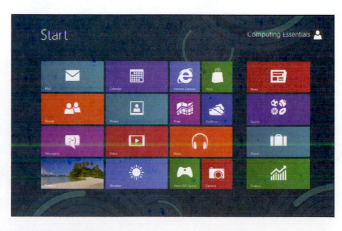

**Figure 4-7** Windows 8

## Mac OS

Apple has been the leader in the development of powerful and easy-to-use microcomputer operating systems since its introduction of the Macintosh microcomputer in 1984. Designed to run only with Apple computers, **Mac OS** is not as widely used as the Windows operating system. As a result, fewer application programs have been written for it. With dramatically increasing sales of Apple computers, however, the use of Mac OS has been rapidly increasing and is widely recognized as one of the most innovative operating systems.

**Mac OS X** is the most widely used Mac OS. Its two most recent versions are:

- **OS X Lion** was released in 2011 and introduced several powerful features, including **Launchpad** to display and provide direct access to applications, **Mission Control** to display all running applications, and gestures.

- **OS X Mountain Lion** was released in 2012 and designed for desktops and laptops. (See Figure 4-8.) Its user interface is very similar to the interface used with its tablets and smartphones. The functionality of Mountain Lion is similar to Windows 8 although it is generally regarded as easier to use.

## UNIX and Linux

The **UNIX** operating system was originally designed to run on minicomputers in network environments. Now, it is widely used by servers on the web, mainframe computers, and very powerful microcomputers. There are a large number of different versions of UNIX.

**Linux** is an operating system that extended one of the UNIX versions. It was originally developed by a graduate student at the University of Helsinki, Linus Torvalds, in 1991. He allowed free distribution of the operating system code and encouraged others to modify and further develop the code. Programs released in this way are

**Figure 4-8  Mac OS X Mountain Lion**

called **open source**. Linux is a popular and powerful alternative to the Windows operating system. (See Figure 4-9.)

Linux has been the basis of several other operating systems. For example, Google's **Chrome OS** is based on Linux. This operating system is designed for netbook computers and other mobile devices. Chrome OS focuses on Internet connectivity and cloud computing.

## Virtualization

As we have discussed, application programs are designed to run with particular operating systems. What if you wanted to run two or more applications each requiring a different operating system? One solution would be to install each of the operating systems on a different computer. There is, however, a way in which a single physical computer can support multiple operating systems that operate independently. This approach is called **virtualization**.

When a single physical computer runs a special program known as **virtualization software**, it operates as though it were two or more separate and independent computers, known as **virtual machines**. Each virtual machine appears to the user as a separate independent computer with its own operating system. The operating system of the physical machine is known as the **host operating system**. The operating system for each virtual machine is known as the **guest operating system**. Users can readily switch between virtual computers and programs running on them. There are several programs that create and run virtual machines. One such program, Microsoft's **Hyper-V**, is included with the Windows 8 Professional version. (See Figure 4-10.)

**Figure 4-9  Linux**

**Figure 4-10  Ubuntu Linux running in a Windows 8 Hyper-V virtual machine**

## concept check

What is Windows? What are the two most recent versions?

What is Mac OS? What are Lion and Mountain Lion?

What is UNIX? What is Linux? What is Chrome OS?

What are virtualization and virtualization software? What are host and guest operating systems?

# Utilities

Ideally, microcomputers would continuously run without problems. However, that simply is not the case. All kinds of things can happen—internal hard disks can crash, computers can freeze up, operations can slow down, and so on. These events can make computing very frustrating. That's where utilities come in. **Utilities** are specialized programs designed to make computing easier. There are hundreds of different utility programs. The most essential are

- **Troubleshooting** or **diagnostic programs** that recognize and correct problems, ideally before they become serious. To learn more about using a troubleshooting program, see Making IT Work for You: Windows Task Manager on pages 105 and 106.
- **Antivirus programs** that guard your computer system against viruses or other damaging programs that can invade your computer system.
- **Backup programs** that make copies of files to be used in case the originals are lost or damaged.
- **File compression programs** that reduce the size of files so they require less storage space and can be sent more efficiently over the Internet.

Most operating systems provide some utility programs. Even more powerful utility programs can be purchased separately or in utility suites.

## tips

Have you ever experienced problems after installing a new program or changing system settings? If so, the System Restore utility can help by reversing the changes and bringing your computer to a previous point in time. For Windows 7:

**1** Click *Start*, and then type *System Restore* in the search box.

**2** Follow the prompts, and choose a restore point.

**3** Click the *Finish* button to start the process.

To see additional tips, visit our website at www.computing 2014.com and enter the keyword tips.

## Windows Utilities

The Windows operating systems are accompanied by several utility programs, including Backup and Restore, Disk Cleanup, and Disk Defragmenter.

**Backup and Restore** is a utility program included with the many versions of Windows that makes a copy of all files or selected files that have been saved onto a disk. It helps protect you from the effects of a disk failure. For example, you can select *Backup and Restore* from the Windows 7 Maintenance menu to create a backup for your hard disk as shown in Figure 4-11.

**1** • Click *Start*, and then select *Maintenance* from the *All Programs* menu.

- Select *Backup and Restore*, and then click *Set up backup*.

- Choose the destination for the backup.

- Choose the files you want to back up.

- Set up Backup Wizard to back up the selected files.

**Figure 4-11  Backup and Restore utility**

# WINDOWS TASK MANAGER

Have you ever been working with a program when it simply stopped working and would not respond to you? Does your computer seem to be getting slower and slower? Windows Task Manager, which gives you a live view of every program that is currently in RAM, is designed to help with these and many other operational problems.

**Starting Task Manager**   You can open Task Manager from anywhere by following these steps:

**1** ● **Press and momentarily hold the Ctrl + Alt + Del keys.**

**2** ● **Select the *Start Task Manager* option.**

As you can see, the Task Manager window provides a menu and several tabs. Please note that it may look slightly different in your version of Windows.

**Closing an Application**   Use Task Manager when a program you are using becomes stuck and stops responding.

**1** ● **Go to the *Applications* tab of Task Manager.**

**2** ● **Find the program that is stuck. Its status should read, "Not Responding."**

**3** ● **Select it and click the *End Task* button.**

The program that was not responding has been closed, and you can now continue using Windows normally.

**Viewing Processes**   This is the most powerful area of Task Manager. Here, you will see a list of every process (running program) that is currently residing in your computer's RAM.

**1** ● **Go to the *Processes* tab of Task Manager.**

**2** ● **Click the *Memory* heading. All the processes will be sorted from highest (occupying the most RAM) to the lowest.**

**3** ● **Click the *CPU* heading. This will show any processes that the CPU is currently working on.**

It is normal for the numbers to fluctuate for running programs, especially those for the CPU. Also note that a very high number on "System Idle Process" is normal.

**Ending a Process**   Some problematic processes could be spyware, while others represent background services you don't need. Other processes are crucial for your system and should never be ended. *Warning:* Before ending a process, you must truly understand the risks (or benefits) of doing so. Using a search engine, type the name of the process, and the results will list several websites that explain what it does. If you want to end a process:

1 • While in the *Processes* tab, click the *Image Name* heading (to avoid the fluctuating positions of each process).

2 • Click the process you want to end.

3 • Select the *End Process* button.

4 • Click *End Process* again to confirm.

That particular program file will be removed from the list and from your computer's memory. Keep in mind that if this program is configured to load automatically, you will see it again when you restart your computer.

**Managing Startup Programs** If you are wondering why you have so many processes running in your computer's memory, it is likely because many of your software titles have small programs or services that begin running each time you start Windows. Some services are crucial, while others are not always needed and do little except slow down your computer. To manage these services:

1 • Click the *Start* button on your Windows Taskbar.

2 • Type "msconfig" in the *Search* box, and press Enter.

3 • Click the *Startup* tab.

4 • Review the list of startup processes, perform research online, and uncheck any programs that you do not want to load automatically each time you start Windows.

5 • Click the *OK* button when finished. This will usually require a system restart.

Before making any changes to startup programs or active processes, be sure that you have carefully researched the program and/or consulted with a professional.

**To learn about other ways to make information technology work for you, visit our website at www.computing2014.com and enter the keyword miw.**

When you surf the web, a variety of programs and files are saved on your hard disk. Many of these and other files are not essential. **Disk Cleanup** is a troubleshooting utility that identifies and eliminates nonessential files. This frees up valuable disk space and improves system performance.

For example, by selecting Disk Cleanup from the Windows 7 System Tools menu, you can eliminate unneeded files on your hard disk as shown in Figure 4-12.

- Click *Start*, and then select *Accessories* from the *All Programs* menu.

- Select *Disk Cleanup* from the *System Tools* menu.

- Review the files suggested for cleanup, and then click *OK*.

**Disk Cleanup : Drive Selection**

Select the drive you want to clean up.

Drives:

SibbittsHDX (C:)

OK          Exit

**Disk Cleanup for SibbittsHDX (C:)**

Disk Cleanup

You can use Disk Cleanup to free up to 57.2 MB of disk space on SibbittsHDX (C:).

Files to delete:

| | |
|---|---|
| ☑ Downloaded Program Files | 0 bytes |
| ☑ Temporary Internet Files | 6.17 MB |
| ☐ Offline webpages | 454 KB |
| ☐ Recycle Bin | 0 bytes |
| ☐ Setup Log Files | 1.73 MB |

Total amount of disk space you gain:          54.1 MB

Description

Downloaded Program Files are ActiveX controls and Java applets downloaded automatically from the Internet when you view certain pages. They are temporarily stored in the Downloaded Program Files folder on your hard disk.

Clean up system files          View Files

How does Disk Cleanup work?

OK          Cancel

- The utility cleans the selected files.

**Disk Cleanup**

The Disk Cleanup utility is cleaning up unnecessary files on your machine.

Cleaning up drive SibbittsHDX (C:).

Cancel

Cleaning:     Temporary Internet Files

**Figure 4-12 Disk Cleanup utility**

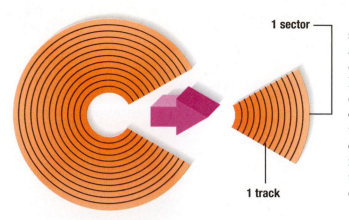

1 sector

1 track

**Figure 4-13** Tracks and sectors

As we will discuss in detail in Chapter 7, files are stored and organized on a disk according to tracks and sectors. A **track** is a concentric ring. Each track is divided into wedge-shaped sections called **sectors**. (See Figure 4-13.) The operating system tries to save a file on a single track across contiguous sectors. Often, however, this is not possible, and the file has to be broken up, or **fragmented**, into small parts that are stored wherever space is available. Whenever a file is retrieved, it is reconstructed from the fragments. After a period of time, a hard disk becomes highly fragmented, slowing operations.

**Disk Defragmenter** is a utility program that locates and eliminates unnecessary fragments and rearranges files and unused disk space to optimize operations. For example, by selecting Disk Defragmenter from the Windows 7 System Tools menu, you can defrag your hard disk as shown in Figure 4-14.

**1** • Click *Start*.

• Select *Accessories* from the *All Programs* menu.

• Select *Disk Defragmenter* from the *System Tools* menu. If necessary, click *Continue*.

**2** • Click the *Defragment disk* button to begin defragging.

• If necessary, choose the drive you want to defragment.

• When defragmentation is complete for the selected drive, view the report or close the window.

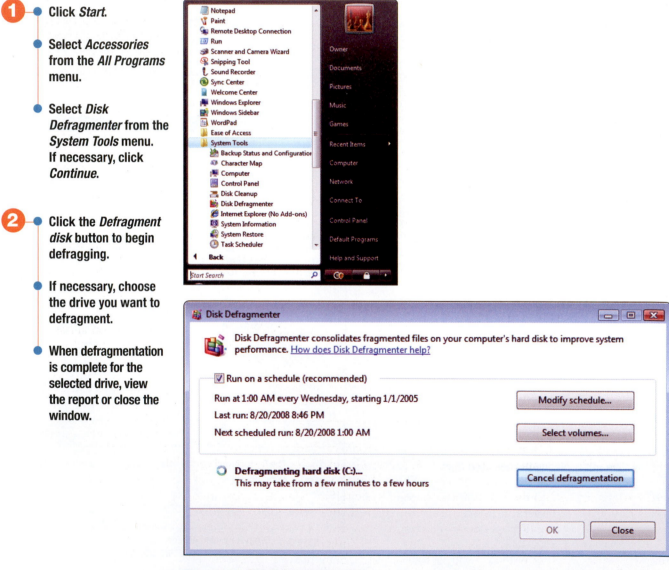

**Figure 4-14** Disk Defragmenter utility

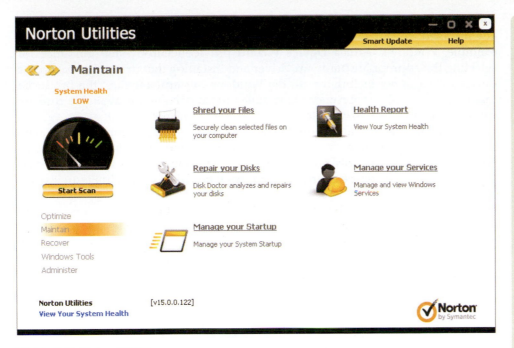

**Figure 4-15** Norton Utilities

### Utility Suites

Like application software suites, **utility suites** combine several programs into one package. Buying the package is less expensive than buying the programs separately. Some of the best-known utility suites are BitDefender, Norton Utilities, and ZoneAlarm. (See Figure 4-15.) These suites provide a variety of utilities, including programs that will protect your system from dangerous programs called computer **viruses**. You can "catch" a computer virus many ways, including by opening attachments to e-mail messages and downloading software from the Internet. (We will discuss computer viruses in detail in Chapter 9.)

 **concept check**

Discuss four essential utilities.

Describe Windows Backup and Restore, Disk Cleanup, and Disk Defragmenter.

What is the difference between a utility and a utility suite?

# Device Drivers

Every device, such as a mouse or printer, that is connected to a computer system has a special program associated with it. This program, called a **device driver** or simply a **driver**, works with the operating system to allow communication between the device and the rest of the computer system. Each time the computer system is started, the operating system loads all of the device drivers into memory.

Whenever a new device is added to a computer system, a new device driver must be installed before the device can be used. Windows supplies hundreds of different device drivers with its system software. For many devices, the appropriate drivers are automatically selected and installed when the device is first

**ethics**

Everyone should worry about getting a computer virus that will corrupt or destroy files. Some suggest that software developers may be taking advantage of this fear by sending out misleading or fake virus alerts. One reported scam encourages users to download a free virus detection program. This free download begins by actually installing a virus onto the user's computer. It then performs a bogus scan, locating the virus and then offering to remove the virus for a fee. Obviously, this is unethical, not to mention illegal. How can you and legitimate antivirus manufacturers protect themselves against viruses and unethical software developers?

To see more ethical issues, visit our website at www .computing2014.com and enter the keyword ethics.

**environment**

Did you know that there are utility suites that help the environment by lowering your computer's energy consumption? These utility programs help you find the hardware components and programs that could be shut off in order to reduce the amount of battery power or electricity being used. By enhancing the power management features of the operating system, these utilities can reduce your energy consumption by as much as 30 percent. To see more environmental facts, visit our website at www.computing2014 .com and enter the keyword environment.

connected to the computer system. For others, the device driver must be manually installed. Fortunately, Windows provides wizards to assist in this process. For example, Windows' **Add a Device Wizard** provides step-by-step guidance for selecting the appropriate hardware driver and installing that driver. If a particular device driver is not included with the Windows system software, the product's manufacturer will supply one. Many times these drivers are available directly from the manufacturer's website.

You probably never think about the device drivers in your computer. However, when your computer behaves unpredictably, you may find reinstalling or updating your device drivers solves your problems. Windows 7 makes it easy to update the drivers on your computer using **Windows Update**, as shown in Figure 4-16.

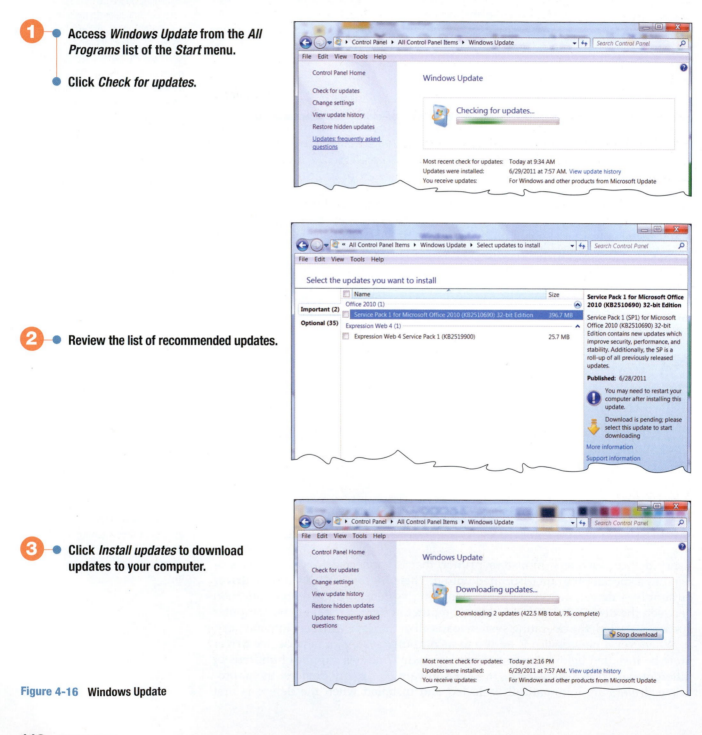

**1** ● Access *Windows Update* from the *All Programs* list of the *Start* menu.

● Click *Check for updates*.

**2** ● Review the list of recommended updates.

**3** ● Click *Install updates* to download updates to your computer.

**Figure 4-16** Windows Update

# Careers in IT

**Computer support specialists** provide technical support to customers and other users. They also may be called technical support specialists or help-desk technicians. Computer support specialists manage the everyday technical problems faced by computer users. They resolve common networking problems and may use troubleshooting programs to diagnose problems. Most computer support specialists are hired to work within a company and provide technical support for other employees and divisions. However, it is increasingly common for companies to provide technical support as an outsourced service.

Employers generally look for individuals with either an advanced associate's degree or a bachelor's degree to fill computer support specialist positions. Degrees in computer science or information systems may be preferred. However, because demand for qualified applicants is so high, those with practical experience and certification from a training program increasingly fill these positions. Employers seek individuals with good analytical and communication skills. Those with good people skills and customer service experience have an advantage in this field.

Computer support specialists can expect to earn an annual salary of $31,000 to $58,000. Opportunities for advancement are very good and may involve design and implementation of new systems. To learn about other careers in information systems, visit us at www.computing2014.com and enter the keyword **careers**.

Now that you know about system software, I'd like to tell you about my career as a computer support specialist.

## Self-Healing Computers Could Mean an End to Computer Crashes and Performance Problems

Wouldn't it be nice if computers could fix themselves? What if your computer could continually fine-tune its operations to maintain peak performance? And wouldn't it be a relief if you never had to help your computer recover after a virus or other intrusion? For many people, this sounds too good to be true. Maintenance and troubleshooting tasks like these can be time-consuming and frustrating.

Now imagine you run a business, and unless these tasks are performed, you will lose time and money. It is not a pleasant daydream, and it quickly becomes a nightmare without properly trained systems administrators to keep servers running smoothly. Yet many experts predict that supercomputers and business systems are not far from becoming too complex for humans to manage and secure. Recent news from IBM makes the dream of a self-repairing, self-updating, and self-protecting server seem closer.

IBM has announced plans to concentrate research efforts on developing just such a server. The project, called the Autonomic Computing Initiative (ACI), hopes to free businesses from time-consuming computer maintenance. IBM hopes the new system will be self-regulating and virtually invisible. It believes autonomic computing has the potential to revolutionize the way businesses run.

Autonomic computing is a system that allows machines to run with little human intervention. Such computers would not have self-awareness but would be self-correcting. Autonomic processes in machines are modeled after autonomic processes in the human body. For example, you are not consciously breathing. Instead, your body monitors and maintains your respiration without your input. Scientists hope autonomic computing will behave in a similar manner and maintain systems without intervention.

Autonomic machines would be able to identify security flaws and repair them. They would be able to sense slow computer operations and take corrective action. They would be able to detect new equipment, format it, and test it. Computer usage will become less complex so that you can focus on getting work done instead of worrying about the machine's operation. These goals are impressive, and the autonomic computer is still in development.

It is important to note that autonomic computing is not artificial intelligence because autonomic machines do not have human cognitive abilities or intelligence. Instead, these machines have knowledge of their own systems and the capability to learn from experience to correct errors.

Given the potential for a self-maintaining server, the possibility of a similar system designed for a microcomputer seems less like a dream and more like a reality. What do you think? Will microcomputers ever care for themselves? Do you think it is possible to have a computer managing its own security? Will hackers find a way to outsmart these "intelligent" systems?

## SYSTEM SOFTWARE

**System software** works with end users, application programs, and computer hardware to handle many details relating to computer operations.

Not a single program but a collection or system of programs, these programs handle hundreds of technical details with little or no user intervention.

Four kinds of systems programs are operating systems, utilities, device drivers, and language translators.

- **Operating systems** coordinate resources, provide an interface between users and the computer, and run programs.
- **Utilities** perform specific tasks related to managing computer resources.
- **Device drivers** allow particular input or output devices to communicate with the rest of the computer system.
- **Language translators** convert programming instructions written by programmers into a language that computers can understand and process.

## OPERATING SYSTEMS

**Operating systems (software environments, software platforms)** handle technical details.

### Functions

Functions include managing resources, providing a **user interface** (most operating systems use a **graphical user interface,** or **GUI**), and running applications. **Multitasking** allows switching between different applications stored in memory; current programs run in **foreground**; other programs run in **background**.

### Features

**Booting** starts (**cold**) or restarts (**warm**) a computer system. The **desktop** provides access to computer resources. Common features include **icons, pointers, windows, menus, tabs, dialog boxes, Help**, and **gesture control**. Data and programs are stored in a system of **files** and **folders**.

### Categories

Three categories of operating systems are

- **Embedded**—used with handheld computers; operating system stored within device.
- **Network (NOS)**—controls and coordinates networked computers; located on the **network server**.
- **Stand-alone (desktop)**—controls a single computer; located on the hard disk.

Operating systems are often called **software environments** or **software platforms**.

To effectively use computers, competent end users need to understand the functionality of system software, including operating systems, utility programs, and device drivers.

## MOBILE OPERATING SYSTEMS

Mobile operating systems (mobile OS) are embedded in every smartphone and tablet. These systems are less complicated and more specialized for wireless communication than desktop operating systems.

Some of the best known are BlackBerry, iOS (iPhone OS), Android, Windows Phone, and WebOS.

- **Android** was originally developed by Android Inc. and later purchased by Google. It is a widely used mobile OS.
- **BlackBerry OS (RIM OS)** originated in Canada. It was designed as the platform for BlackBerry hand-held computers.
- **iOS (iPhone OS)** was developed by Apple to support iPhone, iPod Touch, and iPad.
- **WebOS** was developed by Palm, Inc., and later purchased by **HP**. It has evolved into the operating system for many of **HP**'s mobile devices.
- **Windows Phone 8** was introduced in 2012 by Microsoft to support a variety of mobile devices, including smartphones. It can run many powerful programs designed for laptop and desktop computers.

## DESKTOP OPERATING SYSTEMS

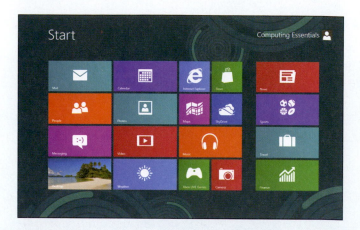

### Windows

**Windows**, the most widely used operating system, is designed to run with many different microprocessors. The two recent versions are **Windows 7** and **Windows 8**. Windows 8 offers an interface very similar to the Windows Phone interface; supports desktops, notebooks, and tablets; uses a **start screen** and **tiles**; and provides support for gestures, cloud integration, and apps. **Windows RT**, a version of Windows 8, is designed to run with ARM tablets.

### Mac OS

**Mac OS**, an innovative, powerful, easy-to-use operating system, runs on Macintosh computers. The two most recent versions are Lion and Mountain Lion. Mountain Lion's interface is very similar to the interfaces on Apple's smartphone and tablets. It is designed for Apple's desktops and laptops. Lion's functionality is similar to Windows 8 but generally considered easier to use.

# DESKTOP OPERATING SYSTEMS

## UNIX and Linux

UNIX was originally designed to run on minicomputers in network environments. Now, it is widely used by servers on the web, mainframe **computers**, and very powerful microcomputers. There are many different versions of UNIX. One version, **Linux**, a popular and powerful alternative to the Windows operating system, is **open source** software. Google's **Chrome OS** is based on Linux and designed for netbooks and other mobile devices. Chrome OS focuses on Internet connectivity and cloud computing.

## Virtualization

**Virtualization** allows a single physical computer to support multiple operating systems. Using a special program (**virtualization software**) allows the single physical computer to operate as two or more separate and independent computers known as **virtual machines**. **Host operating systems** run on the physical machine. **Guest operating systems** operate on virtual machines. Microsoft's **Hyper-V** creates and runs virtual machines.

# UTILITIES

Utilities make computing easier. The most essential are **troubleshooting (diagnostic)**, **antivirus**, **backup**, and **file compression**.

## Windows Utilities

Windows operating systems are accompanied by several utility programs, including **Backup and Restore**, **Disk Cleanup**, and **Disk Defragmenter** (eliminates unnecessary **fragments**; **tracks** are concentric rings; **sectors** are wedge-shaped).

## Utility Suites

**Utility suites** combine several programs into one package. Computer **viruses** are dangerous programs.

# DEVICE DRIVERS

**Device drivers (drivers)** allow communication between hardware devices. **Add a Device Wizard** gives step-by-step guidance to install printer drivers. **Windows Update** automates the process of updating device drivers.

# CAREERS IN IT

**Computer support specialists** provide technical support to customers and other users. Degrees in computer science or information systems are preferred plus good analytical and communication skills. Salary range is $31,000 to $58,000.

# KEY TERMS

Add a Device Wizard   (110)
Android   (100)
antivirus program   (104)
background   (98)
Backup and Restore   (104)
backup program   (104)
BlackBerry OS   (100)
booting   (98)
Chrome OS   (103)
cold boot   (98)
computer support specialist   (111)
desktop   (98)
desktop operating system   (99)
device driver   (96, 109)
diagnostic program   (104)
dialog box   (99)
Disk Cleanup   (107)
Disk Defragmenter   (108)
driver   (109)
embedded operating system   (99)
file   (99)
file compression program   (104)
folder   (99)
foreground   (98)
fragmented   (108)
gesture control   (99)
graphical user interface (GUI)   (97)
guest operating system   (103)
Help   (99)
host operating system   (103)
Hyper-V   (103)
icon   (98)
iOS   (100)
iPhone OS   (100)
language translator   (96)
Launchpad   (102)
Linux   (102)
Mac OS   (102)
Mac OS X   (102)
menu   (99)

Mission Control   (102)
mobile operating system   (100)
mobile OS   (100)
multitasking   (98)
network operating system
(NOS)   (99)
network server   (99)
open source   (103)
operating system   (96, 97)
OS X Lion   (102)
OS X Mountain Lion   (102)
pointer   (98)
RIM OS   (100)
sector   (108)
software environment   (99)
software platform   (99)
stand-alone operating system   (99)
start screen   (101)
system software   (96)
tab   (99)
tile   (101)
track   (108)
troubleshooting program   (104)
UNIX   (102)
user interface   (97)
utilities   (96, 104)
utility suite   (109)
virtual machine   (103)
virtualization   (103)
virtualization software   (103)
virus   (109)
warm boot   (98)
WebOS   (100)
window   (99)
Windows   (101)
Windows 7   (101)
Windows 8   (101)
Windows Phone 8   (100)
Windows RT   (101)
Windows Update   (110)

To test your knowledge of these key terms with animated flash cards, visit our website at www.computing2014.com and enter the keyword terms4. Or use the free *Computing Essentials 2014* app.

# MULTIPLE CHOICE

Circle the correct answer.

1.  What type of software works with users, application software, and computer hardware to handle the majority of technical details?
    a. application
    b. desktop
    c. Linux
    d. system

2.  The programs that convert programming instructions written by programmers into a language that computers understand and process are language:
    a. converters
    b. linguists
    c. managers
    d. translators

3.  The ability to switch between different applications stored in memory is called:
    a. diversion
    b. multitasking
    c. operational interference
    d. programming

4.  Graphic representation for a program, type of file, or function:
    a. app
    b. icon
    c. image
    d. software

5.  This operating system feature is controlled by a mouse and changes shape depending on its current function.
    a. dialog box
    b. menu
    c. mouse
    d. pointer

6.  The operating system based on Linux, designed for Netbook computers, and focused on Internet connectivity through cloud computing:
    a. Chrome
    b. Mac
    c. UNIX
    d. Windows

7.  The mobile operating system developed by Apple and originally called iPhone OS:
    a. Android
    b. BlackBerry OS
    c. iOS
    d. Mac OS

8.  A utility program that makes copies of files to be used in case the originals are lost or damaged:
    a. Backup and Restore
    b. Disk Cleanup
    c. Disk Defragmenter
    d. Compactor

9.  A troubleshooting utility that identifies and eliminates nonessential files, frees up valuable disk space, and improves system performance:
    a. Backup and Restore
    b. Disk Cleanup
    c. Disk Defragmenter
    d. Compactor

10. Windows makes it easy to update drivers with Windows:
    a. Backup
    b. Restore
    c. Driver
    d. Update

For an interactive multiple-choice practice test, visit our website at www.computing2014 .com and enter the keyword multiple4. Or use the free *Computing Essentials 2014* app.

# MATCHING

Match each numbered item with the most closely related lettered item. Write your answers in the spaces provided.

a. Android

b. antivirus

c. driver

d. fragmented

e. Launchpad

f. NOS

g. platform

h. utilities

i. virtualization

j. warm boot

____ 1. Programs that perform specific tasks related to managing computer resources.

____ 2. Restarting a running computer without turning off the power.

____ 3. Type of operating system that controls and coordinates networked computers.

____ 4. An operating system is often referred to as the software environment or software ___.

____ 5. OS X Lion feature to display and provide direct access to applications.

____ 6. A type of software that allows a single physical computer to operate as though it were two or more separate and independent computers.

____ 7. Mobile operating system that is owned by Google and is widely used in many smartphones.

____ 8. Type of program that guards computer systems from viruses and other damaging programs.

____ 9. If a file cannot be saved on a single track, it has to be ___.

____10. Program that works with the operating system to allow communication between a device and the rest of a computer system is called a device ___.

For an interactive matching practice test, visit our website at www.computing2014.com and enter the keyword matching4. Or use the free *Computing Essentials 2014* app.

# OPEN-ENDED

On a separate sheet of paper, respond to each question or statement.

1. Describe system software. Discuss each of the four types of system programs.

2. Define operating systems. Describe the basic features and the three categories of operating systems.

3. What are mobile operating systems? Describe the leading mobile operating systems.

4. What are desktop operating systems? Compare Windows, Mac OS, Linux, and Chrome OS. Discuss virtualization.

5. Discuss utilities. What are the most essential utilities? What is a utility suite?

6. Explain the role of device drivers. Discuss Add a Device Wizard and Windows Update.

# DISCUSSION

Respond to each of the following questions.

## 1 Making IT Work for You: WINDOWS TASK MANAGER

Have you ever been working with a program when it simply stopped working and would not respond to you? Review the Making IT Work for You: Windows Task Manager on pages 105 and 106 and open Task Manager using a Windows-based computer. Then respond to the following: (a) List the top three processes in terms of memory usage. (b) List three processes that are using your CPU, even if it is only for a second or two as you look at that dialog box. (c) Find one process that you do not recognize. Using your favorite search engine, determine what the process does. Write down the name of the process, its description or purpose, and the URL of the website you used to research it.

**Windows Task Manager**

File  Options  View  Help

Applications | Processes | Services | Performance | Networking | Users

| Image Name | User Name | CPU | Memory (... | Description |
|---|---|---|---|---|
| iexplore.exe ... | ComputingEssentials | 00 | 61,492 K | Internet Explorer |
| dwm.exe | ComputingEssentials | 00 | 46,312 K | Desktop Window Manag |
| explorer.exe | ComputingEssentials | 00 | 37,836 K | Windows Explorer |
| msseces.exe | ComputingEssentials | 00 | 29,456 K | Microsoft Security Clien |
| HPPA_Main.exe | ComputingEssentials | 00 | 23,992 K | HP Power Assistant |
| WINWORD.E... | ComputingEssentials | 00 | 19,976 K | Microsoft Word |
| HPWA_Main.exe | ComputingEssentials | 00 | 19,180 K | HP Wireless Assistant |
| NACAgentUI.... | ComputingEssentials | 00 | 12,788 K | Cisco NAC Agent UI |
| PrivacyIconCli... | ComputingEssentials | 00 | 12,624 K | Intel(R) Management a|
| SnippingTool.... | ComputingEssentials | 00 | 12,500 K | Snipping Tool |
| iexplore.exe ... | ComputingEssentials | 00 | 8,616 K | Internet Explorer |
| wisptis.exe | ComputingEssentials | 00 | 8,148 K | Microsoft Pen and Touc |
| sttray64.exe | ComputingEssentials | 00 | 7,796 K | IDT PC Audio |
| wisptis.exe | | 00 | 6,096 K | |

☑ Show processes from all users          End Process

Processes: 133     CPU Usage: 3%     Physical Memory: 40%

## 2 Explorations: LINUX

Did you know that there over a hundred different distributions, or varieties, of Linux? Review the Explorations box on page 102 and then respond to the following: (a) Discuss at least three benefits offered by many Linux distributions. (b) What are some drawbacks of using Linux? (c) Discuss two ways in which you could try Linux without removing your current operating system. (d) What are two of the most popular Linux distributions for home users? In a few sentences, describe some of the key features that make these distributions unique.

## 3 Explorations: UTILITY SOFTWARE

Did you know that there are many types of utility software for both consumers and businesses? Review the Explorations box on page 107 and then respond to the following: (a) Explore Norton Mobile Security. What does this type of utility do? Would you purchase it for your mobile device? Why or why not? (b) Explore Symantec's Web Gateway product. What does this web-filtering software do? What kind of control does it give to managers? (c) Explore Symantec's Ghost Solution Suite. What are some of the benefits of using imaging and deployment software such as this? (d) What are the advantages of using Symantec.cloud for an enterprise? If you were a manager, would you rely on the cloud for your utility software needs? Why or why not?

### 4 Ethics: NEW OPERATING SYSTEMS

Software companies periodically release new versions of their operating systems, and many purchase these programs as soon as they are available. Review the Ethics box on page 101 and respond to the following questions: (a) When a new operating system is introduced, should you purchase it immediately? Why or why not? (b) Do you think the introduction of a new operating system is typically designed to render existing hardware and software obsolete? Defend your position. (c) Is this an ethical issue? If so, develop some ethical guidelines for software manufacturers to consider before they introduce either a new version for their operating systems or application programs. (d) Open source operating systems, such as Linux, often release new versions for free. Do you feel this is a better model for the development of operating systems? Why or why not.

### 5 Ethics: VIRUS PROTECTION SCAMS

Everyone should be concerned about viruses infecting computer systems. Some report that this fear is being used to manipulate users into purchasing new or upgraded antivirus programs. Some even report specific antivirus scams. Review the Ethics box on page 109 and then respond to the following: (a) Have you ever been offered a free virus alert program? If so, describe the offer and whether you accepted the offer. (b) Almost all legitimate antivirus software manufacturers issue new virus alerts. Do you think these alerts are motivated by greed or by good consumer service? Why or why not? (c) Is this an ethical issue for antivirus software manufacturers? If so, create some ethical guidelines for antivirus software manufacturers to follow when issuing virus alerts. (d) What can users do to protect themselves against antivirus scams and against unethical manufacturers of antivirus programs? Be specific and defend your suggestions.

## 6 Environment: OS POWER MANAGEMENT

Did you know that some operating systems help protect the environment? Review the Environment box on page 98 and then respond to the following: (a) In what ways do operating systems help the environment? (b) Do you leave your desktop or notebook computer on all day? Do you use sleep or hibernate modes? Explain the reasons behind your decision. (c) Find the power management options for your operating system. List a few options that you would consider adjusting in order to reduce your computer's energy consumption.

Change settings for the plan: High performance
Choose the sleep and display settings that you want your computer to use.

|  | On battery | Plugged in |
|---|---|---|
| Dim the display: | 2 minutes | 4 minutes |
| Turn off the display: | 5 minutes | 30 minutes |
| Put the computer to sleep: | 10 minutes | 1 hour |
| Adjust plan brightness: | | |

Change advanced power settings

Restore default settings for this plan

Save changes    Cancel

## 7 Environment: GREEN UTILITY SUITES

Did you know that there are utility suites that help the environment? Review the Environment box on page 109 and then respond to the following: (a) Using a search engine, find one utility suite that claims to lower your computer's energy consumption. List the product name and URL of the website. (b) Describe at least three ways in which this utility suite lowers energy consumption. (c) Would you purchase this utility suite? Why or why not?

# The System Unit

▲ Download the free *Computing Essentials 2014* app for videos, key term flashcards, quizzes, and the game, *Over the Edge!*

## Competencies

**After you have read this chapter, you should be able to:**

1 Describe the four basic types of system units.

2 Describe system boards, including sockets, slots, and bus lines.

3 Discuss microprocessors, including microprocessor chips and specialty processors.

4 Discuss memory, including RAM, ROM, and flash memory.

5 Discuss expansion slots and cards.

6 Describe bus lines, bus widths, and expansion buses.

7 Describe ports, including standard and specialized ports.

8 Discuss power supply for desktop, notebook, tablet, and handheld computers.

9 Discuss how a computer can represent numbers and encode characters electronically.

## Why should I read this chapter?

The first computers ever built were too big to fit into a modern home. That was then and this is now. Today's microcomputers fit onto a desk, onto a lap, and even in a hand. They can go almost anywhere and do almost anything. And they are many, many times more powerful than computers of only a few years ago.

This chapter discusses a variety of different types of microcomputers including notebooks, tablets like the iPad, and handheld computers including smartphones like the iPhone. You will learn about the most important computer components including microprocessors and memory. Additionally, you'll learn how to connect external or peripheral devices like a digital video camera and how you can upgrade your computer's speed and power. To be competent and to be competitive in today's professional workplace, you need to know and to understand these things.

## chapter 5

# Introduction

**Hi, I'm Liz, and I'm a computer technician. I'd like to talk with you about the different types of system units for microcomputers. I'd also like to talk about various electronic components that make your computer work.**

Why are some microcomputers more powerful than others? The answer lies in three words: speed, capacity, and flexibility. After reading this chapter, you will be able to judge how fast, powerful, and versatile a particular microcomputer is. As you might expect, this knowledge is valuable if you are planning to buy a new microcomputer system or to upgrade an existing system. (The Computer Buyer's Guide at the end of this book provides additional information.) This knowledge will help you evaluate whether or not an existing microcomputer system is powerful enough for today's new and exciting applications. For example, with the right hardware, you can use your computer to watch TV and to capture video clips for class presentations.

Sometime you may get the chance to watch when a technician opens up a microcomputer. You will see that it is basically a collection of electronic circuitry. While there is no need to understand how all these components work, it is important to understand the principles. Once you do, you will be able to determine how powerful a particular microcomputer is. This will help you judge whether it can run particular kinds of programs and can meet your needs as a user.

Competent end users need to understand the functionality of the basic components in the system unit, including the system board, microprocessor, memory, expansion slots and cards, bus lines, ports, cables, and power supply units.

# System Unit

The **system unit**, also known as the **system chassis**, is a container that houses most of the electronic components that make up a computer system.

At one time all system units were in a separate case. Advances in the miniaturization of electronic components, however, have led to smaller and smaller computers with system units that share containers with other parts of the computer system.

As we have previously discussed, there are four basic microcomputer computer systems: desktop, notebook, tablet, and handheld. Each has a unique type of system unit.

### Desktops

This is the most powerful type of microcomputer. Most **desktops** have their system unit in a separate case. This case contains the system's electronic components and selected secondary storage devices. Input and output devices, such as a mouse, keyboard, and monitor, are located outside the system unit. This type of system unit is designed to be placed either horizontally or vertically. Desktop system units that are placed vertically are sometimes referred to as a **tower unit** or **tower computer**.

Some desktop computers, like Apple's iMac, have their monitor and system unit housed together in the same case. These computers are known as an **all-in-one**. (See Figure 5-1.)

### Notebooks

Although typically not as powerful as desktops, **notebooks** are portable and much smaller. Their system units are housed with selected secondary storage devices

Tower unit

All-in-one

**Figure 5-1** Desktop system units

and input devices (keyboard and pointing device). Located outside the system unit, the monitor is attached by hinges. Notebooks are often called **laptops**.

**Netbooks** are a type of notebook. They are smaller, less powerful, and less expensive than other notebooks. Netbooks are designed to support on-the-go web browsing and e-mail access. They reduce space and weight by leaving out components such as optical drives. (See Figure 5-2.)

## Tablets

**Tablets**, also known as **tablet computers**, are the newest and one of the most popular types of computer. They are effectively a thin slab that is all monitor with the system unit located behind the monitor.

Tablets are smaller, lighter, and generally less powerful than notebooks. Like a notebook, tablets have a flat screen but typically do not have a standard keyboard. Instead, tablets typically use a virtual keyboard that appears on the screen and is touch-sensitive.

Traditional notebook

Netbook

**Figure 5-2** Notebook system units

**Figure 5-3** Microsoft Windows 8 tablet

One distinguishing feature among tablet computers is the operating system that controls their operations. For example, Apple's iPad uses the mobile operating system iOS. It is capable of running apps specifically designed for it. Many other tablets use Microsoft's Windows 8 operating system and can run many general-purpose applications as well as apps specifically designed for it. (See Figure 5-3.)

### Handhelds

**Handheld computers** are the smallest and are designed to fit into the palm of one hand. These systems contain an entire computer system, including the electronic components, secondary storage, and input and output devices. By far the most popular handheld computer is the **smartphone**. These devices are smaller and generally less powerful than tablets.

Smarphones greatly extend the capabilities of a cell phone by providing computing power. In addition to capturing and sending audio and video, smartphones run apps, connect to the Internet, and more. Their system unit is located behind the display screen and keypad.

### Components

While the actual size may vary, each type of system unit has the same basic system components including system board, microprocessor, and memory. (See Figure 5-4.) These components can generate a significant amount of heat that can damage a computer system. To learn more about cooling, see Making IT Work for You: Keeping Your Computer Cool on pages 127 and 128.

**Desktop**

**Tablet**

**Notebook**

**Smartphone**

**Figure 5-4** System unit components

# KEEPING YOUR COMPUTER COOL

Tablets and smartphones do not create significant heat. Desktop and tower system units are easy to cool because of the extensive space for fans and air circulation. Notebook computers, however, can present a challenge when it comes to cooling.

**Checking Processor Temperature** Before exploring cooling solutions, it is useful to check just how hot your processor(s) can become during various activities. *HWMonitor* is a free, useful tool that checks the temperature of your CPU, your graphics processor, and various other parts of your computer.

**1** ● **HWMonitor (free version is recommended) is available at www.cpuid.com/softwares/ hwmonitor.html.**

**2** ● **After installation, start HWMonitor, and observe the current temperatures, as well as the minimum and maximum measured.**

**3** ● **Be sure to try different activities, especially graphics-intensive ones (such as gaming or video editing).**

Note that if your CPU has multiple processors, or cores, they will be listed separately. Your video processor(s) will also be listed separately. Each processor model has a different maximum safe temperature, but generally speaking, temperatures going over 75° Celsius could be cause for concern.

| CPUID Hardware Monitor | | | |
|---|---|---|---|
| File  Edit  View  Help | | | |
| Sensor | Value | Min | Max |
| ⊟ 🖳 | | | |
| ⊟ 🖳 Dell Inc. | | | |
| ⊟ 🗡 Temperatures | | | |
| TZ00 | 27 °C  (80 °F) | 27 °C  (80 °F) | 27 °C  (80 °F) |
| TZ01 | 58 °C  (136 °F) | 55 °C  (131 °F) | 60 °C  (140 °F) |
| ⊟ 🖳 Intel Core i7 720QM | | | |
| ⊟ 🗡 Temperatures | | | |
| Core #0 | 56 °C  (132 °F) | 55 °C  (131 °F) | 62 °C  (143 °F) |
| Core #1 | 56 °C  (132 °F) | 54 °C  (129 °F) | 62 °C  (143 °F) |
| Core #2 | 58 °C  (136 °F) | 56 °C  (132 °F) | 63 °C  (145 °F) |
| Core #3 | 58 °C  (136 °F) | 56 °C  (132 °F) | 65 °C  (149 °F) |
| ⊟ 🔋 Powers | | | |
| Package | 36.50 W | 15.34 W | 55.04 W |
| ⊟ 💠 Hitachi HTS725050A9... | | | |
| ⊟ 🗡 Temperatures | | | |
| Assembly | 37 °C  (98 °F) | 37 °C  (98 °F) | 37 °C  (98 °F) |
| ⊟ 🖳 ATI Mobility Radeon ... | | | |
| ⊟ 〰 Voltages | | | |
| VIN0 | 1.20 V | 1.20 V | 1.20 V |
| ⊟ 🗡 Temperatures | | | |
| TMPIN0 | 54 °C  (129 °F) | 52 °C  (125 °F) | 56 °C  (132 °F) |
| TMPIN0 | 55 °C  (130 °F) | 52 °C  (125 °F) | 57 °C  (133 °F) |
| Ready | | | NUM |

**Laptop Coolers** Although blowing cool air underneath your laptop can help lower the machine's temperature, the most immediate beneficiary will be your legs. Before buying, consider the following:

**1** ● **Will the cooling unit be comfortable on your lap, or will you have to buy a separate *lap desk* to support it?**

**2** ● **How many fans does it have, and how high is its *CFM* (cubic feet per minute)?**

**3** ● **Is the price too good to be true? If so, those units tend to have very cheap construction and poor circulation. Go with top brands, and read reviews carefully before making a decision.**

**Thermal Paste** The most challenging (and rewarding) way to cool a laptop is by applying a special thermal compound (or paste) between the processors and *heat sink* (the mechanism that helps dissipate heat from the processor). This task is usually done by a skilled technician or experienced computer troubleshooter. The paste helps transfer heat more efficiently, thereby expelling more heat through your laptop's vents.

The web is continually changing, and some of the specifics presented in this Making IT Work for You may have changed.

**To learn about other ways to make information technology work for you, visit our website at www.computing2014.com and enter the keyword miw.**

What is the system unit?

Describe and compare the four basic types of microcomputer system units.

What are tower units? What is an all-in-one? What is a netbook?

# System Board

The **system board** is also known as the **mainboard** or **motherboard**. The system board controls communications for the entire computer system. Every component within the system unit connects to the system board. All external devices including the keyboard, mouse, and monitor connect to the system board. It acts as a data path and traffic monitor, allowing the various components to communicate efficiently with one another.

On a desktop computer, the system board is typically located at the bottom of the system unit or along one side. It is a large flat circuit board covered with a variety of different electronic components including sockets, slots, and bus lines. (See Figure 5-5.)

Figure 5-5 System board

Figure 5-6 Chip

Figure 5-7 Chip mounted onto a carrier package

- **Sockets** provide a connection point for small specialized electronic parts called chips. **Chips** consist of tiny circuit boards etched onto squares of sandlike material called silicon. These circuit boards can be smaller than the tip of your finger. (See Figure 5-6.) A chip is also called a **silicon chip**, **semiconductor**, or **integrated circuit**. Chips are mounted on **carrier packages**. (See Figure 5-7.) These packages plug either directly into sockets on the system board or onto cards that are then plugged into slots on the system board. Sockets are used to connect the system board to a variety of different types of chips, including microprocessor and memory chips.

- **Slots** provide a connection point for specialized cards or circuit boards. These cards provide expansion capability for a computer system. For example, a wireless networking card plugs into a slot on the system board to provide a connection to a local area network.

- Connecting lines called **bus lines** provide pathways that support communication among the various electronic components that are either located on the system board or attached to the system board.

Notebook, tablet, and handheld system boards are smaller than desktop system boards. However, they perform the same functions as desktop system boards.

## concept check

What is the system board, and what does it do?

Define and describe sockets, slots, and bus lines.

What are chips? How are chips attached to the system board?

# Microprocessor

In a microcomputer system, the **central processing unit (CPU)** or **processor** is contained on a single chip called the **microprocessor**. The microprocessor is the "brains" of the computer system. It has two basic components: the control unit and the arithmetic-logic unit.

- **Control unit:** The **control unit** tells the rest of the computer system how to carry out a program's instructions. It directs the movement of electronic signals between memory, which temporarily holds data, instructions, and processed information, and the arithmetic-logic unit. It also directs these control signals between the CPU and input and output devices.
- **Arithmetic-logic unit:** The **arithmetic-logic unit**, usually called the **ALU**, performs two types of operations: arithmetic and logical. **Arithmetic operations** are the fundamental math operations: addition, subtraction, multiplication, and division. **Logical operations** consist of comparisons such as whether one item is equal to (=), less than (<), or greater than (>) the other.

### Explorations

There are many types of microprocessors used in servers, home computers, and mobile devices.

To learn more about microprocessors, visit our website at www.computing2014.com and enter the keyword microprocessor.

## Microprocessor Chips

Chip processing capacities are often expressed in word sizes. A **word** is the number of bits (such as 16, 32, or 64) that can be accessed at one time by the CPU. The more bits in a word, the more data a computer can process at one time. Eight bits group together to form a byte. A 32-bit-word computer can access 4 bytes at a time. A 64-bit-word computer can access 8 bytes at a time. Therefore, the computer designed to process 64-bit words has greater processing capacity. Other factors affect a computer's processing capability including how fast it can process data and instructions.

The processing speed of a microprocessor is typically represented by its **clock speed**, which is related to the number of times the CPU can fetch and process data or instructions in a second. Older microcomputers typically process data and instructions in millionths of a second, or microseconds. Newer microcomputers are much faster and process data and instructions in billionths of a second, or nanoseconds. Supercomputers, by contrast, operate at speeds measured in picoseconds—1,000 times as fast as microcomputers. (See Figure 5-8.) Logically, the higher a microprocessor's clock speed, the faster the microprocessor. However, some processors can handle multiple instructions per cycle or tick of the clock; this means that clock speed comparisons can only be made between processors that work the same way.

A recent development is the multicore chip. As mentioned previously, a traditional microcomputer's CPU is typically contained on a single microprocessor chip. A new type of chip, the **multicore chip**, can provide two or more separate and independent CPUs. For example, a quad-core processor could have one core computing a complex Excel spreadsheet, a second core creating a report using Word, a third core locating a record using Access, and a fourth core running a multimedia presentation. More significantly, however, is the potential for microcomputers to run very large, complex programs that previously required expensive and specialized hardware.

For multicore processors to be used effectively, computers must understand how to divide tasks into parts that can be distributed across each core—an operation called **parallel processing**. Operating systems such as Windows 8 and Mac OS X support parallel processing. Software developers use this technology

**tips**

Are you looking to purchase a portable computer? With so many types of notebooks and tablets, do you find yourself confused and undecided? If so, then know you are not alone. Consumers are now faced with various subcategories of notebook computers, and the tablet market has exploded with various brands, operating systems, sizes, and accessories. To get you started, consider these two questions:

**1** Will this portable computer be your main computer? If so, then a notebook computer is generally more versatile and will perform well for home, business, or mobile use.

**2** Do you need a lightweight computer for reading e-books, browsing the web, and viewing photos and videos? If so, a tablet is more comfortable to carry around and hold in your hands for extended periods.

If you would like some help making the best decision, turn to our Computer Buyer's Guide on page 399. To see other tips, visit our website at www.computing2014.com and enter the keyword tips.

| Unit | Speed |
| --- | --- |
| Microsecond | Millionth of a second |
| Nanosecond | Billionth of a second |
| Picosecond | Trillionth of a second |

**Figure 5-8 Processing speeds**

| Processor | Manufacturer |
|-----------|--------------|
| A5 | Apple |
| Phenom | AMD |
| Athlon | AMD |
| A-series | AMD |
| Atom | Intel |
| i7 | Intel |

**Figure 5-9  Popular microprocessors**

for a wide range of applications from scientific programs to sophisticated computer games.

See Figure 5-9 for a table of popular microprocessors.

### Specialty Processors

In addition to microprocessor chips, a variety of more specialized processing chips have been developed.

- **Coprocessors** are specialty chips designed to improve specific computing operations. One of the most widely used is the **graphics coprocessor**, also called a **GPU (graphics processing unit)**. These processors are designed to handle a variety of specialized tasks such as displaying 3-D images and encrypting data.
- Many cars have more than 70 separate specialty processors to control nearly everything from fuel efficiency to satellite entertainment and tracking systems.

### concept check

Name and describe the two components of a microprocessor.

Define word, clock speed, multicore chip, and parallel processing.

What are specialty processors? Describe coprocessors.

# Memory

Memory is a holding area for data, instructions, and information. Like microprocessors, **memory** is contained on chips connected to the system board. There are three well-known types of memory chips: random-access memory (RAM), read-only memory (ROM), and flash memory.

### RAM

**Random-access memory (RAM)** chips hold the program (sequence of instructions) and data that the CPU is presently processing. (See Figure 5-10.) RAM is called temporary or volatile storage because everything in most types of RAM is lost as soon as the microcomputer is turned off. It is also lost if there is a power failure or other disruption of the electric current going to the microcomputer. Secondary storage, which we shall describe in Chapter 7, does not lose its contents. It is permanent or nonvolatile storage, such as the data stored on a hard disk. For this reason, as we mentioned earlier, it is a good idea to frequently save your work in progress to a secondary storage device. That is, if you are working on a document or a spreadsheet, every few minutes you should save, or store, the material.

Cache (pronounced "cash") **memory** improves processing by acting as a temporary high-speed holding area between the memory and the CPU. The computer detects which information in RAM is most frequently used and then copies that information into the cache. When needed, the CPU can quickly access the information from the cache.

Having enough RAM is important! For example, to use Microsoft Office 2010 effectively, you need a minimum of

Chip

Circuit board

**Figure 5-10  RAM chips mounted on circuit board**

256 MB of RAM to hold the program, 512 MB to support graphical features, and another 512 MB–1024 MB of RAM for the operating system.

Some applications, such as photo editing software, may require even more. Fortunately, additional RAM can be added to a computer system by inserting an expansion module called a **DIMM (dual in-line memory module)** into the system board. The capacity or amount of RAM is expressed in bytes. There are three commonly used units of measurement to describe memory capacity. (See Figure 5-11.)

Other types of RAM include DRAM, SDRAM, DDR, and direct RDRAM. To learn more about these other types of RAM, visit our website at www.computing2014.com and enter the keyword ram.

Even if your computer does not have enough RAM to hold a program, it might be able to run the program using **virtual memory**. Most of today's operating systems support virtual memory. With virtual memory, large programs are divided into parts and the parts are stored on a secondary device, usually a hard disk. Each part is then read into RAM only when needed. In this way, computer systems are able to run very large programs. To learn more about how virtual memory works, visit our website at www.computing2014.com and enter the keyword memory.

| Unit | Capacity |
|------|----------|
| Megabyte (MB) | 1 million bytes |
| Gigabyte (GB) | 1 billion bytes |
| Terabyte (TB) | 1 trillion bytes |

**Figure 5-11** Memory capacity

## ROM

**Read-only memory (ROM)** chips have information stored in them by the manufacturer. Unlike RAM chips, ROM chips are not volatile and cannot be changed by the user. "Read only" means that the CPU can read, or retrieve, data and programs written on the ROM chip. However, the computer cannot write—encode or change—the information or instructions in ROM.

Not long ago, ROM chips were typically used to contain almost all the instructions for basic computer operations. For example, ROM instructions are needed to start a computer, to access memory, and to handle keyboard input. Recently, however, flash memory chips have replaced ROM chips for many applications.

## Flash Memory

**Flash memory** offers a combination of the features of RAM and ROM. Like RAM, it can be updated to store new information. Like ROM, it does not lose that information when power to the computer system is turned off.

Flash memory is used for a wide range of applications. For example, it is used to store the start-up instructions for a computer. This information is called the system's **BIOS (basic input/output system)**. This information would include the specifics concerning the amount of RAM and the type of keyboard, mouse, and secondary storage devices connected to the system unit. If changes are made to the computer system, these changes are reflected in flash memory. To learn more about how a computer starts up and BIOS, visit our website at www.computing2014.com and enter the keyword boot.

See Figure 5-12 for a summary of the three types of memory.

| Type | Use |
|------|-----|
| RAM | Programs and data |
| ROM | Fixed start-up instructions |
| Flash | Flexible start-up instructions |

**Figure 5-12** Memory

## concept check

What is memory? Name and describe three types.

What are cache memory, DIMM, and virtual memory?

Define ROM and flash memory.

# Expansion Slots and Cards

As previously mentioned, many microcomputers allow users to expand their systems by providing **expansion slots** on the system board. Users can insert optional devices known as **expansion cards** into these slots. (See Figure 5-13.) Ports on the cards allow cables to be connected from the expansion cards to devices outside the system unit. (See Figure 5-14.) There are a wide range of different types of expansion cards. Some of the most commonly used expansion cards are

- **Graphics cards** provide high-quality 3-D graphics and animation for games and simulations.
- **Sound cards** accept audio input from a microphone and convert it into a form that can be processed by the computer. Also, these cards convert internal electronic signals to audio signals so they can be heard from external speakers or home theater systems.
- **Network interface cards (NIC)**, also known as **network adapter cards**, are used to connect a computer to a network. (See Figure 5-15.) The network allows connected computers to share data, programs, and hardware. The network adapter card typically connects the system unit to a cable that connects to the network.

Slot

- **Wireless network cards** allow computers to be connected without cables. As we will discuss in Chapter 9, wireless networks in the home are widely used to share a common Internet connection. Each device on the network is equipped with a wireless network card that communicates with the other devices.

**Plug and Play** was originally a set of specific hardware and software standards developed by Intel, Microsoft, and others. As hardware and software have evolved, however, Plug and Play has become a generic term that is associated with the ability to plug any

**Figure 5-13** Expansion cards fit into slots on the system board

Ports

**Figure 5-14** Expansion card with three ports

**Figure 5-15** Network interface card

device such as a printer or monitor into a computer and have it play or work immediately. Some devices, however, are not Plug and Play and require that new device drivers be installed, as discussed in Chapter 4.

To meet the size constraints of notebook, tablet, and handheld computers, small credit card–sized expansion cards known as **PC cards** have been developed. These cards plug into **PCMCIA slots** (called **PC card slots**) or, most recently, **ExpressCard** slots. (See Figure 5-16.)

Figure 5-16  PC card

### ☑ concept check

What are expansion slots and cards? Name four expansion cards.

Discuss Plug and Play.

What are PC cards, PCMCIA slots, and ExpressCard slots?

# Bus Lines

As mentioned earlier, a **bus line**—also known simply as a **bus**—connects the parts of the CPU to each other. Buses also link the CPU to various other components on the system board. (See Figure 5-17.) A bus is a pathway for bits representing data and instructions. The number of bits that can travel simultaneously down a bus is known as the **bus width**.

A bus is similar to a multilane highway that moves bits rather than cars from one location to another. The number of traffic lanes determines the bus width. A highway (bus line) with more traffic lanes (bus width) can move traffic (data and instructions) more efficiently. For example, a 64-bit bus can move twice as much information at a time as a 32-bit bus. Why should you even care about what a bus line is? Because as microprocessor chips have changed, so have bus lines. Bus design or bus architecture is an important factor relating to the speed and power for a particular computer. Additionally, many devices, such as expansion cards, will work with only one type of bus.

Every computer system has two basic categories of buses. One category, called **system buses**, connects the CPU to memory on the system board. The other category, called **expansion buses**, connects the CPU to other components on the system board, including expansion slots.

### Expansion Buses

Computer systems typically have a combination of different types of expansion buses. The principal types are USB, FireWire, and PCIe.

Figure 5-17  Bus is a pathway for bits

- **Universal serial bus (USB)** is widely used today. External USB devices are connected from one to another or to a common point or hub and then onto the USB bus. The USB bus then connects to the PCI bus on the system board. The current USB standard is USB 3.0.

- **FireWire buses** are similar to USB buses but more specialized. They are used primarily to connect audio and video equipment to the system board.
- **PCI Express (PCIe)** is widely used in many of today's most powerful computers. Unlike most other buses that share a single bus line or path with several devices, the PCIe bus provides a single dedicated path for each connected device.

## ☑ concept check

What is a bus, and what is bus width?

What is the difference between a system and an expansion bus?

Discuss three types of expansion buses.

# Ports

A **port** is a socket for external devices to connect to the system unit. (See Figure 5-18.) Some ports connect directly to the system board, while others connect to cards that are inserted into slots on the system board. Some ports are standard features of most computer systems, and others are more specialized.

Figure 5-18  Ports

## Standard Ports

Most desktop and notebook microcomputers come with a standard set of ports for connecting a monitor, keyboard, and other peripheral devices. The most common ports include

- **VGA (Video Graphics Adapter)** and **DVI (Digital Video Interface) ports** provide connections to analog and digital monitors, respectively. DVI has become the most commonly used standard, but VGA ports are still provided on almost all systems for compatibility with older/lower-cost monitors.
- **Universal serial bus (USB) ports** can be used to connect several devices to the system unit and are widely used to connect keyboards, mice, printers, storage devices, and a variety of specialty devices. One such device, a USB TV tuner card, allows users to view and record television programs. To learn how you can use a TV tuner card, see Making IT Work for You: TV Tuners on page 138. A single USB port can be used to connect many USB devices to the system unit.
- **FireWire ports** provide high-speed connections to specialized FireWire devices such as camcorders and storage devices.
- **Ethernet ports** are a high-speed networking port that has become a standard for many of today's computers. Ethernet allows you to connect multiple computers for sharing files, or to a DSL or cable modem for high-speed Internet access.

## Specialized Ports

In addition to standard ports, there are numerous specialty ports including eSATA, HDMI, MIDI, MiniDP, and S/PDIF.

- **External Serial Advanced Technology Attachment (eSATA)** ports provide very-high-speed connections for external hard disk drives, optical discs, and other large secondary storage devices.
- **High Definition Multimedia Interface (HDMI)** ports provide high-definition video and audio, making it possible to use a computer as a video jukebox or an HD video recorder.
- **Mini DisplayPort (MiniDP** or **mDP)** ports are an audiovisual port typically used to connect large monitors. These ports are used with many Apple Macintosh computers.
- **Musical instrument digital interface (MIDI)** ports are a special type of port for connecting musical instruments like an electronic keyboard to a sound card. The sound card converts the music into a series of digital instructions. These instructions can be processed immediately to reproduce the music or saved to a file for later processing.
- **Sony/Philips Digital Interconnect Format (S/PDIF)** ports are also known as **optical audio connections**. These ports are used to integrate computers into high-end audio and home theater systems.

## Cables

**Cables** are used to connect exterior devices to the system unit via the ports. One end of the cable is attached to the device and the other end has a connector that is attached to a matching connector on the port. (See Figure 5-19.)

USB     DVI     FireWire   Ethernet

**Figure 5-19 Cables**

# TV TUNERS

Do you already use a DVR (digital video recorder) in order to record your favorite TV shows? Although many cable and satellite companies offer this device, did you know that Windows Media Center can perform the same function? All you need is a device called a TV tuner that connects your antenna or cable to your computer. Below are the steps to turn your Windows-based computer into a DVR.

**Installing a TV Tuner**   A TV tuner is essentially a piece of hardware that allows your computer to process and display a cable or TV signal. Although some (usually pricey) PCs may include this technology, it is usually necessary to purchase it separately. The easiest ones to install are those that connect externally to a USB port, such as the AverTV Hybrid Volar Max.

**1** ● Plug the TV tuner into an available USB port on your computer.

**2** ● Connect a coaxial cable directly from your cable outlet or over-the-air antenna to the back of the TV tuner. If Windows does not automatically install the tuner, consult the user manual for instructions.

**3** ● Start *Windows Media Center.*

**4** ● With your TV tuner installed, it will guide you through a setup process, including a long scan for all available channels from your cable or antenna.

**Using Windows Media Center**   This utility is included with all recent versions of Windows. Although it contains many tools to manage your music, photos, and movies, we focus on its DVR capabilities for TV and cable.

**1** ● Once setup is complete, click the *TV* option from the main menu.

**2** ● Click *Guide,* and scroll up/down and left/right until you find a show you wish to record.

**3** ● Right-click the show, and choose *Record* from the menu.

**4** ● To play back a recorded show, choose *Recorded TV* from the TV menu, and click the show you wish to play back.

**5** ● Once you have watched a recording, choose the *Delete* option to free up space on your hard drive. The number of hours you can record is limited by your available hard drive space.

If you have a high-speed wireless network and several PCs in your home, you will have the capability to watch your recorded shows via Media Center's streaming ability. The web is continually changing, and some of the specifics presented in this Making IT Work for You may have changed.

**To learn about other ways to make information technology work for you, visit our website at www.computing2014.com and enter the keyword miw.**

# Power Supply

Computers require direct current (DC) to power their electronic components and to represent data and instructions. DC power can be provided indirectly by converting alternating current (AC) from standard wall outlets or directly from batteries.

- Desktop computers have a **power supply unit** located within the system unit. (See Figure 5-20.) This unit plugs into a standard wall outlet, converts AC to DC, and provides the power to drive all of the system unit components.

- Notebooks and tablets use **AC adapters** that are typically located outside the system unit. (See Figure 5-21.) AC adapters plug into a standard wall outlet, convert AC to DC, provide power to drive the system unit components, and can recharge the batteries. These computers can be operated either using an AC adapter plugged into a wall outlet or using battery power. Their batteries typically provide sufficient power for 9 to 10 hours before they need to be recharged.

- Like notebooks and tablets, netbooks and handheld computers use AC adapters located outside the system unit. Unlike notebooks and tablets, however, netbooks and handheld computers typically operate only using battery power. The AC adapter is used to recharge the batteries.

## concept check

What are ports? What do they do?

Describe four standard ports and five specialized ports.

What is a power supply unit? What is an AC adapter?

**Figure 5-20  Power supply unit**

**Figure 5-21  AC adapter**

# Electronic Data and Instructions

Have you ever wondered why it is said that we live in a digital world? It's because computers cannot recognize information the same way you and I can. People follow instructions and process data using letters, numbers, and special characters. For example, if we wanted someone to add the numbers 3 and 5 together and record the answer, we might say "please add 3 and 5." The system unit, however, is electronic circuitry and cannot directly process such a request.

Our voices create **analog**, or continuous, signals that vary to represent different tones, pitches, and volume. Computers, however, can recognize only **digital** electronic signals. Before any processing can occur within the system unit, a conversion must occur from what we understand to what the system unit can electronically process.

## Numeric Representation

What is the most fundamental statement you can make about electricity? It is simply this: It can be either on or off. Indeed, there are many forms of technology that can make use of this two-state on/off, yes/no, present/absent arrangement. For instance, a light switch may be on or off, or an electric circuit open or closed. A specific location on a tape or disk may have a positive charge or a negative charge. This is the reason, then, that a two-state or binary system is used to represent data and instructions.

The decimal system that we are all familiar with has 10 digits (0, 1, 2, 3, 4, 5, 6, 7, 8, 9). The **binary system**, however, consists of only two digits—0 and 1. Each 0 or 1 is called a **bit**—short for binary digit. In the system unit, the 1 can be represented by a positive charge and the 0 by no electric charge. In order to represent numbers, letters, and special characters, bits are combined into groups of eight called **bytes**.

Whenever you enter a number into a computer system, that number must be converted into a binary number before it can be processed. To learn more about binary systems and binary arithmetic, visit our website at www.computing2014.com and enter the keyword binary.

Any number can be expressed as a binary number. Binary numbers, however, are difficult for humans to work with because they require so many digits. Instead, binary numbers are often represented in a format more readable by humans. The **hexadecimal system**, or **hex**, uses 16 digits (0, 1, 2, 3, 4, 5, 6, 7, 8, 9, A, B, C, D, E, F) to represent binary numbers. Each hex digit represents four binary digits, and two hex digits are commonly used together to represent 1 byte (8 binary digits). (See Figure 5-22.) You may have already seen hex when selecting a color in a website design or drawing application, or when entering the password for access to a wireless network.

## Character Encoding

As we've seen, computers must represent all numbers with the binary system internally. What about text? How can a computer provide representations of the nonnumeric characters we use to communicate, such as the sentence you are reading now? The answer is character encoding schemes or standards.

**Character encoding standards** assign a unique sequence of bits to each character. Historically, microcomputers used the **ASCII (American Standard Code for Information Interchange)** to represent characters, while mainframe computers used **EBCDIC (Extended Binary Coded Decimal Interchange Code)**. These schemes were

| Decimal | Binary | Hex |
|---------|----------|-----|
| 00 | 00000000 | 00 |
| 01 | 00000001 | 01 |
| 02 | 00000010 | 02 |
| 03 | 00000011 | 03 |
| 04 | 00000100 | 04 |
| 05 | 00000101 | 05 |
| 06 | 00000110 | 06 |
| 07 | 00000111 | 07 |
| 08 | 00001000 | 08 |
| 09 | 00001001 | 09 |
| 10 | 00001010 | 0A |
| 11 | 00001011 | 0B |
| 12 | 00001100 | 0C |
| 13 | 00001101 | 0D |
| 14 | 00001110 | 0E |
| 15 | 00001111 | 0F |

**Figure 5-22** Numeric representations

quite effective; however, they are limited. ASCII, for example, only uses 7 bits to represent each character, which means that only 128 total characters could be represented. This was fine for most characters in the English language but was not large enough to support other languages such as Chinese and Japanese. These languages have too many characters to be represented by the 7-bit ASCII code.

The explosion of the Internet and subsequent globalization of computing have led to a new character encoding called **Unicode**, which uses 16 bits. The Unicode standard is the most widely used character encoding standard and is recognized by virtually every computer system. The first 128 characters are assigned the same sequence of bits as ASCII to maintain compatibility with older ASCII-formatted information. However, Unicode uses a variable number of bits to represent each character, which allows non-English characters and special characters to be represented.

## concept check

What is the difference between an analog and a digital electronic signal?

What are decimal and binary systems? How are they different?

Compare EBCDIC, ASCII, and Unicode.

### ethics

The best protection any consumer can have is to be knowledgeable. Whether you are getting your car or your computer repaired, the more you know, the more likely you will receive fair and ethical treatment. Unfortunately, many times you have to rely on the expertise and morals of service personnel. If a deceitful but skillful computer technician gains access to your computer files, you could be at great personal risk. Given how important computers are in our lives, should we demand a code of ethics for computer technicians? To see more ethical issues, visit our website at www.computing2014.com and enter the keyword ethics.

# Careers in IT

**Computer technicians** repair and install computer components and systems. They may work on everything from personal computers and mainframe servers to printers. Some computer technicians are responsible for setting up and maintaining computer networks. Experienced computer technicians may work with computer engineers to diagnose problems and run routine maintenance on complex systems. Job growth is expected in this field as computer equipment becomes more complicated and technology expands.

Employers look for those with certification in computer repair or associate degrees from professional schools. Computer technicians also can expect to continue their education to keep up with technological changes. Good communication skills are important in this field.

Computer technicians can expect to earn an annual salary in the range of $31,000 to $46,000. Opportunities for advancement typically come in the form of work on more advanced computer systems. Some computer technicians move into customer service positions or go into sales. To learn more about other careers in information technology, visit us at www.computing2014.com and enter the keyword careers.

Now that you know about system units, I'd like to tell you about my career as a computer technician.

## Chips inside Your Brain

Have you ever thought it would be possible to be able to communicate with a computer . . . by merely thinking? Researchers are working with various devices (usually worn on the head) that can use your basic thoughts to move objects, such as wheelchairs. However, the future will lie in implanted microchips that can communicate directly with our nerve cells. Although their initial purpose will be to treat a variety of medical conditions, they could eventually (and controversially) be used to improve various brain functions of otherwise healthy individuals.

For over a decade, doctors have been able to use deep brain stimulation (DBS) to treat several disorders such as Parkinson's disease. As successful as it has been for many patients, those implants simply send preset electrical impulses to the brain. They do not involve an active communication between nerve cells and machines. Researchers working on a chip known as ReNaChip hope to change this by using a programmable computer chip that is responsive to what is going on in the patient's brain. This silicon chip can measure the brain's electrical activity and then deliver the appropriate stimulation when and where it is needed.

Another brain implant that is currently being developed aims to help the blind regain some sight. A microchip is implanted in the brain's visual cortex, which is responsible for processing images. This chip would communicate wirelessly with a camera located inside special eyeglasses worn by the individual. The

images captured by that camera would be processed by the chip and then fed directly to the nerves in this area of the brain.

Getting close to the world of the unbelievable, researchers are improving on the ability of computers to actually read human thoughts. Currently, one research team has been able to use a chip implant and computer to read the thoughts of a stroke victim in order to allow her to move a robotic hand. Although the success rate is not 100 percent and the processing is limited to basic movements, the patient has already been able to get the robotic arm to hold a cup of coffee by thinking about it. This research will hopefully lead to improved, thought-controlled prosthetic devices for millions of disabled individuals.

Many ethicists are concerned by the potential use of such chips to improve human abilities instead of treating medical conditions. For example, with tiny chips being able to store so much, people could use brain implants to improve their memory. This can lead to a variety of scenarios where the individual with the implants could have an unfair advantage over those who don't have them. However, others disagree, arguing that the integration of technology and biology is to be expected, and it is nothing more than the next step in human evolution.

If such a technology became widespread and affordable, would you opt to receive a chip implant? Would you make a distinction between using one for a medical condition versus simply for improving your mental abilities? Do you think the future of humanity lies in the merging of technology with human biology?

## SYSTEM UNIT

System unit (system chassis) contains electronic components. There are four basic categories of system units: **desktop, notebook (laptop), tablet,** and **handheld.**

### Desktop

**Desktop** system units are located in a separate case; **tower unit (tower computer)** has vertical system unit; system unit is housed with monitor in **all-in-one** computers.

### Notebook

**Notebook (laptop)** system units contain secondary storage devices and input devices. **Netbooks** are a smaller, less powerful, and less expensive type of notebook.

### Tablet

**Tablet** system units are located behind the monitor. Tablets are smaller, lighter, and generally less powerful than laptops and use a virtual keyboard.

### Handheld computer

**Smartphones** are most popular **handheld computer.** System unit is located behind the display screen and keypad.

### Components

Each type of system unit has the same basic components including system board, microprocessor, and memory.

## SYSTEM BOARD

The **system board (mainboard** or **motherboard)** connects all system components and allows input and output devices to communicate with the system unit.

- **Sockets** provide connection points for **chips (silicon chips, semiconductors, integrated circuits).** Chips are mounted on **carrier packages.**
- **Slots** provide connection points for specialized cards or circuit boards.
- **Bus lines** provide pathways to support communication.

To be a competent end user, you need to understand the functionality of the basic components in the system unit: system board, microprocessor, memory, expansion slots and cards, bus lines, and ports and cables. Additionally, you need to understand how data and programs are represented electronically.

## MICROPROCESSOR

The **microprocessor** is a single chip that contains the **central processing unit (CPU)** or **microprocessor**. It has two basic components: a **control unit** and **ALU**.

### Microprocessor Chips

A **word** is the number of bits that can be accessed by the microprocessor at one time. **Clock speed** represents the number of times the CPU can fetch and process data or instructions in a second.

**Multicore chips** can provide multiple independent CPUs. **Parallel processing** requires programs that allow multiple processors to work together to run large complex programs.

### Specialty Processors

Specialty processors include **graphics coprocessors**, also known as **GPU** or **graphics processing unit** (processes graphic images), and processors in automobiles (monitor fuel efficiency, satellite entertainment, and tracking systems).

## MEMORY

**Memory** holds data, instructions, and information. There are three types of memory chips.

### RAM

**RAM (random-access memory)** chips are called temporary or volatile storage because their contents are lost if power is disrupted.

- **Cache memory** is a high-speed holding area for frequently used data and information.
- **DIMM (dual in-line memory module)** is used to expand memory.
- **Virtual memory** divides large programs into parts that are read into RAM as needed.

### ROM

**ROM (read-only memory)** chips are nonvolatile storage and control essential system operations.

### Flash Memory

**Flash memory** does not lose its contents when power is removed.

## EXPANSION SLOTS AND CARDS

Most computers allow users to expand their systems by providing **expansion slots** on their system boards to accept **expansion cards**.

Examples of expansion cards include **graphics cards, sound cards, network interface cards (NIC; network adapter cards),** *and* **wireless network cards.**

**Plug and Play** is the ability for a computer to recognize and configure a device without human interaction.

**PC cards** *plug into* **PCMCIA slots,** *and* **ExpressCard** slots accept credit card–sized expansion cards.

## BUS LINES

**Bus lines,** also known as **buses,** provide data pathways that connect various system components. **Bus width** is the number of bits that can travel simultaneously.

**System buses** connect CPU and memory. **Expansion buses** connect CPU and slots.

### Expansion Buses

Three principal expansion bus types are

- **USB (universal serial bus)** can connect from one USB device to another or to a common point (hub) and then onto the system board.
- **FireWire bus** is similar to USB bus but more specialized.
- **PCIe (PCI Express) bus** is widely used; provides a single dedicated path for each connected device.

## PORTS

## POWER SUPPLY

Power supply units convert AC to DC and power desktops. AC adapters power notebooks and tablets and recharge batteries.

Ports are connecting sockets on the outside of the system unit.

### Standard Ports
Four standard ports are

- **VGA (Video Graphics Adapter)** and **DVI (Digital Video Interface)**—provide connections to monitors.
- **USB (universal serial bus)**—widely used to connect keyboards, mice, printers, and storage devices; one port can connect several devices to system unit.
- **FireWire**—provides high-speed connections to specialized FireWire devices such as camcorders and storage devices.
- **Ethernet**—high-speed networking port that has become a standard for many of today's computers.

### Specialized Ports
Five specialty ports are **eSATA (external Serial Advanced Technology Attachment)** for high-speed connections to large secondary storage devices, **HDMI (High Definition Multimedia Interface)** for high-definition digital audio and video, **Mini DisplayPort (MiniDP, mDP)** for large monitors, **MIDI** for digital music, and **S/PDIF (Sony/Philips Digital Interface)** for high-end audio and home theater systems.

### Cables
**Cables** are used to connect external devices to the system unit via ports.

## ELECTRONIC REPRESENTATION

Human voices create **analog** (continuous) signals; computers only recognize **digital** electronic signals.

### Numeric Representation
Data and instructions can be represented electronically with a two-state or **binary system** of numbers (0 and 1). Each 0 or 1 is called a **bit**. A **byte** consists of 8 bits. **Hexadecimal system (hex)** uses 16 digits to represent binary numbers.

### Character Encoding
**Character encoding standards** assign unique sequences of bits to each character. Three standards are **ASCII (American Standard Code for Information Interchange)**, **EBCDIC (Extended Binary Coded Decimal Interchange Code)**, and **Unicode**.

## CAREERS IN IT

**Computer technicians** repair and install computer components and systems. Certification in computer repair or associate degree from professional schools required. Salary range is $31,000 to $46,000.

# KEY TERMS

AC adapter (139)
all-in-one (124)
analog (140)
arithmetic-logic unit
(ALU) (131)
arithmetic operation (131)
ASCII (140)
binary system (140)
BIOS (basic input/output
system) (133)
bit (140)
bus (135)
bus line (130, 135)
bus width (135)
byte (140)
cable (137)
cache memory (132)
carrier package (130)
central processing unit
(CPU) (130)
character encoding
standards (140)
chip (130)
clock speed (131)
computer
technician (141)
control unit (131)
coprocessor (132)
desktop (124)
digital (140)
DIMM (133)
DVI (Digital Video
Interface) port (137)
EBCDIC (140)
Ethernet port (137)
expansion bus (135)
expansion card (134)
expansion slot (134)

ExpressCard (135)
external Serial Advanced
Technology Attachment
(eSATA) (137)
FireWire bus (136)
FireWire port (137)
flash memory (133)
GPU (132)
graphics card (134)
graphics coprocessor (132)
handheld computer (126)
hexadecimal system
(hex) (140)
High Definition
Multimedia Interface
(HDMI) (137)
integrated circuit (130)
laptop (125)
logical operation (131)
mainboard (129)
memory (132)
microprocessor (130)
Mini DisplayPort (MiniDP,
mDP) (137)
motherboard (129)
multicore chip (131)
musical instrument digital
interface (MIDI) (137)
netbook (125)
network adapter card (134)
network interface card
(NIC) (134)
notebook (124)
optical audio
connections (137)
parallel processing (131)
PC card (135)
PC card slot (135)

PCI Express (PCIe) (136)
PCMCIA slot (135)
Plug and Play (134)
port (136)
power supply unit (139)
processor (130)
random-access memory
(RAM) (132)
read-only memory
(ROM) (133)
semiconductor (130)
silicon chip (130)
slot (130)
smartphone (126)
socket (130)
Sony/Philips Digital
Interconnect Format
(S/PDIF) (137)
sound card (134)
system board (129)
system bus (135)
system chassis (124)
system unit (124)
tablet (125)
tablet computer (125)
tower computer (124)
tower unit (124)
Unicode (141)
universal serial bus
(USB) (135)
universal serial bus
(USB) port (137)
VGA (Video Graphics
Adapter) port (137)
virtual memory (133)
wireless network
card (134)
word (131)

To test your knowledge of these key terms with animated flash cards, visit our website at www.computing2014.com and enter the keyword terms5. Or use the free *Computing Essentials 2014* app.

# MULTIPLE CHOICE

Circle the letter or fill in the correct answer.

1. This container houses most of the electrical components for a computer system.

   a. carrier package
   b. system board
   c. system unit
   d. Unicode

2. A type of notebook, this computer specializes in on-the-go web browsing and e-mail access.

   a. chassis
   b. desktop
   c. media center
   d. netbook

3. The mainboard or motherboard is also known as the:

   a. computer
   b. board processor
   c. mobile system
   d. system board

4. How many bytes can a 32-bit-word computer access at one time?

   a. 1
   b. 4
   c. 8
   d. 16

5. In a microcomputer system, the central processing unit is contained on a single:

   a. bus
   b. chip
   c. module
   d. RAM

6. This type of memory divides large programs into parts and stores the parts on a secondary storage device.

   a. direct
   b. expanded
   c. random access
   d. virtual

7. Also known as NIC, this adapter card is used to connect a computer to a(n):

   a. AIA
   b. expansion
   c. graphics
   d. network

8. This provides a pathway to connect parts of the CPU to each other.

   a. bus
   b. Plug and Play
   c. wired
   d. wireless

9. The specialized port that provides very-high-speed connections for large secondary storage devices.

   a. eSATA
   b. HDMI
   c. MIDI
   d. MiniDP

10. Computers can only recognize this type of electronic signal.

    a. analog
    b. bus
    c. digital
    d. maximum

For an interactive multiple-choice practice test, visit our website at www.computing2014 .com and enter the keyword multiple5. Or use the free *Computing Essentials 2014* app.

# MATCHING

Match each numbered item with the most closely related lettered item. Write your answers in the spaces provided.

a. cache
b. flash
c. multicore
d. Plug and Play
e. power supply
f. random access
g. slots
h. sockets
i. system
j. USB

____ 1. A type of multiprocessor chip that provides two or more separate and independent CPUs.

____ 2. A type of memory that is volatile or loses its contents when power is turned off.

____ 3. System board component that provides a connection point for specialized cards or circuit boards.

____ 4. Provide connection points for chips.

____ 5. A type of memory that improves processing by acting as a temporary high-speed holding area between the memory and the CPU.

____ 6. A type of memory that provides a combination of features of RAM and ROM.

____ 7. A generic term that is associated with the ability to attach any device onto a computer and have it play or work immediately.

____ 8. This bus connects the CPU to memory on the system board.

____ 9. This port can be used to connect many USB devices to the system.

____10. This unit plugs into a standard wall outlet and converts AC to DC.

For an interactive matching practice test, visit our website at www.computing2014.com and enter the keyword matching5. Or use the free *Computing Essentials 2014* app.

# OPEN-ENDED

On a separate sheet of paper, respond to each question or statement.

1. Describe the four basic types of microcomputers and microcomputer system units.
2. Describe system boards including sockets, chips, carrier packages, slots, and bus lines.
3. Discuss microprocessor components, chips, and specialty processors.
4. Define computer memory including RAM, ROM, and flash memory.
5. Define expansion slots, cards, Plug and Play, PC cards, PCMCIA slots, and Express-Card slots.
6. Describe bus lines, bus width, system bus, and expansion bus.
7. Define ports including standard and specialized ports. Give examples of each.
8. Describe power supply including power supply units and AC adapters.
9. Discuss electronic data and instructions.

# DISCUSSION

Respond to each of the following questions.

## 1 Making IT Work for You: KEEPING YOUR COMPUTER COOL

Have you noticed how hot the underside of your notebook computer can become after using it for a while? Review the Making IT Work for You: Keeping Your Computer Cool on pages 127 and 128 and then respond to the following: (a) If you have a notebook computer, does it become hot after a period of time? How long? (If you do not have a notebook, consult with people who do and record their responses to this and the following questions.) (b) Do you currently use a laptop cooler or lap desk? If so, which one(s)? If not, would you consider purchasing one? Why or why not? (c) Install the free HWMonitor software discussed in the Making IT Work for You. Record the CPU temperatures when no windows are open, and then record the numbers measured during a graphics-intensive task, such as watching a video or playing a game. Compare your numbers with those of your classmates.

| Sensor | Value | Min | Max |
|---|---|---|---|
| **Dell Inc.** | | | |
| Temperatures | | | |
| TZ00 | 27 °C (80 °F) | 27 °C (80 °F) | 27 °C (80 °F) |
| TZ01 | 58 °C (136 °F) | 55 °C (131 °F) | 60 °C (140 °F) |
| **Intel Core i7 720QM** | | | |
| Temperatures | | | |
| Core #0 | 56 °C (132 °F) | 55 °C (131 °F) | 62 °C (143 °F) |
| Core #1 | 56 °C (132 °F) | 54 °C (129 °F) | 62 °C (143 °F) |
| Core #2 | 58 °C (136 °F) | 56 °C (132 °F) | 63 °C (145 °F) |
| Core #3 | 58 °C (136 °F) | 56 °C (132 °F) | 65 °C (149 °F) |
| Powers | | | |
| Package | 36.50 W | 15.34 W | 55.04 W |
| **Hitachi HTS725050A9...** | | | |
| Temperatures | | | |
| Assembly | 37 °C (98 °F) | 37 °C (98 °F) | 37 °C (98 °F) |
| **ATI Mobility Radeon ...** | | | |
| Voltages | | | |
| VIN0 | 1.20 V | 1.20 V | 1.20 V |
| Temperatures | | | |
| TMPIN0 | 54 °C (129 °F) | 52 °C (125 °F) | 56 °C (132 °F) |
| TMPIN0 | 55 °C (130 °F) | 52 °C (125 °F) | 57 °C (133 °F) |

*CPUID Hardware Monitor — File Edit View Help — Ready — NUM*

## 2 Making IT Work for You: TV TUNERS

Did you know that you can record your favorite TV shows with a computer? Review the Making IT Work for You: TV Tuners on page 138 and then respond to the following: (a) Do you currently have a DVR in your home? If so, who is the manufacturer? If not, have you considered purchasing one? Why or why not? (b) How do the Windows Media Center DVR capabilities compare with the DVR offered by your cable or satellite company? Use a search engine to help you find these differences. (c) Find at least two USB-based TV tuners using any online store. Note their prices and specifications. What are their main differences?

### 3   Explorations: MICROPROCESSORS

Did you know that different micro-processors are used in servers, home computers, and mobile devices? Review the Explorations box on page 131 and then respond to the following: (a) Perform research on one of Intel's Xeon processors. Name the model you chose, and describe why this processor is beneficial for businesses that use it in their servers. (b) Perform research on any AMD processor that includes an integrated graphics processor. What is the benefit of this integration? Would you choose this type of processor? Why or why not? (c) Find one ARM processor that is used in mobile devices. Briefly describe the product and its benefits for mobile computing, and list a few of the companies that license this technology.

### 4   Explorations: GRAPHICS PROCESSING UNITS

Did you know that there are many types of graphics processing units (GPUs) that power today's graphics cards? Review the Explorations box on page 132 and then respond to the following: (a) Find a GPU that is geared toward gaming PCs. Briefly describe the product, and discuss why this processor improves the gaming experience. (b) Find a GPU that is marketed for workstations used in the graphics industry. How does this GPU improve the sort of tasks performed by these workstations? (c) GPUs are often present in the computers that are used for research in science and engineering. Find a GPU used in these computer systems, and describe some of the ways it assists these researchers.

### 5   Ethics: JOB LOSS AND WORKING CONDITIONS

Many computer-related products are produced in China where working conditions are reported to be well below acceptable standards. Review the Ethics box on page 124 and then respond to the following: (a) What do you think about products produced in other countries like China? What are the advantages and disadvantages to consumers? Be specific. (b) What are the ethical issues? Be specific, and defend your list of issues. (c) Would you be willing to pay more for a computer produced entirely in the United States? More specifically, would you be willing to pay three times as much for a smartphone? Why or why not? (d) Do you think consumers have an ethical responsibility to know how goods are produced? More specifically, would your purchase decisions be affected by knowledge about the working conditions of those who make the product? Why or why not?

### 6 Ethics: COMPUTER REPAIR

Most individuals rely on computer repair technicians to fix their expanding collection of computers and electronic devices. With the technicians having such responsibility, some argue that technicians should follow a code of ethics. Review the Ethics box on page 141 and then respond to the following: (a) Should there be a required certification program that enforces a code of ethics among computer technicians? Why or why not? (b) Would you be willing to pay more or wait longer for repairs if you knew the technician you called was bound by a code of ethics? Why or why not? (c) What recourse should you have if a computer technician secretly accesses your personal information and then shares it with others, invents a new problem, or overcharges for a repair? (d) What can you do as a consumer to protect yourself? Be specific.

### 7 Environment: GREEN COMPUTERS

Have you given any thought to buying a greener PC? Review the Environment box on page 126 and then respond to the following: (a) What are some examples of computer components that can contain recycled materials? (b) Does a manufacturer's use (or nonuse) of recycled materials affect your willingness to buy its products? Why or why not? (c) Using a search engine, find at least three computer components that use some recycled materials. Briefly describe the products, and provide the URL of the website where each was found.

### 8 Environment: RECYCLING COMPUTER HARDWARE

Have you ever wondered what you should you do with your old computers, monitors, and mobile devices? Review the Environment box on page 130 and then respond to the following: (a) What do you typically do with your used or broken computers and mobile devices? (b) What are three alternatives to throwing these devices in the trash? (c) Using a search engine, find one nonprofit organization near you that will accept used computers. List the name and URL. (d) Visit the waste management or recycling page of your local government's website. If it does not have a website, contact it. What is its recommended procedure for discarding your computers and other electronic devices?

# Input and Output

▲ Download the free *Computing Essentials 2014* app for videos, key term flashcards, quizzes, and the game, *Over the Edge!*

## Competencies

### After you have read this chapter, you should be able to:

1 Define input.

2 Describe keyboard entry including types and features of keyboards.

3 Discuss pointing devices including game controllers and styluses.

4 Describe scanning devices including optical scanners, RFID readers, and recognition devices.

5 Discuss image capturing and audio-input devices.

6 Define output.

7 Discuss monitor features and types including flat-panels and e-books.

8 Define printing features and types including inkjet and cloud printers.

9 Discuss audio and video devices including portable media devices and Mobile DTV.

10 Define combination input and output devices including multifunctional devices, Internet telephones, robots, and VR headgear and gloves.

11 Discuss ergonomics and ways to minimize physical damage.

## Why should I read this chapter?

Years ago the only way to interact with a computer was through a keyboard, a monitor, and a printer. That was then and this is now. Now, we can input data in a wide variety of ways including pointing, scanning, and photographing. Computers can provide output in many different ways including humanlike voices, monitors that are almost as thin as a piece of paper, and inexpensive high-speed printers.

This chapter discusses a variety of input devices including

wireless and virtual keyboards, touch screens, digital interactive white boards, portable scanners, webcams, and voice recognition systems. Additionally, you'll learn about output devices including e-book readers, HDTV, cloud printers, photo printers, and portable media players. To be competent and to be competitive in today's professional workplace, you need to know and to understand these things.

## chapter .6

# Introduction

Hi, I'm Marie, and I'm a technical writer. I'd like to talk with you about input and output devices. . . . all those devices that help us to communicate with a computer. I'd also like to talk about emerging technologies such as robotics and virtual reality.

How do you send instructions and information to the CPU? How do you get information out? Here we describe one of the most important places where computers interface with people. We input text, music, and even speech, but we probably never think about the relationship between what we enter and what the computer processes. People understand language, which is constructed of letters, numbers, and punctuation marks. However, at a basic level, computers can understand only the binary machine language of 0s and 1s. Input devices are essentially translators. Input devices translate numbers, letters, and actions that people understand into a form that computers can process.

Have you ever wondered how information processed by the system unit is converted into a form that you can use? That is the role of output devices. While input devices convert what we understand into what the system unit can process, output devices convert what the system unit has processed into a form that we can understand. Output devices translate machine language into letters, numbers, sounds, and images that people can understand.

Competent end users need to know about the most commonly used input devices, including keyboards, mice, scanners, digital cameras, voice recognition, and audio-input devices. Additionally, they need to know about the most commonly used output devices, including monitors, printers, and audio-output devices. And end users need to be aware of combination input and output devices such as multifunctional devices and Internet telephones.

## What Is Input?

**Input** is any data or instructions that are used by a computer. They can come directly from you or from other sources. You provide input whenever you use system or application programs. For example, when using a word processing program, you enter data in the form of numbers and letters and issue commands such as to save and to print documents. You also can enter data and issue commands by pointing to items or using your voice. Other sources of input include scanned or photographed images.

**Input devices** are hardware used to translate words, sounds, images, and actions that people understand into a form that the system unit can process. For example, when using a word processor, you typically use a keyboard to enter text and a mouse to issue commands. In addition to keyboards and mice, there are a wide variety of other input devices. These include pointing, scanning, image capturing, and audio-input devices.

## Keyboard Entry

One of the most common ways to input data is by **keyboard**. As mentioned in Chapter 5, keyboards convert numbers, letters, and special characters that people understand into electrical signals. These signals are sent to, and processed by, the system unit. Most keyboards use an arrangement of keys

Function keys are shortcuts for specific tasks; F1, for example, typically displays Help.

Numeric keypad enters numbers and arithmetic symbols and controls cursor or insertion point.

Start key displays the Start menu.

Navigation keys control the cursor or insertion point on the screen.

**Figure 6-1 Traditional keyboard**

given the name QWERTY. This name reflects the keyboard layout by taking the letters of the first six alphabetic characters found on the top row of keys displaying letters.

## Keyboards

There are a wide variety of different keyboard designs. They range from the full-sized to miniature and can even be virtual. There are four basic categories of keyboards: traditional, notebook, virtual, and thumb.

- **Traditional keyboards**—these keyboards are widely used on desktops and larger computers. The standard U.S. traditional keyboard has 101 keys. Some traditional keyboards include a few additional special keys. For example, the Windows keyboard includes a key to directly access the Start menu. Traditional keyboards provide function keys, navigation keys, and a numeric keypad. Some keys, such as the Caps Lock key, are **toggle keys**. These keys turn a feature on or off. Others, such as the Ctrl key, are **combination keys**, which perform a action when held down in combination with another key. (See Figure 6-1.)

- **Notebook keyboards**—these keyboards are widely used on notebook computers including netbooks. While the precise location and number of keys may differ among manufactures, notebook keyboards typically have fewer keys, do not include a numeric keypad, and do not have a standard location for the function and navigation keys. (See Figure 6-2 top.)

- **Virtual keyboards**—these keyboards are widely used on tablets and on some smartphones. Unlike other keyboards, virtual keyboards do not have a physical keyboard. Rather, the keys are typically displayed on a screen and selected by touching their image on the screen. (See Figure 6-2 middle.)

- **Thumb keyboards**—these keyboards are widely used on smartphones and other small portable devices. Designed primarily for communicating via texting and connecting to the web, these keyboards are very small. (See Figure 6-2 bottom.)

**Notebook keyboard**

**Virtual keyboard**

**Thumb keyboard**

**Figure 6-2 Keyboards**

## concept check

What is input? What are input devices?

List and compare the four categories of keyboards.

What are toggle keys? What are combination keys?

# Pointing Devices

Pointing is one of the most natural of all human gestures. **Pointing devices** provide an intuitive interface with the system unit by accepting pointing gestures and converting them into machine-readable input. There are a wide variety of different pointing devices, including the mouse, joystick, touch screen, and stylus.

## Mice

A **mouse** controls a pointer that is displayed on the monitor. The **mouse pointer** usually appears in the shape of an arrow. It frequently changes shape, however, depending on the application. A mouse can have one, two, or more buttons, which are used to select command options and to control the mouse pointer on the monitor. Some mice have a **wheel button** that can be rotated to scroll through information that is displayed on the monitor.

Although there are several different designs, the **optical mouse** is the most widely used. It emits and senses light to detect mouse movement. Traditionally, the detected movements are communicated to the system unit through a cord. Alternatively, the **cordless** or **wireless mouse** uses radio waves or infrared light waves to communicate with the system unit. (See Figure 6-3.) These devices eliminate the mouse cord and free up desk space.

Three devices similar to a mouse are trackballs, touch pads, and pointing sticks.

- **Trackballs** control the pointer by rotating a ball with your thumb. (See Figure 6-4.)

**Figure 6-3 Optical mouse**

**Figure 6-4 Trackball**

**Figure 6-5** Touch pad

**Figure 6-6** Pointing stick

- **Touch pads** control the pointer by moving and tapping your finger on the surface of a pad. (See Figure 6-5.)
- **Pointing sticks**, located in the middle of the keyboard, control the pointer by directing the stick with one finger. (See Figure 6-6.)

### Touch Screens

A **touch screen** allows users to select actions or commands by touching the screen with a finger or penlike device. **Multitouch screens** can be touched with more than one finger, which allows for interactions such as rotating graphical objects on the screen with your hand or zooming in and out by pinching and stretching your fingers. Multitouch screens are commonly used with tablets and smartphones, as well as some notebook computers and desktop monitors. (See Figure 6-7.)

### Game Controllers

**Game controllers** are devices that provide input to computer games. While keyboards and mice can be used as game controllers, the four most popular and specialized game controllers are joysticks, dance pads, gamepads, and motion sensing devices. (See Figure 6-8.)

- **Joysticks** control game actions by users varying the pressure, speed, and direction of a control stick.
- **Dance pads** provide input for dance games. Users move (dance) on a pressure-sensitive mat that provides input to the game.
- **Gamepads** are designed to be held by two hands and provide a wide array of inputs including motion, turning, stopping, and firing.
- **Motion-sensing devices** control games by user movements. For example, Microsoft's Kinect motion-sensing device accepts user movements and spoken commands to control games on the Xbox 360.

### Stylus

A **stylus** is a penlike device commonly used with tablet PCs and PDAs. (See Figure 6-9.) A stylus uses pressure to draw images on a screen. Often, a stylus interacts with the computer through handwriting recognition software. **Handwriting recognition software** translates handwritten notes into a form that the system unit can process.

**Figure 6-7** Multitouch screen

Joystick

Dance pad

Game pad

Motion-sensing device

**Figure 6-8** Game controllers

**Figure 6-9** Stylus

## concept check

What is a pointing device? Describe four pointing devices.

What is an optical mouse? What is a multitouch screen?

Describe four game controllers. What is a stylus?

# Scanning Devices

Scanners move across text and images. **Scanning devices** convert scanned text and images into a form that the system unit can process. There are five types of scanning devices: optical scanners, card readers, RFID readers, bar code readers, and character and mark recognition devices.

### Optical Scanners

An **optical scanner**, also known simply as a **scanner**, accepts documents consisting of text and/or images and converts them to machine-readable form. These devices do not recognize individual letters or images. Rather, they recognize light, dark, and colored areas that make up individual letters or images. Typically, scanned documents are saved in files that can be further processed, displayed, printed, or stored for later use. There are three basic types of optical scanners: flatbed, document, and portable.

- **Flatbed scanner** is much like a copy machine. The image to be scanned is placed on a glass surface, and the scanner records the image from below.
- **Document scanner** is similar to a flatbed scanner except that it can quickly scan multipage documents. It automatically feeds one page of a document at a time through a scanning surface. (See Figure 6-10.)
- **Portable scanner** is typically a handheld device that slides across the image, making direct contact.

**Figure 6-10** Document scanner

Optical scanners are powerful tools for a wide variety of end users, including graphics and advertising professionals who scan images and combine them with text. Lawyers and students use portable scanners as a valuable research tool to record information.

### Card Readers

Nearly everyone uses a credit card, debit card, access (parking or building) card, and/or some type of identification card. These cards typically have the user's name, some type of identification number, and signature on the card. Additionally, encoded information is often stored on the card as well. **Card readers** interpret this encoded information.

Although there are several different types, by far the most common is the **magnetic card reader**. The encoded information is stored on a thin magnetic strip located on the back of the card. When the card is swiped through the magnetic card reader, the information is read.

### Bar Code Readers

You are probably familiar with **bar code readers** or **scanners** from grocery stores. These devices are either handheld **wand readers** or **platform scanners**. They contain photoelectric cells that scan or read **bar codes**, or the vertical zebra-striped marks printed on product containers.

Almost all supermarkets use electronic cash registers and a bar code system called the **Universal Product Code (UPC)**. At the checkout counter, electronic cash registers use a bar code reader to scan each product's UPC code. The codes are sent to the supermarket's computer, which has a description, the latest price, and an inventory level for each product. The computer processes this input to update the inventory level and to provide the electronic cash register with the description and price for each product. These devices are so easy to use that many supermarkets are offering customers self-checkout stations.

Smartphones can also scan bar codes. (See Figure 6-11.) With the appropriate app, you can scan the bar code of a product and get comparative prices. For example, after scanning the bar code from a product you are thinking of buying, the app Price Check by Amazon will provide in-store and online price comparisons as well as provide other customer product reviews.

### RFID Readers

**RFID (radio-frequency identification) tags** are tiny chips that can be embedded in most everything. They can be found in consumer products, driver's licenses, passports, and any number of other items. These chips contain electronically

**Figure 6-11** Smartphone bar code reader

**Figure 6-12** RFID reader

**Figure 6-13** Wand reader

stored information that can be read using an **RFID reader** located several yards away. (See Figure 6-12.) They are widely used to track and locate lost pets; to monitor production and update inventory; and to record prices, product descriptions, and locations of retail items.

Some argue that these tags may one day be inserted into humans to track their locations. Even if the tabs are not embedded into humans, they will likely be embedded into the clothes worn by humans. They argue that RFID tags are a serious threat to our privacy and their use needs to be carefully controlled by legislation.

### Character and Mark Recognition Devices

Character and mark recognition devices are scanners that are able to recognize special characters and marks. They are specialty devices that are essential tools for certain applications. Three types are

- **Magnetic-ink character recognition (MICR)**—used by banks to automatically read those unusual numbers on the bottom of checks and deposit slips. A special-purpose machine known as a reader/sorter reads these numbers and provides input that allows banks to efficiently maintain customer account balances.

- **Optical-character recognition (OCR)**—uses special preprinted characters that can be read by a light source and changed into machine-readable code. A common OCR device is the handheld wand reader. (See Figure 6-13.) These are used in department stores to read retail price tags by reflecting light on the printed characters.

- **Optical-mark recognition (OMR)**—senses the presence or absence of a mark, such as a pencil mark. OMR is often used to score standardized multiple-choice tests.

### concept check

What is a scanner?

Describe five types of scanning devices.

Describe three common character and mark recognition devices.

# Image Capturing Devices

Optical scanners, like traditional copy machines, can make a copy from an original. For example, an optical scanner can make a digital copy of a photograph. *Image capturing devices*, on the other hand, create or capture original images. These devices include digital cameras and **digital video cameras**.

### Digital Cameras

**Digital cameras** are similar to traditional cameras except that images are recorded digitally on a disk or in the camera's memory. Most digital cameras

Figure 6-14 Digital camera

Webcam

Figure 6-15 Attached webcam

are also able to record video as well. (See Figure 6-14.) Almost all tablets and smartphones have built-in digital cameras capable of taking images and video. You can take a picture, view it immediately, and even place it on your own web page, within minutes.

To learn more about how digital photography works, visit us on the web at www.computing2014.com and enter the keyword **photo**. Digital photographs can be shared easily with others over the Internet.

## Webcams

**Webcams** are specialized digital video cameras that capture images and send them to a computer for broadcast over the Internet. Webcams are built into most smartphones and tablets. Desktop and notebook webcams are either built in or attached to the computer's monitor. (See Figure 6-15.) To learn more about webcams, visit our website at www.computing2014.com and enter the keyword **webcam**.

# Audio-Input Devices

*Audio-input devices* convert sounds into a form that can be processed by the system unit. By far the most widely used audio-input device is the microphone. Audio input can take many forms, including the human voice and music.

## Voice Recognition Systems

**Voice recognition systems** use a microphone, a sound card, and special software. These systems allow users to operate computers and other devices as well as to create documents using voice commands. Examples include voice-controlled dialing features on mobile phones,

## tips

Have you ever had trouble communicating with someone who does not speak English? If so, Google Translate may be just what you need.

1. Go to translate.google.com.

2. Using the buttons at the top, select the language you will be speaking, followed by the language you want your words translated to.

3. Click the microphone icon in the box on the left, and begin speaking clearly into your microphone. In a few seconds, you will see the translated text in the box on the right.

4. Click the speaker icon in the box on the right to hear the translation.

If you own a smartphone, consider installing the free Google Translate app. To see other tips, visit our website at www.computing2014.com and enter the keyword tips.

navigation on GPS devices, and control of car audio systems. Specialized portable voice recorders are widely used by doctors, lawyers, and others to record dictation. (See Figure 6-16.) These devices are able to record for several hours before connecting to a computer system to edit, store, and print the dictated information. Some systems are even able to translate dictation from one language to another, such as from English to Japanese.

**Figure 6-16** **Voice recorders**

### ☑ concept check

How are digital cameras different from traditional cameras?

What is a webcam? Describe the two basic designs.

What are voice recognition systems?

# What Is Output?

**Output** is processed data or information. Output typically takes the form of text, graphics, photos, audio, and/or video. For example, when you create a presentation using a presentation graphics program, you typically input text and graphics. You also could include photographs and even add voice narration. The output would be the completed presentation.

**Output devices** are any hardware used to provide or to create output. They translate information that has been processed by the system unit into a form that humans can understand. There are a wide range of output devices. The most widely used are monitors, printers, and audio-output devices.

# Monitors

**Figure 6-17** **Monitor resolution**

| Standard | Pixels |
|----------|--------|
| UXGA | 1,600 × 1,200 |
| QXGA | 2,048 × 1,536 |
| WQXGA | 2,560 × 1,600 |
| QXSGA | 2,560 × 2,048 |
| QWXGA+ | 2,880 × 1,800 |

**Figure 6-18** **Resolution standards**

The most frequently used output device is the **monitor**. Also known as **display screens**, monitors present visual images of text and graphics. The output is often referred to as **soft copy**. Monitors vary in size, shape, and cost. Almost all, however, have some basic distinguishing features.

### Features

The most important characteristic of a monitor is its clarity. **Clarity** refers to the quality and sharpness of the displayed images. It is a function of several monitor features, including resolution, dot pitch, contrast ratio, size, and aspect ratio.

• **Resolution** is one of the most important features. Images are formed on a monitor by a series of dots or **pixels (picture elements)**. (See Figure 6-17.) Resolution is expressed as a matrix of these dots or pixels. For example, many monitors today have a resolution of 1,600 pixel columns by 1,200 pixel rows for a total of 1,920,000 pixels. The higher a monitor's resolution (the more pixels), the clearer the image produced. See Figure 6-18 for the most common monitor resolutions.

- **Dot (pixel) pitch** is the distance between each pixel. Most newer monitors have a dot pitch of 0.31 mm (31/100th of a millimeter) or less. The lower the dot pitch (the shorter the distance between pixels), the clearer the images produced.

- **Contrast ratios** indicate a monitor's ability to display colors. It compares the light intensity of the brightest white to the darkest black. The higher the ratio, the better the monitor. Good monitors typically have contrast ratios between 500:1 and 2000:1.

- **Size**, or **active display area**, is measured by the diagonal length of a monitor's viewing area. Common sizes are 15, 17, 19, 21, and 24 inches.

- **Aspect ratio** is determined by the width of a monitor divided by its height. The most common aspect ratio for standard monitors (similar to traditional television pictures) is 4:3. The most common aspect ratios for wide-screen monitors are 16:9 and 16:10.

### Flat-Panel Monitors

**Flat-panel monitors** are the most widely used type of monitor today. Compared to other types, they are thinner, are more portable, and require less power to operate. (See Figure 6-19.)

**Figure 6-19** Flat-panel monitor

Most of today's flat-panel monitors are **LCD (liquid crystal display)**. One characteristic of LCD technology is that the monitors are backlit, meaning that a common source of light is dispersed over all the pixels on the screen. Although there are many variations of LCD displays, the most common for today's monitors is the **TFT-LC (thin-film transistor liquid crystal)** in which each pixel is independently activated, producing a high-quality and energy-efficient image. **AMOLED (active-matrix organic light-emitting diode)** is a newer technology and is becoming widely used. Compared to LCD, AMOLED technology has the benefits of lower power consumption and longer battery life, as well as possibilities for much thinner displays.

## Explorations

AMOLED is just one type of LED (light-emitting diode).

**To learn more about various LED technologies for monitors and TVs, visit our website at www.computing2014.com and enter the keyword led.**

### E-book Readers

**E-books (electronic books)** are traditional printed books in electronic format. These books are available from numerous sources including many public and private libraries, bookstore websites, and the cloud. **E-book readers (e-readers)** are dedicated mobile devices for storing and displaying e-books and other electronic media including electronic newspapers and magazines.

E-book readers have displays that are typically 6 inches, are limited to black and white output, and use a technology known as e-ink. **E-ink** produces images that reflect light like ordinary paper, making the display easy to read. Two well-known e-book readers are Amazon's Kindle and Barnes & Noble's Nook Simple Touch. (See Figure 6-20.)

Tablets can also display e-books. They are larger, heavier, and more expensive than e-book readers. They are also much more flexible, with displaying e-books being only one of their any number of applications. Unlike dedicated e-book readers, these tablets use LCD displays that provide crisp, colorful images, however, that are difficult to read in bright light due to their reflective nature. Two well-known traditional tablets are Apple's iPad and Samsung's Galaxy Tab.

To learn more about e-books, see Making IT Work for You: E-books, on page 164.

Dedicated e-book reader

**Figure 6-20** E-book reader

# E-BOOKS

Are you tired of carrying a book bag filled with textbooks? Have you ever wished you could have a reference book or text at your fingertips, instead of at home on a bookshelf? E-books are the solutions to these problems, and this guide will discuss their benefits, as well as various options on how to access and read them.

**Benefits of E-books**    Because e-books are digital, they offer a wide range of benefits:

**1** *Transporting.* Books can take up a large volume of space in any home (or your school bag). With e-books, you can store over a thousand books in one small device!

**2** *Searching.* Type any keyword, and you will be taken to the page(s) where that word appears. This is much faster than using an index.

**3** *Bookmarking.* Mark any number of pages as important. This is an improvement over having countless physical bookmarks or folded pages.

**4** *Adding highlights and notes.* All marks on an e-book are digital. They can be added and removed easily. The same could not be said for physical textbooks.

**5** *Purchasing.* Buying an e-book can take less than a minute, as it is downloaded instantly to your device. Prices also tend to be lower than those for physical books.

**Reading E-books**    Once you decide to purchase an e-book, you may be surprised by the number of devices you can use to read it.

**1** *E-book reader.* Dedicated e-book readers, such as the Amazon Kindle and the Barnes & Noble Nook, can be purchased for less than $100. If it is important for you to read in direct sunlight or areas with heavy lighting, the e-ink used by these devices will be desirable.

**2** *Smartphones and tablets.* Do you already own a smartphone or tablet that you take everywhere? If so, you may want to download the free apps from e-book sellers to avoid the cost of a separate e-book reader. The reading experience on these apps is excellent with the touch-screen interface present in these devices.

**3** *Notebook and desktop computers.* Although many e-book retailers make apps for your computer, sellers such as Google allow you to read books purchased from its Google Play store with nothing more than a web browser.

Most e-book sellers offer the synchronization of your e-books and notes with their cloud services. This allows you to start reading a book using your tablet, for example, and pick up where you left off with your smartphone.

The web is continually changing, and some of the specifics presented in this Making IT Work for You may have changed.

**To learn about other ways to make information technology work for you, visit our website at www.computing2014.com and enter the keyword** miw.

Figure 6-21 Digital whiteboard

Figure 6-22 3-D HDTV

### Other Monitors

There are several other types of monitors. Some are used for more specialized applications, such as making presentations and watching television.

- **Digital** or **interactive whiteboards** are specialized devices with a large display connected to a computer or projector. The computer's desktop is displayed on the digital whiteboard and controlled using a special pen, a finger, or some other device. Digital whiteboards are widely used in classrooms and corporate boardrooms. (See Figure 6-21.)

- **High-definition television (HDTV)** delivers a much clearer and more detailed wide-screen picture than regular television. Because the output is digital, users can readily freeze video sequences to create high-quality still images. The video and still images can then be digitized, edited, and stored on disk for later use. This technology is very useful to graphic artists, designers, and publishers. One the most recent and dramatic advances is 3-D HDTV. (See Figure 6-22.) Using special viewing glasses, 3-D HDTV provides theater-quality three-dimensional viewing.

- **Cathode-ray tubes (CRTs)** are similar in size and technology to older televisions. They have been replaced by flat-panel monitors. Discarded CRTs, however, are a serious threat to our environment. Each color CRT contains approximately four pounds of lead and numerous other hazardous materials. Don't just throw out an obsolete CRT. Dispose of it in a responsible manner through an EPA-certified recycling program. Most large cities and manufacturers including IBM, Microsoft, and Dell have certified programs.

### ✓ concept check

What is output? What are output devices?

Define these monitor features: resolution, contrast ratios, refresh rate, size, and aspect ratio.

Describe flat-panel, CRT, and other more specialized monitors.

# Printers

Even as many individuals, schools, and businesses are trying to go paperless, printers remain one of the most used output devices. You probably use a printer to print homework assignments, photographs, and web pages. **Printers** translate information that has been processed by the system unit and present the information on paper. Printer output is often called **hard copy**.

1,200 by 300 dpi

4,800 by 1,200 dpi

**Figure 6-23** DPI comparison

## Features

There are many different types of printers. Almost all, however, have some basic distinguishing features, including resolution, color capability, speed, memory, and duplex printing.

- **Resolution** for a printer is similar to monitor resolution. It is a measure of the clarity of images produced. Printer resolution, however, is measured in **dpi (dots per inch)**. (See Figure 6-23.) Most printers designed for personal use average 4,800 by 1,200 dpi. The higher the dpi, the better the quality of images produced.

- **Color** capability is provided by most printers today. Users typically have the option to print either with just black ink or with color. Because it is more expensive to print in color, most users select black ink for letters, drafts, and homework. The most common black ink selection is **grayscale**, in which images are displayed using many shades of gray. Color is used more selectively for final reports containing graphics and for photographs.

- **Speed** is measured in the number of pages printed per minute. Typically, printers for personal use average 15 to 19 pages per minute for single-color (black) output and 13 to 15 pages per minute for color output.

- **Memory** within a printer is used to store printing instructions and documents waiting to be printed. The more memory in a printer, the faster it will be able to create large documents.

- **Duplex printing** allows automatic printing on both sides of a sheet of paper. Although not currently a standard feature for all printers, it will likely become standard in the future as a way to reduce paper waste and to protect the environment.

## Inkjet Printers

**Inkjet printers** spray ink at high speed onto the surface of paper. This process not only produces a letter-quality image but also permits printing to be done in a variety of colors, making it ideal for printing photos. (See Figure 6-24.) Inkjet printers are the most widely used printers. They are reliable, quiet, and relatively inexpensive. The most costly aspect of inkjet printers is replacing the ink cartridges. For this reason, most users specify black ink for the majority of print jobs and use the more

**Figure 6-24** Inkjet printer

expensive color printing for select applications. Typical inkjet printers produce 17 to 19 pages per minute of black-only output and 13 to 15 pages of color output.

### Laser Printers

The **laser printer** uses a technology similar to that used in a photocopying machine. Laser printers use a laser light beam to produce images with excellent letter and graphics quality. More expensive than inkjet printers, laser printers are faster and are used in applications requiring high-quality output. (See Figure 6-25.)

There are two categories of laser printers. **Personal laser printers** are less expensive and are used by many single users. They typically can print 15 to 17 pages a minute. **Shared laser printers** typically support color, are more expensive, and are used (shared) by a group of users. Shared laser printers typically print over 50 pages a minute.

### Other Printers

There are several other types of printers. These printers include cloud printers, thermal printers, and plotters:

- **Cloud printers** are printers connected to the Internet that provide printing services to others on the Internet. **Google Cloud Print** is a service that supports cloud printing. Once a user activates a printer using the Google Chrome OS, the user can access that printer anywhere with an Internet connection.
- **Thermal printers** use heat elements to produce images on heat-sensitive paper. These printers are widely used with ATMs and gasoline pumps to print receipts.
- **Plotters** are special-purpose printers for producing a wide range of specialized output. Using output from graphics tablets and other graphical input devices, plotters create maps, images, and architectural and engineering drawings. Plotters are typically used by graphic artists, engineers, and architects to print out designs, sketches, and drawings.

**Figure 6-25  Laser printer**

### concept check

Discuss these printer features: resolution, color capability, speed, memory, and duplex printing.

Compare inkjet printers and laser printers.

Discuss cloud, thermal, and plotter printers.

**Figure 6-26** Headset

**Figure 6-27** Digital media player

# Audio and Video Devices

Audio-output devices translate audio information from the computer into sounds that people can understand. The most widely used audio-output devices are **speakers** and **headsets**. (See Figure 6-26.) These devices are connected to an audio jack on the system unit. The sound card is used to capture as well as play back recorded sounds. Audio-output devices are used to play music, vocalize translations from one language to another, and communicate information from the computer system to users.

Creating voice output is not anywhere near as difficult as recognizing and interpreting voice input. In fact, voice output is quite common. It is used with many soft-drink machines, telephones, and cars. It is used as a reinforcement tool for learning, such as to help students study a foreign language. It also is used in many supermarkets at the checkout counter to confirm purchases. One of its most powerful capabilities is to assist the physically challenged.

### Portable Media Players

**Portable media players**, also known as digital media players, are electronic devices for storing and playing digital media. Some of the best-known specialized audio and video players are the Apple iPod, Creative Zen, and Microsoft Zune. (See Figure 6-27.)

One of the most recent applications for portable media players is to watch live TV. This is possible through **mobile digital television (mobile DTV)** technology, which allows television stations to broadcast their programming directly to smartphones, computers, and **digital media players**. Now, many people use their smartphones to provide the functionality of dedicated portable media players.

# Combination Input and Output Devices

Many devices combine input and output capabilities. Sometimes this is done to save space. Other times it is done for very specialized applications. Common combination devices include multifunctional devices, Internet telephones, and robots.

## Multifunctional Devices

**Multifunctional devices (MFD)** typically combine the capabilities of a scanner, printer, fax, and copy machine. These multifunctional devices offer a cost and space advantage. They cost about the same as a good printer or copy machine but require much less space than the single-function devices they replace. Their disadvantage is that the quality and functionality are not quite as good as those of the separate single-purpose devices. Even so, multifunctional devices are widely used in home and small business offices.

## Internet Telephones

**Internet telephones** are specialized input and output devices for receiving and sending voice communication. (See Figure 6-28.)

**Voice over IP (VoIP)** is the transmission of telephone calls over computer networks. Also known as **telephony**, **Internet telephony**, and **IP telephony**, VoIP uses the Internet rather than traditional communication lines to support voice communication. To place telephone calls using Internet telephony requires a high-speed Internet connection and a service provider. Many cable service providers offer bundles including Internet, telephone, and television. While these bundles offer a price break, there are other lower-cost options for VoIP from a variety of providers including Ooma, Vonage, MagicJack, and Skype.

**Skype** provides audio and video service that does not require any dedicated hardware. Once you subscribe to this free service, you can use your computer's existing audio and video devices to connect to any other Skype subscribers. The advantages compared to the other providers are that Skype is free for domestic calls (as well as for international calls), supports video as well as audio, and does not require any special equipment. The disadvantages include that both parties must have their computers on to make or receive calls; calls can only be made between Skype subscribers, although, for an additional fee, you can place calls to non-Skype subscribers; and voice quality and reliability are not as good as traditional telephone communication. To learn more about using Skype, see Making IT Work for You: Skype, on pages 170 and 171.

**Figure 6-28** Internet telephone

## Robots

**Artificial intelligence (AI)** is a field of computer science that attempts to develop computer systems that can mimic or simulate human senses, thought processes, and actions. **Robotics** is an area of AI concerned with developing and using robots. **Robots** are computer-controlled machines that mimic the motor activities of living things. For example, Honda's ASIMO robot resembles a human and is capable of walking upstairs, dancing, shaking hands, playing musical instruments, and much more. (See Figure 6-29.) Robots are used for a wide variety of applications ranging from domestic to manufacturing to military operations. There are four types of robots.

- **Perception system robots** imitate some of the human senses. For example, robots with television-camera vision systems are particularly useful. They can guide machine tools, inspect products, and secure homes.
- **Industrial robots** are used to perform a variety of tasks. For example, in automotive plants, robots are widely used for welding, polishing, and painting.
- **Mobile robots** act as transports and are widely used for a variety of different tasks. For example, the police and military use them to locate and disarm explosive devices.
- **Household robots** are now widely available and are designed to vacuum or scrub floors, mow lawns, patrol the house, or simply provide entertainment.

## Explorations

There are many humanlike robots being developed for research and education.

**To learn more about one of these robots, visit our website at www.computing2014 .com and enter the keyword** robot.

# Making IT work for you

## SKYPE

Do you already use a communication tool that lets you keep in touch with your friends and family? Does that tool include the ability to have face-to-face conversations, share files and screens, and make calls to those not connected to the Internet? Skype is a well-known tool that offers all these services, most of them for free. This section will help you explore some of Skype's features.

**Getting Started** In order to enjoy all the benefits of Skype, it is recommended that your computer have speakers, a microphone, and a webcam. If you have a notebook or tablet, these are all likely integrated. Follow these steps to create your account and install Skype on your machine:

1. Visit www.skype.com, and click the *Join Skype* button at the top right.

2. Enter the required information to create your Skype account. When you are finished, the software will be downloaded automatically. Do not purchase any Skype credits at the moment.

3. Run the downloaded setup file, and follow the prompts to install Skype on your machine.

4. Log in to your Skype account on the welcome screen, and follow the prompts to make sure your audio and video are working.

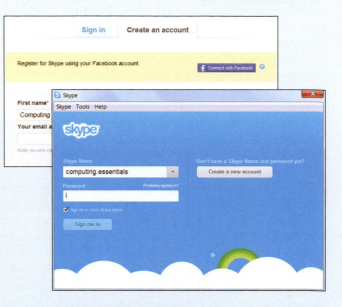

**Adding Contacts** You can find friends or other contacts manually, or you can import them from your address book on Facebook, Outlook, and several other services. To add a contact manually:

1. Click *Add a Contact* at the bottom of the Contacts List on the left side.

2. Enter the information you know about your contact, such as his or her e-mail address.

3. Skype will display matches. Click the one that matches your contact's details, and then click the *Add* button.

Your contact must accept your request before you can see his or her online status.

**Skype-to-Skype Communication** When two individuals have Skype accounts, they can contact each other (for free) using a variety of methods, from voice or video calls to instant messages. They can exchange files and share screens with each other. Please note that for videoconferencing between three or more people, you must have a premium or business account.

**1** Click the contact you wish to communicate with.

**2** Click the *Video Call* or *Call* button. Once your contact accepts the call, your interface will change.

**3** During the call, you have the ability to send instant messages and turn audio and/or video on or off by clicking the buttons at the bottom.

**4** To send files or share screens, click the *Plus* (+) button at the bottom. You could also have initiated the *Send File* feature from the contact screen without having to place a call.

**5** To hang up, press the red *End call* button at the bottom.

**Calling Landline or Mobile Phones (VoIP)** Skype can use your Internet connection to place a call to any phone in the world. This is not a free service, but the costs are low. You can pay as you go with Skype credits, or sign up for a monthly subscription.

**1** Click the *Call* menu and select *Call Phones*.

**2** Click the green *Call* button after entering the phone number.

The web is continually changing, and some of the specifics presented in this Making IT Work for You may have changed.

To learn about other ways to make information technology work for you, visit our website at www.computing2014.com and enter the keyword miw.

**Figure 6-29** ASIMO Robot

**Figure 6-30** Virtual reality

## Virtual Reality Headgear and Gloves

**Virtual reality (VR)** is an artificial, or simulated, reality created in 3-D by computers. It strives to create a virtual or **immersive experience** by using specialized hardware that includes headgear and gloves. (See Figure 6-30.)

The **headgear** has earphones and three-dimensional stereoscopic screens. The **gloves** have sensors that collect data about your hand movements. Coupled with software, this interactive sensory equipment lets you immerse yourself in a computer-generated world.

There are any number of possible applications for virtual reality headgear and gloves. The ultimate recreational use might be something resembling a giant virtual amusement park. More serious applications can simulate important experiences or training environments, such as in aviation, surgical operations, spaceship repair, or nuclear disaster cleanup.

## concept check

What are the two most widely used audio-output devices? What is a portable media player? What is mobile digital television?

What are multifunctional devices? Internet telephones? VoIP?

What is artificial intelligence? Robotics? Virtual reality? Headgear? Gloves?

# Ergonomics

People use computers to enrich their personal and private lives. There are ways, however, that computers can make people less productive and even harm their health. Anyone who frequently uses a computer can be affected. As a result, there has been great interest in a field known as ergonomics.

**Ergonomics** (pronounced "er-guh-nom-ix") is defined as the study of human factors related to things people use. It is concerned with fitting the task to the user rather than forcing the user to contort to do the task. For computer users and manufacturers this means designing input and output devices to increase ease of use and to avoid health risks.

Sitting in front of a screen in awkward positions for long periods may lead to physical problems such as eyestrain, headaches, and back pain. Computer users can alleviate these problems by taking frequent rest breaks and by using

**Figure 6-31** Ergonomic recommendations

well-designed computer furniture. Some recommendations by ergonomics experts are illustrated in Figure 6-31.

Other recommendations to avoid physical discomfort are

- **Eyestrain and headache:** To make the computer easier on the eyes, take a 15-minute break every hour or two. Keep everything you're focusing on at about the same distance. For example, the computer screen, keyboard, and a document holder containing your work might be positioned about 20 inches away. Clean the screen of dust from time to time.

- **Back and neck pain:** To help avoid back and neck problems, make sure your equipment is adjustable. You should be able to adjust your chair for height and angle, and the chair should have good back support. The monitor should be at eye level or slightly below eye level. Use a footrest, if necessary, to reduce leg fatigue.

- **Repetitive strain injury: Repetitive strain injury (RSI)** is any injury that is caused by fast, repetitive work that can generate neck, wrist, hand, and arm pain. RSI is by far the greatest cause of workplace illnesses, resulting in compensation claims totaling billions of dollars and lost productivity every year. One particular type of RSI, **carpal tunnel syndrome**, found among heavy computer users, consists of damage to nerves and tendons in the hands. Some victims report the pain is so intense that they cannot open doors or shake hands and that they require corrective surgery. Ergonomically correct keyboards have been developed to help prevent injury from heavy computer use. (See Figure 6-32.) In addition to using ergonomic keyboards, you should take frequent short rest breaks and gently massage your hands.

**Figure 6-32** Ergonomic keyboard

## concept check

What is ergonomics? How does it relate to input and output devices?

What can be done to minimize eyestrain, headache, back pain, and neck pain?

What is RSI? What is carpal tunnel syndrome?

# Careers in IT

**Technical writers** prepare instruction manuals, technical reports, and other scientific or technical documents. Most technical writers work for computer software firms, government agencies, or research institutions. They translate technical information into easily understandable instructions or summaries. As new technology continues to develop and expand, the need for technical writers who can communicate technical expertise to others is expected to increase.

Technical writing positions typically require an associate or a college degree in communications, journalism, or English and a specialization in, or familiarity with, a technical field. However, individuals with strong writing skills sometimes transfer from jobs in the sciences to positions in technical writing.

Technical writers can expect to earn an annual salary in the range of $41,000 to $78,000. Advancement opportunities can be limited within a firm or company, but there are additional opportunities in consulting. To learn about other careers in information technology, visit us at www.computing2014.com and enter the keyword careers.

**Now that you've learned about input and output devices, I'd like to tell you about my career as a technical writer.**

# A LOOK TO THE FUTURE

## Augmented Reality Displays

Have you ever run into someone who looks familiar, but you cannot remember her name or where you know her from? What about finding yourself in an unfamiliar town, constantly having to look at your smartphone or GPS to get directions? Don't you wish the information would appear instantly, right before your eyes? With wearable augmented reality displays, this wish will become a reality. Data from your computer and the Internet will become instantly accessible and viewable without having to access another device. The reality you see in front of you is improved, or augmented, with additional visual information using projected images.

Bringing up information about a visual image is not new. Several search engines already have the ability to identify an image simply by looking for similar images in their databases. In addition, many types of software can do the same with faces, looking at key points in the image in order identify that individual. These augmented reality displays will take that technology one step further by integrating it with wearable glasses or contact lenses. Whether you look at a landmark, textbook, or person, the computer connected to that display will be able to retrieve the information you need and place it in your field of vision. So if you forgot the name of the person greeting you in the coffee shop, do not worry. Her name and brief biography will be retrieved from her social networking account and be displayed in front of you in time to properly return the greeting.

Identification of people and objects is not the only use of augmented reality. As technology continues to shrink in size, the device will be able to perform all the tasks of your smartphone. You will be able to look at the sky and see information about today's weather. Text message and incoming call notifications

can appear in front of you. Prices from various online stores will appear by the time you ask your friend where he got that new T-shirt. And of course, integrated GPS will display arrows in front of you and guide you as you walk through unfamiliar city streets.

Although this technology will likely be available in the next few years, there are some challenges. First, you have the issue of powering the device. Something as small as a pair of glasses or contact lenses may not have room for a battery large enough to power it all day. Another issue involves limitations of human vision. Normally, our eyes find it difficult to focus on objects that are placed very close to them. Researchers have come up with various solutions to fix this problem, but they need to make it comfortable for the eyes to shift focus between the information being projected up close to the real-world object that could be far away. Lastly, there is the issue of comfort. Will these glasses or contact lenses be comfortable to wear all day? Will they make you look strange to those that do not know about augmented reality?

Many companies and universities are working on various types of augmented reality displays. There are a few that have received funding from the military in order to assist soldiers and pilots. The ones that seem closest to release for the general public are from Google. Prototype eyeglasses from its "Project Glass" division are already being tested by various Google employees. To learn more about this project, visit our website at www.computing2014.com and enter the keyword projectglass.

Now that you have learned more about augmented reality, do you see yourself wearing these sorts of eyeglasses when they become affordable? Do you think that they can end up being a dangerous distraction?

## KEYBOARDS

Input is any data or instructions that are used by a computer. **Input devices** are hardware used to translate words, sounds, images, and actions that people understand into a form that the system unit can process. These include keyboards, pointing, scanning, image capturing, and audio-input devices.

**Keyboards** convert numbers, letters, and special characters that people understand into electrical signals. These signals are sent to, and processed by, the system unit.

### Keyboards

There are four basic categories of keyboards: traditional, notebook, virtual, and thumb.

- **Traditional keyboards**, used on desktop and larger computers. Standard keyboard has 101 keys. **Toggle keys** turn features on and off. **Combination keys** perform actions when combinations of keys are held down.
- **Notebook keyboards**, used on notebook computers. Smaller than traditional keyboard with fewer keys. Typically does not have numeric keypad or standard location for function and navigation keys.
- **Virtual keyboard**, used on tablets and smartphones. Does not have a physical keyboard. Keys displayed on screen and selected by pressing a key's image.
- **Thumb keyboard**, used on smartphones and small portable devices. Very small devices primarily used for texting and connecting to the web.

## POINTING DEVICES

**Pointing devices** provide an intuitive interface with the system unit by accepting pointing gestures and converting them into machine-readable input.

### Mice

A **mouse** controls a pointer that is displayed on the monitor. The **mouse pointer** usually appears in the shape of an arrow. Some mice have a **wheel button** that rotates to scroll through information on the monitor. **Optical mouse** is the most widely used. A **cordless** or **wireless mouse** uses radio waves or infrared light waves. Three devices similar to a mouse are **trackballs**, **touch pads**, and **pointing sticks**.

### Touch Screens

**Touch screens** allow users to select actions by touching the screen with a finger or penlike device. **Multitouch screens** accept multiple-finger commands.

### Game Controllers

**Game controllers** provide input to computer games. Widely used controllers include **joysticks**, **dance pads**, **gamepads**, and **motion-sensing devices**.

### Stylus

A **stylus** is a penlike device commonly used with tablets and PDAs. Often, a stylus interacts with the computer through **handwriting recognition software** that translates handwritten notes into a form that the system unit can process.

To be a competent end user, you need to be aware of the most commonly used input and output devices. These devices are translators for information into and out of the system unit. Input devices translate words, sounds, and actions into symbols the system unit can process. Output devices translate symbols from the system unit into words, images, and sounds that people can understand.

## SCANNING DEVICES

Scanning devices move across text and images to convert them into a form that the system unit can process.

### Optical Scanners

An **optical scanner (scanner)** converts documents into machine-readable form. The three basic types are **flatbed**, **document**, and **portable**.

### Card Readers

**Card readers** interpret encoded information located on a variety of cards. The most common is the **magnetic card reader** that reads information from a thin magnetic strip on the back of a card.

### Bar Code Readers

**Bar code readers** or **scanners** (either handheld **wand readers** or **platform scanners**) read **bar codes** on products. The bar code system **Universal Product Code (UPC)** is widely used in supermarkets.

### RFID Readers

**RFID readers** read **RFID (radio-frequency identification) tags**. These tags are widely used for tracking lost pets, production, and inventory and for recording prices and product descriptions.

### Character and Mark Recognition Devices

Character and mark recognition devices are scanners that are able to recognize special characters and marks. Three types are **magnetic-ink character recognition (MICR)**, **optical-character recognition (OCR)**, and **optical-mark recognition (OMR)**.

## IMAGE CAPTURING DEVICES

Image capturing devices create or capture original images. These devices include digital cameras and webcams.

### Digital Cameras

**Digital cameras** are similar to traditional cameras except that images are recorded digitally on a disk or in the camera's memory. Most digital cameras record video too.

### Webcams

**Webcams** are specialized digital video cameras that capture images and send them to a computer for broadcast over the Internet. Webcams are built into many smartphones and tablets, while others are attached to the computer monitor.

## AUDIO-INPUT DEVICES

Audio-input devices convert sounds into a form that can be processed by the system unit. By far the most widely used audio-input device is the microphone.

### Voice Recognition Systems

**Voice recognition systems** use a microphone, a sound card, and special software. These systems allow users to operate computers and other devices as well as create documents by using voice commands. Specialized portable voice recorders are widely used by doctors, lawyers, and others to record dictation. Some systems are able to translate dictation from one language to another, such as from English to Japanese.

Output is processed data or information. **Output devices** are any hardware used to provide or to create output.

Monitors (**display screens**) are the most used output device. Output is often referred to as **soft copy**. Monitors vary in size, shape, and cost. Almost all, however, have some basic distinguishing features.

## Features

The most important characteristic of a monitor is its **clarity**, which relates to the quality and sharpness of images. It is a function of several monitor features, including **resolution** (matrix of **pixels** or **picture elements**), **dot pitch, contrast ratio, size,** and **aspect ratio.**

## Flat Panel

**Flat-panel monitors** are the most widely used monitor; most are **LCD** (**liquid crystal display**). Most common type is **TFT-LC** (**thin-film transistor liquid crystal**). **AMOLED** (**active-matrix organic light-emitting diode**) is a newer flat-panel technology.

## E-book Readers

**E-books** (**electronic books**) are traditional printed books in electronic format. **E-book readers** (**e-readers**) are mobile devices to store and display e-books and other electronic media. They use **e-ink** technology. Tablets can display e-books and have a larger display area but are heavier, more expensive, and more difficult to read in bright light.

## Other Monitors

Other types of monitors include **digital** (**interactive**) **whiteboards** to project output; **high-definition television** (**HDTV**) to display clear detailed images; and older monitors using **cathode-ray tubes** (**CRTs**).

**Printers** translate information processed by the system unit and present the information on paper. Printer output is often called **hard copy**.

## Features

Most printers have the same basic features, including **resolution** measured in **dpi** (**dots per inch**), color capability (most common black ink selection is **grayscale**), speed (measured in the number of pages printed per minute), memory, and **duplex** (both sides of paper) **printing.**

## Inkjet

**Inkjet printers** spray ink at high speed onto the surface of paper. Most widely used type of printer, reliable, quiet, and inexpensive. The most costly aspect of inkjet printers is replacing the ink cartridges.

## Laser

**Laser printers** use technology similar to photocopying machine involving laser light beam to produce high-quality images. There are two categories: **personal** (less expensive, used by single user) and **shared** (supports color, more expensive, and supports group of users).

## Other Printers

There are several other types of printers. These printers include cloud printers, thermal printers, and plotters.

- **Cloud printers** provide printing services to others on the Internet. **Google Cloud Print** is a service that supports cloud printing.
- **Thermal printers** use heat elements to produce images on heat-sensitive paper.
- **Plotters** are special-purpose printers for producing a wide range of specialized output including output from graphics tablets and other graphical input devices.

## AUDIO AND VIDEO DEVICES

Audio-output devices translate audio information from the computer into sounds that people can understand. The most widely used are **speakers** and **headsets**.

### Portable Media Players

**Portable media players (digital media players)** are electronic devices for storing and playing digital media. **Mobile digital television (mobile DTV)** technology allows direct broadcast to digital media players as well as smartphones and other computers.

## COMBINATION INPUT AND OUTPUT DEVICES

Many devices combine input and output capabilities.

### Multifunctional Devices

**Multifunctional devices (MFD)** typically combine the capabilities of a scanner, printer, fax, and copy machine.

### Internet Telephones

**Internet telephones** send and receive voice communication over the computer networks using **voice over IP (VoIP, telephony, Internet telephony, IP telephony)**. **Skype** is a widely used VoIP service.

### Robots

**Artificial intelligence (AI)** attempts to mimic human senses, thought processes, and actions. **Robotics**, an area of AI, uses **robots** (computer-controlled machines that mimic the motor activities of living things). Four types of robots: **perception system, industrial, mobile, and household**.

### Virtual Reality Headgear and Gloves

**Virtual reality (VR)** creates 3-D simulated **immersive experiences**. Virtual reality hardware includes **headgear** and **gloves**. Applications include training environments, such as in aviation, surgery, spaceship repair, or nuclear disaster cleanup.

## ERGONOMICS

**Ergonomics** is the study of human factors related to things people use. Concerned with fitting the task to the user rather than forcing the user to contort to do the task, it involves devising ways that input and output devices can be used and designed to increase ease of use and decrease health risks.

### Recommendations

Some recommendations to avoid physical discomfort are

- **Eyestrain and headache.** To make the computer easier on the eyes, take a 15-minute break every hour or two; keep everything you're focusing on at about the same distance; and clean the screen periodically.

- **Back and neck pain.** To help avoid back and neck problems, use adjustable equipment; chairs should adjust for height, angle, and back support; monitors should be at eye level or slightly below. Use a footrest, if necessary, to reduce leg fatigue.

- **Repetitive strain injury. Repetitive strain injury (RSI)** is caused by fast, repetitive work and can generate neck, wrist, hand, and arm pain. One particular type of RSI, **carpal tunnel syndrome**, found among heavy computer users, consists of damage to nerves and tendons in the hands. Ergonomically correct keyboards help prevent injury. Take frequent, short rest breaks and gently massage hands.

## CAREERS IN IT

**Technical writers** prepare instruction manuals, technical reports, and other documents. An associate or a college degree in communication, journalism, or English and a specialization in, or familiarity with, a technical field are required. Salary range is $41,000 to $78,000.

# KEY TERMS

active display area  (163)
active-matrix organic
light-emitting diode
(AMOLED)  (163)
artificial intelligence
(AI)  (169)
aspect ratio  (163)
bar code  (159)
bar code reader  (159)
bar code scanner  (159)
card reader  (159)
carpal tunnel
syndrome  (173)
cathode-ray tube
(CRT)  (165)
clarity  (162)
cloud printer  (167)
combination key  (155)
contrast ratio  (163)
cordless mouse  (156)
dance pad  (157)
digital camera  (160)
digital media player  (168)
digital video camera  (160)
digital whiteboard  (165)
display screen  (162)
document scanner  (159)
dot pitch  (163)
dots per inch (dpi)  (166)
duplex printing  (166)
e-book reader  (163)
e-books  (163)
e-ink  (163)
e-reader  (163)
electronic books  (163)
ergonomics  (172)
flat-panel monitor  (163)
flatbed scanner  (159)
game controller  (157)
gamepads  (157)
gloves  (172)
Google Cloud Print  (167)
grayscale  (166)
handwriting recognition
software  (157)
hard copy  (165)
headgear  (172)
headsets  (168)

high-definition television
(HDTV)  (165)
household robot  (169)
immersive
experience  (172)
industrial robot  (169)
inkjet printer  (166)
input  (154)
input device  (154)
interactive
whiteboard  (165)
Internet telephone  (169)
Internet telephony  (169)
IP telephony  (169)
joystick  (157)
keyboard  (154)
laser printer  (167)
liquid crystal display
(LCD)  (163)
magnetic card reader  (159)
magnetic-ink character
recognition (MICR)  (160)
mobile digital
television  (168)
mobile DTV  (168)
mobile robot  (169)
monitor  (162)
motion-sensing
device  (157)
mouse  (156)
mouse pointer  (156)
multifunctional device
(MFD)  (169)
multitouch screen  (157)
notebook keyboard  (155)
optical-character
recognition (OCR)  (160)
optical-mark recognition
(OMR)  (160)
optical mouse  (156)
optical scanner  (158)
output  (162)
output device  (162)
perception system
robot  (169)
personal laser
printer  (167)
photo printer  (161)

picture element  (162)
pixel  (162)
pixel pitch  (163)
platform scanner  (159)
plotter  (167)
pointing device  (156)
pointing stick  (157)
portable media
player  (168)
portable scanner  (159)
printer  (165)
repetitive strain injury
(RSI)  (173)
resolution  (162, 166)
RFID reader  (160)
RFID (radio-frequency
identification) tag  (159)
robot  (169)
robotics  (169)
scanner  (158)
scanning devices  (158)
shared laser printer  (167)
Skype  (169)
soft copy  (162)
speakers  (168)
stylus  (157)
technical writer  (174)
telephony  (169)
thermal printer  (167)
thin-film transistor liquid
crystal (TFT-LC)  (163)
thumb keyboard  (155)
toggle key  (155)
touch pad  (157)
touch screen  (157)
trackball  (156)
traditional keyboard  (155)
Universal Product Code
(UPC)  (159)
virtual keyboard  (155)
virtual reality (VR)  (172)
voice over IP (VoIP)  (169)
voice recognition
system  (161)
wand reader  (159)
webcam  (161)
wheel button  (156)
wireless mouse  (156)

To test your knowledge of these key terms with animated flash cards, visit our website at www.computing2014.com and enter the keyword terms6. Or use the free *Computing Essentials 2014* app.

# MULTIPLE CHOICE

Circle the correct answer.

1. Most keyboards use an arrangement of keys known as:
   a. Alpha
   b. Daisy
   c. OptiKey
   d. QWERTY

2. The device that controls a pointer displayed on the monitor.
   a. cord
   b. mouse
   c. printer
   d. scanner

3. The type of screen that can be touched with more than one finger and supports zooming in and out by pinching and stretching your fingers.
   a. digital
   b. dynamic
   c. multitouch
   d. AMOLED

4. Flatbed and document are types of:
   a. headsets
   b. HDTVs
   c. monitors
   d. scanners

5. Device used by banks to automatically read those unusual numbers on the bottom of checks and deposit slips.
   a. MICR
   b. FDIC
   c. OMR
   d. UPC

6. The most widely used audio-input device.
   a. mouse
   b. VR
   c. microphone
   d. TFT

7. The monitor feature that indicates the ability to display colors.
   a. aspect ratio
   b. contrast ratio
   c. dot pitch
   d. resolution rate

8. Mobile devices able to store and display electronic media.
   a. e-book readers
   b. HDTV
   c. lasers
   d. whiteboards

9. This technology allows television stations to broadcast their programming directly to smartphones, computers, and digital media players.
   a. CRT
   b. HDTV
   c. LED
   d. mobile DTV

10. The study of human factors related to things people use is:
    a. ergonomics
    b. RFID
    c. RSI
    d. telephony

For an interactive multiple-choice practice test, visit our website at www.computing2014 .com and enter the keyword multiple6. Or use the free *Computing Essentials 2014* app.

# MATCHING

Match each numbered item with the most closely related lettered item. Write your answers in the spaces provided.

a. active display area
b. digital camera
c. dot pitch
d. MagicJack
e. mouse
f. plotters
g. scanners
h. stylus
i. toggle key
j. UPC

____ 1. Pressing this key turns a feature on or off.
____ 2. Input device that controls a pointer that is displayed on the monitor.
____ 3. A penlike device commonly used with tablet PCs and PDAs.
____ 4. Bar code readers use either handheld wand readers or platform _____.
____ 5. Bar code system used by many electronic cash registers.
____ 6. Records images digitally on a disk or in its memory.
____ 7. The distance between each pixel.
____ 8. A monitor feature that is measured by the diagonal length of the viewing area.
____ 9. Special-purpose printers for creating maps, images, and architectural and engineering drawings.
____10. A provider of lower-cost options for VoIP.

For an interactive matching practice test, visit our website at www.computing2014.com and enter the keyword matching6. Or use the free *Computing Essentials 2014* app.

# OPEN-ENDED

On a separate sheet of paper, respond to each question or statement.

1. Define input and input devices.
2. Describe the different types of keyboard, pointing, scanning, image capturing, and audio-input devices.
3. Define output and output devices.
4. Describe the features and different types of monitors and printers.
5. Describe audio and video devices including portable media devices and mobile DTV.
6. Discuss combination input and output devices, including multifunctional devices, Internet telephones, robots, and virtual reality headgear and gloves.
7. Define ergonomics, and describe ways to minimize physical discomfort.

# DISCUSSION

Respond to each of the following questions.

### 1 Making IT Work for You: E-BOOKS

Are you tired of carrying a book bag filled with textbooks? Review the Making IT Work for You: E-books on page 164 and then respond to the following: (a) Have you ever purchased or read an e-book? If so, what was your most recent one? If not, have you considered it? Why or why not? (b) Download and install an e-book app (desktop, tablet, or smartphone version), and then download a free e-book for that particular service. Identify the e-book you selected, and describe your experience with that e-book service, as well as some of the in-book features of its app. (c) Based on your experience, will you be purchasing more e-books in the future? Why or why not? (d) Would you consider buying future textbooks as e-books? Discuss the advantages and disadvantages of e-book textbooks.

### 2 Making IT Work for You: SKYPE

Do you already use a communication tool that lets you keep in touch with your friends and family? Review the Making IT Work for You: Skype on pages 170 and 171 and then respond to the following: (a) Have you ever used Skype or a similar service? If so, what service have you used, and what do you typically use it for? If you have not used Skype or a similar service, do you expect to in the future? Why or why not? (b) If you do not have a Skype account, create a free one, and add one of your classmates as a contact. Try a few of Skype's features after connecting with your classmate, and then describe your experience with those features. (c) Discuss the advantages and disadvantages of using Skype or a similar service for communication. (d) Do you currently use VoIP with your Internet provider or any other online service? Why or why not?

### 3 Explorations: LED TECHNOLOGY

Did you know that AMOLED is just one of several types of LED monitors and TVs? Review the Explorations box on page 163 and then respond to the following: (a) What is the primary difference between LCD and LED? Why does the article claim that many LED TVs are not actually LED TVs? (b) What is the technical difference between LED and OLED? What benefits does OLED offer? (c) What is AMOLED? Where do you typically find this technology? (d) Do you see yourself buying an LED monitor or TV? Why or why not?

### 4 Explorations: ROBOTS

Did you know that humanlike robots are being developed for research and education? Review the Explorations box on page 169 and then respond to the following: (a) How does this robot move? How is it able to maintain humanlike balance and stability? (b) How does this robot "see"? How does it "hear"? Can it recognize human voices and faces? If so, how? (c) How does this robot sense nearby objects? Can it sense if it is being touched? If so, how? (d) Do think this robot can be beneficial in education? Why or why not?

### 5 Ethics: WEBCAMS

Webcams can be set up almost anywhere by anyone. Once in place, these webcams can continuously broadcast images to the Internet. Some images can be very embarrassing to the individuals who were recorded. Review the Ethics box on page 161 and respond to the following: (a) Would you feel uncomfortable if a hidden webcam was recording you when you entered a private home or business? What if the video was broadcast online? Why or why not? (b) Do you think recording and broadcasting images without permission is an ethical or a privacy concern? What if that person is in a public place at the moment the recording took place? In your response, consider whether such ethical concerns are significant enough to warrant new laws and regulations. (c) Many cities use webcams or video cameras for traffic control purposes. If those cameras record a person engaged in an illegal or questionable activity that is not related to traffic, should law enforcement be able to use the video in court? Should a concerned parent or jealous spouse be able to access that video? Defend your responses.

## 6 Ethics: VIRTUAL REALITY

Virtual reality environments can allow individuals to engage in violent or sexual aggression toward another actor in order to reach a goal. Even though the situation is simulated, there are ethical concerns about the actions a person chooses in such environments. Review the Ethics box on page 172 and then respond to the following: (a) Are there any dangers of using the virtual world to escape the rules of the real world? Can such a person become dangerous when coming out of the virtual environment? Defend your answers. (b) Do you think accepted ethical standards in the real world should also govern behavior in virtual environments? Should they apply to those who write the software? How about the users? Why or why not? (c) Instead of sending criminals to prison, what if they were required to spend extended time in a virtual environment that functioned as a reprogramming tool to change their attitude and behavior? Would this be ethical? Why or why not?

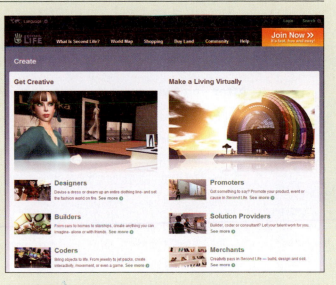

## 7 Environment: INKJET PRINTERS

Have you considered the environmental impact of using your inkjet printer? Review the Environment box on page 166 and then respond to the following: (a) How often do you use your printer at home? What sort of items do you typically print? (b) Have you considered any alternatives to printing? If so, what are those alternatives? Why would or wouldn't you use these alternatives? (c) Does the manufacturer of your ink cartridges use recycled plastic? Support your answer with details from the manufacturer's website. (d) Find a store near you that accepts used ink cartridges. Name the store, and provide details on the benefits it gives you for turning in cartridges.

## 8 Environment: ROBOTS AND POLLUTION

Did you know that robots are already being used to help the environment? Review the Environment box on page 169 and then respond to the following: (a) List two ways in which robots are helping the environment. (b) Using a search engine, find additional information on the robotic fish that will help detect pollution. Briefly describe how the robot will perform its function. Do you believe that this robot will eventually enjoy widespread use? Why or why not? (c) Do you see robots providing additional help with the environment in the future? Do you feel that future robots could harm the environment in any way? Explain your responses.

# Secondary Storage

▲ Download the free *Computing Essentials 2014* app for videos, key term flashcards, quizzes, and the game, *Over the Edge!*

## Competencies

**After you have read this chapter, you should be able to:**

1 Distinguish between primary and secondary storage.

2 Discuss the important characteristics of secondary storage including media, capacity, storage devices, and access speed.

3 Describe hard-disk platters, tracks, sectors, cylinders, and head crashes.

4 Compare internal and external hard drives.

5 Discuss performance enhancements including disk caching, RAID, file compression, and file decompression.

6 Define optical storage including compact discs, digital versatile discs, and Blu-ray discs.

7 Define solid-state storage including solid-state drives, flash memory cards, and USB drives.

8 Define cloud storage and cloud storage services.

9 Discuss mass storage, mass storage devices, enterprise storage systems, and storage area networks.

## Why should I read this chapter?

One of the earliest secondary storage materials was the floppy disk, capable of storing less than one-half megabyte of data. That's not even enough to store one digital photograph! That was then and this is now. Now, we can store data and information using a variety of different types of media including hard disks, optical discs, and solid-state devices like flash memory and USB drives.

This chapter discusses a variety of different types of secondary storage including internal and external hard disks and a variety of optical discs including CDs, DVDs, and Blu-ray discs. Additionally, you'll learn about the advantages and disadvantages of cloud storage. Also, you'll learn about very large capacity storage devices including file servers, network application servers, and RAID systems. To be competent and to be competitive in today's professional workplace, you need to know and to understand these things.

## chapter 7

# Introduction

Secondary storage devices are used to save, to back up, and even to transport files consisting of data or programs from one location or computer to another. At one time, almost all files contained only numbers and letters. The demands for saving these files were easily met with low-capacity storage devices.

Data storage has expanded from text and numeric files to include digital music files, photographic files, video files, and much more. These new types of files require secondary storage devices that have much greater capacity.

Secondary storage devices have always been an indispensable element in any computer system. They have similarities to output and input devices. Like output devices, secondary storage devices receive information from the system unit in the form of the machine language of 0s and 1s. Rather than translating the information, however, secondary storage devices save the information in machine language for later use. Like input devices, secondary storage devices send information to the system unit for processing. However, the information, since it is already in machine form, does not need to be translated. It is sent directly to memory (RAM), where it can be accessed and processed by the CPU.

Competent end users need to be aware of the different types of secondary storage. They need to know the capabilities, limitations, and uses of hard disks, solid-state drives, optical discs, cloud storage, and other types of secondary storage. Additionally, they need to be aware of specialty storage devices for portable computers and to be knowledgeable about how large organizations manage their extensive data resources.

**Hi, I'm James, and I'm a disaster recovery specialist. I'd like to talk with you about secondary storage, one of the most critical parts of any computer system. I'd also like to talk about various cloud storage services.**

# Storage

An essential feature of every computer is the ability to save, or store, information. As discussed in Chapter 5, random-access memory (RAM) holds or stores data and programs that the CPU is presently processing. Before data can be processed or a program can be run, it must be in RAM. For this reason, RAM is sometimes referred to as **primary storage**.

Unfortunately, most RAM provides only temporary or volatile storage. That is, it loses all of its contents as soon as the computer is turned off. Its contents also are lost if there is a power failure that disrupts the electric current going into the system unit. This volatility results in a need for more permanent or nonvolatile storage for data and programs. We also need external storage because users need much more storage capacity than is typically available in a computer's primary or RAM memory.

**Secondary storage** provides permanent or nonvolatile storage. Using **secondary storage devices** such as a hard-disk drive, data and programs can be retained after the computer has been shut off. This is accomplished by *writing* files to and *reading* files from secondary storage devices. Writing is the process of saving information *to* the secondary storage device. Reading is the process of accessing information *from* secondary storage. This chapter focuses on secondary storage devices.

Some important characteristics of secondary storage include

- **Media** are the actual physical material that holds the data and programs. (See Figure 7-1.)
- **Capacity** measures how much a particular storage medium can hold.
- **Storage devices** are hardware that reads data and programs from storage media. Most also write to storage media.
- **Access speed** measures the amount of time required by the storage device to retrieve data and programs.

Most desktop microcomputer systems have hard-disk and optical disc drives, as well as ports where additional storage devices can be connected.

# Hard Disks

Hard disks save files by altering the magnetic charges of the disk's surface to represent 1s and 0s. Hard disks retrieve data and programs by reading these charges from the magnetic disk. Characters are represented by positive (+) and negative (−) charges using the ASCII, EBCDIC, or Unicode binary codes. For example, the letter A would require a series of 8 charges. (See Figure 7-2.) **Density** refers to how tightly these charges can be packed next to one another on the disk.

**Hard disks** use rigid metallic **platters** that are stacked one on top of another. Hard disks store and organize files using tracks, sectors, and cylinders. **Tracks** are rings of concentric circles without visible grooves. Each track is divided into invisible wedge-shaped sections called **sectors**. (See Figure 7-3.) A **cylinder** runs through each track of a stack of platters. Cylinders are necessary to differentiate files stored on the same track and sector of different platters. When a hard disk is formatted, tracks, sectors, and cylinders are assigned.

**Figure 7-1  Secondary storage media**

**Figure 7-2  How charges on a disk surface store the letter A**

**Figure 7-3  Tracks and sectors**

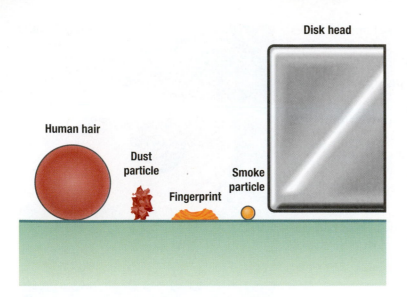

Disk head

Human hair

Dust particle

Fingerprint

Smoke particle

**Figure 7-4** Materials that can cause a head crash

Hard disks are sensitive instruments. Their read/write heads ride on a cushion of air about 0.000001 inch thick. It is so thin that a smoke particle, fingerprint, dust, or human hair could cause what is known as a head crash. (See Figure 7-4.)

A **head crash** occurs when a read/write head makes contact with the hard disk's surface or with particles on its surface. A head crash is a disaster for a hard disk. The disk surface is scratched, and some or all of the data is destroyed. At one time, head crashes were commonplace. Now, fortunately, they are rare.

There are two basic types of hard disks: internal and external.

### Internal Hard Disk

An **internal hard disk** is located inside the system unit. These hard disks are able to store and retrieve large quantities of information quickly. They are used to store programs and data files. For example, nearly every microcomputer uses its internal hard disk to store its operating system and major applications such as Word and Excel.

To see how a hard disk works, visit our website at www.computing2014.com and enter the keyword **disk**.

To ensure adequate performance of your internal hard disk and the safety of your data, you should perform routine maintenance and periodically make backup copies of all important files. For hard-disk maintenance and backup procedures, refer to Chapter 4's coverage of the Windows utilities Backup and Restore, Disk Cleanup, and Disk Defragmenter.

### External Hard Drives

While internal hard disks provide fast access, they have a fixed amount of storage and cannot be easily removed from the system unit. External hard disks typically connect to a USB or FireWire port on the system unit and are easily removed. Like an internal hard disk, external hard disks have a fixed amount of storage. However, since each removable hard disk can be easily replaced by another removable hard disk, a single port on the system unit can provide access to an unlimited amount of storage. (See Figure 7-5.)

**Figure 7-5** External hard drive

**External hard drives** use the same basic technology as internal hard disks and are used primarily to complement an internal hard disk. Because they are easily removed, they are particularly useful to protect or secure sensitive information. Other uses for external drives include backing up the contents of the internal hard disk and providing additional hard-disk capacity.

### Performance Enhancements

Three ways to improve the performance of hard disks are disk caching, redundant arrays of inexpensive disks, and file compression/decompression.

**Disk caching** improves hard-disk performance by anticipating data needs. It performs a function similar to cache memory discussed in Chapter 5. While cache memory improves processing by acting as a temporary high-speed holding area between memory and the CPU, disk caching improves processing by acting as a temporary high-speed holding area between a secondary storage device and the CPU. Disk caching requires a combination of hardware and software. During idle processing time, frequently used data is automatically identified and read from the hard disk into memory (cache). When needed, the data is then accessed directly from memory. The transfer rate from memory is much faster than from the hard disk. As a result, overall system performance is often increased by as much as 30 percent.

Figure 7-6 **RAID storage device**

**Redundant arrays of inexpensive disks (RAID)** improve performance by expanding external storage, improving access speed, and providing reliable storage. Several inexpensive hard-disk drives are connected to one another. These connections can be by a network or within specialized RAID devices. (See Figure 7-6.) The connected hard-disk drives are related or grouped together, and the computer system interacts with the RAID system as though it were a single large-capacity hard-disk drive. The result is expanded storage capability, fast access speed, and high reliability. For these reasons, RAID is often used by Internet servers and large organizations.

**File compression** and **file decompression** increase storage capacity by reducing the amount of space required to store data and programs. File compression is not limited to hard-disk systems. It is frequently used to compress files on DVDs, CDs, and flash drives as well. File compression also helps to speed up transmission of files from one computer system to another. Sending and receiving compressed files across the Internet is a common activity.

File compression programs scan files for ways to reduce the amount of required storage. One way is to search for repeating patterns. The repeating patterns are replaced with a token, leaving enough tokens so that the original can be rebuilt or decompressed. These programs often shrink files to a quarter of their original size. To learn more about file compression, visit our website at www.computing2014.com and enter the keyword **compression**.

You can compress and decompress files using specialized utilities such as WinZip. Or, if a specialized utility is not available, you can use utility programs in Windows. For a summary of performance enhancement techniques, see Figure 7-7.

| Technique | Description |
|---|---|
| Disk caching | Uses cache and anticipates data needs |
| RAID | Linked, inexpensive hard-disk drives |
| File compression | Reduces file size |
| File decompression | Expands compressed files |

Figure 7-7 **Performance enhancement techniques**

**concept check**

Discuss four important characteristics of secondary storage.

What are the two types of hard disks? Briefly describe each.

What is density? What are tracks, sectors, cylinders, and head crashes?

List and describe three ways to improve the performance of hard disks.

# Optical Discs

## ethics

Almost all music and movies are protected by copyright laws that prohibit unauthorized copying and distribution. However, there are numerous websites and file-sharing services that allow individuals to download illegal copies of these files, which can then be recorded to a CD or DVD. Individuals and organizations owning the copyrights argue that those who engage in these actions are acting unethically and that they should be prosecuted for violating copyright law. What do you think? To see more ethical issues, visit our website at www.computing2014.com and enter the keyword ethics.

Today's **optical discs** can hold over 100 gigabytes of data. (See Figure 7-8.) That is the equivalent of millions of typewritten pages or a medium-sized library all on a single disc. Optical discs are having a great impact on storage today, but we are probably only beginning to see their effects.

In optical disc technology, a laser beam alters the surface of a plastic or metallic disc to represent data. Unlike hard disks, which use magnetic charges to represent 1s and 0s, optical discs use reflected light. The 1s and 0s are represented by flat areas called **lands** and bumpy areas called **pits** on the disc surface. The disc is read by an **optical disc drive** using a laser that projects a tiny beam of light on these areas. The amount of reflected light determines whether the area represents a 1 or a 0. To see how an optical disc drive works, visit our website at www.computing2014.com and enter the keyword optical.

Like hard disks, optical discs use tracks and sectors to organize and store files. Unlike the concentric tracks and wedge-shaped sectors used for hard disks, however, optical discs typically use a single track that spirals toward the center of the disc. This single track is divided into equally sized sectors.

The most widely used optical discs are CD, DVD, and Blu-ray discs.

### Compact Disc

**Compact disc**, or as it is better known, **CD**, was the most widely used optical format. CD drives were standard on many microcomputer systems. Typically, CD drives can store 700 MB (megabytes) of data on one side of a CD.

There are three basic types of CDs: read only, write once, and rewritable:

**Figure 7-8** Optical disc

- **Read only—CD-ROM**, which stands for **compact disc–read-only memory**, is similar to a commercial music CD. *Read only* means it cannot be written on or erased by the user. Thus, you as a user have access only to the data imprinted by the publisher. CD-ROMs are used to distribute large databases and references. They also are used to distribute software application packages.

- **Write once—CD-R**, which stands for **CD-recordable**, can be written to once. After that it can be read many times without deterioration but cannot be written on or erased. CD-R drives often are used to archive data and to record music downloaded from the Internet.

- **Rewritable—CD-RW** stands for **compact disc rewritable**. Also known as **erasable optical discs**, these discs are very similar to CD-Rs except that the disc surface is not permanently altered when data is recorded. Because they can be changed, CD-RWs are often used to create and edit multimedia presentations.

### Digital Versatile Disc

**DVD** stands for **digital versatile disc** or **digital video disc**. This disc has replaced CDs as the standard optical disc. DVDs are very similar to CDs except that more data can be packed into the same amount of space. (See Figure 7-9.) Typically, DVD discs can store 4.7 GB (gigabytes) on one side of a DVD disc—7 times the capacity of CDs. There are three basic types of DVDs, similar to CDs: read only, write once, and rewritable.

**Figure 7-9** DVD disc drive

- **Read only—DVD-ROM** stands for **digital versatile disc–read-only memory**. DVD-ROM drives are also known as **DVD players**. DVD-ROMs are having a major impact on the video market. While CD-ROMs are effective for distributing music, they can only contain just over an hour of fair-quality video. DVD-ROMs can provide over two hours of high-quality video and sound comparable to that found in motion picture theaters. DVD-ROMs are widely used to distribute videos and software.
- **Write once—DVD+R** and **DVD-R** are two competing write-once formats. Both stand for **DVD recordable**. Each has a slightly different way in which it formats its discs. Fortunately, most new DVD players can use either format. These drives are typically used to create permanent archives for large amounts of data and to record videos. DVD recordable drives are rapidly replacing CD-R drives due to their massive capacity.
- **Rewritable**—The three most widely used rewritable formats are **DVD+RW (DVD rewritable)**, **DVD-RW (DVD rewritable)**, and **DVD-RAM (DVD random-access memory)**. Each format has a unique way of storing data. Unfortunately, older DVD players typically can read only one type of format. Newer DVD players, however, are able to read and use any of the formats. Rewritable DVD disc drives have rapidly replaced CD rewritable drives. Applications range from recording video from camcorders to developing multimedia presentations that include extensive graphics and video.

### Blu-ray Disc

While CDs and DVDs represent the past and the present for optical disc storage, the future belongs to discs of even greater capacity. While DVD discs have sufficient capacity to record standard-definition movies and music, they are insufficient for recording high-definition video, which requires about four times as much storage. This next generation of optical disc is called **hi def (high definition)**, with a far greater capacity than DVDs. The hi-def standard is **Blu-ray disc (BD)**. The name comes from the blue-colored laser that is used to read the disc.

## environment

Did you know that many companies are now working to minimize the environmental impact of their products? Sony, which makes Blu-ray players, strives to make these products smaller in order to reduce the materials used in production. Furthermore, smaller products fit in smaller boxes, which reduce the amount of shipping containers needed for transportation. This, in turn, lowers emissions from vehicles used in shipping and distribution. Lastly, improvements in circuits and processors result in more energy-efficient devices. For example, one recent Blu-ray player from Sony uses 55 percent less energy than its predecessor. To see more environmental facts, visit our website at www.computing2014 .com and enter the keyword environment.

| Format | Typical Capacity | Description |
|--------|------------------|-------------|
| CD | 700 MB | Once the standard optical disc |
| DVD | 4.7 GB | Current standard |
| Blu-ray | 50 GB | Hi-def format, large capacity |

**Figure 7-10 Types of optical discs**

Typically, Blu-ray discs have a capacity of 50 GB on one side, more than 10 times the capacity of a standard single-layer DVD. Although Blu-ray media are the same size as other optical media, the discs require special drives. Most of these drives are capable of reading standard DVDs and CDs in addition to Blu-ray.

Like CDs and DVDs, Blu-ray has three basic types: read only, write once, and rewritable. As with any optical disc, a device with recording capabilities is required for writing data.

For a summary of the different types of optical discs, see Figure 7-10.

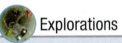

## concept check

How is data represented on optical discs?

Compare CD and DVD formats. Why did DVDs replace CDs?

What is hi def? What is Blu-ray? Compare Blu-ray to standard DVD.

# Solid-State Storage

Unlike hard disks, which rotate and have read/write heads that move in and out, **solid-state storage** devices have no moving parts. Data and information are stored and retrieved electronically directly from these devices much as they would be from conventional computer memory.

### Solid-State Drives

**Solid-state drives (SSDs)** are designed to be connected inside a microcomputer system the same way an internal hard disk would be but contain solid-state memory instead of magnetic disks to store data. (See Figure 7-11.) SSDs are faster and more durable than hard disks. SSDs also require less power, which can lead to increased battery life for laptops and mobile devices. SSDs are more expensive and generally have a lower capacity than hard disks, but this is changing as the popularity of SSDs continues to increase. SDDs are widely used for tablet PCs, such as the iPad.

### Flash Memory Cards

**Flash memory cards** are small solid-state storage devices widely used in portable devices. Some of the cards are used within devices such as smartphones, digital media players, and GPS navigation systems. (See Figure 7-12.) Other cards provide removable storage. For example, flash memory is used to store images captured from digital cameras and then to transfer the images

**Figure 7-11 Solid-state drive**

**Figure 7-12** Flash memory card

**Figure 7-13** USB drive

to desktop and other computers. Flash memory is used in digital media players like the iPod to store and play music and video files.

### USB Drives

**USB drives**, or **flash drives**, are so compact that they can be transported on a key ring. (See Figure 7-13.) These drives conveniently connect directly to a computer's USB port to transfer files and can have capacities ranging from 1 GB to 256 GB, with a broad price range to match. Due to their convenient size and large capacities, USB drives have become a very popular option for transporting data and information between computers, specialty devices, and the Internet.

**tips**

Have you ever accidentally deleted or lost important files from your flash drive? Do you have a USB flash drive that is no longer being recognized by your computer? Here are a few suggestions that might help.

**1** **Recovery/undelete software.** If you accidentally deleted files from a USB drive, it is unlikely that you can recover them using your operating system or searching through your recycle bin. Fortunately, there are several recovery (or undelete) programs that might help and some are even free. For example, two free programs are *Undelete 360* and *Recuva*. These programs will scan your flash drives for deleted files and offer you a chance to recover the ones you want back.

**2** **Testing USB ports.** If your computer does not recognize your USB flash drive, there could be a problem with your USB port. Try plugging another device into that same port to see if it works. If this device does not work, then your computer's USB is most likely defective and needs to be replaced. If the device works, then most likely your USB flash drive is damaged and you should try the professional recovery services discussed in the next step.

**3** **Professional recovery services.** For damaged flash drives, there is a possibility that your data could be recovered by several companies that are dedicated to data recovery. Although the fees are high, they can rescue data from the actual memory chip, even if the drive or supporting circuits are damaged.

To see other tips, visit our website at www.computing2014.com and enter the keyword tips.

### concept check

What is solid-state storage?

Compare solid-state technology to that used in hard disks.

What are solid-state storage devices?

What are flash memory cards? What are they used for?

What are USB drives? What are they used for?

# Cloud Storage

Recently, many applications that would have required installation on your computer to run have moved to the web. Numerous websites now exist to provide application services. As we discussed in Chapter 2, this is known as **cloud computing**,

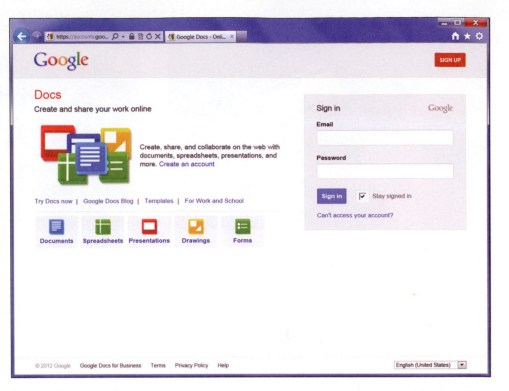

**Figure 7-14 Google Docs**

| Company | Location |
|---------|----------|
| Dropbox | www.dropbox.com |
| Google | drive.google.com |
| Microsoft | www.skydrive.com |
| Amazon | amazon.com/cloud |
| SugarSync | www.sugarsync.com |

**Figure 7-15 Cloud storage services**

where the Internet acts as a "cloud" of servers that supply applications to clients as a *service* rather than a *product*. Additionally, these servers provide **cloud storage**, also known as **online storage**.

If you have used Google Docs to create a word processing document or a spreadsheet, used Mint.com to manage your financial information, or stored data using Amazon S3, you have already used cloud computing. (See Figure 7-14.) The processing power of the service provider's server is used to run the applications, and your local computer is responsible only for displaying the results. The applications and data can be accessed from any Internet-ready device. This means that even devices with little storage, memory, or processing power, such as mobile smartphones, can run the same powerful applications as a desktop computer.

The benefits to this arrangement are numerous. Imagine how much easier it would be to install or upgrade software in a large company. In the past, a software technician would need to visit every computer the company owned to install the software from disk and manage licensing for the number of computers the software was purchased for. With software delivered from the cloud as a service, the company can simply purchase the appropriate number of accounts from the service provider and direct employees to use the provider's website.

There are numerous websites that provide cloud storage services. (See Figure 7-15.) To learn more about how you could use cloud storage, see Making IT Work for You: Cloud Storage on pages 197 and 198.

 **concept check**

What is cloud computing?

What is cloud storage?

What are the benefits of cloud storage?

## CLOUD STORAGE

Have you ever found yourself e-mailing files back and forth between two of your computers as a way to transport them? Do you keep forgetting your USB drive at school or work? Have you ever wished that you had some of your files readily available on your smartphone? If so, then you should sign up for Dropbox.

**Getting Started**   To use Dropbox, you need to create an account. To take advantage of the synchronization feature, you will need to install the software on each of your computers.

1. ● Go to www.dropbox.com, and click the *Download Dropbox* button.

2. ● Select the "I don't have a Dropbox account" option during the installation process (if this is your first installation).

3. ● Enter your information to create a new account.

4. ● Select the *Free* option when asked for a Dropbox size, and then choose the *Typical* setup.

5. ● Continue clicking the *Next* button to view the important tour.

   If you have a tablet or smartphone, be sure to install its free app in order to access your files.

**The Dropbox Folder**   After installation, a folder named "Dropbox" will be created on your hard drive and connected to your computer's user account. This folder is the basis for all synchronization—any files placed here will immediately be uploaded to your Dropbox account and will be kept synchronized between all your computers. A good use of this folder would be to place all of your schoolwork and favorite photos, so that you can access them from any Internet-connected computer, tablet, or smartphone. Follow these steps to use your Dropbox folder:

1. ● Open Windows Explorer, and look at your *Favorites* area.

2. ● Click the *Dropbox* folder, and notice the files and folders already in there. Open the *Photos* subfolder.

3. ● Create a subfolder in this location named "Practice" (this will serve as a photo gallery or album).

4. ● Copy any photo from your computer and paste it in this new folder.

**197**

Notice the tiny, blue *synchronization icon* at the bottom left of your file. When this icon turns into a green check mark, it means that the file has finished uploading to the Dropbox server. The same system is used for the Dropbox icon in your Windows notification area.

**Sharing Files**  Any file or folder in your Dropbox account can be shared with anyone via a unique link. This method is superior to sending large e-mail attachments that can be subject to the limits of the e-mail service. To share a file or folder:

**1**  Go to your Dropbox folder using Windows Explorer.

**2**  Right-click any file or folder, click *Dropbox,* and click *Get link.* Your browser will automatically navigate to the Dropbox website, where you will see a unique URL in the address bar. This is the URL that you will give to anyone with whom you want to share this file or folder.

**3**  Click the button that looks like a gear (top right of the website), and select the *Remove link* option if you no longer wish to share this content.

**Getting More Storage Space**  Dropbox's free service includes all its features, but with a limited amount of storage space. You can increase that space with a paid account or by inviting friends and colleagues to join. (Dropbox increases your storage each time one of them signs up.)

**1**  Go to the Dropbox website, and log in to your account.

**2**  Click the *Get free space!* link at the top right of the page. Follow the instructions to invite others to use Dropbox.

**3**  Alternatively, click the *Get Started* link on the left. This area helps you keep track of your progress toward receiving a 250 MB bonus.

The web is continually changing, and some of the specifics presented in this Making IT Work for You may have changed.

**To learn about other ways to make information technology work for you, visit our website at www .computing2014.com and enter the keyword miw.**

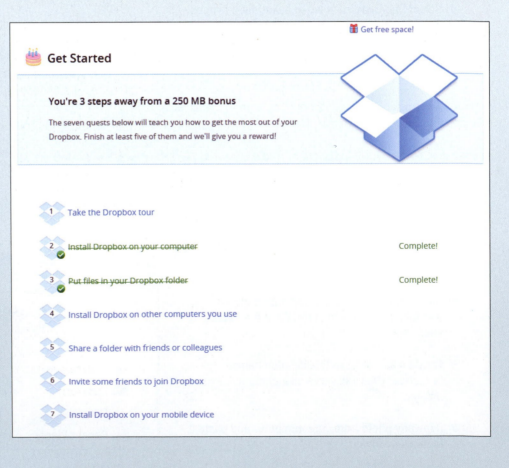

# Mass Storage Devices

It is natural to think of secondary storage media and devices as they relate to us as individuals. It may not be as obvious how important these matters are to organizations. **Mass storage** refers to the tremendous amount of secondary storage required by large organizations. **Mass storage devices** are specialized high-capacity secondary storage devices designed to meet organizational demands for data.

### Enterprise Storage System

Most large organizations have established a strategy called an **enterprise storage system** to promote efficient and safe use of data across the networks within their organizations. (See Figure 7-16.) Some of the mass storage devices that support this strategy are

- **File servers**—dedicated computers with very large storage capacities that provide users access to fast storage and retrieval of data.
- **Network attached storage (NAS)**—similar to a file server except simpler and less expensive; widely used for home and small business storage needs.
- **RAID systems**—larger versions of the specialized devices discussed earlier in this chapter that enhance organizational security by constantly making backup copies of files moving across the organization's networks.

Figure 7-16 Enterprise storage system

- **Tape library**—device that provides automatic access to data archived on a library of tapes.
- **Organizational cloud storage**—high-speed Internet connection to a dedicated remote organizational cloud storage server.

### Storage Area Network

A recent mass storage development is **storage area network (SAN)** systems. SAN is an architecture to link remote computer storage devices, such as enterprise storage systems, to computers such that the devices are as available as locally attached drives. In a SAN system, the user's computer provides the file system for storing data, but the SAN provides the disk space for data.

The key to a SAN is a high-speed network, connecting individual computers to mass storage devices. Special file systems prevent simultaneous users from interfering with each other. SANs provide the ability to house data in remote locations and still allow efficient and secure access.

### Explorations

Are SANs going to make tape libraries obsolete?

**To learn more about tapes and other storage devices used for archiving, visit our website at www.computing2014.com and enter the keyword tape.**

## concept check

Define mass storage and list five mass storage devices.

What is an enterprise storage system?

What is a storage area network system?

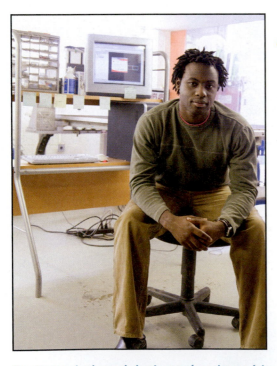

Now that you've learned about secondary storage, let me tell you a little bit about my career as a disaster recovery specialist.

# Careers in IT

**Disaster recovery specialists** are responsible for recovering systems and data after a disaster strikes an organization. In addition, they often create plans to prevent and prepare for such disasters. A crucial part of that plan is to use storage devices and media in order to ensure that all company data is backed up and, in some cases, stored off-site.

Employers typically look for candidates with a bachelor's or advanced specialized associate's degree in information systems or computer science. Experience in this field is usually required, and additional skills in the areas of networking, security, and database administration are desirable. Disaster recovery specialists should possess good communication skills and be able to handle high-stress situations.

Disaster recovery specialists can expect to earn an annual salary of $70,000 to $103,000. Opportunities for advancement typically include upper-management positions. With so many types of threats facing organizations, demand for these types of specialists is expected to grow. To learn about other careers in information technology, visit us at www.computing2014.com and enter the keyword **careers**.

# A LOOK TO THE FUTURE

## Next-Generation Storage

Have you already started to use a cloud storage service for your files? Have your friends and family members used one also? With millions of individuals and businesses all signing up for these services, how do these companies keep up with the amount of storage required to accommodate all these users? The answer is simple: They keep adding more hard drives. However, at some point, hard drives will no longer be able to increase in capacity, and companies may run out of the physical space to keep adding more. Therefore, researchers are looking into new technology to increase the capacity of existing storage solutions, as well as reduce the size of current storage media.

The first product that will receive a huge improvement is the hard drive. When it comes to the primary storage of your computer and the millions of servers throughout the world, nothing beats hard drives. They are the most affordable solution when it comes to the price per gigabyte. Therefore, researchers are looking at ways of increasing their capacity without increasing their size. Current hard drive technology will max out at approximately 128 GB per square inch. Seagate, a manufacturer of hard drives, is working on two new technologies that hope to increase that limit: heat-assisted magnetic recording (HAMR) and bit-patterned media (BPM). The idea is to keep making the bits smaller so that more of them fit in the same area. Once these technologies are implemented, the capacity could reach 6.25 TB (or 6,250 GB) per square inch. With a density like that, Seagate estimates that you could hold the entire contents of the U.S. Library of Congress on a disk that is no bigger than a coin.

The latest optical disc, Blu-ray, is commercially available as 25- or 50-GB discs. Although several companies have achieved higher limits by adding more layers, a ceiling will soon be hit. GE Global Research is currently developing a disc made up of tiny holograms, stored over dozens of layers, that react to light. These discs will store 1 TB of data, and the drives that read them will also be able to read your DVD and Blu-ray discs.

Advancements in chemistry have led to the speculation that circuits and storage media could soon be working with carbon-containing molecules. Researchers have discovered that a group of compounds known as *metallofullerenes* can be oriented in various ways, allowing them to represent 0 and 1 bits just as other storage media currently do. The biggest advantage of working with organic molecules involves size. These molecules are so small that storage devices created with them could be extremely tiny, allowing the creation of much smaller computers and gadgets.

You may be wondering why solid-state storage, or flash memory, has not yet been mentioned. This type of media has definitely been improving over the years. Your flash drives and memory cards keep getting smaller and capacities keep going up. However, the price per gigabyte is still much higher than that of hard drives. Furthermore, they have a limited life span because they can only support approximately 10,000 write operations. These two issues may not be a problem for individuals, but they make it impossible for large businesses and cloud storage companies to rely on them.

Now that several types of future technologies have been explored, which do you see yourself using in five years? Do you believe that solid-state storage will completely replace the hard drive in desktop and notebook computers? Do you think that molecule-sized storage solutions will ever be affordable enough to be used in all computers?

## STORAGE

## HARD DISKS

A

RAM is **primary storage**. Most RAM is volatile, meaning that it loses its contents whenever power is disrupted. **Secondary storage** provides nonvolatile storage. Secondary storage retains data and information after the computer system is turned off.

Writing is the process of saving information to **secondary storage devices**. Reading is the process of accessing information from secondary storage devices.

Important characteristics of secondary storage include

- **Media**—actual physical material that retains data and programs.
- **Capacity**—how much a particular storage medium can hold.
- **Storage devices**—hardware that reads and writes to storage media.
- **Access speed**—time required to retrieve data from a secondary storage device.

**Hard disks** use rigid metallic **platters** that provide a large amount of capacity. They store data and programs by altering the electromagnetic charges on the platter's surface. Files are organized according to

- **Tracks**—concentric rings without visible grooves.
- **Sectors**—wedge-shaped sections.
- **Cylinders**—run through each track of a stack of platters.

**Density** refers to how tightly electromagnetic charges can be packed next to one another on the disk.

A **head crash** occurs when the hard disk makes contact with the drive's read/write heads.

Two types of hard disks are internal and external hard disks.

### Internal Hard Disk

**Internal hard disks** are located within the system unit. Used to store programs and data files.

To be a competent end user, you need to be aware of the different types of secondary storage. You need to know their capabilities, limitations, and uses. There are four widely used storage media: hard disk, optical disc, solid-state, and cloud storage.

## HARD DISKS

### External Hard Drives

Unlike internal hard disks, **external hard drives** are removable. External drives use the same basic technology as internal disks.

### Performance Enhancements

Three ways to improve hard-disk performance are disk caching, RAID, and file compression and decompression.

- **Disk caching**—provides a temporary high-speed holding area between a secondary storage device and the CPU; improves performance by anticipating data needs and reducing time to access data from secondary storage.
- **RAID (redundant array of inexpensive disks)**— several inexpensive hard-disk drives are connected together; improves performance by providing expanded storage, fast access, and high reliability.
- **File compression and decompression**—files compressed before storing and then decompressed before being used again; improves performance through efficient storage.

## OPTICAL DISCS

**Optical discs** use laser technology. 1s and 0s are represented by **pits** and **lands**. **Optical disc drives** project light and measure the reflected light.

### Compact Disc

**Compact discs (CDs)** have typical capacity of 700 MB on one side. Three types are **CD-ROM (compact disc–read-only memory)**, **CD-R (CD-recordable; CD-R** drives are also known as CD burners), and **CD-RW (compact disc rewritable, erasable optical discs)**.

### Digital Versatile Disc

**DVDs (digital versatile discs, digital video discs)** have far greater capacity than CDs with a typical capacity of 4.7 GB on one side. Three types are **DVD-ROM (digital versatile disc–read-only memory; DVD players** are drives), write once (**DVD+R, DVD-R**), and rewritable (**DVD+RW, DVD-RW, DVD-RAM**).

### Blu-ray Disc

Hi-def (high-definition) Blu-ray discs are the next standard optical disc. **Blu-ray discs (BDs)** have a capacity of 50 GB on one side. Same size as other optical media, but much greater capacity and requires special drives. Three basic types: read only, write once, and rewritable.

## SOLID-STATE STORAGE

Solid-state storage devices have no moving parts and are more reliable and require less power than hard disks.

### Solid-State Drives

Solid-state drives are similar to internal hard-disk drives except they use solid-state memory; are faster, more durable, and more expensive; and generally provide less capacity.

### Flash Memory Cards

Flash memory cards are small solid-state storage devices that are widely used with notebook computers. They are used with a variety of specialized input devices including digital cameras to store and transfer images and digital media players like the iPod to store and transfer music and video files.

### USB Drives

USB drives (flash drives) are so small that they fit onto a key ring. These drives connect to a computer's USB port and are widely used to transfer data and information between computers, specialty devices, and the Internet.

## CLOUD STORAGE

With cloud computing, the Internet acts as a "cloud" of servers that supply applications to clients as a service rather than a product. Cloud storage (online storage) is supplied by servers.

- Examples include Google Docs for word processing and spreadsheets, Mint.com for financial management, and Amazon S3 for storing data.
- Cloud servers provide storage, processing, and memory.
- With cloud computing software, installation and upgrade are avoided.

## MASS STORAGE DEVICES

Mass storage refers to the tremendous amount of secondary storage required by large organizations. Mass storage devices are specialized high-capacity secondary storage devices.

Most large organizations have established a strategy called an enterprise storage system to promote efficient and safe use of data across the networks within their organizations.

Mass storage devices that support this strategy are file servers, network attached storage (NAS), RAID systems, tape libraries, and organizational cloud storage. A storage area network (SAN) is a method of using enterprise-level remote storage systems as if they were local to your computer.

## CAREERS IN IT

Disaster recovery specialists are responsible for recovering systems and data after a disaster strikes an organization. Bachelor's or advanced specialized associate's degree in information systems or computer science, experience, and additional skills in the areas of networking, security, and database administration are desirable. Salary range is $70,000 to $103,000.

# KEY TERMS

access speed (189)
Blu-ray disc (BD) (193)
capacity (189)
CD (compact disc) (192)
CD-R (CD-recordable) (192)
CD-ROM (compact disc–read-only memory) (192 )
CD-RW (compact disc rewritable) (193)
cloud computing (195)
cloud storage (196)
cylinder (189)
density (189)
disaster recovery specialist (200)
disk caching (190)
DVD (digital versatile disc or digital video disc) (193)
DVD player (193)
DVD-R (DVD recordable) (193)
DVD+R (DVD recordable) (193)
DVD-RAM (DVD random-access memory) (193)
DVD-ROM (DVD–read-only memory) (193)
DVD-RW (DVD rewritable) (193)
DVD+RW (DVD rewritable) (193)
enterprise storage system (199)
erasable optical disc (192)
external hard drive (190)
file compression (191)
file decompression (191)
file server (199)

flash drive (195)
flash memory card (194)
hard disk (189)
head crash (190)
hi def (high definition) (193)
internal hard disk (190)
land (192)
mass storage (199)
mass storage devices (199)
media (189)
network attached storage (NAS) (199)
online storage (196)
optical disc (192)
optical disc drive (192)
organizational cloud storage (200)
pit (192)
platter (189)
primary storage (188)
RAID system (199)
redundant array of inexpensive disks (RAID) (191)
secondary storage (188)
secondary storage device (188)
sector (189)
solid-state drive (SSD) (194)
solid-state storage (194)
storage area network (SAN) (200)
storage device (189)
tape library (200)
track (189)
USB drive (195)

To test your knowledge of these key terms with animated flash cards, visit our website at www.computing2014.com and enter the keyword terms7. Or use the free *Computing Essentials 2014* app.

# MULTIPLE CHOICE

Circle the letter of the correct answer.

1. RAM is sometimes referred to as:
   - **a.** primary storage
   - **b.** ratio active memory
   - **c.** read-only memory
   - **d.** secondary storage

2. The actual physical material that holds the data and programs.
   - **a.** primary storage
   - **b.** media
   - **c.** capacity
   - **d.** access

3. Measures how tightly the magnetic charges can be packed next to one another on the disk.
   - **a.** density
   - **b.** cylinders
   - **c.** tracks
   - **d.** sectors

4. When a read/write head makes contact with the hard disk's surface, it causes a head:
   - **a.** crash
   - **b.** land
   - **c.** pit
   - **d.** scratch

5. This hard-disk performance enhancement anticipates data needs.
   - **a.** disk caching
   - **b.** file compression
   - **c.** file decompression
   - **d.** RAID

6. This type of storage uses pits and lands to represent 1s and 0s.
   - **a.** cloud
   - **b.** hard disk
   - **c.** optical
   - **d.** solid state

7. DVD stands for:
   - **a.** digital versatile disc
   - **b.** digital video data
   - **c.** dynamic versatile disc
   - **d.** dynamic video disc

8. USB drives are also known as:
   - **a.** flash drives
   - **b.** optical drives
   - **c.** ports
   - **d.** universal state bus

9. An organizational strategy to promote efficient and safe use of data across the networks.
   - **a.** cloud dynamic
   - **b.** data mission statement
   - **c.** enterprise storage system
   - **d.** RAID

10. A mass storage device that provides access to data archived on tapes.
    - **a.** file system
    - **b.** NAS
    - **c.** RAID system
    - **d.** tape library

For an interactive multiple-choice practice test, visit our website at www.computing2014.com and enter the keyword multiple7. Or use the free *Computing Essentials 2014* app.

# MATCHING

Match each numbered item with the most closely related lettered item. Write your answers in the spaces provided.

a. CD-R
b. file compression
c. formats
d. network attached storage
e. secondary storage
f. sectors
g. solid-state drives
h. storage area network
i. storage devices
j. tracks

____ 1. Provides permanent or nonvolatile storage.

____ 2. Hardware that reads data and programs from storage media.

____ 3. Rings of concentric circles without visible grooves on a hard-disk platter.

____ 4. Each track is divided into invisible wedge-shaped sections called _____.

____ 5. Increases storage capacity by reducing the amount of space required to store data and programs.

____ 6. Discs that can be written only one time.

____ 7. DVD+R and DVD-R are two competing write-once _____.

____ 8. Designed to be connected inside a microcomputer system the same way an internal hard disk would be but contains solid-state memory instead of magnetic disks to store data.

____ 9. Mass storage device that is similar to a file server and widely used for home and small business storage.

____ 10. An architecture to link remote computer storage devices, such as enterprise storage systems, to computers such that the devices are as available as locally attached drives.

For an interactive matching practice test, visit our website at www.computing2014.com and enter the keyword matching7. Or use the free *Computing Essentials 2014* app.

# OPEN-ENDED

On a separate sheet of paper, respond to each question or statement.

1. Compare primary storage and secondary storage, and discuss the most important characteristics of secondary storage.
2. Discuss hard disks including density, platters, tracks, sectors, cylinders, head crashes, internal, external, and performance enhancements.
3. Discuss optical discs including pits, lands, CDs, DVDs, Blu-ray, and hi def.
4. Discuss solid-state storage including solid-state drives, flash memory, and USB drives.
5. Discuss cloud computing and cloud storage.
6. Describe mass storage devices including enterprise storage systems, file servers, network attached storage, RAID systems, tape libraries, organizational cloud storage, and storage area network systems.

# DISCUSSION

Respond to each of the following questions.

### **1** Making IT Work for You: CLOUD STORAGE

Have you ever found yourself e-mailing files back and forth between two of your computers or with others as a way to transport them? Review the Making IT Work for You: Cloud Storage on pages 197 and 198. Then respond to the following: (a) Have you ever used Dropbox or a similar service? If so, what service have you used, and what do you typically use it for? If you have not used Dropbox or a similar service, describe how and why you might use one. (b) If you do not have a Dropbox account, set up a free one and create a Dropbox folder. Use Dropbox to either (1) access a file from another computer or (2) share a file with one of your classmates. Describe your experience. (c) Try a few of Dropbox's features, and describe your experience with these features. (d) Do you see yourself using Dropbox on an everyday basis? Why or why not?

### **2** Explorations: SD MEMORY CARDS

There are many capacities, sizes, and speeds for the popular SD memory cards. Review the Explorations box on page 194 and then respond to the following: (a) What are the three sizes for SD cards? (b) What is the difference between SD, SDHC, and SDXC? (c) What are the different speed classes for these cards? Which one(s) would you choose if you needed to record full HD video? (d) Look for any portable device, such as a smartphone or digital camera, that you currently own or would like to own. What type of memory card does it require? What capacity and speed would you consider buying for this device? Explain your answer.

### **3** Explorations: SYSTEM AREA NETWORK

Are SANs going to make tape libraries obsolete? Review the Explorations box on page 200 and then respond to the following: (a) What are some of the reasons to replace tape with SAN? (b) What is the main feature of tape storage that SAN cannot compete with? Why is this feature so crucial? (c) What are the disadvantages of using hot-swappable SATA drives? (d) Do you think solid-state drives will replace tapes one day? Why or why not?

### **4** Ethics: CUSTOM CDS AND DVDS

Creating a custom CD of your favorite music is a common activity. Although many sites on the web offer free music that you can download, not all music files can be legally copied. Review the Ethics box on page 192 and then respond to the following: (a) Why do you suppose that making and distributing music and movies on CDs and DVDs is receiving so much attention? (b) Is it legal to make a copy of a CD you have purchased? How about converting the music on the CD into MP3 files that are saved onto your computer? Defend your position. (c) Is this an ethical as well as a legal issue? Specifically, do you think it would be ethical to create a custom CD or DVD and then give it to a friend? What if you created the CD or DVD for your own use? Defend your position. (d) Do you believe that those who illegally download music and movies are behaving unethically? Why or why not? Would your answer change if you were an artist who produced music or movies? Explain your response.

 ## 5 Ethics: CLOUD STORAGE AND CONFIDENTIALITY

When individuals and businesses store files using cloud services, they expect the cloud company to behave ethically by providing adequate security to protect confidential files. What if this expectation is not met? Review the Ethics box on page 196 and then respond to the following: (a) Would you be comfortable if your attorney stored digital copies of your legal documents in the cloud? What about your doctor or psychologist? Why or why not? (b) Who should be responsible if files stored on the cloud are stolen or viewed by hackers or unethical employees? Who would suffer the consequences? Defend your position. (c) Should laws be created that require cloud storage companies to operate ethically and to assume responsibility for security and confidentiality of stored data? Why or why not? (d) Cloud computers are not necessarily located within the borders of the United States and therefore may not be subject to the same regulations as U.S.-based computers. Do you think that all U.S. companies should be required to keep their cloud servers in this country? Defend your response. (e) How do you feel about storing personal and confidential information in the cloud? Do you currently do it? Why or why not?

## 6 Environment: ECO-CONSCIOUS PRODUCTS

Did you know that many companies are now working to minimize the environmental impact of their products? Review the Environment box on page 193 and then respond to the following: (a) In what ways are Sony's newer Blu-ray players more environmentally friendly? (b) When purchasing a new product, do you consider its environmental impact? Why or why not? (c) If given the option to watch Blu-ray-quality movies online, would you choose this option over purchasing Blu-ray discs? Why or why not? Is one option more environmentally friendly than the other? Discuss your answer.

## 7 Environment: SOLID-STATE STORAGE

Did you know that traditional, magnetic hard-disk storage requires more energy than solid-state storage? Review the Environment box on page 194 and then respond to the following: (a) Why do you suppose that less energy is required for solid-state drives? (b) Why are not all hard drives being replaced with solid-state drives? (c) Do you think hard drives will become obsolete in the near future? Why or why not? (d) Would you be willing to pay more for a solid-state drive? If so, how much? If not, why not?

# Communications and Networks

▲ Download the free *Computing Essentials 2014* app for videos, key term flashcards, quizzes, and the game, *Over the Edge!*

## Competencies

**After you have read this chapter, you should be able to:**

1  Discuss connectivity, the wireless revolution, and communication systems.

2  Describe physical and wireless communications channels.

3  Discuss connection devices and services including dial-up, DSL, cable, satellite, and cellular.

4  Describe data transmission factors, including bandwidth and protocols.

5  Discuss networks and key network terminology including network interface cards and network operating systems.

6  Describe different types of networks, including local, home, wireless, personal, metropolitan, and wide area networks.

7  Describe network architectures, including topologies and strategies.

8  Discuss the organization issues related to Internet technologies and network security.

## Why should I read this chapter?

At one time, the wiring for computers was incredibly complicated with wires seemingly going everywhere. That was then and this is now. Do you know what is driving today's mobile computing? The iPhone, iPad, and other mobile computing devices use today's communication and network technologies. Specifically, it is the wireless revolution that is driving mobile computing.

This chapter discusses the wireless revolution, wireless connections including Wi-Fi, Bluetooth, and satellite connections. You'll also learn about hotspots, GPS, 4G networks, and protocols or rules that control the Internet. Additionally, you'll learn about home wireless networks and about firewalls to protect the privacy and security of networks. To be competent and to be competitive in today's professional workplace, you need to know and to understand these things.

## chapter .8

# Introduction

Hi, I'm Michael, and I'm a network administrator. I'd like to talk with you about computer communications and networks. I'd also like to talk about technologies that support mobile computing including global positioning systems, Wi-Fi, and 3G and 4G networks.

We live in a truly connected society. We can communicate almost instantaneously with others worldwide; changing events from the smallest of countries and places are immediately broadcast to the world; our e-mail messages are delivered to handheld devices; cars access the Internet to receive driving instructions and solve mechanical problems. Even household appliances can connect to the Internet and be remotely controlled. The communications and information options we have at our fingertips have changed how we react and relate to the world around us.

As the power and flexibility of our communication systems have expanded, the sophistication of the networks that support these systems has become increasingly critical and complex. The network technologies that handle our cellular, business, and Internet communications come in many different forms. Satellites, broadcast towers, telephone lines, even buried cables and fiber optics carry our telephone messages, e-mail, and text messages. These different networks must be able to efficiently and effectively integrate with one another.

Competent end users need to understand the concept of connectivity, wireless networking, and the elements that make up network and communications systems. Additionally, they need to understand the basics of communications channels, connection devices, data transmission, network types, network architectures, and organizational networks.

# Communications

Computer communications is the process of sharing data, programs, and information between two or more computers. We have discussed numerous applications that depend on communication systems, including

- **E-mail**—provides a fast, efficient alternative to traditional mail by sending and receiving electronic documents.
- **Texting**—provides very efficient direct text communication between individuals using short electronic messages.
- **Internet telephone**—provides a very low-cost alternative to long-distance telephone calls using electronic voice and video delivery.
- **Electronic commerce**—buying and selling goods electronically.

In this chapter, we will focus on the communication systems that support these and many other applications. Connectivity, the wireless revolution, and communication systems are key concepts and technologies for the 21st century.

### Connectivity

**Connectivity** is a concept related to using computer networks to link people and resources. For example, connectivity means that you can connect your microcomputer to other computers and information sources almost anywhere. With this connection, you are linked to the world of larger computers and the Internet. This includes hundreds of thousands of web servers and their extensive information resources. Thus, becoming computer competent and knowledgeable becomes a matter of knowing not only about connectivity through networks to microcomputers but also about larger computer systems and their information resources.

## The Wireless Revolution

The single most dramatic change in connectivity and communications in the past few years has been the widespread use of mobile devices like smartphones and tablets with wireless Internet connectivity. Students, parents, teachers, businesspeople, and others routinely talk and communicate with these devices. It is estimated that over 1.5 billion smartphones are in use worldwide. This wireless technology allows individuals to stay connected with one another from almost anywhere at any time.

**Figure 8-1  Wireless revolution**

So what's the revolution? While wireless technology was originally used primarily for voice communications, today's mobile computers support e-mail, web access, and a variety of Internet applications. In addition, wireless technology allows a wide variety of nearby devices to communicate with one another without any physical connection. You can share a high-speed printer, share data files, and collaborate on working documents with a nearby co-worker without having your computers connected by cables or telephone—wireless communication. High-speed Internet wireless technology allows individuals to connect to the Internet and share information from almost anywhere in the world. (See Figure 8-1.) But is it a revolution? Most experts say yes and that the revolution is just beginning.

## Communication Systems

**Communication systems** are electronic systems that transmit data from one location to another. Whether wired or wireless, every communication system has four basic elements. (See Figure 8-2.)

- **Sending and receiving devices**. These are often a computer or specialized communication device. They originate (send) as well as accept (receive) messages in the form of data, information, and/or instructions.
- **Connection devices**. These devices act as an interface between the sending and receiving devices and the communication channel. They convert outgoing messages into packets that can travel across the communication channel. They also reverse the process for incoming messages.

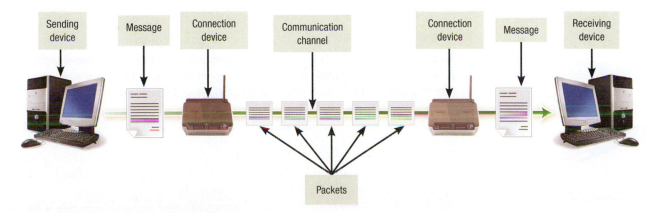

**Figure 8-2  Basic elements of a communication system**

- **Data transmission specifications**. These are rules and procedures that coordinate the sending and receiving devices by precisely defining how the message will be sent across the communication channel.
- **Communication channel**. This is the actual connecting or transmission medium that carries the message. This medium can be a physical wire or cable, or it can be wireless.

For example, if you wanted to send an e-mail to a friend, you could create and send the message using your computer, the *sending device.* Your modem, a *connection device,* would modify and format the message so that it could travel efficiently across *communication channels,* such as telephone lines. The specifics describing how the message is modified, reformatted, and sent would be described in the *data transmission specifications.* After your message traveled across the channel, the receiver's modem, a connection device, would reform it so that it could be displayed on your friend's computer, the *receiving device.* (Note: This example presents the basic communication system elements involved in sending e-mail. It does not and is not intended to demonstrate all the specific steps and equipment involved in an e-mail delivery system.)

## concept check

Define computer communications and connectivity.

What is the wireless revolution?

Describe the four elements of every communication system.

# Communication Channels

**Communication channels** are an essential element of every communication system. These channels actually carry the data from one computer to another. There are two categories of communication channels. One category connects sending and receiving devices by providing a physical connection, such as a wire or cable. The other category is wireless.

### Physical Connections

Physical connections use a solid medium to connect sending and receiving devices. These connections include telephone lines (twisted pair), coaxial cable, and fiber-optic cable.

**Figure 8-3  Twisted-pair cable**

**Figure 8-4  Coaxial cable**

**Figure 8-5  Fiber-optic cable**

- **Twisted-pair cable** consists of pairs of copper wire that are twisted together. Both standard **telephone lines** and **Ethernet cables** use twisted pair. (See Figure 8-3.) Ethernet cables are often used in networks and to connect a variety of components to the system unit.
- **Coaxial cable**, a high-frequency transmission cable, replaces the multiple wires of telephone lines with a single solid-copper core. (See Figure 8-4.) In terms of the number of telephone connections, a coaxial cable has over 80 times the transmission capacity of twisted pair. Coaxial cable is used to deliver television signals as well as to connect computers in a network.
- **Fiber-optic cable** transmits data as pulses of light through tiny tubes of glass. (See Figure 8-5.) In terms of the number of telephone connections,

fiber-optic cable has over 26,000 times the transmission capacity of twisted-pair cable. Compared to coaxial cable, it is lighter, faster, and more reliable at transmitting data. Fiber-optic cable is rapidly replacing twisted-pair cable telephone lines.

| Standard | Maximum speed |
|----------|---------------|
| 802.11b  | 11 Mbps       |
| 802.11g  | 54 Mbps       |
| 802.11n  | 600 Mbps      |

**Figure 8-6** Wi-Fi standards

## Wireless Connections

Wireless connections do not use a solid substance to connect sending and receiving devices. Rather, they move data through the air.

Most wireless connections use radio waves to communicate. For example, smartphones and many other Internet-enabled devices use radio waves to place telephone calls and to connect to the Internet. Primary technologies used for wireless connections are Bluetooth, Wi-Fi, microwave, WiMax, LTE, and satellite connections.

- **Bluetooth** is a short-range radio communication standard that transmits data over short distances of up to approximately 33 feet. Bluetooth is widely used for wireless headsets, printer connections, and handheld devices.
- **Wi-Fi (wireless fidelity)** uses high-frequency radio signals to transmit data. A number of standards for Wi-Fi exist, and each can send and receive data at a different speed. (See Figure 8-6.) Most home and business wireless networks use Wi-Fi.
- **Microwave** communication uses high-frequency radio waves. It is sometimes referred to as line-of-sight communication because microwaves can only travel in a straight line. Because the waves cannot bend with the curvature of the earth, they can be transmitted only over relatively short distances. Thus, microwave is a good medium for sending data between buildings in a city or on a large college campus. For longer distances, the waves must be relayed by means of microwave stations with microwave dishes or antennas. (See Figure 8-7.)
- **WiMax (Worldwide Interoperability for Microwave Access)** is a new standard that extends the range of Wi-Fi networks using microwave connections. WiMax is commonly used by universities and others to extend the capability of existing Wi-Fi networks.
- **LTE (Long Term Evolution)** is one of the newest wireless standards. Currently, LTE and WiMax connections provide similar performance. LTE, however, promises to provide greater speed and quality transmissions in the near future.
- **Satellite** communication uses satellites orbiting about 22,000 miles above the earth as microwave relay stations. Many of these are offered by Intelsat, the International Telecommunications Satellite Consortium, which is owned by 114 governments and forms a worldwide communication system. Satellites orbit at a precise point and speed above the earth. They can amplify and relay microwave signals from one transmitter on the ground to another. Satellites can be used to send and receive large volumes of data. **Uplink** is a term relating to sending data to a satellite. **Downlink** refers to receiving data from a satellite. The major drawback to satellite communication is that bad weather can sometimes interrupt the flow of data.

One of the most interesting applications of satellite communications is for global positioning. A network of satellites owned and managed by the Department of Defense continuously sends location information to earth. **Global positioning system (GPS)** devices use that information to uniquely determine the geographic location of the device. Available in many automobiles to provide navigational support, these systems are often mounted into the dash with a monitor to display maps and speakers to provide spoken directions.

**Figure 8-7** Microwave dish

# environment

Did you know that GPS technology might help protect the environment? Many cars and mobile devices now have GPS capabilities, and these tools can help save fuel by providing drivers with the shortest route to a destination. Most devices now provide real-time traffic avoidance data, which will reduce the carbon emissions and pollution of cars stuck in traffic. By finding the best routes and avoiding congested areas, you can maximize your fuel efficiency and help protect the environment. To see more environmental facts, visit our website at www.computing2014.com and enter the keyword environment.

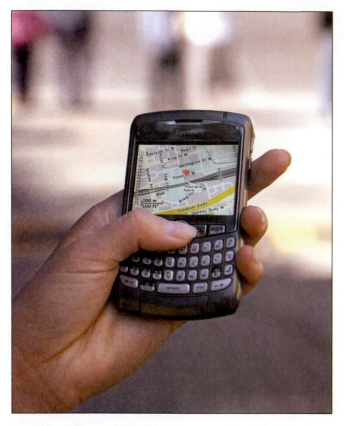

**Figure 8-8** GPS navigation

Most of today's smartphones and tablets use GPS technology for handheld navigation. (See Figure 8-8.)

Unlike radio waves, **infrared** uses infrared light waves to communicate over short distances. Like microwave transmissions, infrared is a line-of-sight communication. Because light waves can only travel in a straight line, sending and receiving devices must be in clear view of one another without any obstructions blocking that view. One of the most common infrared devices is the TV remote control.

☑ **concept check**

- What are communication channels? List three physical connections.
- What is Bluetooth? Wi-Fi? Microwave communication? WiMax?
- What is LTE? Satellite communications? GPS? Infrared?

# Connection Devices

At one time nearly all computer communication used telephone lines. However, because the telephone was originally designed for voice transmission, telephones typically send and receive **analog signals**, which are continuous electronic waves. Computers, in contrast, send and receive **digital signals**. (See Figure 8-9.) These represent the presence or absence of an electronic pulse—the on/off binary signals we mentioned in Chapter 5. To convert the digital signals to analog signals and vice versa, you need a modem.

## Modems

The word **modem** is short for *modulator-demodulator*. **Modulation** is the name of the process of converting from digital to analog. **Demodulation** is the process of converting from analog to digital. The modem enables digital microcomputers to communicate across different media, including telephone wires, cable lines, and radio waves.

The speed with which modems transmit data varies. This speed, called **transfer rate**, is typically measured in millions of bits **(megabits) per second (Mbps)**. (See Figure 8-10.) The higher the speed, the faster you can send and receive information. For example, to download a complete full-length motion picture (700 MB) on a 1.5-Mbps modem would take about 1 hour. Using a 6.0-Mbps modem would take about 15 minutes. To learn more about transfer rates, visit our website at www.computing2014.com and enter the keyword rate.

There are four commonly used types of modems: telephone, DSL, cable, and wireless. (See Figure 8-11.)

- A **telephone modem** is used to connect a computer directly to a telephone line. These modems can be either internal or external. Internal modems are on an expansion card that plugs into a slot on the system board. An external modem is typically connected to the system unit through a USB port. Of the four types of modems, the telephone modem is the slowest and least used.

- A **DSL (digital subscriber line)** modem uses standard phone lines to create a high-speed connection directly to your phone company's offices. These devices are usually external and connect to the system unit using either a USB or an Ethernet port.

**Analog**

**Digital**

**Figure 8-9** Analog and digital signals

| Unit | Speed |
|------|-------|
| Kbps | thousand bits per second |
| Mbps | million bits per second |
| Gbps | billion bits per second |

**Figure 8-10** Typical transfer rates

Telephone    DSL    Cable    Wireless

**Figure 8-11** Basic types of modems

- A **cable modem** uses the same coaxial cable as your television. Like a DSL modem, a cable modem creates high-speed connections using the system unit's USB or Ethernet port.
- A **wireless modem** is also known as a **WWAN (wireless wide area network) modem**. It is usually a small plug-in USB or ExpressCard device that provides very portable high-speed connectivity from virtually anywhere.

## Connection Service

For years, large corporations have been leasing special high-speed lines from telephone companies. Originally, these were copper lines, known as **T1** lines, that could be combined to form higher-capacity options known as **T3** or **DS3** lines. These lines have largely been replaced by faster **optical carrier (OC)** lines.

While the special high-speed lines are too costly for most individuals, Internet service providers (as discussed in Chapter 2) do provide affordable connections. For years, individuals relied on **dial-up services** using existing telephones and telephone modems to connect to the Internet. This type of service has been replaced by higher-speed connection services including DSL, cable, satellite, and cellular services.

- **Digital subscriber line (DSL) service** is provided by telephone companies using existing telephone lines to provide high-speed connections. **ADSL (asymmetric digital subscriber line)** is one of the most widely used types of DSL. DSL is much faster than dial-up.
- **Cable service** is provided by cable television companies using their existing television cables. These connections are faster than DSL.
- **Satellite connection services** use satellites to provide wireless connections. While slower than DSL and cable modem, satellite connections are available almost anywhere using a satellite-receiving disk.

### Explorations

There are many different types of DSL technology.

**To learn more about one of these technologies, visit our website at www.computing2014.com and enter the keyword dsl.**

- **Cellular service providers**, including Verizon, AT&T, Sprint, and T-Mobile, support voice and data transmission to wireless devices. Cellular services have gone through different generations. **First-generation mobile telecommunications (1G)** started in the 1980s using analog radio signals to provide analog voice transmission service. **Second-generation mobile telecommunications (2G)** stared in the 1990s using digital radio signals. This generation focused on voice transmission and was too slow for effective Internet connectivity. **Third-generation mobile telecommunications (3G)** started in the 2000s and provided services capable of effective connectivity to the Internet, marking the beginning of smartphones.

  While **fourth-generation mobile telecommunications (4G)** has been widely marketed by several cellular services, not everyone acknowledges that this generation has begun. Most experts, however, do agree that 4G has entered into its infancy with providers using WiMax and LTE connections to provide faster transmission speeds. While current speeds are only marginally faster than 3G, 4G technologies promise to provide speeds up to 10 times faster than 3G in the near future.

To learn more about how can use mobile communications, see Making IT Work for You: Mobile Internet on page 219.

## concept check

What is the function of a modem? Compare the four types of modems.

What is a connection service? Compare the four high-speed connection services.

Describe the four generations of mobile communications.

# Data Transmission

Several factors affect how data is transmitted. These factors include bandwidth and protocols.

### Bandwidth

**Bandwidth** is a measurement of the width or capacity of the communication channel. Effectively, it means how much information can move across the communication channel in a given amount of time. For example, to transmit text documents, a slow bandwidth would be acceptable. However, to effectively transmit video and audio, a wider bandwidth is required. There are four categories of bandwidth.

- **Voiceband**, also known as **low bandwidth**, is used for standard telephone communication. Microcomputers with telephone modems and dial-up service use this bandwidth. While effective for transmitting text documents, it is too slow for many types of transmission, including high-quality audio and video.
- **Medium band** is used in special leased lines to connect midrange computers and mainframes as well as to transmit data over long distances. This bandwidth is capable of very high speed data transfer.
- **Broadband** is widely used for DSL, cable, and satellite connections to the Internet. Several users can simultaneously use a single broadband connection for high-speed data transfer.
- **Baseband** is widely used to connect individual computers that are located close to one another. Like broadband, it is able to support high-speed transmission. Unlike broadband, however, baseband can only carry a single signal at one time.

## MOBILE INTERNET

Is your smartphone or tablet always connected to the Internet? Millions have this always-on connection to access their e-mail, favorite websites, cloud services, and apps from anywhere at any time. What can be confusing to many is the variety of connection devices, data plans, and penalties for exceeding usage limits.

**Devices**  There are many devices that can help you get Internet access from wherever you are.

**①** *Smartphones.* Most modern smartphones are capable of accessing the Internet via Wi-Fi and 3G or 4G networks.

**②** *Tablets.* Most tablets will provide Wi-Fi access, but to get 3G or 4G capabilities, you will generally have to purchase a higher-priced model.

**③** *Notebooks.* By inserting a USB modem, almost all notebooks can access the Internet through a 3G or 4G network.

**④** *Mobile hotspot device.* This is a stand-alone device that connects to a 3G or 4G network. It will then allow multiple devices near it to access the Internet via a Wi-Fi connection.

It is worth noting that many smartphones have a Wi-Fi sharing, or tethering, ability that is similar to the mobile hotspot device. However, to use that capability, you may have to pay a monthly fee in addition to your regular data plan.

**Data Plans**  A data plan essentially tells you how many megabytes or gigabytes of data you can download using your 3G or 4G connection. These plans can be very confusing, but for most individuals, the plan that gives you a few gigabytes per month is best. Although a few providers have unlimited data plans, they may slow down, or throttle, your connection speed significantly if they deem that your usage is excessive.

**Overage Charges**  If you exceed the monthly data limit, wireless providers will start charging overage fees. For example, one provider charges $10 for every extra gigabyte used. To minimize overage charges, consider the following:

**①** *Wi-Fi access points.* Whenever possible, use a Wi-Fi connection. These connections are not subject to your data plan limits. So if you are in a coffee shop that offers free Wi-Fi, use it!

**②** *Streaming music/video.* Streaming too much of any media while using 3G or 4G can quickly become a problem. The solution: Be particularly selective when watching TV shows, movies, and YouTube videos, and try to store some of your music on your device.

**③** *Downloading.* Limit your downloading of new apps and music to Wi-Fi connections only. Many programs and MP3 files can reach (or even exceed) a size of 10 MB.

**④** *Monitor your data usage.* Most wireless companies provide a free app that helps you monitor your minutes, text messages, and data. Keep an eye on this.

The web is continually changing, and some of the specifics presented in this Making IT Work for You may have changed. **To learn about other ways to make information technology work for you, visit our website at www.computing2014.com and enter the keyword miw.**

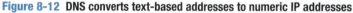

**Figure 8-12 DNS converts text-based addresses to numeric IP addresses**

### Protocols

For data transmission to be successful, sending and receiving devices must follow a set of communication rules for the exchange of information. These rules for exchanging data between computers are known as **protocols**.

As discussed in Chapter 2, **http**, or **hypertext transfer protocol**, is a widely used protocol used for web traffic. Another protocol, **https**, or **hypertext transfer protocol secure**, is becoming widely used to protect the transfer of sensitive information. Another widely used Internet protocol is **TCP/IP (transmission control protocol/Internet protocol)**. The essential features of this protocol involve (1) identifying sending and receiving devices and (2) breaking information into small parts for transmission across the Internet.

- **Identification:** Every computer on the Internet has a unique numeric address called an **IP address (Internet protocol address)**. Similar to the way a postal service uses addresses to deliver mail, the Internet uses IP addresses to deliver e-mail and to locate websites. Because these numeric addresses are difficult for people to remember and use, a system was developed to automatically convert text-based addresses to numeric IP addresses. This system uses a **domain name server (DNS)** that converts text-based addresses to IP addresses. For example, whenever you enter a URL, say www.computing2014.com, a DNS converts this to an IP address before a connection can be made. (See Figure 8-12.)

- **Packetization:** Information sent or transmitted across the Internet usually travels through numerous interconnected networks. Before the message is sent, it is reformatted or broken down into small parts called **packets**. Each packet is then sent separately over the Internet, possibly traveling different routes to one common destination. At the receiving end, the packets are reassembled into the correct order.

## concept check

What is bandwidth? Describe the four categories.

What are protocols? What is the standard protocol for the Internet?

Define TCP/IP, IP address, and packets.

# Networks

A **computer network** is a communication system that connects two or more computers so that they can exchange information and share resources. Networks can be set up in different arrangements to suit users' needs. (See Figure 8-13.)

## Terms

There are a number of specialized terms that describe computer networks. These terms include

- **Node**—any device that is connected to a network. It could be a computer, printer, or data storage device.
- **Client**—a node that requests and uses resources available from other nodes. Typically, a client is a user's microcomputer.
- **Server**—a node that shares resources with other nodes. Dedicated servers specialize in performing specific tasks. Depending on the specific task, they may be called an application server, communication server, database server, file server, printer server, or web server.

**Figure 8-13  Computer network**

- **Directory server**—a specialized server that manages resources, such as user accounts, for an entire network.
- **Host**—any computer system that can be accessed over a network.
- **Router**—a node that forwards or routes data packets from one network to their destination in another network.
- **Switch**—central node that coordinates the flow of data by sending messages directly between sender and receiver nodes. A **hub** previously filled this purpose by sending a received message to all connected nodes, rather than just the intended node.
- **Network interface cards (NIC)**—as discussed in Chapter 5, these are expansion cards located within the system unit that connect the computer to a network. Sometimes referred to as a LAN adapter.
- **Network operating systems (NOS)**—control and coordinate the activities of all computers and other devices on a network. These activities include electronic communication and the sharing of information and resources.
- **Network administrator**—a computer specialist responsible for efficient network operations and implementation of new networks.

A network may consist only of microcomputers, or it may integrate microcomputers or other devices with larger computers. Networks can be controlled by all nodes working together equally or by specialized nodes coordinating and supplying all resources. Networks may be simple or complex, self-contained or dispersed over a large geographic area.

## ☑ concept check

What is a computer network? What are nodes, clients, servers, directory servers, hosts, routers, and switches?

What is the function of an NIC and an NOS?

What is a network administrator?

# Network Types

Clearly, different types of channels—wired or wireless—allow different kinds of networks to be formed. Telephone lines, for instance, may connect communications equipment within the same building or within a home. Networks also may be citywide and even international, using both cable and wireless connections. Local area, metropolitan area, and wide area networks are distinguished by the geographic area they serve.

## Local Area Networks

Networks with nodes that are in close physical proximity—within the same building, for instance—are called **local area networks (LANs)**. Typically, LANs span distances less than a mile and are owned and operated by individual organizations. LANs are widely used by colleges, universities, and other types of organizations to link microcomputers and to share printers and other resources. For a simple LAN, see Figure 8-14.

The LAN represented in Figure 8-14 is a typical arrangement and provides two benefits: economy and flexibility. People can share costly equipment. For instance, the four microcomputers share the laser printer and the file server, which are expensive pieces of hardware. Other equipment or nodes also may be added to

Microcomputer     Microcomputer

Laser printer     File server     Network gateway

Microcomputer     Microcomputer

**Figure 8-14** Local area network

the LAN—for instance, more microcomputers, a mainframe computer, or optical disc storage devices. Additionally, the **network gateway** is a device that allows one LAN to be linked to other LANs or to larger networks. For example, the LAN of one office group may be connected to the LAN of another office group.

There are a variety of different standards or ways in which nodes can be connected to one another and ways in which their communications are controlled in a LAN. The most common standard is known as **Ethernet**. LANs using this standard are sometimes referred to as Ethernet LANs.

### Home Networks

While LANs have been widely used within organizations for years, they are now being commonly used by individuals in their homes and apartments. These LANs, called **home networks**, allow different computers to share resources, including a common Internet connection. Computers can be connected in a variety of ways, including electrical wiring, telephone wiring, and special cables. One of the simplest ways, however, is without cables, or wireless.

### Wireless LAN

A wireless local area network is typically referred to as a **wireless LAN (WLAN)**. It uses radio frequencies to connect computers and other devices. All communications pass through the network's centrally located **wireless access point** or **base station**. This access point interprets incoming radio frequencies and routes communications to the appropriate devices. To see how wireless home networks work, visit our website at www.computing2014 .com and enter the keyword **network**.

Would you like to share files or view photos from anywhere in your home? Here are some typical ways in which this can be accomplished.

**1** **Home network.** Most operating systems now make it relatively simple to set up a home network. In Windows, for example, the *HomeGroup* feature makes it easy to share photos, music, videos, documents, and printers between all the computers in your home.

**2** **Public folders.** Certain folders in the operating system are designated as public folders. Any files placed in those are accessible to any user account in your computer and usually to anyone in your home network.

**3** **File sharing.** You can configure the sharing settings for individual files (or folders) in your computer. This is typically done by right-clicking the file. When sharing, you can limit others to simply viewing the file (read only), or you can give them the ability to edit and delete it (read/write).

**4** **Media server/streaming.** Many devices (including gaming consoles and new TVs) have the ability to look for media stored on your home computer. Follow the manufacturer's instructions to set up the streaming on your computer and then accessing the shared content from your console or TV.

To see other tips, visit our website at www.computing2014.com and enter the keyword tips.

**Figure 8-15** Wireless adapter

Wireless access points that provide Internet access are widely available in public places such as coffee shops, libraries, bookstores, colleges, and universities. These access points are known as **hotspots** and typically use Wi-Fi technology. Many of these services are free and easy to find using free locator sites such as www.hotspot-locations.com. Most mobile computing devices have an internal wireless network card to connect to hotspots. If your mobile device does not have an internal wireless network card, you can use an external wireless adapter (see Figure 8-15) that plugs into your computer's USB port or PC card slot.

### Personal Area Network

A **personal area network (PAN)** is a type of wireless network that works within a very small area—your immediate surroundings. PANs connect cell phones to headsets, PDAs to other PDAs, keyboards to cell phones, and so on. These tiny, self-configuring networks make it possible for all our gadgets to interact wirelessly with each other. The most popular PAN technology is Bluetooth, with a maximum range of around 33 feet. Virtually all wireless peripheral devices available today use Bluetooth, including the controllers on popular game systems like the PlayStation and Wii.

### Metropolitan Area Networks

The next step up from the LAN is the **MAN**—the **metropolitan area network**. MANs span distances up to 100 miles. These networks are frequently used as links between office buildings that are located throughout a city.

Unlike a LAN, a MAN is typically not owned by a single organization. Rather, it is owned either by a group of organizations that operate the network or by a single network service provider that provides network services for a fee.

### Wide Area Networks

**Wide area networks (WANs)** are countrywide and worldwide networks. These networks provide access to regional service (MAN) providers and typically span distances greater than 100 miles. They use microwave relays and satellites to reach users over long distances—for example, from Los Angeles to Paris. Of course, the widest of all WANs is the Internet, which spans the entire globe.

The primary difference between a LAN, MAN, and WAN is the geographic range. Each may have various combinations of hardware, such as microcomputers, midrange computers, mainframes, and various peripheral devices.

For a summary of network types, see Figure 8-16.

---

**tips**

Do you use your notebook to connect to wireless networks at school or in public places such as coffee shops, airports, or hotels? If so, it is important to use caution to protect your computer and your privacy. Here are a few suggestions:

**1 Use a firewall.** A personal firewall is essential when connecting your computer directly to public networks. Some firewalls, such as the one built into Windows 7 and Windows 8, will ask whether a new network should be treated as home, work, or a public network.

**2 Avoid fake hotspots.** Thieves are known to set up rogue (or fake) hotspots in popular areas where users expect free Wi-Fi, such as coffee shops and airports. Since many operating systems automatically connect to the access point with the strongest signal, you could be connecting to the one set up by the thief. Always confirm that you are connecting to the access point of that establishment. Ask an employee if you are unsure.

**3 Turn off file sharing.** Turning off file-sharing features in your operating system will ensure that no one can access or modify your files.

**4 Check if connection is encrypted.** If the hotspot you are using is protected with a password, then it is likely encrypted. If it is not, then be very careful with websites you visit and the information you provide.

To see additional tips, visit our website at www.computing2014.com and enter the keyword tips.

---

✔ **concept check**

● Describe LANs, home networks, wireless LAN, and PAN.

● What is a MAN? What is a WAN?

| Type | Description |
| --- | --- |
| LAN | Local area network; located within close proximity |
| Home | Local area network for home and apartment use; typically wireless |
| WLAN | Wireless local area network; all communication passes through access point |
| PAN | Personal area network; connects digital devices, such as PDAs |
| MAN | Metropolitan area network; typically spans cities with coverage up to 100 miles |
| WAN | Wide area network for countrywide or worldwide coverage; the Internet is the largest WAN |

Figure 8-16 **Types of networks**

# Network Architecture

**Network architecture** describes how a network is arranged and how resources are coordinated and shared. It encompasses a variety of different network specifics, including network topologies and strategies. Network topology describes the physical arrangement of the network. Network strategies define how information and resources are shared.

## Topologies

A network can be arranged or configured in several different ways. This arrangement is called the network's **topology**. Five of the most common topologies are ring, bus, star, tree, and mesh.

- **Bus network**—each device is connected to a common cable called a **bus** or **backbone**, and all communications travel along this bus.
- **Ring network**—each device is connected to two other devices, forming a ring. (See Figure 8-17.) When a message is sent, it is passed around the ring until it reaches the intended destination.
- **Star network**—each device is connected directly to a central network switch. (See Figure 8-18.) Whenever a node sends a message, it is routed to the switch,

Figure 8-17 **Ring network**

Figure 8-18 **Star network**

**Figure 8-19** Tree network

**Figure 8-20** Mesh network

which then passes the message along to the intended recipient. The star network is the most widely used network topology today. It is applied to a broad range of applications from small networks in the home to very large networks in major corporations.

- **Tree network**—each device is connected to a central node, either directly or through one or more other devices. The central node is connected to two or more subordinate nodes that in turn are connected to other subordinate nodes, and so forth, forming a treelike structure. (See Figure 8-19.) This network, also known as a **hierarchical network**, is often used to share corporatewide data.

- **Mesh network**—this topology is the newest type and does not use a specific physical layout (such as a star or a tree). Rather, the mesh network requires that each node have more than one connection to the other nodes. (See Figure 8-20.) The resulting pattern forms the appearance of a mesh. If a path between two nodes is somehow disrupted, data can be automatically rerouted around the failure using another path. Wireless technologies are frequently used to build mesh networks.

### Strategies

Every network has a **strategy**, or way of coordinating the sharing of information and resources. Two of the most common network strategies are client/server and peer-to-peer.

**Figure 8-21** Client/server network

**Client/server networks** use central computers to coordinate and supply services to other nodes on the network. The server provides access to resources such as web pages, databases, application software, and hardware. (See Figure 8-21.) This strategy is based on specialization. Server nodes coordinate and supply specialized services, and client nodes request the services. Commonly used server operating systems are Windows Server, Mac OS X Server, Linux, and Solaris.

Client/server networks are widely used on the Internet. For example, each time you open a web browser, your computer (the client) sends out a request for a specific web page. This request is routed over the Internet to a server. This server locates and sends the requested material back to your computer.

One advantage of the client/server network strategy is the ability to handle very large networks efficiently. Another advantage is the availability of powerful network management software to monitor and control network activities. The major disadvantages are the cost of installation and maintenance.

In a **peer-to-peer (P2P) network**, nodes have equal authority and can act as both clients and servers. The most common way to share games, movies, and music over the Internet is to use a P2P network. For example, special file-sharing software such as eDonkey or BitTorrent can be used to obtain files located on another microcomputer and also can provide files to other microcomputers.

P2P networks are rapidly growing in popularity as people continue to share information with others around the world. The primary advantage is that they are easy and inexpensive (often free) to set up and use. One disadvantage of P2P networks is the lack of security controls or other common management functions. For this reason, few businesses use this type of network to communicate sensitive information.

## Explorations

BitTorrent is a file-sharing protocol used to distribute large files across the Internet.

**To learn more about BitTorrent, visit our website at www.computing2014.com and enter the keyword torrent.**

## ☑ concept check

What is a network topology?

Compare bus, ring, star, tree, and mesh topologies.

What is a network strategy?

Compare client/server and peer-to-peer strategies.

# Organizational Networks

Computer networks in organizations have evolved over time. Most large organizations have a complex and wide range of different network configurations, operating systems, and strategies. These organizations face the challenge of making these networks work together effectively and securely.

### Internet Technologies

Many organizations today employ Internet technologies to support effective communication within and between organizations using intranets and extranets.

- An **intranet** is a *private* network within an organization that resembles the Internet. Like the *public* Internet, intranets use browsers, websites, and web pages. Typical applications include electronic telephone directories, e-mail addresses, employee benefit information, internal job openings, and much more. Employees find surfing their organizational intranets to be as easy and as intuitive as surfing the Internet.

- An **extranet** is a *private* network that connects *more than one* organization. Many organizations use Internet technologies to allow suppliers and others limited access to their networks. The purpose is to increase efficiency and reduce costs. For example, an automobile manufacturer has hundreds of suppliers for the parts that go into making a car. By having access to the car production schedules, suppliers can schedule and deliver parts as they are needed at the assembly plants. In this way, operational efficiency is maintained by both the manufacturer and the suppliers.

## environment

Did you know that Cisco, one of the worldwide leaders in networking solutions, helps companies achieve environmental sustainability? The Cisco Networked Sustainability Framework is an approach that seeks to reduce greenhouse gas emissions, increase operational efficiency, and attain sustainable business behavior. One of the key components is its EnergyWise technology—an energy management protocol that helps measure, report, and reduce energy consumption across an entire company's network infrastructure. To see more environmental facts, visit our website at www.computing2014.com and enter the keyword environment.

## Network Security

Large organizations face the challenge of ensuring that only authorized users have access to network resources, sometimes from multiple geographic locations or across the Internet. Securing large computer networks requires specialized technology. Three technologies commonly used to ensure network security are firewalls, intrusion detection systems, and virtual private networks.

- A **firewall** consists of hardware and software that control access to a company's intranet and other internal networks. Most use software or a special computer called a **proxy server**. All communications between the company's internal networks and the outside world pass through this server. By evaluating the source and the content of each communication, the proxy server decides whether it is safe to let a particular message or file pass into or out of the organization's network. (See Figure 8-22.)

- **Intrusion detection systems (IDS)** work with firewalls to protect an organization's network. These systems use sophisticated statistical techniques to analyze all incoming and outgoing network traffic. Using advanced pattern matching and heuristics, an IDS system can recognize signs of a network attack and disable access before an intruder can do damage.

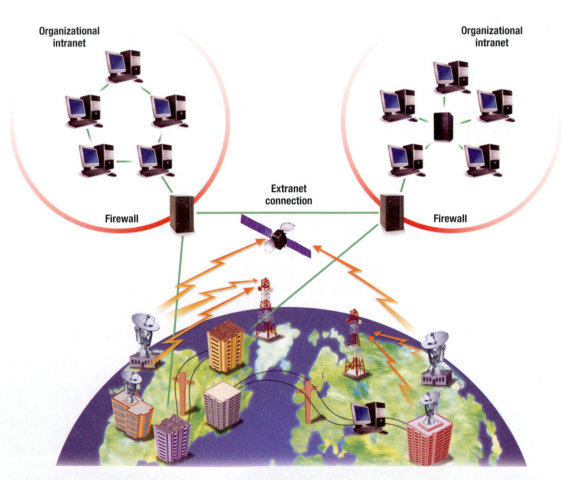

**Figure 8-22** Intranets, extranets, firewalls, and proxy servers

- **Virtual private networks (VPN)** create a secure private connection between a remote user and an organization's internal network. Special VPN protocols create the equivalent of a dedicated line between a user's home or notebook computer and a company server. The connection is heavily encrypted, and, from the perspective of the user, it appears that the workstation is actually located on the corporate network. To see how you can set up remote access, see Making IT Work for You: Remote Access on page 230.

Like organizations, end users have security challenges and concerns. We need to be concerned about the privacy of our personal information. In the next chapter, we will discuss personal firewalls and other ways to protect personal privacy and security.

## concept check

What are Internet technologies? Compare intranets and extranets.

What is a firewall? What is a proxy server?

What are intrusion detection systems?

What are virtual private networks?

# Careers in IT

**Network administrators** manage a company's LAN and WAN networks. They may be responsible for design, implementation, and maintenance of networks. Responsibilities usually include maintenance of both hardware and software related to a company's intranet and Internet networks. Network administrators are typically responsible for diagnosing and repairing problems with these networks. Some network administrators are responsible for planning and implementation of network security as well.

Employers typically look for candidates with a bachelor's or an advanced specialized associate's degree in computer science, computer technology, or information systems as well as practical networking experience. Experience with network security and maintenance is preferred. Technical certification also may be helpful in obtaining this position. Because network administrators are involved directly with people in many departments, good communication skills are essential.

Network administrators can expect to earn an annual salary of $46,000 to $84,000. Opportunities for advancement typically include upper-management positions. This position is expected to be among the fastest-growing jobs in the near future. To learn about other careers in information technology, visit us at www.computing2014.com and enter the keyword **careers**.

Now that you have learned about computer communications and networks, let me tell you about my career as a network administrator.

## REMOTE ACCESS

Have you ever been using someone else's computer and wished you could open a program installed on your home computer? Have you found yourself at school when you realized that you left an important file on your desktop? There are countless reasons why you may need full access to your computer when away from home, and LogMeIn provides a free way to do so.

**Getting Started**    To use this service, you need an account and a special piece of software on your home computer. You also need to have administrator privileges on your machine.

**1** ● Go to www.logmein.com, and click the *Create an account* link on the right side.

**2** ● Click the *Access Computers Remotely* button.

**3** ● Enter your information in the form. Select the *Personal/Business* option.

**4** ● Click *Continue*, and then proceed to download and install the software. By default, LogMeIn sets you up with a trial version of its Pro software. You can, however, continue using its free version once your trial expires.

**5** ● Choose the *Typical* settings when asked during installation.

When installation finishes, the LogMeIn software will automatically start. Your computer can now be accessed remotely.

**Accessing your Computer**    The LogMeIn software must be running on your home computer (which must be connected to the Internet) in order to access it from any other computer. All you need on the remote computer is a web browser and an Internet connection.

**1** ● On the remote computer, go to www.logmein.com and log into your account. You will be taken to LogMeIn Central, which is a console that is used to manage all the computers connected to your account.

**2** ● Find your computer in the list, and click it in order to start the connection. Depending on which web browser you use, you may be prompted to install a plug-in. This step is optional, since it is possible to use Java for the remote session.

**3** ● Enter your user name and password for your remote machine. Since you are logging into Windows or Mac OS, you must enter your credentials exactly as if you were sitting in front of your computer.

You are now logged into your computer. You can move around, click, and type as if you were sitting in front of it. You can also move outside this area to access your web browser and some options from the LogMeIn interface. Click the *Disconnect* button on the left side to end the session.

The web is continually changing, and some of the specifics presented in this Making IT Work for You may have changed.

**To learn about other ways to make information technology work for you, visit our website at www.computing2014.com and enter the keyword miw.**

# A LOOK TO THE FUTURE

## Telepresence Lets You Be There without Actually Being There

How would you like to speak with distant friends or family as though they were in the same room at the touch of a button? Can you imagine receiving a physical examination from a doctor thousands of miles away? All this and more could be possible in the future thanks to the emerging technology known as telepresence.

Telepresence seeks to create the illusion that you are actually at a remote location, seeing, hearing, and, someday maybe, even feeling as though you were really there. Today's early implementations, such as Cisco TelePresence, mainly focus on an extension of video conferencing, allowing people in different locations to conduct meetings as though they are sitting across a table from one another. This illusion is created with very high definition video, acoustically tuned audio systems, and high-speed networks. However, telepresence could someday go beyond the simple voice and video conferencing available today, and the applications seem endless.

Robots are quickly becoming a key part of many telepresence applications. In addition to audio and video feeds from another location, robots will bring you the ability to manipulate objects at the remote location. Such robots are already being used in the medical field. In one system, a surgeon uses special controls and screens in one room to control robotic arms that operate on the patient in another room. This type of system could be used to allow expert surgeons to perform several procedures on various patients located throughout the world in just one day!

In addition to manipulating objects, users may one day wear special gloves and other sensors that permit them to feel the objects being touched by the robot. This technology might be used to allow people to work in hazardous areas or perform search and rescue operations from a safe, remote location. A more casual application may see individuals using telepresence as a substitute for traditional vacations. Imagine touring remote cities or touching objects from a shipwreck on a deep-sea diving expedition without the expense, hassle, or risk of travel.

Various research institutions are currently experiencing breakthroughs in the areas of holography, which is technology that creates 3-D images called holograms that might pave the way to advanced telepresence. In the coming decade, you might be able to interact virtually with others via a projected, 3-D hologram of yourself.

How would you use telepresence? What benefits do you see from this technology? How might telepresence affect traveling? Do you see any disadvantages?

## COMMUNICATIONS

Communications is the process of sharing data, programs, and information between two or more computers. Applications include e-mail, texting, Internet telephones, and electronic commerce.

### Connectivity

Connectivity is a concept related to using computer networks to link people and resources. You can link or connect to large computers and the Internet, providing access to extensive information resources.

### The Wireless Revolution

Mobile devices like smartphones and tablets have brought dramatic changes in connectivity and communications. These wireless devices are becoming widely used for computer communication.

### Communication Systems

Communication systems transmit data from one location to another. Four basic elements are

- Sending and receiving devices
- Communication channel (transmission medium)
- Connection (communication) devices
- Data transmission specifications

## COMMUNICATION CHANNELS

Communication channels carry data from one computer to another.

### Physical Connections

Physical connections use a solid medium to connect sending and receiving devices. Connections include twisted pair (telephone lines and Ethernet cables), coaxial cable, and fiber-optic cable.

### Wireless Connections

Wireless connections do not use a solid substance to connect devices. Most use radio waves.

- Bluetooth—transmits data over short distances; widely used for wireless headsets, printers, and handheld devices.
- Wi-Fi (wireless fidelity)—uses high-frequency radio signals; most home and business wireless networks use Wi-Fi.
- Microwave—line-of-sight communication; used to send data between buildings; longer distances require microwave stations.
- WiMax (Worldwide Interoperability for Microwave Access)—extends the range of Wi-Fi networks using microwave connections.
- LTE (Long Term Evolution)—currently has similar performance to WiMax; promises to provide greater speed and quality transmissions in the near future.
- Satellite—uses microwave relay stations in the sky; GPS (global positioning system) tracks geographic locations.
- Infrared—uses light waves over a short distance; line-of-sight communication.

To be a competent end user you need to understand the concepts of connectivity, the wireless revolution, and communication systems. Additionally, you need to know the essential parts of communication technology, including channels, connection devices, data transmission, networks, network architectures, and network types.

## CONNECTION DEVICES

Many communication systems use standard telephone lines and **analog signals**. Computers use **digital signals**.

### Modems

**Modems** **modulate** and **demodulate**. Transfer rate is measured in **megabits per second**. Four types are **telephone, DSL, cable**, and **wireless (wireless wide area network, WWAN)**.

### Connection Service

**T1, T3 (DS3)**, and **OC (optical carrier)** lines provide support for very high speed, all-digital transmission for large corporations. More affordable technologies include **dial-up, DSL (digital subscriber line), ADSL** (widely used), **cable, satellite**, and **cellular services**. **4G (fourth-generation mobile telecommunications)** promises 10 times faster speeds than 3G.

## DATA TRANSMISSION

**Bandwidth** measures a communication channel's width or capacity. Four bandwidths are **voiceband (low bandwidth), medium band, broadband (high-capacity transmissions)**, and **baseband**. **Protocols** are rules for exchanging data. Widely used Internet protocols include **http, https**, and **TCP/IP. IP addresses (Internet protocol addresses)** are unique numeric Internet addresses. **DNS (domain name server)** converts text-based addresses to and from numeric IP addresses. **Packets** are small parts of messages.

## NETWORKS

**Computer networks** connect two or more computers. Some specialized network terms include

- **Node**—any device connected to a network.
- **Client**—node requesting resources.
- **Server**—node providing resources.
- **Directory server**—specialized node that manages resources.
- **Host**—any computer system that can be accessed over a network.
- **Router**—a node that forwards data packets from one network to another network.
- **Switch**—node that coordinates direct flow of data between other nodes. **Hub** is an older device that directed flow to all nodes.
- **NIC (network interface card)**—LAN adapter card for connecting to a network.
- **NOS (network operating system)**—controls and coordinates network operations.
- **Network administrator**—network specialist responsible for network operations.

## NETWORK TYPES

Networks can be citywide or even international, using both wired and wireless connections.

- **Local area networks (LANs)** connect nearby devices. **Network gateways** connect networks to one another. **Ethernet** is a LAN standard. These LANs are called Ethernet LANs.
- **Home networks** are LANs used in homes.
- **Hotspots** provide Internet access typically using Wi-Fi technology.
- **Wireless LANs (WLANs)** use a **wireless access point (base station)** as a hub.
- **Personal area networks (PANs)** are wireless networks for PDAs, cell phones, and other small gadgets.
- **Metropolitan area networks (MANs)** link office buildings within a city, spanning up to 100 miles.
- **Wide area networks or WANs** are the largest type. They span states and countries or form worldwide networks. The Internet is the largest wide area network in the world.

**Network architecture** describes how networks are arranged and resources are shared.

## Topologies

A network's **topology** describes the physical arrangement of a network.

- **Bus network**—each device is connected to a common cable called a **bus** or **backbone**.
- **Ring network**—each device is connected to two other devices, forming a ring.
- **Star network**—each device is connected directly to a central network switch; most common type today.
- **Tree (hierarchical) network**—a central node is connected to subordinate nodes forming a treelike structure.
- **Mesh network**—newest; each node has two or more connecting nodes.

## Strategies

Every network has a **strategy**, or way of sharing information and resources. Common network strategies include client/server and peer-to-peer.

- **Client/server (hierarchical) network**—central computers coordinate and supply services to other nodes; based on specialization of nodes; widely used on the Internet; able to handle very large networks efficiently; powerful network management software available.
- **Peer-to-peer network**—nodes have equal authority and act as both clients and servers; widely used to share games, movies, and music over the Internet; easy to set up and use; lacks security controls.

## Internet Technologies

Internet technologies support effective communication using intranets and extranets.

- **Intranet**—private network within an organization; uses browsers, websites, and web pages. Typical applications include electronic telephone directories, e-mail addresses, employee benefit information, internal job openings, and much more.
- **Extranet**—like intranet except connects *more than one* organization; typically allows suppliers and others limited access to their networks.

## Network Security

Three technologies commonly used to ensure network security are firewalls, intrusion detection systems, and virtual private networks.

- **Firewall**—controls access; all communications pass through **proxy server**.
- **Intrusion detection systems (IDS)**—work with firewalls; use sophisticated statistical techniques to recognize and disable network attacks.
- **Virtual private network (VPN)**—creates secure private connection between remote user and organization's internal network.

## CAREERS IN IT

**Network administrators** manage a company's LAN and WAN networks. Bachelor's or specialized advanced associate's degree in computer science, computer technology, or information systems and practical networking experience required. Salary range is $46,000 to $84,000.

# KEY TERMS

1G (first-generation mobile telecommunications) (218)

2G (second-generation mobile telecommunications) (218)

3G (third-generation mobile telecommunications) (218)

4G (fourth-generation mobile telecommunications) (218)

analog signal (216)

asymmetric digital subscriber line (ADSL) (217)

backbone (225)

bandwidth (218)

base station (223)

baseband (218)

Bluetooth (215)

broadband (218)

bus (225)

bus network (225)

cable modem (217)

cable service (217)

cellular service provider (218)

client (221)

client/server network (226)

coaxial cable (214)

communication channel (214)

communication system (213)

computer network (221)

connectivity (212)

demodulation (216)

dial-up service (217)

digital signal (216)

digital subscriber line (DSL) (216)

digital subscriber line (DSL) service (217)

directory server (222)

domain name server (DNS) (220)

downlink (215)

DS3 (217)

Ethernet (223)

Ethernet cable (214)

extranet (227)

fiber-optic cable (214)

firewall (228)

global positioning system (GPS) (215)

hierarchical network (226)

home network (223)

host (222)

hotspot (224)

http (hypertext transfer protocol) (220)

https (hypertext transfer protocol secure) (220)

hub (222)

infrared (216)

intranet (227)

intrusion detection system (IDS) (228)

IP address (Internet protocol address) (220)

local area network (LAN) (222)

low bandwidth (218)

LTE (Long Term Evolution) (215)

medium band (218)

megabits per second (Mbps) (216)

mesh network (226)

metropolitan area network (MAN) (224)

microwave (215)

modem (216)

modulation (216)

network administrator (222, 229)

network architecture (225)

network gateway (223)

network interface card (NIC) (222)

network operating system (NOS) (222)

node (221)

optical carrier (OC) (217)

packet (220)

peer-to-peer (P2P) network (227)

personal area network (PAN) (224)

protocol (220)

proxy server (228)

ring network (225)

router (222)

satellite (215)

satellite connection service (217)

server (221)

star network (225)

strategy (226)

switch (222)

T1 (217)

T3 (217)

telephone line (214)

telephone modem (216)

topology (225)

transfer rate (216)

transmission control protocol/Internet protocol (TCP/IP) (220)

tree network (226)

twisted-pair cable (214)

uplink (215)

virtual private network (VPN) (229)

voiceband (218)

wide area network (WAN) (224)

Wi-Fi (wireless fidelity) (215)

WiMax (Worldwide Interoperability for Microwave Access) (215)

wireless access point (223)

wireless LAN (WLAN) (223)

wireless modem (217)

wireless wide area network (WWAN) modem (217)

To test your knowledge of these key terms with animated flash cards, visit our website at www.computing2014.com and enter the keyword terms8. Or use the free *Computing Essentials 2014* app.

# MULTIPLE CHOICE

Circle the letter of the correct answer.

1. The concept related to using computer networks to link people and resources.
   - a. connectivity
   - b. GPS
   - c. TCP/IP
   - d. Wi-Fi

2. A high-frequency transmission cable that delivers television signals as well as connects computers in a network.
   - a. coaxial
   - b. hi def
   - c. 3-D
   - d. twisted pair

3. A short-range radio communication standard that transmits data over short distances of up to approximately 33 feet.
   - a. Bluetooth
   - b. broadband
   - c. DSL
   - d. TCP/IP

4. The speed with which a modem transmits data is called its:
   - a. digital velocity
   - b. dynamic rate
   - c. modular rating
   - d. transfer rate

5. The bandwidth typically used for DSL, cable, and satellite connections to the Internet.
   - a. baseband
   - b. broadband
   - c. medium band
   - d. voiceband

6. Every computer on the Internet has a unique numeric address called a(n):
   - a. IP address
   - b. DNS
   - c. broadcast
   - d. packet

7. Sometimes referred to as a LAN adapter, these expansion cards connect a computer to a network.
   - a. PCMCIA
   - b. NIC
   - c. server
   - d. VPN

8. A device that allows one LAN to be linked to other LANs or to larger networks.
   - a. IDS
   - b. network gateway
   - c. PAN
   - d. switch

9. Typically using Wi-Fi technology, these wireless access points are available from public places such as coffee shops, libraries, bookstores, colleges, and universities.
   - a. hotspots
   - b. extranets
   - c. PANs
   - d. LANs

10. Bus, ring, star, tree, and mesh are five types of network:
    - a. topologies
    - b. protocols
    - c. strategies
    - d. devices

For an interactive multiple-choice practice test, visit our website at www.computing2014 .com and enter the keyword multiple8. Or use the free *Computing Essentials 2014* app.

# MATCHING

Match each numbered item with the most closely related lettered item. Write your answers in the spaces provided.

a. analog
b. bus
c. intrusion detection systems
d. microwave
e. network administrator
f. node
g. peer-to-peer
h. protocols
i. RF
j. tree

___ 1. Type of network topology in which each device is connected to a common cable called a backbone.

___ 2. Uses radio signals to communicate between wireless devices.

___ 3. Uses high-frequency radio waves.

___ 4. Signals that are continuous electronic waves.

___ 5. Rules for exchanging data between computers.

___ 6. Any device that is connected to a network.

___ 7. A computer specialist responsible for efficient network operations and implementation of new networks.

___ 8. This network, also known as a hierarchical network, is often used to share corporatewide data.

___ 9. In this network, nodes have equal authority and can act as both clients and servers.

___ 10. Work with firewalls to protect an organization's network.

For an interactive matching practice test, visit our website at www.computing2014.com and enter the keyword matching8. Or use the free *Computing Essentials 2014* app.

# OPEN-ENDED

On a separate sheet of paper, respond to each question or statement.

1. Define communications including connectivity, the wireless revolution, and communication systems.
2. Discuss communication channels including physical connections (twisted-pair, coaxial, and fiber-optic cable) and wireless connections (Bluetooth, Wi-Fi, microwave, WiMax, LTE, satellite, and infrared).
3. Discuss connection devices including modems (telephone, DSL, cable, and wireless modems) and connection services (DSL, ADSL, cable, satellite, and cellular connection services).
4. Discuss data transmission including bandwidths (voiceband, medium band, broadband, and baseband) as well as protocols (IP addresses, domain name servers, and packetization).
5. Discuss networks by identifying and defining specialized terms that describe computer networks.
6. Discuss network types including local area, home, wireless, personal, metropolitan, and wide area networks.
7. Define network architecture including topologies (bus, ring, star, tree, and mesh) and strategies (client/server and peer-to-peer).
8. Discuss organization networks including Internet technologies (intranets and extranets) and network security (firewalls, proxy servers, intrusion detection systems, and virtual private networks).

# DISCUSSION

Respond to each of the following questions.

### 1 Making IT Work for You: MOBILE INTERNET

Is your smartphone or tablet always connected to the Internet? Review the Making IT Work for You: Mobile Internet on page 219 and then respond to the following: (a) What mobile Internet devices do you currently use? If you do not own any, which device do you feel would be most beneficial to you? (b) Do you currently have a 3G or 4G data plan for your mobile device? If so, provide details on your plan and why you chose it. Otherwise, describe what your ideal data plan would include. (c) Have you, a friend, or a family member ever gone over the data limit and/or been throttled? What sorts of activities are typically responsible for excessive data usage? (d) Go to the websites of at least two wireless companies and compare their data plans. How are they similar? How are they different?

### 2 Making IT Work for You: REMOTE ACCESS

Have you ever needed to access your home computer while away from home? Review the Making IT Work for You: Mobile Internet on page 230 and then respond to the following: (a) Have you ever used LogMeIn or a similar remote access service? If so, what service have you used, and what do you typically use it for? If you have not used LogMeIn or a similar service, describe how and why you might use one. (b) If you do not have a LogMeIn account, set up a free one and install LogMeIn on your home computer or one that you have authorization and access to use. Go to another computer and remotely access the other computer. Describe your experience with this process. (c) Describe the advantages and disadvantages of using a service like LogMeIn. (d) Do you see yourself using LogMeIn in the future? Why or why not?

### 3 Explorations: DSL

Did you know that there are many different types of DSL technology? Review the Explorations box on page 217 and then respond to the following: (a) What is VDSL? What advantages does it have over ADSL? (b) What kinds of services can run on this type of technology? (c) How do telecommunication companies overcome the short-distance limitation of VDSL? (d) Do any of your local ISPs offer VDSL? If so, which ones? If not, find any ISP in the United States that offers it. Briefly describe some of the plans and their costs, and whether you would consider purchasing this type of service.

### 4 Explorations: BITTORRENT

Did you know that many large files are distributed across the Internet using the BitTorrent protocol? Review the Explorations box on page 227 and then respond to the following: (a) What makes BitTorrent so unique in the way it handles file sharing? (b) How do you download files using BitTorrent? How is downloading related to the process of seeding? (c) List at least three organizations that distribute their software via BitTorrent. (d) Can using BitTorrent be risky for your computer? Can it be illegal? Explain your responses.

### 5 Ethics: ELECTRONIC MONITORING

Many companies, websites, and law enforcement and various government agencies engage in monitoring or tracking Internet activity. Review the Ethics box on page 214 and respond to the following: (a) Is it unethical for an organization or corporation to use programs to monitor communications on its network? Why or why not? (b) Is it unethical for a government agency (such as the FBI) to monitor communications on the Internet or gather your records from the websites you visit? Why or why not? (c) Do you feel that new laws are needed to handle these issues? How would you balance the needs of companies and the government with the needs of individuals? Explain your answers.

### 6 Ethics: UNAUTHORIZED NETWORK INTRUSION

Attempting to access another organization's network is a common activity today. Some say all attempts are unethical regardless of the circumstances. Review the Ethics box on page 228 and then respond to the following: (a) Can you think of any circumstances in which unauthorized access to a network can be considered ethical? Be specific and defend your position. (b) Would it be unethical for a firm that provides network security to attempt to penetrate a prospective client's network without authorization in order to demonstrate vulnerabilities and to market its services? Why or why not? (c) Would it be ethical for a member of an organization to gain unauthorized access to the organization's network to obtain evidence demonstrating the firm's involvement in illegal and/or dangerous activities? Why or why not? (d) Is it ethical for the U.S. government to support unauthorized network access to obtain information about other countries? What about information about terrorist activities? Conversely, is it ethical for other countries to attempt to gain unauthorized access to U.S. government networks? Why or why not?

### 7 Environment: GPS

Did you know that GPS technology might help protect the environment? Review the Environment box on page 215 and then respond to the following: (a) Identify ways in which GPS could benefit the environment. You need not limit your response to applications in motor vehicles. (b) Have you used a GPS device or mobile navigation app? If so, describe what you used it for. If not, do you think that you will in the near future? (c) Do you think that GPS should be standard equipment for every new car? Why or why not? (d) Do you think that they should be required by law? Why or why not?

### 8 Environment: CISCO

Did you know that Cisco helps companies achieve environmental sustainability? Review the Environment box on page 227 and then respond to the following: (a) What is the goal of Cisco's Networked Sustainability Framework? (b) What does its EnergyWise technology do? (c) Using a search engine, find Cisco's "Environmental Sustainability" web page. Besides the solutions listed in this chapter's Environment box, in what other ways is Cisco helping businesses achieve environmental sustainability? (d) Do you believe that Cisco's network technology can help the environment in the long run? Why or why not?

# Privacy, Security, and Ethics

▲ Download the free *Computing Essentials 2014* app for videos, key term flashcards, quizzes, and the game, *Over the Edge!*

## Competencies

**After you have read this chapter, you should be able to:**

**1** Identify the most significant concerns for effective implementation of computer technology.

**2** Discuss the primary privacy issues of accuracy, property, and access.

**3** Describe the impact of large databases, private networks, the Internet, and the web on privacy.

**4** Discuss online identity and the major laws on privacy.

**5** Discuss cybercrimes including creation of malicious programs such as viruses, worms, Trojan horses, and zombies as well as denial of service attacks, Internet scams, social networking risks, cyberbullying, rogue Wi-Fi hotspots, theft, and data manipulation.

**6** Detail ways to protect computer security including restricting access, encrypting data, anticipating disasters, and preventing data loss.

**7** Discuss computer ethics including copyright law, software piracy, digital rights management, the Digital Millennium Copyright Act, as well as plagiarism and ways to identify plagiarism.

## Why should I read this chapter?

In the past, protecting your privacy and security was pretty simple. You needed a paper shredder and perhaps an unlisted phone number. That was then and this is now. Now, in the digital age, personal security and privacy are much more complicated and difficult. Every minute there are thousands of malicious programs that are being spread across the Internet.

This chapter discusses privacy including identity theft, cookies, web bugs, and keystroke loggers.

Additionally, you'll learn about viruses, worms, rogue Wi-Fi hotspots, and the risks associated with Facebook and other social networking sites. You will also learn how to protect your computer security using a variety of techniques including biometric scanners and encryption. To be competent and to be competitive in today's professional workplace, you need to know and to understand these things.

## chapter .9

# Introduction

Hi, I'm Anthony, and I'm an IT security analyst. I'd like to talk with you about privacy, security, and ethics, three critical topics for anyone who uses computers today. I would also like to talk about how you can protect your privacy, ensure your security, and act ethically.

The tools and products of the information age do not exist in a world by themselves. As we said in Chapter 1, an information system consists not only of procedures, software, hardware, data, and connectively but also of people. Because of people, computer systems may be used for both good and bad purposes.

There are more than one billion microcomputers in use today. What are the consequences of the widespread presence of this technology? Does technology make it easy for others to invade our personal privacy? When we apply for a loan or for a driver's license, or when we check out at the supermarket, is that information about us being distributed and used without our permission? When we use the web, is information about us being collected and shared with others?

This technology prompts lots of questions—very important questions. Perhaps these are some of the most important questions for the 21st century. Competent end users need to be aware of the potential impact of technology on people and how to protect themselves on the web. They need to be sensitive to and knowledgeable about personal privacy and organizational security.

# People

As we have discussed, information systems consist of people, procedures, software, hardware, data, and connectivity. This chapter focuses on people. (See Figure 9-1.) While most everyone agrees that technology has had a very positive impact on people, it is important to recognize the negative, or potentially negative, impacts as well.

Effective implementation of computer technology involves maximizing its positive effects while minimizing its negative effects. The most significant concerns are

- **Privacy:** What are the threats to personal privacy, and how can we protect ourselves?

**Figure 9-1 People are part of an information system**

- **Security:** How can access to sensitive information be controlled, and how can we secure hardware and software?
- **Ethics:** How do the actions of individual users and companies affect society?

Let us begin by examining privacy.

# Privacy

As you have seen, computing technology makes it possible to collect and use data of all kinds, including information about people. The websites you visit, the stores where you shop, and the television shows you watch are all examples of information about you. How would you feel if you learned such information was being collected or shared? Would it matter who was collecting it, or how it was being used, or whether it was even correct?

**Privacy** concerns the collection and use of data about individuals. There are three primary privacy issues:

- **Accuracy** relates to the responsibility of those who collect data to ensure that the data is correct.
- **Property** relates to who owns data and rights to software.
- **Access** relates to the responsibility of those who have data to control who is able to use that data.

## Large Databases

Large organizations are constantly compiling information about us. The federal government alone has over 2,000 databases. Every day, data is gathered about us and stored in large databases. For example, telephone companies compile lists of the calls we make, the numbers called, and so on. A special telephone directory (called a **reverse directory**) lists telephone numbers sequentially. (See Figure 9-2.)

**Figure 9-2 Reverse directory website**

By entering just a telephone number, you can determine the name, address, and more information about the person registered with that number.

Credit card companies maintain user databases that track cardholder purchases, payments, and credit records. Supermarket scanners in grocery checkout counters record what we buy, when we buy it, how much we buy, and the price. Financial institutions, including banks and credit unions, record how much money we have, what we use it for, and how much we owe. Publishers of magazines, newspapers, and mail-order catalogues have our names, addresses, phone numbers, and what we order. Search engines record the search histories of their users including search topics and sites visited.

A vast industry of data gatherers known as **information resellers** or **information brokers** now exists that collects and sells such personal data. Using publicly available databases and in many cases nonpublic databases, information resellers create **electronic profiles** or highly detailed and personalized descriptions of individuals. Very likely, you have an electronic profile that includes your name, address, telephone number, Social Security number, driver's license number, bank account numbers, credit card numbers, telephone records, and shopping and purchasing patterns. Information resellers sell these electronic profiles to direct marketers, fund-raisers, and others. Many provide these services on the web for free or for a nominal cost. (See Figure 9-3.)

Your personal information, including preferences, habits, and financial data, has become a marketable commodity. This raises many issues, including

- **Collecting public, but personally identifying information:** What if people anywhere in the world could view detailed images of you, your home, or your vehicle? Using detailed images captured with a specially equipped van, Google's Street View project allows just that. Street View makes it possible to take a virtual tour of many cities and neighborhoods from any computer with a connection to the Internet. (See Figure 9-4.) Although the images available on Street View are all taken in public locations, some have objected to the project as being an intrusion on their privacy.

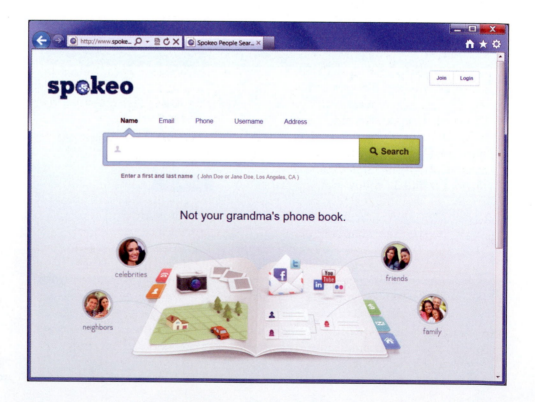

**Figure 9-3 Information reseller's website**

**Figure 9-4**  Google Street View

As digital cameras and webcams become cheaper and software becomes more sophisticated, it is likely that many more issues involving personal privacy in public spaces will need to be addressed. Such a combination of computing technologies could, for example, make real-time tracking of individuals in public places possible.

- **Spreading information without personal consent:** How would you feel if an employer were using your Facebook, Google+, or other social networking profiles to make decisions about hiring, placement, promotion, and firing? It is a common practice today for many organizations.

How would you feel if someone obtained a driver's license and credit cards in your name? What if that person then assumed your identity to buy clothes, cars, and a house? It happens every day. Every year, nearly 10 million people are victimized in this way. It is called **identity theft**. Identity theft is the illegal assumption of someone's identity for the purposes of economic gain. It is one of the fastest-growing crimes in the country. To learn more about identity theft and how to minimize your risk, visit our website at www.computing2014.com and enter the keyword **theft**.

- **Spreading inaccurate information:** How would you like to be turned down for a home loan because of an error in your credit history? This is much more common than you might expect. What if you could not find a job or were fired from a job because of an error giving you a serious criminal history?

**tips**

Identity theft is a growing problem, and can be financially devastating if you are a victim. Thieves are after anything that can help them steal your identity, from your Social Security number and date of birth to account information and passwords. Here are some steps to help protect your identity.

**1** Be careful what you write on the Internet. Never post personal information on forums or social networking areas that are public or in response to an e-mail from someone you do not know or trust.

**2** Only do business on the Internet with companies you know to be legitimate.

**3** When selling a computer, be sure to completely remove all personal information from the hard drive.

**4** Monitor your credit. Each year, you are entitled to a free personal credit report from each of the three major credit reporting agencies. Monitor your credit by requesting a report every four months from a different reporting agency. The official site for this service is www.annualcreditreport.com.

To see more tips, visit our website at www.computing2014.com and enter the keyword tips.

This can and has happened due to simple clerical errors. In one case, an arresting officer while completing an arrest warrant incorrectly recorded the Social Security number of a criminal. From that time forward, this arrest and the subsequent conviction became part of another person's electronic profile. This is an example of **mistaken identity** in which the electronic profile of one person is switched with another.

It's important to know that you have some recourse. The law allows you to gain access to those records about you that are held by credit bureaus. Under the **Freedom of Information Act**, you are also entitled to look at your records held by government agencies. (Portions may be deleted for national security reasons.)

## concept check

What are the three primary privacy issues?

What are information resellers, electronic profiles, identity theft, and mistaken identity?

What is the Freedom of Information Act?

### Private Networks

Suppose you use your company's electronic mail system to send a co-worker an unflattering message about your supervisor or to send a highly personal message to a friend. Later you find the boss has been spying on your exchange. This is legal, and a recent survey revealed that nearly 75 percent of all businesses search employees' electronic mail and computer files using so-called **employee-monitoring software**. (See Figure 9-5.) These programs record virtually everything you do on your computer. One proposed law would not prohibit

**Figure 9-5** Employee-monitoring software

this type of electronic monitoring but would require employers to provide prior written notice. Employers also would have to alert employees during the monitoring with some sort of audible or visual signal. If you are employed and would like to know your company's current policy on monitoring electronic communication, contact your human relations department.

## The Internet and the Web

When you send e-mail on the Internet or browse the web, do you have any concerns about privacy? Most people do not. They think that as long as they are using their own computer and are selective about disclosing their names or other personal information, then little can be done to invade their personal privacy. Experts call this the **illusion of anonymity** that the Internet brings.

As we discussed in Chapter 8, every computer on the Internet is identified by a unique number known as an IP address. IP addresses can be used to trace Internet activities to their origin, allowing computer security experts and law enforcement officers to investigate computer crimes such as unauthorized access to networks or sharing copyright files without permission.

When you browse the web, your browser stores critical information onto your hard disk, typically without you being aware of it. This information, which contains records about your Internet activities, includes history and temporary Internet files.

- **History files** include the locations, or addresses, of sites that you have recently visited. This history file can be displayed by your browser in various locations, including the address bar (as you type) and the *History* tab. To view your browsing history using Internet Explorer 9, follow the steps in Figure 9-6.

- **Temporary Internet files**, also known as the **browser cache**, contain web page content and instructions for displaying this content. Whenever you visit a website, these files are saved by your browser. If you leave a site and then return later, these files are used to quickly redisplay web content.

Another way your web activity can be monitored is with **cookies**. Cookies are small data files that are deposited on your hard disk from websites you have visited. Based on your browser's settings, these cookies can be accepted or blocked. (See Figure 9-7). Although you will generally not be aware when a website generates a cookie, the personalized experiences you enjoy on the web are often a result of those cookies. While cookies are harmless in and of themselves, what makes them a potential privacy risk is that they can store information about you, your preferences, and your browsing habits. The information stored generally depends on whether the cookie is a first-party or a third-party cookie.

- A **first-party cookie** is one that is generated (and then read) only by the website you are currently visiting. Many websites use first-party cookies to store information about the current session, your general preferences, and your activity on the site. The intention of these cookies is to provide a personalized experience on a particular site. For example, when you revisit a particular electronic commerce site, a previously deposited cookie can provide information so that you can be greeted by name and presented with sales and promotions that interest you.

**1** ● Select the *Favorites* button.

**2** ● Select *History*.

**Figure 9-6** Viewing history files

**1** ● Select the *Tools* button.

   ● Choose *Internet Options.*

**2** ● Select the *Privacy* tab.

   ● Move the slide to the desired level of protection.

   ● Click *OK*.

**Figure 9-7** Blocking cookies

- A **third-party cookie** is usually generated by an advertising company that is affiliated with the website you are currently visiting. They are used by the advertising company to keep track of your web activity as you move from one site to the next. For this reason, they are often referred to as **tracking cookies**. Critics of this practice claim that your privacy is being violated because your activity is being recorded across multiple websites. Defenders of this practice argue that these cookies are beneficial because it helps websites deliver ads that interest you. For example, suppose you visit four different websites that employ the same advertising agency. The first three sites are about cars, but the fourth is a search engine. When you visit the fourth site, you will likely see a car advertisement because your cookie showed that you had been visiting car-related websites.

Some users are not comfortable with idea of web browsers storing so much information in the form of cookies, history, and temporary Internet files. For this reason, browsers now offer users an easy way to delete their browsing history. (See Figure 9-8.) In addition, most browsers also offer a **privacy mode**, which ensures that your browsing activity is not recorded on your hard disk. For example, Internet Explorer 9 provides **InPrivate Browsing** accessible from the *Tools* button, and Safari provides **Private Browsing** accessible from the *Safari* option on the main menu.

Although these web browser files can concern many individuals, several other threats could potentially violate your privacy. **Web bugs**, which are invisible images or HTML code hidden within a web page or e-mail message, can be used to transmit information without your knowledge. When a user opens an e-mail containing a web bug, information is sent back to the source of the bug. The receiving server will now know that this e-mail address is active. One of the most common web bugs is used by companies that sell active mailing lists to spammers. Because of this deception, many e-mail programs now block images and HTML code from unknown senders. It is up to the user to decide whether or not to allow such content to be displayed for current and future messages. To see how web bugs work, visit our website at www.computing2014.com and enter the keyword bugs.

The most dangerous type of privacy threat comes in the form of spyware. The term **spyware** is used to describe a wide range of programs that are designed to secretly record and report an individual's activities on the Internet. Some of these programs can even make changes to your browser in order to deceive you and manipulate what you see online. **Computer monitoring software**, also known as **keystroke loggers**, is perhaps the most invasive and dangerous type of spyware. These programs record every activity and keystroke made on your computer system, including credit card numbers, passwords, and e-mail messages. Computer monitoring software can be deposited onto your hard drive without your knowledge by a malicious website or by someone installing the program directly onto your computer. While such software is deadly in the hands of criminals, it can be legally used by companies monitoring employees or law enforcement officials who are collecting evidence.

Unfortunately, many spyware programs go undetected, largely because users have no idea they are infected. Spyware will run in the background, invisible to the average user. Other times, it disguises itself as useful software, such as a security program. Various studies have demonstrated that an alarming number of computers are infected with spyware. The financial impact to individuals, companies, and financial institutions is estimated at billions of dollars.

One of the best defenses against spyware is to exercise caution when visiting new websites and downloading software from an unknown source. Another defense involves using a category of software known as **antispyware** or **spy removal programs**, which are designed to detect and remove various types of privacy threats. (See Figure 9-9.) For a list of some of these programs, see Figure 9-10.

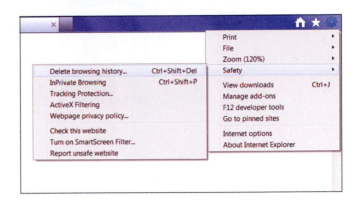

- **1** ● Select the *Tools* button.
  ● Choose *Safety*.
  ● Choose *Delete browsing history*.

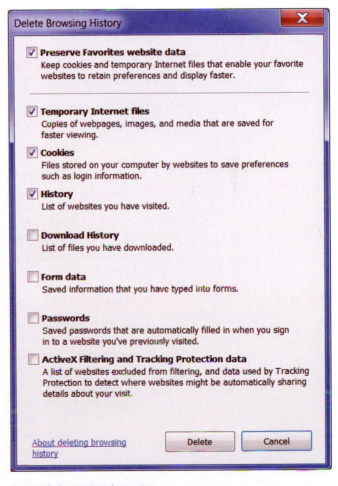

- **2** ● Select check boxes for items to be deleted.
  ● Choose *Delete*.

**Figure 9-8 Deleting browsing**

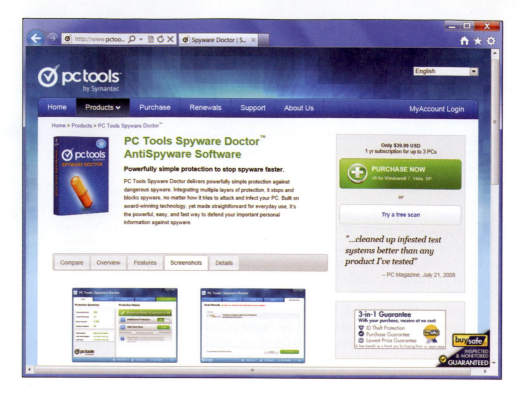

**Figure 9-9** Antispyware

| Program | Website |
|---------|---------|
| Ad-Aware | www.lavasoft.com |
| SUPERAntiSpyware | www.superantispyware.com |
| Spyware Doctor | www.spydoctor.com |
| Windows Defender | www.microsoft.com |

**Figure 9-10** Antispyware programs

## Online Identity

Another aspect of Internet privacy comes from **online identity**, the information that people voluntarily post about themselves online. With the popularity of social networking, blogging, and photo- and video-sharing sites, many people post intimate details of their lives without considering the consequences. Although it is easy to think of online identity as something shared between friends, the archiving and search features of the web make it available indefinitely to anyone who cares to look. There are any number of cases of people who have lost their jobs on the basis of posts on social media websites. These job losses range from a teacher (using off-color language and photos showing drinking) to a chief financial officer of a major corporation (discussing corporate dealings and financial data). The cases include college graduates being refused a job because of Facebook posts. How would you feel if information you posted about yourself on the web kept you from getting a job?

## Major Laws on Privacy

Some federal laws governing privacy matters have been created. For example, the **Gramm-Leach-Bliley Act** protects personal financial information, the **Health Insurance Portability and Accountability Act (HIPAA)** protects medical records, and the **Family Educational Rights and Privacy Act (FERPA)** restricts disclosure of educational records. To learn more about existing privacy laws, visit our website at www.computing2014.com and enter the keyword law.

Most of the information collected by private organizations is not covered by existing laws. However, as more and more individuals become concerned about controlling who has the right to personal information and how that information is used, companies and lawmakers will respond.

## concept check

- What is employee-monitoring software? Describe the illusion of anonymity.

- What is a history file? What are temporary Internet files? Compare first- and third-party cookies. What is privacy mode?

- Define spyware, web bugs, keystroke loggers, antispyware programs, and online identity.

- Describe three federal laws to protect privacy.

# Security

We are all concerned with having a safe and secure environment to live in. We are careful to lock our car doors and our homes. We are careful about where we walk at night and whom we talk to. This is personal security. What about computer security? What if someone gains unauthorized access to our computer or other computers that contain information about us? These people are commonly known as computer **hackers**. It should be noted that not all hackers are intent on malicious actions and that not all are criminals. **Security** involves protecting individuals and organizations from theft and danger. Computer security specifically focuses on protecting information, hardware, and software from unauthorized use, as well as preventing or limiting the damage from intrusions, sabotage, and natural disasters.

## Cybercrime

**Cybercrime** or **computer crime** is any criminal offense that involves a computer and a network. It was recently estimated that cybercrime affects over 400 million people and costs over $400 billion each year. Cybercrimes can take various forms including the creation of malicious programs, denial of service attacks, Internet scams, theft, and data manipulation.

**Malicious Programs** A **cracker** is someone who creates and distributes malicious programs. These programs are called **malware**, which is short for **mal**icious soft**ware**. They are specifically designed to damage or disrupt a computer system. The three most common types of malware are viruses, worms, and Trojan horses.

- **Viruses** are programs that migrate through networks and operating systems, and most attach themselves to different programs and databases. While some viruses are relatively harmless, many can be quite destructive. Once activated, these destructive viruses can alter and/or delete files. Creating and knowingly spreading a virus is a very serious crime and a federal offense punishable under the **Computer Fraud and Abuse Act**.

  Unfortunately, new computer viruses are appearing all the time. The best way to stay current is through services that keep track of viruses on a daily basis. For example, Symantec tracks the most serious virus threats. See Figure 9-11.

- **Worms** are programs that simply replicate themselves over and over again. Once active in a network, the self-replicating activity clogs computers and networks until their operations are slowed or stopped. A recent worm traveled across the world within hours, stopping tens of thousands of computers along its way. Unlike a virus, a worm typically does not attach itself to a program or alter and/or delete files. Worms, however, can carry a virus. Once a virus has been deposited by a worm onto an unsuspecting computer system, the virus

## environment

Did you know that the U.S. Department of Defense considers certain environmental issues to be potential threats to national security? There are currently two environmental research programs that are being funded by this department. The Strategic Environmental Research and Development Program (SERDP) focuses on research on innovative technology that can help to reduce environmental risks while enhancing and sustaining military readiness. The Environmental Security Technology Certification Program (ESTCP) is responsible for demonstrating and validating the most promising technologies. To see more environmental facts, visit our website at www.computing2014 .com and enter the keyword environment.

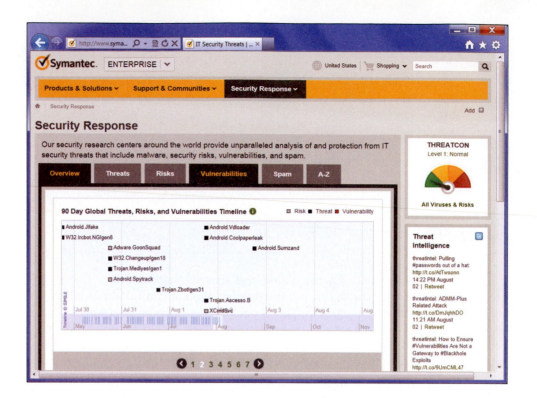

**Figure 9-11** Tracking viruses

will either activate immediately or lie dormant until some future time. For example in 2010, the Stuxnet worm infected several networks in Iran. One of these networks was used by Iran's nuclear program. Soon after the infection, several key pieces of nuclear equipment became permanently disabled.

Viruses and worms typically find their way into microcomputers through e-mail attachments and programs downloaded from the Internet. Because viruses can be so damaging, computer users are advised to never open an e-mail attachment from an unknown source and to exercise great care in accepting new programs and data from any source.

As we discussed in Chapter 4, antivirus programs alert users when certain kinds of viruses and worms enter their system. Two of the most widely used are McAfee VirusScan and Norton AntiVirus. Unfortunately, new viruses are being developed all the time, and not all viruses can be detected.

- **Trojan horses** are programs that come into a computer system disguised as something else. Trojan horses are not viruses. Like worms, however, they can be carriers of viruses. The most common types of Trojan horses appear as free computer games and free screen saver programs that can be downloaded from the Internet. When a user downloads one of these programs, a virus is deposited on the computer system. The virus then begins its mischief. One of the most dangerous types of Trojan horse claims to provide free antivirus programs. When a user downloads one of these programs, the Trojan horse starts with a virus that locates and disables any existing virus protection programs before depositing other viruses.

**Zombies** are computers infected by a virus, worm, or Trojan horse that allows them to be remotely controlled for malicious purposes. A collection of zombie computers is known as a **botnet**, or **robot network**. Botnets harness the combined power of many zombies for malicious activities like password cracking or sending junk e-mail. Because they are formed by many computers distributed across the Internet, botnets are hard to shut down even after they are detected. Unfortunately for individual computer owners, it also can be difficult to detect when a personal computer has been compromised.

| Type | Description |
|------|-------------|
| Identity theft | Individuals pose as ISPs, bank representatives, or government agencies requesting personal information. Once obtained, criminals assume a person's identity for a variety of financial transactions. |
| Chain letter | Classic chain letter instructing recipient to send a nominal amount of money to each of five people on a list. The recipient removes the first name on the list, adds his or her name at the bottom, and mails the chain letter to five friends. This is also known as a pyramid scheme. Almost all chain letters are fraudulent and illegal. |
| Auction fraud | Merchandise is selected and payment is sent. Merchandise is never delivered. |
| Vacation prize | "Free" vacation has been awarded. Upon arrival at vacation destination, the accommodations are dreadful but can be upgraded for a fee. |
| Advance fee loans | Guaranteed low-rate loans available to almost anyone. After applicant provides personal loan-related information, the loan is granted subject to payment of an "insurance fee." |

**Figure 9-12  Common Internet scams**

**Denial of Service**  A **denial of service (DoS) attack** attempts to slow down or stop a computer system or network by flooding a computer or network with requests for information and data. The targets of these attacks are usually Internet service providers (ISPs) and specific websites. Once under attack, the servers at the ISP or the website become overwhelmed with these requests for service and are unable to respond to legitimate users. As a result, the ISP or website is effectively shut down.

**Internet Scams**  A **scam** is a fraudulent or deceptive act or operation designed to trick individuals into providing personal information or spending their time and money for little or no return. An **Internet scam** is simply a scam using the Internet. Internet scams are becoming a serious problem and have created financial and legal problems for many thousands of people. Almost all the scams are initiated by a mass mailing to unsuspecting individuals.

A technique often employed by scammers is **phishing** (pronounced "fishing"). Phishing attempts to trick Internet users into thinking a fake but official-looking website or e-mail is legitimate. Phishing has grown in sophistication, replicating entire websites like PayPal to try to lure users into divulging their financial information.

See Figure 9-12 for a list of common types of Internet scams.

**Social Networking Risks**  As we have discussed in Chapter 2, social networking is designed for open sharing of information among individuals that share a common interest. Unfortunately, this openness can put individuals using social networking sites at risk. Some have lost their jobs after posting unflattering remarks about their supervisor or after discussing their dislike of their current job. Others post detailed personal information such as their birth dates, family member names, home addresses, and photos of their children. This information can be used by others to steal personal identities and commit other types of crimes. Always exercise caution when providing information on Facebook, Twitter, and other social networking sites. Always use the privacy settings and controls that are provided at the social networking sites you use. (See Figure 9-13.)

**Cyberbullying**  A fairly recent and all-too-common phenomenon, **cyberbullying** is the use of the Internet, cell phones, or other devices to send or post content intended

**Figure 9-13** Facebook privacy controls

to hurt or embarrass another person. Although not always a crime, it can lead to criminal prosecution. Cyberbullying includes sending repeated unwanted e-mails to an individual who has stated that he or she wants no further contact with the sender, ganging up on victims in electronic forums, posting false statements designed to injure the reputation of another, maliciously disclosing personal data about a person that could lead to harm to that person, and sending any type of communication that is threatening or harassing. Never participate in cyberbullying, and discourage others from participating in this dangerous and hateful activity.

**Rogue Wi-Fi Hotspots** Free Wi-Fi networks are available almost everywhere from libraries to fast-food restaurants and coffee shops. **Rogue Wi-Fi hotspots** imitate these free networks. These rogue networks operate close to the legitimate free hotspots and typically provide stronger signals that many users unsuspectingly connect to. Once connected, the rogue networks capture any and all information sent by the users to legitimate sites including user names and passwords.

**Theft** Theft can take many forms—of hardware, of software, of data, of computer time. Thieves steal equipment and programs, of course, but there are also white-collar crimes. These crimes include the theft of data in the form of confidential information such as preferred-client lists. Another common crime is the use (theft) of a company's computer time by an employee to run another business.

**Data Manipulation** Finding entry into someone's computer network and leaving a prankster's message may seem like fun, which is why hackers do it. It is still against the law. Moreover, even if the manipulation seems harmless, it may cause a great deal of anxiety and wasted time among network users.

The **Computer Fraud and Abuse Act** makes it a crime for unauthorized persons even to view—let alone copy or damage—data using any computer across state lines. It also prohibits unauthorized use of any government computer or a computer used by any federally insured financial institution. Offenders can be sentenced to up to 20 years in prison and fined up to $100,000.

| Computer Crime | Description |
| --- | --- |
| Malicious programs | Include viruses, worms, and Trojan horses |
| DoS | Causes computer systems to slow down or stop |
| Internet scams | Are scams over the Internet usually initiated by e-mail and involving phishing |
| Social networking risks | Includes posting work-related criticisms and disclosure of personal information |
| Cyberbullying | Is using the Internet, cell phones, or other devices to send/post content intended to hurt or embarrass another person |
| Rogue Wi-Fi hotspots | Imitate legitimate Wi-Fi hotspot in order to capture personal information |
| Theft | Includes hardware, software, and computer time |
| Data manipulation | Involves changing data or leaving prank messages |

**Figure 9-14** Computer crimes

For a summary of computer crimes, see Figure 9-14. For a brief history of computer crimes, visit our website at www.computing2014.com and enter the keyword **crime**.

## concept check

What is cybercrime? What are malicious programs?

Compare viruses, worms, and Trojan horses. What are zombies?

What are denial of service attacks? Internet scams? Social networking risks?

What is cyberbullying? A rogue Wi-Fi hotspot? Data theft and manipulation?

## Measures to Protect Computer Security

There are numerous ways in which computer systems and data can be compromised and many ways to ensure computer security. Some of the principal measures to ensure computer security are restricting access, encrypting messages, anticipating disasters, and preventing data loss.

**Restricting Access** Security experts are constantly devising ways to protect computer systems from access by unauthorized persons. Sometimes security is a matter of putting guards on company computer rooms and checking the identification of everyone admitted. Other times it is using **biometric scanning** devices such as fingerprint and iris (eye) scanners. (See Figure 9-15.) There are numerous applications that use face recognition to allow access to a computer system.

With so many security threats out there, as well as tools to counter those threats, you can easily feel helpless and overwhelmed. Here is an easy-to-follow list of best practices that can help protect the security of your computer and valuable data:

**1** **Security tools.** An Internet security suite (which includes an antivirus program), together with the firewall that is included with most operating systems, will keep most threats from harming your computer.

**2** **Software updates.** Always ensure that your operating system, security suites, and other crucial programs are set to receive updates as soon as the companies make them available.

**3** **E-mail and attachments.** Avoid opening any e-mail that seems suspicious or is from a person or organization you do not know. Be even more careful with links and attachments. Also remember that the e-mail accounts belonging to your friends and family members could be compromised, so be careful with attachments and links from them that seem suspicious.

**4** **Passwords.** Use a strong password for your operating system log-in, and a different strong password for each website log-in. Do not share passwords with anyone and do not leave them in obvious places, such as on a notebook next to your computer or in an unencrypted Word document.

**5** **Wireless encryption.** Use WPA2 encryption for your home's wireless router.

To see other tips, visit our website at www.computing2014.com and enter the keyword tips.

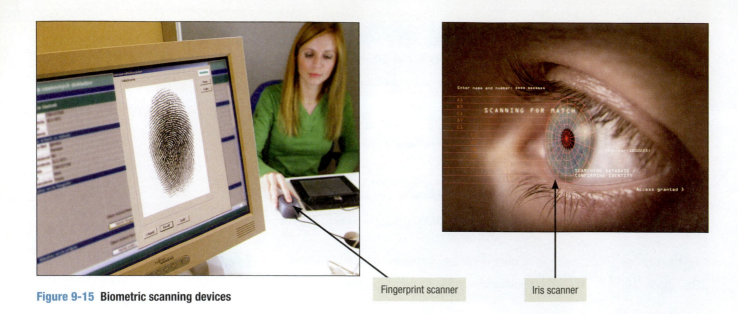

**Figure 9-15 Biometric scanning devices**

Fingerprint scanner

Iris scanner

For example, many microcomputer systems use Dell's FastAccess face recognition application to prevent unauthorized access. There are also several face recognition apps for mobile devices including Face Recognition by iNFINITE Studios LLC.

Oftentimes it is a matter of being careful about assigning passwords to people and of changing the passwords when people leave a company. **Passwords** are secret words or phrases (including numbers, letters, and special characters) that must be keyed into a computer system to gain access. For many applications on the web, users assign their own passwords. Windows 8 includes an application, Picture Password, that accepts a series of gestures over a picture of the users choice to gain access.

The strength of a password depends on how easily it can be guessed. A **dictionary attack** uses software to try thousands of common words sequentially in an attempt to gain unauthorized access to a user's account. For this reason, words, names, and simple numeric patterns make weak or poor passwords. Strong passwords have at least eight characters and use a combination of letters, numbers, and punctuation marks. It is also important not to reuse passwords for different accounts. If one account is compromised, that password might be tried for access to other systems as well. For example, if a low-security account such as an online web forum is compromised, that password could also be tried on higher-security accounts such as banking websites.

As mentioned in previous chapters, individuals and organizations use security suites and firewalls to protect and control access to their computers.

- **Security suites** provide a collection of utility programs designed to protect your privacy and security while you are on the web. To learn more about selecting and using security suites, see Making IT Work for You: Security Suites on pages 257 and 258.

- **Firewalls** act as a security buffer between a corporation's private network and all external networks, including the Internet. All electronic communications coming into and leaving the corporation must be evaluated by the firewall. Security is maintained by denying access to unauthorized communications.

**Encrypting Data** Whenever information is sent over a network or stored on a computer system, the possibility of unauthorized access exists. The solution is **encryption**, the process of coding information to make it unreadable except to

## SECURITY SUITES

Do you currently have software that protects you and your computer from various types of threats? Are they separate programs that have to be managed individually? If so, then you may find that a security suite is a more convenient solution. These suites are software packages that include various utilities that help protect your computer from malware, hackers, and many other types of threats.

**Standard Utilities**   Most security suites provide the following features to protect you and your computer:

- **Antivirus**
- **Antispyware**
- **Firewall**
- **Phishing detection**
- **Privacy/identity protection**
- **Parental controls**

At a minimum, all products will have antivirus and antispyware capabilities. You will be protected by a real-time scanner that is loaded into your computer's RAM each time you log into your system.

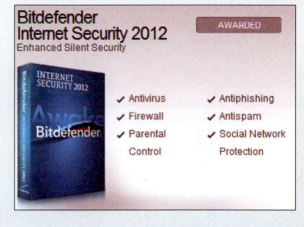

**Factors to Consider**   With so many security suites, it may be difficult to make a choice. Experts generally consider the following factors:

- *Detection.* **How well does it detect threats? Does it miss too many?**
- *False-positives.* **How many times does it mistake a safe file for a threat?**
- *Threat removal.* **How well does it eliminate malicious files from your machine?**
- *Performance.* **Does it slow down your system significantly while it is in RAM? How fast does it complete a system scan?**
- *Interface.* **Is the software easy to use and configure?**

For specific recommendations and rankings, it is useful to read expert reviews and test results. Search for "security suites" on reliable online sources such as pcworld.com and cnet.com.

**Free Resources** There are several ways to obtain security tools at no cost:

- *Free antivirus.* Many reputable companies, such as Avast and AVG, create free antivirus products in order to promote their more feature-rich versions (which do cost money). Although they are offered as free downloads, these tools will generally perform their detection and removal jobs quite well.

- *ISP provided.* Most Internet service providers include a security suite with your Internet subscription. Make sure this offer is a permanent and not a limited trial. Many individuals have found themselves unprotected because their antivirus subscription expired!

- *Microsoft Security Essentials.* Windows does not include an antivirus; however, Microsoft does offer this product as a free download on its website if you are running a genuine copy of Windows.

| Free Antivirus | Pro Antivirus | Internet Security |
|:---:|:---:|:---:|
| ✓ | ✓ | ✓ |
| ✓ | ✓ | ✓ |
|  | ✓ | ✓ |
|  | ✓ | ✓ |
|  | ✓ | ✓ |
|  |  | ✓ |
|  |  | ✓ |
|  |  | ✓ |
|  |  | ✓ |
|  |  | ✓ |
|  |  | ✓ |

- *Online scans.* Several products, such as Trend Micro's *HouseCall* and Panda Security's *ActiveScan,* offer web-based scanning of your computer when you visit their websites. Generally speaking, this is useful only when you suspect that your computer is already infected.

The web is continually changing, and some of the specifics presented in this Making IT Work for You may have changed.

**To learn about other ways to make information technology work for you, visit our website at www.computing2014.com and enter the keyword miw.**

**Figure 9-16** Encrypted e-mail

those who have a special piece of information known as an **encryption key**, or, simply, a **key**. Some common uses for encryption include

- **E-mail encryption:** Protects e-mail messages as they move across the Internet. One of the most widely used personal e-mail encryption programs is Pretty Good Privacy. (See Figure 9-16.)

- **File encryption:** Protects sensitive files by encrypting them before they are stored on a hard drive. Files can be encrypted individually, or specialized software can be used to encrypt all files automatically each time they are saved to a certain hard drive location. (See Figure 9-17.)

- **Website encryption:** Secures web transactions, especially financial transactions. Web pages that accept passwords or confidential information like a credit card number are often encrypted.

**Figure 9-17** File encryption

The most common protocol for website encryption is **https (hypertext transfer protocol secure)**. As we discussed in Chapter 2, **http (hypertext transfer protocol)** is the most widely used Internet protocol. The https adds a security level to http. Every URL that begins with *https* requires that the browser and the connecting site encrypt all messages, providing a safer and more secure transmission.

- **Virtual private networks: Virtual private networks (VPNs)** encrypt connections between company networks and remote users such as workers connecting from home. This connection creates a secure virtual connection to a company LAN across the Internet.
- **Wireless network encryption:** Restricts access to authorized users on wireless networks. **WPA2 (Wi-Fi Protected Access)** is the most widely used wireless network encryption for home wireless networks. WPA2 is typically established for a wireless network through the network's wireless router. While the specifics vary between routers, WPA2 is usually set through the router's settings options.

**Anticipating Disasters** Companies (and even individuals) should prepare themselves for disasters. **Physical security** is concerned with protecting hardware from possible human and natural disasters. **Data security** is concerned with protecting software and data from unauthorized tampering or damage. Most large organizations have a **disaster recovery plan** describing ways to continue operating until normal computer operations can be restored.

**Preventing Data Loss** Equipment can always be replaced. A company's *data*, however, may be irreplaceable. Most companies have ways of trying to keep software and data from being tampered with in the first place. They include careful screening of job applicants, guarding of passwords, and auditing of data and programs from time to time. Some systems use redundant storage to prevent loss of data even when a hard drive fails. We discussed RAID in Chapter 7, which is a commonly used type of redundant storage. Backup batteries protect against data loss due to file corruption during unexpected power outages.

Making frequent backups of data is essential to prevent data loss. Backups are often stored at an off-site location to protect data in case of theft, fires, floods, or other disasters. Students and others often use flash drives and cloud storage as discussed in Chapter 7 to back up homework and important papers. Incremental backups store multiple versions of data at different points in time to prevent data loss due to unwanted changes or accidental deletion. To see how you could use a cloud-based backup service, see Making IT Work for You: Cloud-Based Backup on pages 261 and 262.

See Figure 9-18 for a summary of the different measures to protect computer security.

| Measure | Description |
|---|---|
| Restricting access | Limit access to authorized persons using such measures as passwords and firewalls. |
| Encrypting data | Code all messages sent over a network. |
| Anticipating disasters | Prepare for disasters by ensuring physical security and data security through a disaster recovery plan. |
| Preventing data loss | Routinely copy data and store it at a remote location. |

**Figure 9-18 Measures to protect computer security**

## CLOUD-BASED BACKUP

Do you remember to make frequent backups of your irreplaceable data files, such as photos and documents? Would you like a service that remembers to do the backups for you and places them in a very reliable location? If so, then a cloud-based backup service, such as Carbonite, is the solution for you.

**Getting Started**  Carbonite offers a free trial to its backup service. Once the trial ends, you will have to pay an annual fee to continue using it. To get started with the trial:

**1**  Visit www.carbonite.com, and click the *Try It For Free* button for home users.

**2**  Create an account, and then click the *Install Now* button to download the software.

**3**  Start the installation process, and when prompted, select the *Automatic* backup settings for easy setup.

After installation, Carbonite InfoCenter will launch and begin scanning your system for files to back up.

**Managing Files for Backup**  During the free trial, Carbonite will not automatically back up certain types of files (such as music and video). Regardless, you can still select these files manually and request that they be backed up.

**1**  Go to a folder that contains photos, such as *Sample Pictures* in Windows. If you see an orange or a green icon at the bottom left of the files, that means they have been backed up (green) or are waiting to be backed up (orange).

**2**  Now, go to a folder where you have music files. Notice that they do not have an icon in the corner.

**3**  Right-click a music file, select *Carbonite,* and click *Back this up.* This file is now marked with an orange icon (you may have to refresh your window) and will be backed up in due time.

**Restoring your Files**   Both your files and folder structure are securely backed up on Carbonite's servers. Although the Carbonite InfoCenter window has a restore area, this guide will show you how to view your backups on Carbonite's website for easy downloading from wherever you are.

**1** ● Go to Carbonite's website, and click the *Log In* button. Enter your log-in information. You will be taken to a screen where you can see both computer and account information.

**2** ● Click the *Restore* button, and you will be given a choice to restore all your files or to select individual files to be downloaded.

**3** ● Click the *Remote Access* button.

**4** ● Browse your backups by drives, folders, or users on your machine.

**5** ● Select a particular file or folder, and then click the *Download* button.

Home-Computer (edit)

TRIAL
Carbonite Home
Expires on June 8, 2012 (B

Backup Status: **Normal** ✓
Last backed up May 24, 2012

View Files
Restore

My Computers
Home-Computer
Guest
ComputingEssentials
Local Disk (C:)
Local Disk (F:)

Computer Summary

My Account
• Account summary
• Personal info
• Credit card info
• Payment history

Search ComputingEssentials

C ▸ Users ▸ ComputingEssentials

Share photos   Download   Select all

Name ▲                                    Size    Date Modified
AppData
Contacts
Desktop
Documents
Downloads
Favorites
Links
Music
Pictures

To maintain access to your files, you will have to sign up for a yearly subscription once the free trial ends. The affordable "Home" option is sufficient for most users. However, if you need to back up files that are stored on an external hard drive, the "HomePlus" plan may be best.

The web is continually changing, and some of the specifics presented in this Making IT Work for You may have changed.

**To learn about other ways to make information technology work for you, visit our website at www.computing2014.com and enter the keyword miw.**

## concept check

Discuss biometric scanning, passwords, dictionary attack, and firewalls.

What is encryption? What is WPA2?

Define physical security, data security, and disaster recovery plans.

# Ethics

What do you suppose controls how computers can be used? You probably think first of laws. Of course, that is right, but technology is moving so fast that it is very difficult for our legal system to keep up. The essential element that controls how computers are used today is *ethics*.

**Ethics**, as you may know, are standards of moral conduct. **Computer ethics** are guidelines for the morally acceptable use of computers in our society. Ethical treatment is critically important to us all, and we are all entitled to ethical treatment. This includes the right to keep personal information, such as credit ratings and medical histories, from getting into unauthorized hands. These issues, largely under the control of corporations and government agencies, were covered earlier in this chapter. These issues and many more have been addressed in the Ethics boxes throughout this book. Now we'll examine two important issues in computer ethics where average users have a role to play.

## Copyright and Digital Rights Management

**Copyright** is a legal concept that gives content creators the right to control use and distribution of their work. Materials that can be copyrighted include paintings, books, music, films, and even video games. Some users choose to make unauthorized copies of digital media, which violates copyright. For example, making an unauthorized copy of a digital music file for a friend might be a copyright violation.

**Software piracy** is the unauthorized copying and/or distribution of software. According to a recent study, software piracy costs the software industry over $30 billion annually. To prevent copyright violations, corporations often use **digital rights management (DRM)**. DRM encompasses various technologies that control access to electronic media and files. Typically, DRM is used to (1) control the number of devices that can access a given file and (2) limit the kinds of devices that can access a file. Although some companies see DRM as a necessity to protect their rights, some users feel they should have the right to use the media they buy—including movies, music, software, and video games—as they choose.

The **Digital Millennium Copyright Act** makes it illegal to deactivate or otherwise disable any antipiracy technologies including DRM technologies. The act also establishes that copies of commercial programs may not be legally resold or given away. It further makes it a crime to sell or to use programs or devices that are used to illegally copy software. This may come as a surprise to those who copy software including music and games from a friend or from the Internet. The law is clear: It is illegal to copy or download copyright-protected music and videos from the Internet without appropriate authorization.

Today, there are many legal sources for digital media. Television programs can be watched online, often for free, on television-network-sponsored sites. Sites like

**Figure 9-19 iTunes Music Store**

Pandora allow listeners to enjoy music at no cost. There are several online stores for purchasing music and video content. A pioneer in this area is Apple's iTunes Music Store. (See Figure 9-19.)

### Plagiarism

Another ethical issue is **plagiarism**, which means representing some other person's work and ideas as your own without giving credit to the original source. Although plagiarism was a problem long before the invention of computers, computer technology has made plagiarism easier. For example, simply cutting and pasting content from a web page into a report or paper may seem tempting to an overworked student or employee.

Correspondingly, computer technology has made it easier than ever to recognize and catch **plagiarists**. For example, services such as Turnitin are dedicated to preventing Internet plagiarism. This service will examine the content of a paper and compare it to a wide range of known public electronic documents including web page content. In this way, Turnitin can identify an undocumented paper or even parts of an undocumented paper. (See Figure 9-20.)

## ✓ concept check

What is the distinction between ethics and computer ethics?

Define copyright, software privacy, digital rights management, and the Digital Millennium Copyright Act.

What is plagiarism? What is Turnitin and what does it do?

## ethics

Do you know of anyone who has copied parts of a web page from a variety of sites and combined the parts to form a term paper? Of course, such a practice is unethical and most likely illegal. Many schools and universities now use a program that can compare the content of a student's paper to published material on the web and previously submitted papers. Do you think it is ethical for instructors to employ a program that checks for plagiarism? Is there a risk that the program may confuse proper citations from the web with obvious cases of plagiarism? To see more ethical issues, visit our website at www.computing2014.com and enter the keyword ethics.

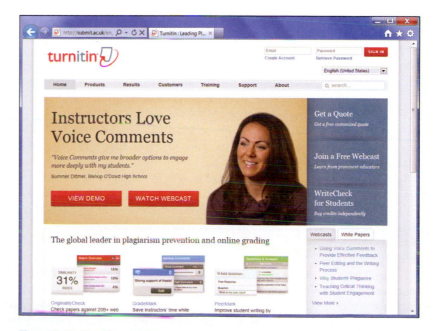

**Figure 9-20 Turnitin website**

# Careers in IT

**IT security analysts** are responsible for maintaining the security of a company's network, systems, and data. Their goal is to ensure the confidentiality, integrity, and availability of information. These analysts must safeguard information systems against a variety of external threats, such as hackers and viruses, as well be vigilant of threats that may come from within the company.

Employers typically look for candidates with a bachelor's or advanced specialized associate's degree in information systems or computer science. Experience in this field or in network administration is usually required. IT security analysts should possess good communication and research skills, and be able to handle high-stress situations.

IT security analysts can expect to earn an annual salary of $62,000 to $101,000. Opportunities for advancement typically depend on experience. Demand for this position is expected to grow as malware, hackers, and other types of threats become more complex and prevalent. To learn about other careers in information technology, visit us at www.computing2014.com and enter the keyword careers.

Now that you have learned about privacy, security, and ethics, let me tell you about my career as an IT security analyst.

# A LOOK TO THE FUTURE

## The End of Anonymity

Do you enjoy the ability to interact with others on the web anonymously? Is there a sense of comfort knowing that you can express yourself freely without others knowing your identity? Anonymity has been a way of life on the Internet since the very beginning. However, various organizations, ranging from advertisers to governments, are questioning whether the Internet can continue like this. And based on the amount of information currently shared by people online, one wonders whether anonymity will be valued at all in the future.

There are many factors that are causing many to question the value of anonymity. First is the issue of harassment. Most forums and comment areas on websites allow users to post messages anonymously. Some individuals use this ability to write abusive or threatening comments. Many children and teenagers have been victims of online harassment, or cyberbullying, at some point in their lives. Others have been stalked online to the point where they have experienced psychological harm. Experts feel that if anonymous comments were disallowed, those same individuals would not be willing to write those types of messages, as their anonymity would be stripped. The other area where anonymity has become a problem is the legal field. Some anonymous web users have posted lies about individuals or businesses that have damaged the target's reputation. In the real world, those types of false and damaging comments could lead to lawsuits. For these reasons, many legislators are proposing laws aimed at discouraging the sort of anonymity that allows various online crimes to occur. In the future, it may even be a requirement to provide a real-world ID in order to use the Internet.

Many online companies are also fighting to end anonymity. This is because they make most of their money off targeted advertising. For these companies to deliver the proper advertisement to you, they need to know quite a bit about you and your online activities. By having a profile with your real name and interests, they can follow your activity throughout the web to get to know you better. At present, many advertisements you see online are for a product or service that does not interest you. In the future, every advertisement you see will interest you, as marketing companies develop a complete profile that lets them know everything about you. Now, many online businesses do aim to protect your privacy, but this is only with respect to what the public knows about you. When it comes to their advertising partners, they don't hide much because it is not in their interest to do so. Essentially, it is a trade-off for users, whether to give up some (or all) of your anonymity in return for targeted advertising.

Although many organizations are working toward ending or severely limiting anonymity, some would like to keep the Internet the way it is. Many civil rights groups and journalists support anonymity as a basic right. If you cannot be anonymous, then it would be difficult, for example, to post information that uncovers abuses in government or in a business. Some psychologists also support anonymity, stating that creating a separate online identity can be useful for personal development, allowing an individual to explore interests without leaving a record that is tied to his or her own life.

How do you feel about the possible end to anonymity? Do you agree that there will be less negativity on the web if everyone had to provide real names? Since advertisements pay for free services, will you at least tolerate future ads more if they contain something that interests you?

## PRIVACY

Privacy concerns the collection and use of data about individuals. There are three primary privacy issues: **accuracy** (who is responsible to ensure data is correct), **property** (who owns data and rights to software), **access** (who controls access to data).

### Large Databases

Large organizations are constantly compiling information about us. **Reverse directories** list telephone numbers followed by subscriber names. **Information resellers (information brokers)** collect and sell personal data. **Electronic profiles** are compiled from databases to provide highly detailed and personalized descriptions of individuals.

**Identity theft** is the illegal assumption of someone's identity for the purposes of economic gain. **Mistaken identity** occurs when an electronic profile of one person is switched with another. **The Freedom of Information Act** entitles individuals access to governmental records relating to them.

### Private Networks

Many organizations monitor employee e-mail and computer files using special software called **employee-monitoring software**.

### The Internet and the Web

Many people believe that, while using the web, little can be done to invade their privacy. This is called the **illusion of anonymity**.

## PRIVACY

Information stored by browsers includes **history files** (record sites visited) and **temporary Internet files** or **browser cache** (contain website content and display instructions). **Cookies** store and track information. **Privacy mode (InPrivate Browsing; Private Browsing)** ensures that your browsing activity is not recorded.

**Spyware** secretly records and reports Internet activities. **Computer monitoring software** (or **keystroke loggers**) are particularly dangerous. **Antispyware (spy removal programs)** detects and removes various privacy threats.

### Online Identity

Many people post personal information and sometimes intimate details of their lives without considering the consequences. This creates an **online identity**. With the archiving and search features of the web, this identity is indefinitely available to anyone who cares to look for it.

### Major Laws on Privacy

The **Gramm-Leach-Bliley Act** protects personal financial information; the **Health Insurance Portability and Accountability Act (HIPAA)** protects medical records; and the **Family Educational Rights and Privacy Act (FERPA)** restricts disclosure of educational records.

To be a competent end user, you need to be aware of the potential impact of technology on people. You need to be sensitive to and knowledgeable about personal privacy, organizational security, and ethics.

## SECURITY

Computer **security** focuses on protecting information, hardware, and software from unauthorized use as well as preventing damage from intrusions, sabotage, and natural disasters. Someone who gains unauthorized access to computers that contain information about us is commonly known as a computer **hacker**. Not all hackers are intent on malicious actions and not all are criminals.

### Cybercrime

**Cybercrime (computer crime)** is an illegal action involving special knowledge of computer technology.

- Malicious programs (**malware**) include **viruses** (the **Computer Fraud and Abuse Act** makes spreading a virus a federal offense), **worms**, and **Trojan horses. Zombies** are remotely controlled infected computers used for malicious purposes. A collection of zombie computers is known as a **botnet**, or **robot network**.
- **Denial of service (DoS) attack** is an attempt to shut down or stop a computer system or network. It floods a computer or network with requests for information and data.
- **Scams** are designed to trick individuals into spending their time and money with little or no return. Common **Internet scams** include identity theft, chain letters, auction fraud, vacation prizes, and advance fee loans. These are frequently coupled with **phishing** websites or e-mails.

## SECURITY

- Social networking risks include posting work-related criticisms and disclosure of personal information.
- **Cyberbullying** is the use of the Internet, cell phones, or other devices to send or post content intended to hurt or embarrass another person.
- **Rogue Wi-Fi hotspots** imitate legitimate hotspots to capture personal information.
- Theft takes many forms including stealing hardware, software, data, and computer time.
- Data manipulation involves changing data or leaving prank messages. **The Computer Fraud and Abuse Act** helps protect against data manipulation.

### Measures to Protect Computer Security

There are numerous ways in which computer systems and data can be compromised and many ways to protect computer security. These measures include

- Access can be restricted through **biometric scanning** devices and **passwords** (secret words or phrases; **dictionary attacks** use thousands of words to attempt to gain access).
- **Encrypting** is coding information to make it unreadable except to those who have the **encryption key. Virtual private networks (VPNs)** encrypt connections between company networks and remote users. **WPA2 (Wi-Fi Protected Access)** is the most widely used wireless network encryption for home wireless networks.
- Anticipating disasters involves physical security, data security, and disaster recovery plans.
- Preventing data loss involves protecting data by screening job applicants, guarding passwords, and auditing and backing up data.

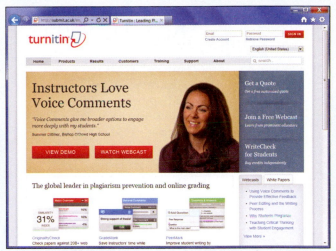

What do you suppose controls how computers can be used? You probably think first of laws. Of course, that is right, but technology is moving so fast that it is very difficult for our legal system to keep up. The essential element that controls how computers are used today is *ethics*.

**Ethics** are standards of moral conduct. **Computer ethics** are guidelines for the morally acceptable use of computers in our society. We are all entitled to ethical treatment. This includes the right to keep personal information, such as credit ratings and medical histories, from getting into unauthorized hands.

### Copyright and Digital Rights Management

**Copyright** is a legal concept that gives content creators the right to control use and distribution of their work. Materials that can be copyrighted include paintings, books, music, films, and even video games.

**Software piracy** is the unauthorized copying and distribution of software. The software industry loses over $30 billion annually to software piracy. Two related topics are the Digital Millennium Copyright Act and digital rights management.

- **Digital Millennium Copyright Act** establishes the right of a program owner to make a backup copy of any program and disallows the creation of copies to be sold or given away. It is also illegal to download copyright-protected music and videos from the Internet.

- **Digital rights management (DRM)** is a collection of technologies designed to prevent copyright violations. Typically, DRM is used to (1) control the number of devices that can access a given file and (2) limit the kinds of devices that can access a file.

Today, many legal sources for digital media exist, including

- Television programs that can be watched online, often for free, on television-network-sponsored sites.
- Sites like Pandora that allow listeners to enjoy music at no cost.
- Online stores that legally sell music and video content. A pioneer in this area is Apple's iTunes Music Store.

### Plagiarism

**Plagiarism** is the illegal and unethical representation of some other person's work and ideas as your own without giving credit to the original source. Examples of plagiarism include cutting and pasting web content into a report or paper.

Recognizing and catching **plagiarists** is relatively easy. For example, services such as **Turnitin** are dedicated to preventing Internet plagiarism. This service examines a paper's content and compares it to a wide range of known public electronic documents including web page content. Exact duplication or paraphrasing is readily identified.

## CAREERS IN IT

**IT security analysts** are responsible for maintaining the security of a company's network, systems, and data. Employers look for candidates with a bachelor's or advanced specialized associate's degree in information systems or computer science and network experience. Salary range is $62,000 to $101,000.

# KEY TERMS

access   (243)
accuracy   (243)
antispyware   (249)
biometric scanning   (255)
botnet   (252)
browser cache   (247)
computer crime   (251)
computer ethics   (263)
Computer Fraud and Abuse
Act   (251, 254)
computer monitoring software   (249)
cookies   (247)
copyright   (263)
cracker   (251)
cyberbullying   (253)
cybercrime   (251)
data security   (260)
denial of service (DoS) attack   (253)
dictionary attack   (256)
Digital Millennium Copyright
Act   (263)
digital rights management (DRM)   (263)
disaster recovery plan   (260)
electronic profile   (244)
employee-monitoring software   (246)
encryption   (256)
encryption key   (259)
ethics   (263)
Family Educational Rights and
Privacy Act (FERPA)   (250)
firewall   (256)
first-party cookie   (247)
Freedom of Information Act   (246)
Gramm-Leach-Bliley Act   (250)
hacker   (251)
Health Insurance Portability and
Accountability Act (HIPAA)   (250)
history file   (247)
http (hypertext transfer protocol)   (260)
https (hypertext transfer protocol
secure)   (260)

identity theft   (245)
illusion of anonymity   (247)
information broker   (244)
information reseller   (244)
InPrivate Browsing   (248)
Internet scam   (253)
IT security analyst   (265)
key   (259)
keystroke loggers   (249)
malware   (251)
mistaken identity   (246)
online identity   (250)
password   (256)
phishing   (253)
physical security   (260)
plagiarism   (264)
plagiarist   (264)
privacy   (243)
privacy mode   (248)
Private Browsing   (248)
property   (243)
reverse directory   (243)
robot network   (252)
rogue Wi-Fi hotspot   (254)
scam   (253)
security   (251)
security suites   (256)
software piracy   (263)
spy removal program   (249)
spyware   (249)
temporary Internet file   (247)
third-party cookie   (248)
tracking cookies   (248)
Trojan horse   (252)
virtual private network (VPN)   (260)
virus   (251)
web bugs   (249)
wireless network encryption   (260)
worm   (251)
WPA2 (Wi-Fi Protected Access 2)   (260)
zombie   (252)

To test your knowledge of these key terms with animated flash cards, visit us at
www.computing2014.com and enter the keyword terms9. Or use the free *Computing
Essentials 2014* app.

# MULTIPLE CHOICE

Circle the letter of the correct answer.

1. The three primary privacy issues are accuracy, property, and:
   a. access
   b. ethics
   c. ownership
   d. security

2. To get the name, address, and other details about a person using only his or her telephone number, you could use a:
   a. third-party cookie
   b. keystroke logger
   c. reverse directory
   d. worm

3. Browsers store the locations of sites visited in a:
   a. history file
   b. menu
   c. tool bar
   d. firewall

4. The browser mode that ensures your browsing activity is not recorded.
   a. detect
   b. insert
   c. privacy
   d. sleep

5. The information that people voluntarily post in social networking sites, blogs, and photo- and video-sharing sites is used to create their:
   a. access approval
   b. firewall
   c. online identity
   d. phish

6. Computer criminals who create and distribute malicious programs.
   a. antispies
   b. crackers
   c. cyber traders
   d. identity thieves

7. Programs that come into a computer system disguised as something else are called:
   a. Trojan horses
   b. viruses
   c. web bugs
   d. zombies

8. The use of the Internet, cell phones, or other devices to send or post content intended to hurt or embarrass another person is known as:
   a. cyberbullying
   b. online harassment
   c. social media discrimination
   d. unethical communication

9. Special hardware and software used to control access to a corporation's private network is known as a(n):
   a. antivirus program
   b. communication gate
   c. firewall
   d. spyware removal program

10. To prevent copyright violations, corporations often use:
    a. ACT
    b. DRM
    c. VPN
    d. WPA2

For an interactive multiple-choice practice test, visit us at www.computing2014.com and enter the keyword multiple9. Or use the free *Computing Essentials 2014* app.

# MATCHING

Match each numbered item with the most closely related lettered item. Write your answers in the spaces provided.

a. accuracy
b. biometric
c. cookies
d. encryption
e. information brokers
f. malware
g. phishing
h. plagiarism
i. spyware
j. zombies

____ 1. Privacy concern that relates to the responsibility to ensure correct data collection.

____ 2. Individuals who collect and sell personal data.

____ 3. Small data files deposited on your hard disk from websites you have visited.

____ 4. Wide range of programs that secretly record and report an individual's activities on the Internet.

____ 5. Malicious programs that damage or disrupt a computer system.

____ 6. Infected computers that can be remotely controlled.

____ 7. Used by scammers to trick Internet users with official-looking websites.

____ 8. A type of scanning device such as fingerprint and iris (eye) scanner.

____ 9. Process of coding information to make it unreadable except to those who have a key.

____ 10. An ethical issue relating to using another person's work and ideas as your own without giving credit to the original source.

For an interactive matching practice test, visit our website at www.computing2014.com and enter the keyword matching9. Or use the free *Computing Essentials 2014* app.

# OPEN-ENDED

On a separate sheet of paper, respond to each question or statement.

1. Define privacy, and discuss the impact of large databases, private networks, the Internet, and the web.

2. Define and discuss online identity and the major privacy laws.

3. Define security. Define computer crime and the impact of malicious programs, including viruses, worms, Trojan horses, and zombies, as well as cyberbullying, denial of service attacks, Internet scams, social networking risks, rogue Wi-Fi hotspots, theft, data manipulation, and other hazards.

4. Discuss ways to protect computer security including restricting access, encrypting data, anticipating disasters, and preventing data loss.

5. Define ethics, and describe copyright law and plagiarism.

# DISCUSSION

Respond to each of the following questions.

## ① Making IT Work for You: SECURITY SUITES

Do you currently have software that protects you and your computer from various types of threats? Review the Making IT Work for You: Security Suites on pages 257 and 258 and then respond to the following: (a) Do you have a security suite installed on your computer? If so, which one do you have and describe its functionality. If you do not, have you ever experienced any security or virus issues? (b) Does your Internet service provider offer a security suite or antivirus with your subscription? If so, which one(s) does it offer? If it does not, contact your ISP and ask its advice on how to protect your computer. What was its advice? (c) Find an article that reviews current security suites. (*PCWorld, CNET*, and *PCMag* are good places to start.) List three products that earned the highest marks, and document your source(s). (d) Based on your experience and research, do you plan on using a security suite in the future? If so, which one and why that one? If you do not plan to use a security suite, why not? (e) Do you think free security suites are as effective as those that must be purchased? Discuss.

## ② Making IT Work for You: CLOUD-BASED BACKUP

Do you remember to make frequent backups of your irreplaceable data files, such as photos and documents? Review the Making IT Work for You: Cloud-Based Backup on pages 261 and 262 and then respond to the following: (a) How do you currently back up your important files? How often do you create these backups? (b) Have you ever used Carbonite or a similar cloud-based service? If so, which service have you used, and what do you typically use it for? If you have not used Carbonite or a similar service, describe how and why you might use one. (c) If you do not have a Carbonite account, set up a free one. Did you find the Carbonite software easy to set up and use? Briefly describe your opinion of the process. (d) Do you see yourself signing up for a paid, yearly subscription to a service such as Carbonite? Why or why not?

## ③ Explorations: PRIVACY MONITORS

Did you know that several organizations actively monitor privacy-related issues? Review the Explorations box on page 247 and then respond to the following: (a) What are the nature and goal of this organization? (b) Find and briefly explain one privacy issue related to cloud computing. Do you agree with this organization's concerns? Why or why not? (c) Find and briefly explain one privacy issue related to social networking. Do you agree with this organization's concerns? Why or why not? (d) Overall, do you believe that these organizations are valuable when it comes to privacy and the Internet? Why or why not?

### 4 Explorations: PASSWORDS

To learn more about creating strong passwords, review the Explorations box on page 256. Then respond to the following: (a) What are the problems with using passwords such as "internet" or "computer"? (b) Does the password strength improve if you add two digits, such as in "computer99"? Do any weaknesses remain in such a password? (c) Using some of the tips you have discovered, create a password that will not result in any warnings (do not use any of your actual, current passwords). What was this password? How long will it take to break such a password?

### 5 Ethics: SOCIAL NETWORKING

Social networking companies are often criticized for having misleading or confusing policies regarding the sharing of personal information. Review the Ethics box on page 253 and then answer the following: (a) Which social network(s) do you currently use? Do you feel that you fully understand how your posts and photos are shared on the network? Support your answer with a few examples. (b) Do you believe that social networks act unethically when they share information with advertisers? Why or why not? (c) Suppose that a high school teacher shares photos of her Halloween party, in which she is having alcoholic drinks with her social networking friends. Somehow, the school board obtains these photos and decides to suspend her. Is this ethical? Does this violate her right to act as she wishes on her own time? Why or why not? (d) In late 2009, Facebook's privacy settings underwent a major change in which each user's name, picture, and basic information appeared in Google search results and was visible to the entire Internet by default. Are there any ethical concerns here? Or by joining Facebook, does one waive the right to privacy? What do you think? Defend your position.

### 6 Ethics: PLAGIARISM

Some argue that when writing a paper using research from the Internet, it is difficult to draw a distinction between using information found on a website and plagiarizing its content. Many schools use special software to help professors make this distinction. Review the Ethics box on page 264 and then respond to the following: (a) Do you think it is ethical for instructors to employ a program that checks for plagiarism? Why or why not? (b) Do you think it is ethical for students or any individuals to copy all or part of a web page's content and then present the information as his or her original work? Why or why not? (c) How would you distinguish between using the web for research and plagiarizing web content? Be as specific as possible. (d) Does your school have a policy specifically regarding plagiarism of web content? If yes, what is the policy? If not, what would you suggest would be an appropriate policy?

### 7 ⃝ Environment: DEPARTMENT OF DEFENSE

Did you know that the U.S. Department of Defense considers certain environmental issues to be potential threats to national security? Review the Environment box on page 251 and then respond to the following: (a) What are the two environmental research programs sponsored by the Department of Defense? (b) Why do you feel that environmental issues could be threats to national security? (c) Do you feel that the U.S. government should spend money on these types of research programs? Why or why not?

### 8 ⃝ Environment: ENVIRONMENTAL ETHICS AND IT

Many technology companies and IT professionals are already taking their responsibility to the environment very seriously. Review the Environment box on page 263 and then respond to the following: (a) Do you feel that IT professionals should receive training or education in environmental issues? Why or why not? (b) Can a person be considered unethical if failing to consider the environment in any decisions? Discuss your response. (c) Do you feel  that governments should create laws that govern the energy consumption of computers and other electronic devices? Why or why not? (d) Using a search engine, find the website of the Energy Star program. Which government agencies are responsible for this program? What environmental benefits has this program already given us?

# The Evolution of the Computer Age

Many of you probably can't remember a world without computers, but for some of us, computers were virtually unknown when we were born and have rapidly come of age during our lifetime.

Although there are many predecessors to what we think of as the modern computer—reaching as far back as the 18th century, when Joseph Marie Jacquard created a loom programmed to weave cloth and Charles Babbage created the first fully modern computer design (which he could never get to work)—the computer age did not really begin until the first computer was made available to the public in 1951.

The modern age of computers thus spans slightly more than 60 years (so far), which is typically broken down into five generations. Each generation has been marked by a significant advance in technology.

- **First Generation (1951–57):** During the first generation, computers were built with vacuum tubes— electronic tubes that were made of glass and were about the size of lightbulbs.

- **Second Generation (1958–63):** This generation began with the first computers built with transistors—small devices that transfer electronic signals across a resistor. Because transistors are much smaller, use less power, and create less heat than vacuum tubes, the new computers were faster, smaller, and more reliable than the first-generation machines.

- **Third Generation (1964–69):** In 1964, computer manufacturers began replacing transistors with integrated circuits. An integrated circuit (IC) is a complete electronic circuit on a small chip made of silicon (one of the most abundant elements in the earth's crust). These computers were more reliable and compact than computers made with transistors, and they cost less to manufacture.

- **Fourth Generation (1970–90):** Many key advances were made during this generation, the most significant being the microprocessor—a specialized chip developed for computer memory and logic. Use of a single chip to create a smaller "personal" computer (as well as digital watches, pocket calculators, copy machines, and so on) revolutionized the computer industry.

- **Fifth Generation (1991–2012 and beyond):** Our current generation has been referred to as the "Connected Generation" because of the industry's massive effort to increase the connectivity of computers. The rapidly expanding Internet, World Wide Web, and intranets have created an information superhighway that has enabled both computer professionals and home computer users to communicate with others across the globe.

This appendix provides you with a timeline that describes in more detail some of the most significant events in each generation of the computer age.

# First Generation: The Vacuum Tube Age

**1951** Dr. John W. Mauchly and J. Presper Eckert Jr. introduce the first commercially available electronic digital computer—the UNIVAC—built with vacuum tubes. This computer was based on their earlier ENIAC (Electronic Numerical Integrator and Computer) design completed in 1946.

**1951–53** IBM adds computers to its business equipment products and sells over 1,000 IBM 650 systems.

**1952** Development team led by Dr. Grace Hopper, former U.S. Navy programmer, introduces the A6 Compiler—the first example of software that converts high-level language symbols into instructions that a computer can execute.

**1957** Introduction of first high-level programming language—FORTRAN (FORmula TRANslator).

| 1951 | 1952 | 1953 | 1954 | 1955 | 1956 | 1957 |

# Second Generation: The Transistor Age

**1958** Introduction of computers built with transistors—a 1947 Bell Laboratories invention.

**1959** Introduction of the removable disk pack, providing users with fast access to stored data.

**1960** Introduction of the first business application programming language—COBOL (Common Business Oriented Language)—based on English-like phrases.

**1963** Introduction of the first computer industry standard character set—ASCII (American Standard Code for Information Interchange)—that enables computers to exchange information.

**1959** General Electric Corporation introduces ERMA (Electronic Recording Machine Accounting)—the first technology that can read special characters, such as digitized information.

| 1958 | 1959 | 1960 | 1961 | 1962 | 1963 |

# Third Generation: The Integrated Circuit Age

**1964** Introduction of computers built with an integrated circuit (IC), which incorporates multiple transistors and electronic circuits on a single silicon chip.

**1965** Digital Equipment Corporation (DEC) introduces the first minicomputer.

**1969** Introduction of ARPANET and the beginning of the Internet.

| 1964 | 1965 | 1966 | 1967 | 1968 | 1969 |

**1965** Introduction of the BASIC programming language.

**1969** IBM announces its decision to offer unbundled software, priced and sold separately from the hardware.

**1964** IBM introduces its System/360 line of compatible computers, which can all use the same programs and peripherals.

# Fourth Generation: The Microprocessor Age

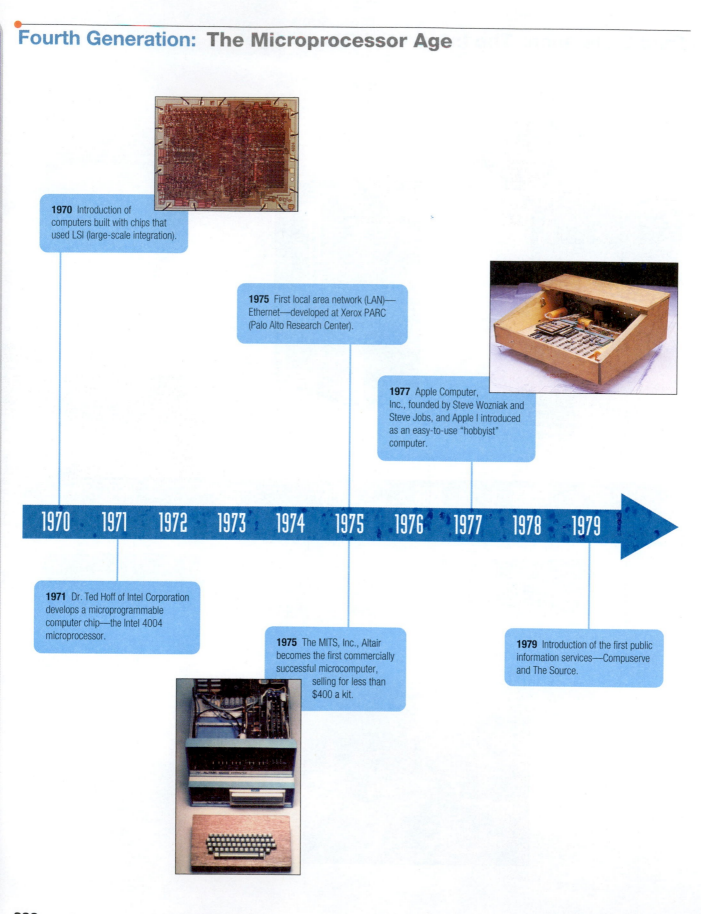

**1970** Introduction of computers built with chips that used LSI (large-scale integration).

**1975** First local area network (LAN)—Ethernet—developed at Xerox PARC (Palo Alto Research Center).

**1977** Apple Computer, Inc., founded by Steve Wozniak and Steve Jobs, and Apple I introduced as an easy-to-use "hobbyist" computer.

1970 1971 1972 1973 1974 1975 1976 1977 1978 1979

**1971** Dr. Ted Hoff of Intel Corporation develops a microprogrammable computer chip—the Intel 4004 microprocessor.

**1975** The MITS, Inc., Altair becomes the first commercially successful microcomputer, selling for less than $400 a kit.

**1979** Introduction of the first public information services—Compuserve and The Source.

**1980** IBM asks Microsoft founder, Bill Gates, to develop an operating system—MS-DOS—for the soon-to-be-released IBM personal computer.

**1981** Introduction of the IBM PC, which contains an Intel microprocessor chip and Microsoft's MS-DOS operating system.

**1989** Introduction of Intel 486—the first 1,000,000-transistor microprocessor.

1980 1981 1982 1983 1984 1985 1986 1987 1988 1989 1990

**1984** Apple introduces the Macintosh Computer, with a unique, easy-to-use graphical user interface.

**1985** Microsoft introduces its Windows graphical user interface.

**1990** Microsoft releases Windows 3.0, with an enhanced graphical user interface and the ability to run multiple applications.

The Evolution of the Computer Age    **281**

# Fifth Generation: The Age of Connectivity

**1991** Release of World Wide Web standards that describe the framework of linking documents on different computers.

**1992** Apple introduces the Newton MessagePad—a personal digital assistant (PDA) that incorporates a pen interface and wireless communications.

**1993** Introduction of computer systems built with Intel's Pentium microprocessor.

**1995** Intel begins shipping the Pentium Pro microprocessor.

| 1991 | 1992 | 1993 | 1994 | 1995 |
|------|------|------|------|------|

**1991** Linus Torvalds, a graduate student at the University of Helsinki, develops a version of UNIX called the Linux operating system.

**1993** Introduction of the Mosaic graphical web browser, which led to the organization of Netscape Communications Corporation.

**1995** Microsoft releases Windows 95, a major upgrade to its Windows operating system.

**1994** Yahoo is launched and quickly becomes a popular web directory.

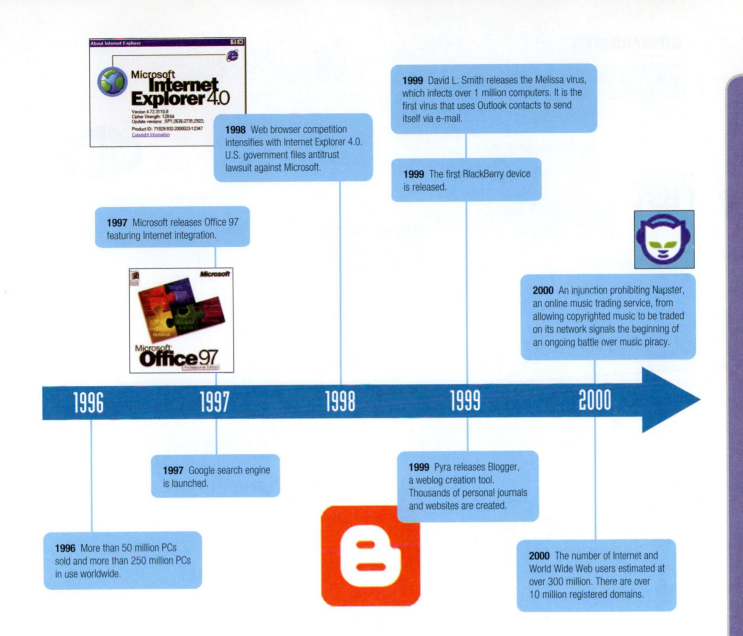

**1999** David L. Smith releases the Melissa virus, which infects over 1 million computers. It is the first virus that uses Outlook contacts to send itself via e-mail.

**1998** Web browser competition intensifies with Internet Explorer 4.0. U.S. government files antitrust lawsuit against Microsoft.

**1999** The first BlackBerry device is released.

**1997** Microsoft releases Office 97 featuring Internet integration.

**2000** An injunction prohibiting Napster, an online music trading service, from allowing copyrighted music to be traded on its network signals the beginning of an ongoing battle over music piracy.

**1996**     **1997**     **1998**     **1999**     **2000**

**1997** Google search engine is launched.

**1999** Pyra releases Blogger, a weblog creation tool. Thousands of personal journals and websites are created.

**1996** More than 50 million PCs sold and more than 250 million PCs in use worldwide.

**2000** The number of Internet and World Wide Web users estimated at over 300 million. There are over 10 million registered domains.

**amazon**.com.

**2002** Amazon.com, the largest online retailer, announces its first profitable quarter nearly 10 years after the company was founded.

**2004** Facebook is launched by Mark Zuckerberg and a few schoolmates from Harvard.

Microsoft
**.net**

**2002** Microsoft initiates its .NET platform that allows users to create a profile for use across platforms and allows developers to create web services quickly.

**2003** Apple opens the iTunes music store with a catalog of over 700,000 songs. Users can buy and then download songs for 99¢.

**WiFi**™

**2005** Wi-Fi use continues to grow, with over 8,500 cafés offering connections to customers. Several cities add citywide Wi-Fi coverage.

**2001** Microsoft releases Windows XP and Office XP with enhanced user interfaces, better integration and collaboration tools, and increased stability.

**2001** | **2002** | **2003** | **2004** | **2005** ➔

**2002** Internet2, with over 200 university affiliates, regularly broadcasts live theater and HDTV transmissions.

**2004** Google releases invitations to test Gmail, its e-mail service that includes a search function and 1 GB of storage.

**2001** Apple releases Mac OS X with a UNIX backbone and new interface.

Mac OS **X**

**G**mail™
by Google  BETA

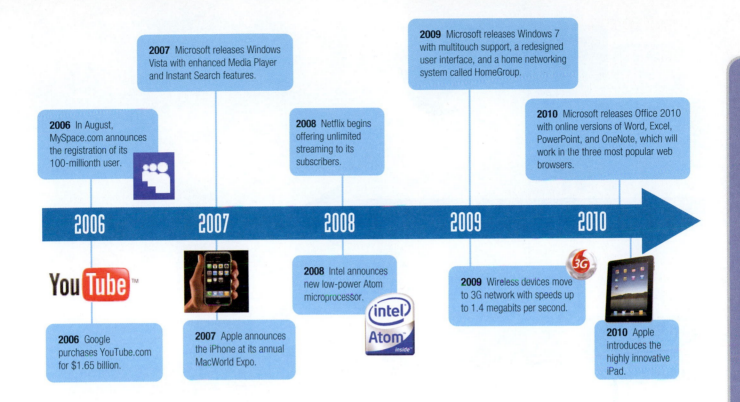

**2006** In August, MySpace.com announces the registration of its 100-millionth user.

**2007** Microsoft releases Windows Vista with enhanced Media Player and Instant Search features.

**2008** Netflix begins offering unlimited streaming to its subscribers.

**2009** Microsoft releases Windows 7 with multitouch support, a redesigned user interface, and a home networking system called HomeGroup.

**2010** Microsoft releases Office 2010 with online versions of Word, Excel, PowerPoint, and OneNote, which will work in the three most popular web browsers.

2006    2007    2008    2009    2010

**2006** Google purchases YouTube.com for $1.65 billion.

**2007** Apple announces the iPhone at its annual MacWorld Expo.

**2008** Intel announces new low-power Atom microprocessor.

**2009** Wireless devices move to 3G network with speeds up to 1.4 megabits per second.

**2010** Apple introduces the highly innovative iPad.

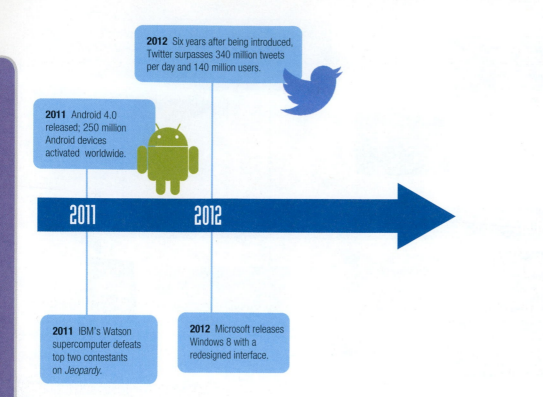

**2012** Six years after being introduced, Twitter surpasses 340 million tweets per day and 140 million users.

**2011** Android 4.0 released; 250 million Android devices activated worldwide.

2011

2012

**2011** IBM's Watson supercomputer defeats top two contestants on *Jeopardy*.

**2012** Microsoft releases Windows 8 with a redesigned interface.

# The Computer Buyer's Guide

## PART 1: WHICH TYPES OF COMPUTERS SHOULD YOU PURCHASE?

Many individuals feel confused and overwhelmed when it comes to buying a new computer. In today's market, there are various categories of computers ranging from desktops and notebooks to ultraportable tablets and smartphones. And within each category, there are countless choices and a wide range of prices. This buying guide will help you choose the best combination of computers for your needs, as well as point out some key specifications that they should have.

### NOTEBOOKS COMPUTERS: TODAY'S STANDARD

*Typical Recommendation: Buy a $500 to $700 notebook with a 15-inch screen.*

The notebook computer has become the must-have device that can do everything you need, wherever you need it. They are powerful enough to be your primary home computer (replacing desktops) while portable enough to take to school, work, the local coffee shop, and even on your next trip. Many students are bringing them to classes to take notes and perform research. If you can only own one computer, make it a notebook. Affordable ones start at under $500.

If you have decided that you want to buy a notebook computer, be sure to read Part 2 for additional tips and recommendations.

### SMARTPHONES: COMPUTERS IN YOUR POCKET

*Typical Recommendation: Obtain a free or low-cost smartphone by signing a two-year wireless contract with a data plan.*

For many individuals, the smartphone has become much like a wallet, purse, or keys—you don't leave home without it. This single, pocket-sized device fills many roles. It is a mobile phone, digital camera, video recorder, gaming device, and personal digital assistant. Most individuals purchase a smartphone because they need to access information quickly and easily, regardless of where they are.

With many smartphones now available for free with two-year contracts, it is easier than ever to replace your older cell phone. The biggest drawback to owning a smartphone is that its "use anywhere" benefit is limited if it is not paired with a wireless data plan, which can often cost around $30 per month.

Although Apple's iPhone was once the clear leader in the smartphone market, various Android devices include competitive features and are enjoying favorable reviews. If you have decided that you want to buy a smartphone, be sure to read Part 2 for additional tips and recommendations.

### TABLETS: THE RISING STARS

*Typical Recommendation: Buy a 10-inch tablet with 16 GB of storage.*

The release of the iPad has revived this category of computers. With an attractive, 10-inch touch-screen surface, it has quickly become a popular device for watching videos, playing games, reading e-books, and browsing the web. Tablets are light enough to hold comfortably for many hours, yet powerful enough to use a variety of apps. They generally have a much longer battery life than notebook computers.

If you are a typical computer user, then you may not benefit much from purchasing a tablet computer. Most of your computing time will be spent on your notebook computer (at home and at school, for example) or on your smartphone. Although tablets are very popular right now, you must remember that they cost several hundred dollars. You should have a very clear need for this sort of device before you decide to spend the money on it.

Many students consider buying tablets because the low weight makes a tablet easy to carry around. Although this is true, there are lightweight notebook computers that weigh only one or two pounds more and are much more versatile than tablets. Such versatility is crucial for various types of software that are not available as apps and require installation on a Windows or Mac computer. Before you decide between a tablet and lightweight notebook, consider the type of software you will need for your schoolwork, business, or personal use. If everything you need is available as a mobile app, then a tablet (paired with a wireless keyboard) will be more affordable than a lightweight notebook computer.

In conclusion, purchase a tablet computer only if see yourself using it often. The touch-screen interface, low weight, and long battery life do indeed make it easy to carry around and use almost anywhere you go. However, the price tag does not make the decision an obvious one if you already own a notebook computer and smartphone. If you have decided that you want to buy a tablet, be sure to read Part 2 for additional tips and recommendations.

## DESKTOPS

### Typical Recommendation: Buy a tower system with a 20- to 24-inch monitor for approximately $600.

Desktop (or tower) computers have been around for a long time. You will still find them in many offices and homes. However, they are steadily losing popularity because notebook computers have become very powerful and affordable. Why have a computer that remains stuck in your home or office when you can have a notebook that can be taken almost anywhere?

Although notebook computers seem to be the better choice, there are several reasons why you might want to purchase a desktop computer. First, the use of a notebook computer as your primary computer can be uncomfortable. After prolonged use, it can place stress on your neck, back, and wrists. Desktops typically come with large monitors, and various types of ergonomic keyboards are available. However, desktop critics will point out that notebook computers can be connected to external monitors and keyboards as well. The only downside is that a notebook requires the purchase of extra equipment.

The other reason to get a desktop is if you have a specific need that cannot be addressed by a notebook computer. For example, some families have a media center computer that holds all the videos, photos, and music for the entire home network. Another example involves gamers, who often seek to build or customize extremely powerful computers. They often choose desktops for this endeavor.

Most users will not need to purchase a desktop computer. In fact, they are currently the least popular of the four categories in this buying guide. However, if you have decided that you want to buy a desktop, be sure to read Part 2 for additional tips and recommendations.

## PART 2: PERSONALIZED BUYING GUIDE

Now that you have decided which types of computers you need, it is time to explore computer specifications. The areas below explore the decision-making process from the perspective of various buyers.

### NOTEBOOKS

There are two basic categories of notebooks: the traditional notebook and the ultrabook. Although these two categories of notebook computers have the same general appearance, they vary greatly in power, storage capacity, weight, and battery life. The following section helps you find the device that best meets your needs.

*User #1:* *I am a power user. I need a portable computer that can handle the latest video games or process-intensive operations such as video editing, engineering, and design.*

*Response #1:* Purchase a traditional notebook computer that includes the following minimum specs:

- **The fastest categories of processors with large number of cores and high GHz count**
- **A graphics processor (GPU) outside of the main CPU**
- **8-GB RAM**
- **750-GB hard drive**
- **17-inch screen**

Expect to pay approximately $1000, perhaps more. For games, many individuals choose Windows-based PCs. The video and design industries usually use Macs.

*User #2:* *I am a regular user. I need a desktop replacement and portable computer. I typically run office software, use the Internet, and listen to music.*

*Response #2:* Purchase an affordable traditional notebook computer that includes the following specs:

- **Middle-tier processors—not the fastest but not the slowest either**
- **4- to 8-GB RAM**
- **500-GB hard drive**
- **15-inch screen**

Expect to pay approximately $500 to $700. For maximum savings, as well as compatibility with most software, many buyers choose Windows-based PCs. Be sure to purchase an external monitor, keyboard, and mouse if you plan on heavy use while at home.

*User #3:* I want a small, lightweight computer that I can carry anywhere. I would like long battery life for extended use.

*Response #3:* Purchase an ultrabook with

- **11- to 13-inch screen**
- **Solid-state hard drive**
- **4-GB RAM**
- **Weight under 4 pounds**

Expect to pay $700 to $1000. Many ultrabooks will not include a DVD drive. Windows-based ultrabooks tend to be more affordable. The MacBook Air is slightly more expensive, but it has always been considered a leader in the lightweight notebook field.

## SMARTPHONES

Shopping for a smartphone involves three separate processes: (1) choosing an operating system, such iOS, Android, or Windows; (2) choosing a device; and (3) choosing a wireless carrier. Although the following section does not review different wireless companies or data plans, it presents a list of smartphone features that you should always consider before making your choice. In addition, it presents each smartphone operating system from the perspective of typical users.

### Features to Consider

- *Screen and device size:* **Consider a size (and weight) that is comfortable for you to use and carry around. Four-inch screens are now typical.**
- *Screen resolution:* **Some devices deliver HD quality for sharp photos and videos.**
- *Integrated keyboard:* **consider one if you type often on these devices.**
- *Storage:* **Having 8 GB is enough for most users. Choose 16 GB or more if you plan to store large quantities of music, photos, and videos. Some devices allow you to increase storage by using memory cards.**
- *Battery life:* **About 7 to 8 hours is typical. Some devices have removable batteries.**
- *Cameras:* **Many include front- and rear-facing cameras. Compare megapixels and photo quality.**
- *App market:* **Consider the number of apps, and ensure that any apps you need are available for this operating system.**

### Operating Systems

- *iOS:* **The iPhone is considered by many to be the standard against which all smartphones are** measured. Buyers typically choose the iPhone if they are Mac owners or prefer a tightly controlled "ecosystem" from Apple where stability and ease of use are favored over heavy customization.
- *Android:* **There are many Android devices available from various manufacturers, some free with a wireless contract. Buyers who enjoy customizing their interface typically choose Android. In addition, this operating system is tightly integrated with many of Google's products and services.**
- *BlackBerry:* **Many of these devices contain integrated keyboards for faster and more comfortable typing. Many business users choose BlackBerry for typing e-mail and notes on the go.**
- *Windows Phone:* **The newcomer to the smartphone market features an interface that will seem familiar to those using Windows 8 notebooks and tablets. Users enjoy the "live tiles" which constantly update information, such as social network activity.**

Remember that smartphones can cost very little when you sign a two-year contract with a wireless company. Consider whether you want to make that sort of commitment.

## TABLET COMPUTERS

Because of their increased popularity, tablets are available in several sizes from many different companies. The following section helps you find the device that best meets your needs.

*User #1:* I want to watch videos, play games, create notes, and browse websites.

*Response #1:* Purchase a 10-inch tablet. Expect to pay $400 to $500. Most weigh about 1.5 pounds. Apple's iPad was very popular when first released, and it continues to be a popular choice among buyers today. Other things to consider:

- **For greater customization, consider an Android-based tablet. There are several models that are comparable to the iPad, which is considered by many reviewers to be the standard bearer.**
- **The Microsoft Surface tablet includes a keyboard that is integrated into the cover. However, any tablet can be paired with a Bluetooth keyboard, which is crucial if you plan to type often.**
- **Make sure the apps you plan on using are available for the tablet's operating system.**
- **Having 16 GB of storage is typical. Some tablets let you expand this by using flash memory cards.**

**User #2:** *I want to read e-books, browse websites, and have a lightweight device that I can hold with one hand.*

**Response #2:** Purchase a 7-inch tablet. Expect to pay around $200. Most weigh less than 1 pound. Google's Nexus 7 and Amazon's Kindle Fire are popular Android-based tablets.

## DESKTOP COMPUTERS

Desktops remain popular for offices, both at home and in many companies. In addition, many power users require them for graphics-intensive tasks. The following section helps you find the device that best meets your needs.

**User #1:** *I need a powerful computer that can handle the latest video games or process-intensive operations such as video editing, engineering, and design.*

**Response #1:** Purchase a tower-based computer with the following minimum specs:

- **The fastest categories of processors with large number of cores and high GHz count**
- **High-performance video card**
- **16-GB RAM**
- **2-TB hard drive**

- **24-inch monitor**
- **Specialty peripherals (such as game controllers) when needed**

Expect to pay at least $1,500 for these powerful computers. For games, many individuals choose Windows-based PCs. The video and design industries usually use Macs.

**User #2:** *I would like a computer that can be used by the entire family for many years.*

**Response #2:** Purchase a tower or all-in-one computer with the following minimum specs:

- **Middle-tier processor**
- **4 GB RAM**
- **500 GB hard drive (increase to 2 TB if you plan to store a large number of videos)**
- **20- to 24-inch monitor**
- **Ergonomic keyboard**

Tower-based systems are usually offered in a package that includes the monitor and several peripherals. All-in-one systems will, of course, include the monitor, some of which are touch screens. Spending approximately $600 to $800 will help ensure that the components remain relevant for several years. For a stylish and powerful all-in-one computer, consider the slightly more expensive iMac from Apple.

# Glossary

**3G and 4G cellular network:** A network that allows portable devices such as cell phones and properly equipped laptop computers to download data from the Internet.

**3GLs (third-generation languages):** High-level procedural language. *See* Procedural language.

**4G (fourth-generation mobile telecommunications):** Provides faster transmission speeds than 3G. 3G started in the 2000s providing services capable of effective connectivity to the Internet and marked the beginning of smartphones.

**4GLs (fourth-generation languages):** Very high-level or problem-oriented languages. *See* Task-oriented language.

**5GLs (fifth-generation languages):** *See* Fifth-generation language.

**802.11:** *See* Wi-Fi (wireless fidelity).

## a

**AC adapter:** Notebook computers use AC adapters that are typically outside the system unit. They plug into a standard wall outlet, convert AC to DC, provide power to drive the system components, and can recharge batteries.

**Access:** Refers to the responsibility of those who have data to control who is able to use that data.

**Access speed:** Measures the amount of time required by the storage device to retrieve data and programs.

**Accounting:** The organizational department that records all financial activity from billing customers to paying employees.

**Accounts payable:** The activity that shows the money a company owes to its suppliers for the materials and services it has received.

**Accounts receivable:** The activity that shows what money has been received or is owed by customers.

**Accuracy:** Relates to the responsibility of those who collect data to ensure that the data is correct.

**Active display area:** The diagonal length of a monitor's viewing area.

**Active-matrix monitor:** Type of flat-panel monitor in which each pixel is independently activated. Displays more colors with better clarity; also known as thin film transistor (TFT) monitor.

**Active-matrix organic light-emitting diode (AMOLED):** A monitor technology that has the benefits of lower-power consumption and longer battery life, as well as possibilities for much thinner displays.

**Add a Device Wizard:** A Windows wizard that provides step-by-step guidance for selecting and installing an appropriate printer driver for a new printer.

**Address:** Located in the header of an e-mail message; the e-mail address of the persons sending, receiving, and, optionally, anyone else who is to receive copies.

**Advanced Research Project Agency Network (ARPANET):** A national computer network from which the Internet developed.

**Agile development:** A development methodology that starts by getting core functionality of a program working, then expands on it until the customer is satisfied with the results.

**AJAX:** An advanced use of JavaScript found on many interactive sites. This technology is used to create interactive websites that respond quickly like traditional desktop application software.

**All-in-one:** A desktop computer that has the monitor and system unit housed together in the same case (e.g., Apple's iMac).

**Analog:** Continuous signals that vary to represent different tones, pitches, and volume.

**Analog signals:** Signals that represent a range of frequencies, such as the human voice. They are a continuous electronic wave signal as opposed to a digital signal that is either on or off. To convert the digital signals of your computer to analog and vice versa, you need a modem. Another cable connects the modem to the telephone wall jack.

**Analytical graphs or charts:** Form of graphics used to put numeric data into objects that are easier to analyze, such as bar charts, line graphs, and pie charts.

**Android:** Mobile operating system originally developed by Android Inc. and later purchased by Google.

**Animation:** Feature involving special visual and sound effects like moving pictures, audio, and video clips that play automatically when selected.

**Antispyware:** *See* Spy removal programs.

**Antivirus program:** A utility program that guards a computer system from viruses or other damaging programs.

**App:** *See* Application software.

**App store:** A website that provides access to specific mobile apps that can be downloaded either for a nominal fee or free of charge.

**Applets:** Web pages contain links to programs called applets, which are written in a programming language called Java. These programs are used to add interest to a website by presenting animation, displaying graphics, providing interactive games, and so forth.

**Application generation subsystem:** Provides tools to create data entry forms and specialized programming languages that interface or work with common languages, such as C or Visual Basic.

**Application generator:** Also called program coder; provides modules of prewritten code to accomplish various tasks, such as calculation of overtime pay.

**Application software:** Also referred to as apps. Software that can perform useful work, such as word processing, cost estimating, or accounting tasks. The user primarily interacts with application software.

**Arithmetic-logic unit (ALU):** The part of the CPU that performs arithmetic and logical operations.

**Arithmetic operation:** Fundamental math operations: addition, subtraction, multiplication, and division.

**Artificial intelligence (AI):** A field of computer science that attempts to develop computer systems that can mimic or simulate human thought processes and actions.

**Artificial reality:** *See* Virtual reality.

**ASCII (American Standard Code for Information Interchange):** Binary coding scheme widely used on all computers, including microcomputers. Eight bits form each byte, and each byte represents one character.

**Aspect ratio:** The width of a monitor divided by its height. Common aspect ratios for monitors are 4:3 (standard) and 16:9 (wide screen).

**Assembly language:** A step up from machine language, using names instead of numbers. These languages use abbreviations or mnemonics, such as ADD, that are automatically converted to the appropriate sequence of 1s and 0s.

**Asymmetric digital subscriber line (ADSL):** One of the most widely used types of telephone high-speed connections (DSL).

**Attachment:** A file, such as a document or worksheet, that is attached to an e-mail message.

**Attribute:** A data field represents an attribute (description or characteristic) of some entity (person, place, thing, or object). For example, an employee is an entity with many attributes, including his or her last name, address, phone, etc.

**Auction house sites:** Websites that operate like a traditional auction to sell merchandise to bidders.

**Audio editing software:** Allows you to create and edit audio clips like filtering out pops and scratches in an old recording.

**Automated design tool:** Software package that evaluates hardware and software alternatives according to requirements given by the systems analyst. Also called computer-aided software engineering (CASE) tools.

# b

**Backbone:** *See* Bus.

**Background:** Other programs running simultaneously with the program being used in an operating system. *See* foreground.

**Backup:** A Windows utility program. *See* Backup program.

**Backup and Restore:** A utility program included with many versions of Windows that makes a copy of all files or selected files that have been saved onto a disk.

**Backup program:** A utility program that helps protect you from the effects of a disk failure by making a copy of selected or all files that have been saved onto a disk.

**Balance sheet:** Lists the overall financial condition of an organization.

**Bandwidth:** Bandwidth determines how much information can be transmitted at one time. It is a measurement of the communication channel's capacity. There are three bandwidths: voice band, medium band, and broadband.

**Bar code:** Code consisting of vertical zebra-striped marks printed on product containers, read with a bar code reader.

**Bar code reader:** Photoelectric scanner that reads bar codes for processing.

**Bar code scanner:** *See* Bar code reader.

**Base station:** *See* Wireless access point.

**Baseband:** Bandwidth used to connect individual computers that are located close to one another. Though it supports high-speed transmission, it can only carry a single signal at a time.

**Batch processing:** Processing performed all at once on data that has been collected over time.

**BD (Blu-ray disc):** A type of high-definition disc with a capacity of 25 to 50 gigabytes.

**Beta testing:** Testing by a select group of potential users in the final stage of testing a program.

**Binary system:** Numbering system in which all numbers consist of only two digits: 0 and 1.

**Biometric scanning:** Devices that check fingerprints or retinal scans.

**BIOS (basic input/output system):** Information including the specifics concerning the amount of RAM and the type of keyboard, mouse, and secondary storage devices connected to the system unit.

**Bit (binary digit):** Each 1 or 0 is a bit; short for binary digit.

**Bitmap image:** Graphic file in which an image is made up of thousands of dots (pixels).

**BitTorrent:** A peer-to-peer file-sharing protocol used for distributing large amounts of data over the Internet.

**BlackBerry OS:** Mobile phone operating system originally designed for the BlackBerry handheld computer.

**Blog:** *See* Web log.

**Bluetooth:** A wireless technology that allows nearby devices to communicate without the connection of cables or telephone systems.

**Boot Camp:** Feature of Leopard, a version of Mac OS, that allows appropriately equipped Apple computers to run both Mac OS and Windows.

**Booting:** Starting or restarting your computer.

**Botnet:** A collection of zombie computers.

**Broadband:** Bandwidth that includes microwave, satellite, coaxial cable, and fiber-optic channels. It is used for very-high-speed computers.

**Browser:** Special Internet software connecting you to remote computers; opens and transfers files, displays text and images, and provides an uncomplicated interface to the Internet and web documents. Examples of browsers are Internet Explorer, Mozilla Firefox, and Google Chrome.

**Browser cache:** A collection of temporary Internet files that contain web page content and instructions for displaying this content.

**Bulleted list:** The sequence of topics arranged on a page and organized by bullets.

**Bus:** All communication travels along a common connecting cable called a bus or a backbone. As information passes along the bus, it is examined by each device on the system board to see if the information is intended for that device. *See* Bus line and Ethernet.

**Bus line:**   Electronic data roadway, along which bits travel; connects the parts of the CPU to each other and links the CPU with other important hardware. The common connecting cable in a bus network.

**Bus network:**   Each device is connected to a common cable called a bus or backbone, and all communications travel along this bus.

**Bus width:**   The number of bits traveling simultaneously down a bus is the bus width.

**Business suite:**   *See* Productivity suites.

**Business-to-business (B2B):**   A type of electronic commerce that involves the sale of a product or service from one business to another. This is typically a manufacturer–supplier relationship.

**Business-to-consumer (B2C):**   A type of electronic commerce that involves the sale of a product or service to the general public or end users.

**Button:**   A special area you can click to make links that "navigate" through a presentation.

**Byte:**   Unit consisting of eight bits. There are 256 possible bit combinations in a byte and each byte represents one character.

# C

**Cable:**   Cords used to connect input and output devices to the system unit.

**Cable modem:**   Allows all-digital communication, which is a speed of 27 million bps.

**Cable service:**   Service provided by cable television companies using existing television cables.

**Cache memory:**   Area of random-access memory (RAM) set aside to store the most frequently accessed information. Cache memory improves processing by acting as a temporary high-speed holding area between memory and the CPU, allowing the computer to detect which information in RAM is most frequently used.

**Capacity:**   Capacity is how much data a particular storage medium can hold and is another characteristic of secondary storage.

**Card reader:**   A device that interprets the encoded information contained on credit, debit, access, and identification cards.

**Carpal tunnel syndrome:**   A repetitive strain injury consisting of damage to the nerves and tendons in the hands.

**Carrier package:**   The material that chips are mounted on that then plugs into sockets on the system board.

**Cathode-ray tube (CRT) monitor:**   Desktop-type monitor built in the same way as a television set.

**Cascading style sheets (CSS):**   Files inserted into an HTML document that control the appearance of web pages including layout, colors, and fonts.

**CD:**   *See* Compact disc.

**CD-R:**   Stands for CD-recordable. This optical disc can be written to only once. After that it can be read many times without deterioration but cannot be written on or erased. Used to create custom music CDs and to archive data.

**CD-ROM (compact disc–read-only memory):**   Optical disc that allows data to be read but not recorded. Used to distribute large databases, references, and software application packages.

**CD-RW (compact disc rewriteable):**   A reusable, optical disc that is not permanently altered when data is recorded. Used to create and edit large multimedia presentations.

**Cell:**   The space created by the intersection of a vertical column and a horizontal row within a worksheet in a program like Microsoft Excel. A cell can contain text or numeric entries.

**Cellular service provider:**   Links car phones and portable phones.

**Center for European Nuclear Research (CERN):**   In Switzerland, where the web was introduced in 1992.

**Central processing unit (CPU):**   The part of the computer that holds data and program instructions for processing the data. The CPU consists of the control unit and the arithmetic-logic unit. In a microcomputer, the CPU is on a single electronic component called a microprocessor chip.

**Character:**   A single letter, number, or special character, such as a punctuation mark or $.

**Character effect:**   Changes the appearance of font characters by using bold, italic, shadow, and colors.

**Character encoding standards:**   Assign unique sequence of bits to each character.

**Chart:**   Displaying numerical data in a worksheet as a pie chart or a bar chart, making it easier to understand.

**Checklist:**   In analyzing data, a list of questions helps guide the systems analyst and end user through key issues for the present system.

**Child node:**   A node one level below the node being considered in a hierarchical database or network. *See* Parent node.

**Chip:**   A tiny circuit board etched on a small square of sandlike material called silicon. A chip is also called a silicon chip, semiconductor, or integrated circuit.

**Chrome OS:**   An operating system designed by Google for netbook computers and Internet connectivity through cloud computing.

**Circles:**   A service offered through Google Plus, for grouping individuals according to common interests or other criteria.

**Clarity:**   Indicated by the resolution, or number of pixels, on a monitor. The greater the resolution, the better the clarity.

**Class:**   In an object-oriented database, classes are similar objects grouped together.

**Client:**   A node that requests and uses resources available from other nodes. Typically, a client is a user's microcomputer.

**Client-based e-mail account:**   An account that requires a special program known as an e-mail client to be installed on your computer.

**Client/server network:**   Network in which one powerful computer coordinates and supplies services to all other nodes on the network. Server nodes coordinate and supply specialized services, and client nodes request the services.

**Clip art:**   Graphic illustrations representing a wide variety of topics.

**Clock speed:** Also called clock rate. It is measured in giga-hertz, or billions of beats per second. The faster the clock speed, the faster the computer can process information and execute instructions.

**Cloud computing:** Data stored at a server on the Internet and available anywhere the Internet can be accessed.

**Cloud printer:** A printer connected to the Internet that provides printing services to others on the Internet.

**Cloud storage:** Also known as online storage. An Internet-based space for storing data and files.

**Cloud suite:** Suite stored at a server on the Internet and available anywhere from the Internet.

**Coaxial cable:** High-frequency transmission cable that replaces the multiple wires of telephone lines with a single solid-copper core. It is used to deliver television signals as well as to connect computers in a network.

**Code:** Writing a program using the appropriate computer language.

**Code review:** *See* Desk checking.

**Coding:** Actual writing of a computer program, using a programming language.

**Cold boot:** Starting the computer after it has been turned off.

**Column:** Using Microsoft Excel, for example, a vertical block of cells one cell wide all the way down the worksheet.

**Combination key:** Keys such as the Ctrl key that perform an action when held down in combination with another key.

**Commercial database:** Enormous database an organization develops to cover certain particular subjects. Access to this type of database is usually offered for a fee or subscription. Also known as data bank and informational utility.

**Common data item:** In a relational database, all related tables must have a common data item or key field.

**Communication channel:** The actual connecting medium that carries the message between sending and receiving devices. This medium can be a physical wire, cable, or wire-less connection.

**Communication device:** Computer systems that communicate with other computer systems using modems. For example, it modifies computer output into a form that can be transmitted across standard telephone lines.

**Communication system:** Electronic system that transmits data over communication lines from one location to another.

**Compact disc (CD):** Widely used optical disc format. It holds 650 MB (megabytes) to 1 GB (gigabyte) of data on one side of the CD.

**Compact disc–read-only memory:** *See* CD-ROM.

**Compact disc rewriteable:** *See* CD-RW.

**Company database:** Also called shared database. Stored on a mainframe, users throughout the company have access to the database through their microcomputers linked by a network.

**Compiler:** Software that converts the programmer's procedural-language program (source code) into machine language (object code). This object code can then be saved and run later.

**Computer-aided design/computer-aided manufacturing (CAD/CAM) system:** Knowledge work systems that run programs to integrate the design and manufacturing activities. CAD/CAM is widely used in manufacturing automobiles.

**Computer-aided software engineering (CASE) tool:** A type of software development tool that helps provide some automation and assistance in program design, coding, and testing. *See* Automated design tool.

**Computer competency:** Becoming proficient in computer-related skills.

**Computer crime:** *See* Cybercrime.

**Computer ethics:** Guidelines for the morally acceptable use of computers in our society.

**Computer Fraud and Abuse Act:** Law allowing prosecution of unauthorized access to computers and databases.

**Computer monitoring software:** The most invasive and dangerous type of spyware. These programs record every activity made on your computer, including credit card numbers, bank account numbers, and e-mail messages.

**Computer network:** Communications system connecting two or more computers and their peripheral devices to exchange information and share resources.

**Computer support specialist:** Specialists include technical writers, computer trainers, computer technicians, and help-desk specialists who provide technical support to customers and other users.

**Computer technician:** Specialist who installs hardware and software and troubleshoots problems for users.

**Computer trainer:** Computer professional who provides classes to instruct users.

**Connectivity:** Capability of the microcomputer to use information from the world beyond one's desk. Data and information can be sent over telephone or cable lines and through the air so that computers can talk to each other and share information.

**Consumer-to-consumer (C2C):** A type of electronic commerce that involves individuals selling to individuals.

**Content-markup language:** Also known as markup language. Uses symbols, words, and phrases that instruct a computer on how to display information to the user. For example, HTML is a content-markup language used to display web pages.

**Content template:** Includes suggested content for each slide in a PowerPoint presentation.

**Contextual tab:** A type of tab found in Microsoft Word that only appears when needed and anticipates the next operations to be performed by the user.

**Contrast ratio:** Indicates a monitor's ability to display colors. It compares the light intensity of the brightest white to the darkest black.

**Control unit:** Section of the CPU that tells the rest of the computer how to carry out program instructions.

**Conversion:** Also known as systems implementation; four approaches to conversion: direct, parallel, pilot, and phased. *See* Systems implementation.

**Cookies:** Programs that record information on website visitors.

**Coprocessor:** Specialized processing chip designed to improve specific computer operations, such as the graphics coprocessor.

**Copyright:** A legal concept that gives content creators the right to control use and distribution of their work.

**Cordless mouse:** A battery-powered mouse that typically uses radio waves or infrared light waves to communicate with the system unit. Also known as wireless mouse.

**Cracker:** One who gains unauthorized access to a computer system for malicious purposes.

**Cryptographer:** Designs, tests, and researches encryption procedures.

**Cryptography:** The science of disguising and revealing encrypted information.

**Cyberbullying:** The use of the Internet, a cell phone, or other device to deliver content intended to hurt or embarrass another person.

**Cybercash:** *See* Digital cash.

**Cybercrime:** Any criminal offens that involves a computer and a network. Criminals may be employees, outside users, hackers and crackers, or organized crime members.

**Cylinder:** Hard disks store and organize files using tracks, sectors, and cylinders. A cylinder runs through each track of a stack of platters. Cylinders differentiate files stored on the same track and sector of different platters.

**Cynic:** Individual who feels that the idea of using a microcomputer is overrated and too troublesome to learn.

# d

**Dance pad:** An input device for dance games where signals are sent via a pressure-sensitive mat.

**Dashboard Widgets:** A collection of specialized programs on the Mac OS X operating system that constantly updates and displays information such as stock prices and weather information.

**Data:** Raw, unprocessed facts that are input to a computer system that will give compiled information when the computer processes those facts. Data is also defined as facts or observations about people, places, things, and events.

**Data administration subsystem:** Helps manage the overall database, including maintaining security, providing disaster recovery support, and monitoring the overall performance of database operations.

**Data bank:** *See* Commercial database.

**Data cube:** A multidimensional data model. *Also see* Multi-dimensional database.

**Data definition subsystem:** This system defines the logical structure of the database by using a data dictionary.

**Data dictionary:** Dictionary containing a description of the structure of data in a database.

**Data entry worker:** Inputs customer information, lists, and other types of data.

**Data flow diagram:** Diagram showing data or information flow within an information system.

**Data integrity:** Database characteristics relating to the consistency and accuracy of data.

**Data maintenance:** Maintaining data includes adding new data, deleting old data, and editing existing data.

**Data manipulation subsystem:** Provides tools to maintain and analyze data.

**Data mining:** Technique of searching data warehouses for related information and patterns.

**Data processing system (DPS):** Transaction processing system that keeps track of routine operations and records these events in a database. Also called transaction processing system (TPS).

**Data redundancy:** A common database problem in which data is duplicated and stored in different files.

**Data security:** Protection of software and data from unauthorized tampering or damage.

**Data warehouse:** Data collected from a variety of internal and external databases and stored in a database called a data warehouse. Data mining is then used to search these databases.

**Data worker:** Person involved with the distribution and communication of information, such as secretaries and clerks.

**Database:** A collection of related information, like employee names, addresses, and phone numbers. It is organized so that a computer program can quickly select the desired pieces of information and display them for you.

**Database administrator (DBA):** Uses database management software to determine the most efficient way to organize and access data.

**Database file:** File containing highly structured and organized data created by database management programs.

**Database management system (DBMS):** To organize, manage, and retrieve data. DBMS programs have five subsystems: DBMS engine, data definition, data manipulation, applications generation, and data administration. An example of a database management system is Microsoft Access. *See* Database manager.

**Database manager:** Software package used to set up, or structure, a database such as an inventory list of supplies. It also provides tools to edit, enter, and retrieve data from the database.

**Database model:** Defines rules and standards for all data in a database. There are five database models: hierarchical, network, relational, multidimensional, and object-oriented. For example, Access uses the relational data model.

**DBMS engine:** Provides a bridge between the logical view of data and the physical view of data.

**Debugging:** Programmer's word for testing and then eliminating errors in a program. Programming errors are of two types: syntax and logic errors.

**Decision model:** The decision model gives the decision support system its analytical capabilities. There are three types of models included in the decision model: tactical, operational, and strategic.

**Decision support system (DSS):** Flexible analysis tool that helps managers make decisions about unstructured problems, such as effects of events and trends outside the organization.

**Decision table:**   Table showing decision rules that apply when certain conditions occur and what action should take place as a result.

**Demand report:**   A demand report is produced on request. An example is a report on the numbers and types of jobs held by women and minorities done at the request of the government.

**Demodulation:**   Process performed by a modem in converting analog signals to digital signals.

**Denial of service (DoS) attack:**   A variant virus in which websites are overwhelmed with data and users are unable to access the website. Unlike a worm that self-replicates, a DoS attack floods a computer or network with requests for information and data.

**Density:**   Refers to how tightly the bits (electromagnetic charges) can be packed next to one another on a disk.

**Design template:**   Provides professionally selected combinations of color schemes, slide layouts, and special effects for presentation graphics.

**Desk checking:**   Process of checking out a computer program by studying a printout of the program line by line, looking for syntax and logic errors.

**Desktop:**   (1) The screen that is displayed on the monitor when the computer starts up. All items and icons on the screen are considered to be on your desktop and are used to interact with the computer. (2) A system unit that typically contains the system's electronic components and selected secondary storage devices. Input and output devices, such as the mouse, keyboard, and monitor, are located outside the system unit.

**Desktop computer:**   Computer small enough to fit on top of or along the side of a desk and yet too big to carry around.

**Desktop operating system:**   *See* Stand-alone operating system.

**Desktop publisher:**   One who creates and formats publication-ready material.

**Desktop publishing program:**   Program that allows you to mix text and graphics to create publications of professional quality.

**Device driver:**   Every device that is connected to the computer has a special program associated with it called a device driver that allows communication between the operating system and the device.

**Diagnostic program:**   *See* Troubleshooting program.

**Dial-up service:**   Antiquated method of connecting to the Internet using telephones and telephone modems, which has been replaced with higher-speed connection services.

**Dialog box:**   Provides additional information and requests user input.

**Dictionary attack:**   Uses software to try thousands of common words sequentially in an attempt to gain unauthorized access to a user's account.

**Digital:**   Computers are digital machines because they can only understand 1s and 0s. It is either on or off. For example, a digital watch states the exact time on the face, whereas an analog watch has the second hand moving in constant motion as it tells the time.

**Digital camera:**   Similar to a traditional camera except that images are recorded digitally in the camera's memory rather than on film.

**Digital cash:**   Currency for Internet purchases. Buyers purchase digital cash from a third party (a bank that specializes in electronic currency) by transferring funds from their banks.

**Digital media player:**   *See* Portable media player.

**Digital Millennium Copyright Act:**   Law that makes it legal for a program owner to make only his or her own backup copies of a software program. However, it is illegal for those copies to be resold or given away.

**Digital rights management (DRM):**   Encompasses various technologies that control access to electronic media and files.

**Digital signal:**   Computers can only understand digital signals. Before processing can occur within the system unit, a conversion must occur from what we understand (analog) to what the system unit can electronically process (digital). *See* Analog signals.

**Digital subscriber line (DSL):**   Provides high-speed connection using existing telephone lines.

**Digital subscriber line (DSL) service:**   Service provided by telephone companies using existing telephone lines to provide high-speed connections.

**Digital versatile disc (DVD):**   A type of optical disc similar to CD-ROMs except that more data can be packed into the same amount of space. *Also see* DVD (digital versatile disc).

**Digital video camera:**   Input device that records motion digitally.

**Digital video disc:**   *See* DVD (digital versatile disc).

**Digital wallet:**   Information to make online shopping more convenient. A digital wallet typically resides on a user's smartphone and contains an individual's mailing address, credit card, and other information typically required to make an online purchase.

**Digital whiteboard:**   A specialized device with a large display connected to a computer or projector.

**DIMM (dual in-line memory module):**   An expansion module used to add memory to the system board.

**Direct approach:**   Approach for systems implementation whereby the old system is simply abandoned for the new system.

**Directory server:**   A specialized server that manages resources such as user accounts for an entire network.

**Disaster recovery plan:**   Plan used by large organizations describing ways to continue operations following a disaster until normal computer operations can be restored.

**Disaster recovery specialist:**   Workers responsible for recovering systems and data after a disaster strikes an organization.

**Disk caching:**   Method of improving hard-disk performance by anticipating data needs. Frequently used data is read from the hard disk into memory (cache). When needed, data is then accessed directly from memory, which has a much faster transfer rate than from the hard disk. Increases performance by as much as 30 percent.

**Disk Cleanup:**   A Windows troubleshooting utility that eliminates nonessential files.

**Disk Defragmenter:**   A Windows utility that optimizes disk performance by eliminating unnecessary fragments and rearranging files.

**Display screen:** *See* Monitor.

**Distributed database:** Database that can be made accessible through a variety of communications networks, which allow portions of the database to be located in different places.

**DO UNTIL structure:** Loop structure in programming that appears at the end of a loop. The DO UNTIL loop means that the loop statements will be executed at least once. In other words, this program tells you to DO option one UNTIL it is no longer true.

**DO WHILE structure:** Loop structure in programming that appears at the beginning of a loop. The DO WHILE loop will keep executing as long as there is information to be processed. For example, DO option one WHILE (or as long as) option one remains true.

**Document:** Any kind of text material.

**Document file:** File created by a word processor to save documents such as letters, research papers, and memos.

**Document scanner:** Similar to a flatbed scanner except that it can quickly scan multipage documents. It automatically feeds one page of a document at a time through a scanning surface.

**Documentation:** Written descriptions and procedures about a program and how to use it. *See* Program documentation.

**Domain name:** The second part of the URL; it is the name of the server where the resource is located. For example, www.mtv.com.

**Domain name server (DNS):** Internet addressing method that assigns names and numbers to people and computers. Because the numeric IP addresses are difficult to remember, the DNS server was developed to automatically convert text-based addresses to numeric IP addresses.

**Dot-matrix printer:** A type of printer that forms characters and images using a series of small pins on a print head. Used where high-quality output is not required.

**Dot pitch:** Distance between each pixel. The lower the dot pitch, the shorter the distance between pixels, and the higher the clarity of images produced.

**Dots-per-inch (dpi):** Printer resolution is measured in dpi. The higher the dpi, the better the quality of images produced.

**Downlink:** To receive data from a satellite.

**Downloading:** Process of transferring information from a remote computer to the computer one is using.

**Drawing program:** Program used to help create artwork for publications. *See* Illustration program.

**Driver:** *See* Device driver.

**DS3:** Provides support for very high speed, all-digital transmission for large corporations.

**DSL:** *See* Digital subscriber line.

**Dual-scan monitor:** *See* Passive-matrix monitor.

**Duplex printing:** Allows automatic printing on both sides of a sheet of paper.

**DVD (digital versatile disc or digital video disc):** Similar to CD-ROMs except that more data can be packed into the same amount of space. DVD drives can store a typical capacity of 4.7 GB on one side.

**DVD player:** Also known as DVD-ROM drives. *See* DVD.

**DVD-R (DVD recordable):** A DVD with a write-once format that differs slightly from the format of DVD+R. Typically used to create permanent archives for large amounts of data and to record videos.

**DVD+R (DVD recordable):** A DVD with a write-once format that differs slightly from the format of DVD-R. Typically used to create permanent archives for large amounts of data and to record videos.

**DVD-RAM (DVD random-access memory):** A high-capacity, maximum-performance disc that allows the user to read the information, write over it, and erase the data if necessary. Used like a floppy disk to copy, delete files, and run programs. It has up to 8 times the storage capacity of a CD and also can be used to read CD and DVD formats.

**DVD-ROM (DVD–read-only memory):** Used to distribute full-length feature films with theater-quality video and sound. Also known as DVD players. Are read-only.

**DVD-RW (DVD rewriteable):** A type of reusable DVD disc that is more flexible than the DVD-RAM. DVD-RW is able to create and read CD discs along with creating and editing large-scale multimedia presentations.

**DVD+RW (DVD rewriteable):** Another DVD format to record and erase repeatedly. Able to create and read CD discs along with creating and editing large-scale multimedia presentations.

**DVI (Digital Video Interface) port:** A type of port that provides a connection to a digital monitor.

# e

**E-book:** *See* E-book reader.

**E-book reader:** Handheld, book-sized device that displays text and graphics. Using content downloaded from the web or special cartridges, these devices are used to read newspapers, magazines, and books.

**E-commerce:** Buying and selling goods over the Internet.

**E-ink:** A black and white output from some e-book readers producing images that reflect light like ordinary paper.

**E-learning:** A web application that allows one to take educational courses online.

**E-mail:** Communicate with anyone in the world who has an Internet address or e-mail account with a system connected to the Internet. You can include a text message, graphics, photos, and file attachments.

**E-mail client:** A special program that communicates with the e-mail service provider and must be installed on the computer first.

**E-paper:** Requires power only when changing pages, and not the entire time a page is displayed on the screen.

**E-reader:** Dedicated mobile devices for storing and displaying e-books and other electronic media including electronic newspapers and magazines.

**EBCDIC (Extended Binary Coded Decimal Interchange Code):** Binary coding scheme that is a standard for minicomputers and mainframe computers.

**Economic feasibility:** Comparing the costs of a new system to the benefits it promises.

**Editing:** Features that modify a document such as using a thesaurus, find and replace, or spell check.

**Electronic books:** Traditional printed books in electronic format.

**Electronic commerce (e-commerce):** Buying and selling goods over the Internet.

**Electronic mail:** Transmission of electronic messages over the Internet. Also known as e-mail.

**Electronic paper:** *See* E-paper.

**Electronic profile:** Using publicly and privately available databases, information resellers create electronic profiles, which are highly detailed and personalized descriptions of individuals.

**Embedded operating system:** An operating system that is completely stored within the ROM (read-only memory) of the device that it is in; used for handheld computers and smaller devices like PDAs.

**Employee-monitoring software:** Programs that record virtually every activity on a computer system.

**Encryption:** Coding information so that only the user can read or otherwise use it.

**Encryption key:** A binary number used to gain access to encrypted information.

**End user:** Person who uses microcomputers or has access to larger computers.

**Enterprise storage system:** Using mass storage devices, a strategy designed for organizations to promote efficient and safe use of data across the networks within their organizations.

**Entity:** In an object-oriented database, a person, place, thing, or event that is to be described.

**Erasable optical disc:** Optical disc on which the disk drive can write information and also erase and rewrite information. Also known as CD-RW or compact disc rewriteable.

**Ergonomic keyboard:** Keyboard arrangement that is not rectangular and has a palm rest, which is designed to alleviate wrist strain.

**Ergonomics:** The study of human factors related to things people use.

**Ethernet:** Otherwise known as Ethernet bus or Ethernet LAN. The Ethernet bus is the pathway or arterial to which all nodes (PCs, file servers, print servers, web servers, etc.) are connected. All of this is connected to a local area network (LAN) or a wide area network (WAN). *See* Bus network.

**Ethernet cable:** Twisted-pair cable commonly used in networks and to connect a variety of components to the system unit.

**Ethernet port:** A high-speed networking port that allows multiple computers to be connected for sharing files or for high-speed Internet access.

**Ethics:** Standards of moral conduct.

**Exception report:** Report that calls attention to unusual events.

**Executive information system (EIS):** Sophisticated software that can draw together data from an organization's databases in meaningful patterns and highly summarized forms.

**Executive support system (ESS):** *See* Executive information system.

**Expansion bus:** Connects the CPU to slots on the system board. There are different types of expansion buses such as industry standard architecture (ISA), peripheral component interconnect (PCI), accelerated graphics port (AGP), universal serial bus (USB), and FireWire buses. *See* System bus.

**Expansion card:** Optional device that plugs into a slot inside the system unit to expand the computer's abilities. Ports on the system board allow cables to be connected from the expansion board to devices outside the system unit.

**Expansion slots:** Openings on a system board. Users can insert optional devices, known as expansion cards, into these slots, allowing users to expand their systems. *See* Expansion card.

**Expert system:** Computer program that provides advice to decision makers who would otherwise rely on human experts. It's a type of artificial intelligence that uses a database to provide assistance to users.

**ExpressCard:** Technology replacing the PC card to provide a direct connection to the system bus. *Also see* PC card slots.

**External data:** Data gathered from outside an organization. Examples are data provided by market research firms.

**External hard drive:** Uses the same technology as an internal hard disk but is used primarily to complement an internal hard disk by providing additional storage. They are typically connected to a USB or FireWire port on the system unit and are easily removed.

**External Serial Advanced Technology Attachment (eSATA):** A port that provides very high speed connections for external hard-disk drives, optical disks, and other large secondary storage devices.

**Extranet:** Private network that connects more than one organization.

# f

**Facebook:** The most widely used social networking site, as of 2008.

**Facebook groups:** Communities of individuals who share common interest on Facebook.

**Facebook Pages:** Often used by businesses and public figures to promote ideas, products, and services.

**Facebook Profile:** An individual's Facebook page, which may include photos, lists of personal interests, contact information, and other personal information.

**Family Educational Rights and Privacy Act (FERPA):** A federal law that restricts disclosure of educational records.

**Fax machine:** A device for sending and receiving images over telephone lines.

**Fiber-optic cable:** Special transmission cable made of glass tubes that are immune to electronic interference. Data is transmitted through fiber-optic cables in the form of pulses of light.

**Field:** Each column of information within a record is called a field. A field contains related information on a specific item like employee names within a company department.

**Fifth-generation language (5GL):** Computer language that incorporates the concept of artificial intelligence to allow direct human communication.

**File:** A collection of related records that can store data and programs. For example, the payroll file would include payroll information (records) for all of the employees (entities).

**File compression:** Process of reducing the storage requirements for a file.

**File compression program:** Utility program that reduces the size of files so they require less storage on the computer and can be sent more efficiently over the Internet. Examples of such programs are WinZip and Wizard.

**File decompression:** Process of expanding a compressed file.

**File server:** Dedicated computer with large storage capacity providing users access to shared folders or fast storage and retrieval of information used in that business.

**File transfer protocol (FTP):** Internet service for uploading and downloading files.

**Filter:** (1) A filter blocks access to selected websites. (2) A filter will locate or display records from a table that fit a set of conditions or criteria when using programs like Excel.

**Find and replace:** An editing tool that finds a selected word or phrase and replaces it with another. Click *edit, find*.

**Firewall:** Security hardware and software. All communications into and out of an organization pass through a special security computer, called a proxy server, to protect all systems against external threats.

**FireWire bus:** Operates much like USB buses on the system board but at higher speeds.

**FireWire port:** Used to connect high-speed printers, and even video cameras, to system unit.

**First-party cookie:** A cookie that is generated and then read only by the website you are currently visiting.

**Flash:** An interactive animation program from Adobe that is usually full screen and highly dynamic, displaying moving text or complicated interactive features.

**Flash drive:** *See* USB drive.

**Flash memory:** RAM chips that retain data even when power is disrupted. Flash memory is an example of solid-state storage and is typically used to store digitized images and record MP3 files.

**Flash memory card:** A solid-state storage device widely used in notebook computers. Flash memory also is used in a variety of specialized input devices to capture and transfer data to desktop computers.

**Flat-panel monitor:** Or liquid crystal display (LCD) monitor. These monitors are much thinner than CRTs and can be used for desktop systems as well.

**Flatbed scanner:** An input device similar to a copying machine.

**Folder:** A named area on a disk that is used to store related subfolders and files.

**Font:** Also known as typeface, is a set of characters with a specific design.

**Font size:** The height of a character measured in points, with each point being 1/72 inch.

**Foreground:** The current program when multitasking or running multiple programs at once.

**Form:** Electronic forms reflecting the contents of one record or table. Primarily used to enter new records or make changes to existing records.

**Format:** Features that change the appearance of a document like font, font sizes, character effects, alignment, and bulleted and numbered lists.

**Formula:** Instructions for calculations in a spreadsheet. It is an equation that performs calculations on the data contained within the cells in a worksheet or spreadsheet.

**Fourth-generation language (4GL):** Task-oriented language designed to solve a specific problem and requiring little special training on the part of the end user.

**Fragmented:** Storage technique that breaks up large files and stores the parts wherever space is available in adjacent sectors and clusters.

**Freedom of Information Act of 1970:** Law giving citizens the right to examine data about them in federal government files, except for information restricted for national security reasons.

**Friend:** An individual on a list of contacts for an instant messaging server.

**Frustrated:** Person who feels it is an imposition to have to learn something new like computer technology.

**Function:** A built-in formula in a spreadsheet that performs calculations automatically.

**Fuzzy logic:** Used by expert systems to allow users to respond by using qualitative terms, such as *great* and *OK*.

# g

**Galleries:** Feature of Microsoft Office 2007, 2010, and 2013 that simplifies the process of making selections from a list of alternatives by replacing dialog boxes with visual presentations of results.

**Game controller:** A device that provides input to computer games.

**Gamepad:** An input device designed to be held by two hands and provide a wide array of inputs including motion, turning, stopping, and firing.

**General ledger:** Activity that produces income statements and balance sheets based on all transactions of a company.

**General-purpose application:** Application used for doing common tasks, such as browsers and word processors, spreadsheets, databases, management systems, and presentation graphics. Also known as productivity applications.

**Generations (of programming languages):** The five generations are machine languages, assembly languages, procedural languages, problem-oriented languages, and natural languages. *See* Levels.

**Gesture control:** The ability to control operations with finger movements, such as swiping, sliding, and pinching.

**Gestures:** A feature of Mac OS 10.7 that allows the use of fingers to run programs and to control the content of a display screen.

**Global positioning system (GPS):** Devices that use location information to determine the geographic location of your car, for example.

**Google+:** *See* Google Plus.

**Google Cloud Print:** A Google service that supports cloud printing.

**Google Plus:** A combination of some of Google's previously existing services with some new services, many of which are similar to Facebook's services.

**GPU (graphics processing unit):** *See* Graphics coprocessor.

**Gramm-Leach-Bliley Act:** A law that protects personal financial information.

**Grammar checker:** In word processing, a tool that identifies poorly worded sentences and incorrect grammar.

**Graphical site map:** Diagram of a website's overall design.

**Graphical user interface (GUI):** Special screen that allows software commands to be issued through the use of graphic symbols (icons) or pull-down menus.

**Graphics card:** Device that provides high-quality 3-D graphics and animation for games and simulations.

**Graphics coprocessor:** Designed to handle requirements related to displaying and manipulating 2-D and 3-D graphic images.

**Graphics suite:** Group of graphics programs offered at a lower cost than if purchased separately, like CorelDraw.

**Grayscale:** The most common black ink selection in which images are displayed using many shades of gray.

**Grid chart:** Chart that shows the relationship between input and output documents.

**Group decision support system (GDSS):** System used to support the collective work of a team addressing large problems.

**Groups:** In Microsoft Word, each tab is organized into groups that contain related items.

**Guest operating system:** Operating system that operates on virtual machines.

# h

**Hacker:** Person who gains unauthorized access to a computer system for the fun and challenge of it.

**Handheld computer:** *See* Personal digital assistant (PDA).

**Handheld computer system unit:** Smallest type of system unit, designed to fit into the palm of one hand.

**Handwriting recognition software:** Translates handwritten notes into a form that the system unit can process.

**Hangouts:** A service offered through Google Plus, for communicating with up to 10 people at a time.

**Hard copy:** Information presented on paper; also referred to as printer output.

**Hard disk:** Enclosed disk drive containing one or more metallic disks. Hard disks use magnetic charges to record data and have large storage capacities and fast retrieval times.

**Hardware:** Equipment that includes a keyboard, monitor, printer, the computer itself, and other devices that are controlled by software programming.

**Head crash:** When a read-write head makes contact with the hard disk's surface or particles on its surface, the disk surface becomes scratched and some or all data is destroyed.

**Header:** A typical e-mail has three elements: header, message, and signature. The header appears first and includes addresses, subject, and attachments.

**Headsets:** Audio-output devices connected to a sound card in the system unit. The sound card is used to capture as well as play back recorded sound.

**Health Insurance Portability and Accountability Act (HIPAA):** A federal law that protects medical records.

**Help:** A feature in most application software providing options that typically include an index, a glossary, and a search feature to locate reference information about specific commands.

**Hexadecimal system (hex):** Uses 16 digits to represent binary numbers.

**Hi def (high definition):** The next generation of optical disc, with increased storage capacity. See BD (Blue-ray disc).

**Hierarchical database:** Database in which fields or records are structured in nodes. Organized in the shape of a pyramid, and each node is linked directly to the nodes beneath it. Also called one-to-many relationship.

**Hierarchical network:** *See* Tree network.

**High Definition Multimedia Interface (HDMI):** Port that provides high-definition video and audio, making it possible to use a computer as a video jukebox or an HD video recorder.

**High-definition television (HDTV):** All-digital television that delivers a much clearer and more detailed widescreen picture.

**Higher level:** Programming languages that are closer to the language humans use.

**History file:** Created by the browser to store information on websites visited by your computer system.

**Hits:** The sites that a search engine returns after running a keyword search, ordered from most likely to least likely to contain the information requested.

**Home network:** LAN network for homes allowing different computers to share resources, including a common Internet connection.

**Home software:** *See* Integrated package.

**Host:** Also called a server or provider, is a large centralized computer.

**Host operating system:** Operating system that runs on the physical machine.

**Hotspot:** Wireless access points that provide Internet access and are often available in public places such as coffee shops, libraries, bookstores, colleges, and universities.

**Household robot:** Robot designed to vacuum or scrub floors, mow lawns, patrol the house, or simply provide entertainment.

**HTML:** *See* Hypertext Markup Language.

**HTML editor:** *See* Web authoring program.

**Hub:** The center or central node for other nodes. This device can be a server or a connection point for cables from other nodes.

**Human resources:** The organizational department that focuses on the hiring, training, and promoting of people, as well as any number of human-centered activities within the organization.

**Hyper-V:** A program created by Microsoft used to create and run a virtual machine.

**Hyperlink:** Connection or link to other documents or web pages that contain related information.

**Hypertext Markup Language (HTML):** Programming language that creates document files used to display web pages.

**Hypertext transfer protocol (http):** A widely used protocol for web traffic.

**Hypertext transfer protocol secure (https):** A widely used protocol for web traffic and to protect the transfer of sensitive information.

# i

**Icons:** Graphic objects on the desktop used to represent programs and other files.

**Identity theft:** The illegal assumption of someone's identity for the purpose of economic gain.

**IF-THEN-ELSE structure:** Logical selection structure whereby one of two paths is followed according to IF, THEN, and ELSE statements in a program. *See* Selection structure.

**IFPS (interactive financial planning system):** A 4GL language used for developing financial models.

**Illusion of anonymity:** The misconception that being selective about disclosing personal information on the Internet can prevent an invasion of personal privacy.

**Illustration program:** Also known as drawing programs; used to create digital illustrations and modify vector images and thus create line art, 3-D models, and virtual reality.

**Image editor:** An application for modifying bitmap images.

**Image gallery:** Libraries of electronic images.

**Immersive experience:** Allows the user to walk into a virtual reality room or view simulations on a virtual reality wall.

**Income statement:** A statement that shows a company's financial performance, income, expenses, and the difference between them for a specific time period.

**Individual database:** Collection of integrated records used mainly by just one person. Also called microcomputer database.

**Industrial robot:** Robot used in factories to perform a variety of tasks. For example, machines used in automobile plants to do painting and polishing.

**Information:** Data that has been processed by a computer system.

**Information broker:** *See* Information reseller.

**Information reseller:** Also known as information broker. It gathers personal data on people and sells it to direct marketers, fund-raisers, and others, usually for a fee.

**Information system:** Collection of hardware, software, people, data, and procedures that work together to provide information essential to running an organization.

**Information systems manager:** Oversees the work of programmers, computer specialists, systems analysts, and other computer professionals.

**Information technology (IT):** Computer and communication technologies, such as communication links to the Internet, that provide help and understanding to the end user.

**Information utility:** *See* Commercial database.

**Information worker:** Employee who creates, distributes, and communicates information.

**Infrared:** Uses infrared light waves to communicate over short distances. Sometimes referred to as line-of-sight communication because light waves can only travel in a straight line.

**Inkjet printer:** Printer that sprays small droplets of ink at high speed onto the surface of the paper, producing letter-quality images, and can print in color.

**InPrivate Browsing:** A privacy mode provided by Internet Explorer that eliminates history files as well as blocks most cookies.

**Input:** Any data or instructions used by a computer.

**Input device:** Piece of equipment that translates data into a form a computer can process. The most common input devices are the keyboard and the mouse.

**Instant messaging (IM):** A program allowing communication and collaboration for direct, "live" connections over the Internet between two or more people.

**Integrated circuit:** *See* Silicon chip.

**Integrated package:** A single program providing functionality of a collection of programs but not as extensive as a specialized program like Microsoft Word. Popular with home users who are willing to sacrifice some advanced features for lower cost and simplicity.

**Interactive whiteboard:** *See* Digital whiteboard.

**Interactivity:** User participation in a multimedia presentation.

**Internal data:** Data from within an organization consisting principally of transactions from the transaction processing system.

**Internal hard disk:** Storage device consisting of one or more metallic platters sealed inside a container. Internal hard disks are installed inside the system cabinet of a microcomputer. It stores the operating system and major applications like Word.

**Internet:** A huge computer network available to everyone with a microcomputer and a means to connect to it. It is the actual physical network made up of wires, cables, and satellites as opposed to the web, which is the multimedia interface to resources available on the Internet.

**Internet scam:** Using the Internet, a fraudulent act or operation designed to trick individuals into spending their time and money for little or no return.

**Internet security suite:** Collection of utility programs designed to make using the Internet easier and safer.

**Internet service provider (ISP):** Provides access to the Internet.

**Internet telephone:** Low-cost alternative to long-distance telephone calls using electronic voice delivery.

**Internet telephony:** *See* Telephony.

**Interpreter:** Software that converts a procedural language one statement at a time into machine language just before the statement is executed. No object code is saved.

**Intranet:** Like the Internet, it typically provides e-mail, mailing lists, newsgroups, and FTP services, but it is accessible only to those within the organization. Organizations use intranets to provide information to their employees.

**Intrusion detection system (IDS):** Using sophisticated statistical techniques to analyze all incoming and outgoing network traffic, this system works with firewalls to protect an organization's network.

**Inventory:** Material or products that a company has in stock.

**Inventory control system:** A system that keeps records of the number of each kind of part or finished good in the warehouse.

**iOS:** Previously known as iPhone, mobile operating system developed for Apple's iPhone, iPod Touch, and iPad.

**IP address (Internet Protocol address):** The unique numeric address of a computer on the Internet that facilitates the delivery of e-mail.

**IP telephony:** *See* Telephony.

**iPhone OS:** *See* iOS.

**IT security analyst:** Person responsible for maintaining the security of a company's network, systems, and data. Employers look for candidates with a bachelor's or advanced specialized associate's degree in information systems or computer science and network experience.

# j

**JavaScript:** A scripting language that adds basic interactivity to web pages.

**Joystick:** Popular input device for computer games. You control game actions by varying the pressure, speed, and direction of the joystick.

# k

**Key:** Another term for encryption key.

**Key field:** The common field by which tables in a database are related to each other. This field uniquely identifies the record. For example, in university databases, a key field is the Social Security number. Also known as primary key.

**Keyboard:** Input device that looks like a typewriter keyboard but has additional keys.

**Keystroke logger:** Also known as computer monitoring software and sniffer programs. They can be loaded onto your computer without your knowledge.

**Knowledge base:** A system that uses a database containing specific facts, rules to relate these facts, and user input to formulate recommendations and decisions.

**Knowledge-based systems:** Programs duplicating human knowledge. A type of artificial intelligence that uses a database to provide assistance to users.

**Knowledge work system (KWS):** Specialized information system used to create information in a specific area of expertise.

**Knowledge worker:** Person involved in the creation of information, such as an engineer or a scientist.

# l

**Label:** Provides structure to a worksheet by describing the contents of the rows and columns. *See* Text entry.

**Land:** *See* Lands and pits.

**Lands and pits:** Flat and bumpy areas, respectively, that represent 1s and 0s on the optical disc surface to be read by a laser.

**Language translator:** Converts programming instructions into a machine language that can be processed by a computer.

**Laptop computer:** *See* Notebook computer and Notebook system unit.

**Laser printer:** Printer that creates dotlike images on a drum, using a laser beam light source.

**Launchpad:** A feature of Mac OS X Lion that displays and provides direct access to all apps installed on your computer.

**Levels:** Generations or levels of programming languages ranging from "low" to "high." *See* Generations (of programming languages).

**Link:** A connection to related information.

**LinkedIn:** The premier business-oriented social networking site.

**Linux:** Type of UNIX operating system initially developed by Linus Torvalds, it is one of the most popular and powerful alternatives to the Windows operating system.

**Lion:** Also known as Mac OS 10.7, this operating system introduced Launchpad, Mission Control, and gesture support.

**Liquid crystal display (LCD):** A technology used for flat-panel monitors.

**Local area network (LAN):** Network consisting of computers and other devices that are physically near each other, such as within the same building.

**Location:** For browsers to connect to resources, locations or addresses must be specified. Also known as uniform resource locators or URLs.

**Logic error:** Error that occurs when a programmer has used an incorrect calculation or left out a programming procedure.

**Logic structure:** Programming statements or structures called sequence, selection, or loop that control the logical sequence in which computer program instructions are executed.

**Logical operation:** Comparing two pieces of data to see whether one is equal to (=), less than (<), or greater than (>) the other.

**Logical view:** Focuses on the meaning and content of the data. End users and computer professionals are concerned with this view as opposed to the physical view, with which only specialized computer professionals are concerned.

**Loop structure:** Logic structure in which a process may be repeated as long as a certain condition remains true. This structure is called a "loop" because the program loops around or repeats again and again. There are two variations: DO UNTIL and DO WHILE.

**Low bandwidth:** *See* Voiceband.

**Lower level:** Programming language closer to the language the computer itself uses. The computer understands the 0s and 1s that make up bits and bytes.

**LTE (Long Term Evolution):** A wireless standard, comparable to WiMax.

# m

**Mac OS:** Operating system designed for Macintosh computers.

**Mac OS X:** Macintosh operating system featuring a user interface called Aqua.

**Machine language:** Language in which data is represented in 1s and 0s. Most languages have to be translated into machine language for the computer to process the data. Either a compiler or an interpreter performs this translation.

**Magnetic card reader:** A card reader that reads encoded information from a magnetic strip on the back of a card.

**Magnetic-ink character recognition (MICR):** Direct-entry scanning devices used in banks. This technology is used to automatically read the numbers on the bottom of checks.

**Mainboard:** See Motherboard or System board.

**Mainframe computer:** This computer can process several million program instructions per second. Sizeable organizations rely on these room-size systems to handle large programs and a great deal of data.

**Maintenance programmer:** Programmers who maintain software by updating programs to protect them from errors, improve usability, standardize, and adjust to organizational changes.

**Malware:** Short for malicious software.

**MAN:** See Metropolitan area network.

**Management information system (MIS):** Computer-based information system that produces standardized reports in a summarized and structured form. Generally used to support middle managers.

**Many-to-many relationship:** In a network database, each child node may have more than one parent node and vice versa.

**Marketing:** The organizational department that plans, prices, promotes, sells, and distributes an organization's goods and services.

**Markup language:** See Content-markup language.

**Mass storage:** Refers to the tremendous amount of secondary storage required by large organizations.

**Mass storage devices:** Devices such as file servers, RAID systems, tape libraries, optical jukeboxes, and more.

**Mechanical mouse:** Traditional and most widely used type of mouse. It has a ball on the bottom and is attached with a cord to the system unit.

**Media:** Media are the actual physical material that holds the data, such as a floppy disk, which is one of the important characteristics of secondary storage. Singular of media is medium.

**Medium:** See Media.

**Medium band:** Bandwidth of special leased lines, used mainly with minicomputers and mainframe computers.

**Megabits per second (Mbps):** The transfer rate of millions of bits per second.

**Memory:** Memory is contained on chips connected to the system board and is a holding area for data instructions and information (processed data waiting to be output to secondary storage). RAM, ROM, and CMOS are three types of memory chips.

**Menu:** List of commands.

**Menu bar:** Menus are displayed in a menu bar at the top of the screen.

**Mesh network:** A topology requiring each node to have more than one connection to the other nodes so that if a path between two nodes is disrupted, data can be automatically rerouted around the failure using another path.

**Message:** The content portion of e-mail correspondence.

**Metasearch engine:** Program that automatically submits your search request to several indices and search engines and then creates an index from received information. One of the best known is Dogpile.

**Method:** In an object-oriented database, description of how the data is to be manipulated.

**Metropolitan area network (MAN):** These networks are used as links between office buildings in a city.

**Microblog:** Publishes short sentences that only take a few seconds to write, rather than long stories or posts like a traditional blog.

**Microcomputer:** Small, low-cost computer designed for individual users. These include desktop, notebook, and personal digital assistant computers.

**Microcomputer database:** See Individual database.

**Microprocessor:** The central processing unit (CPU) of a microcomputer controls and manipulates data to produce information. The microprocessor is contained on a single integrated circuit chip and is the brains of the system.

**Microwave:** Communication using high-frequency radio waves that travel in straight lines through the air.

**Middle management:** Middle-level managers deal with control and planning. They implement the long-term goals of the organization.

**MIDI:** See Musical instrument digital interface.

**Midrange computer:** Refrigerator-sized machines falling in between microcomputers and mainframes in processing speed and data-storing capacity. Medium-sized companies or departments of large companies use midrange computers.

**Mini DisplayPort (MiniDP or mDP):** A port that an audio-visual device typically uses to connect large monitors. These ports are used with many Apple Macintosh computers.

**Mission Control:** A feature of Mac OS Lion that displays all running programs at one time.

**Mistaken identity:** When the electronic profile of one person is switched with another.

**Mobile apps (applications):** Add-on features for a variety of mobile devices, including smartphones, netbooks, and tablets.

**Mobile browser:** Special browsers designed to run on portable devices.

**Mobile digital television:** A technology that allows television stations to broadcast their programming directly to smartphones, computers, and digital media players.

**Mobile DTV:** See Mobile digital television.

**Mobile operating system:** Embedded operating system that controls a smartphone.

**Mobile OS:** *See* Mobile operating system.

**Mobile robots:** Robots that act as transports and are used for a variety of different tasks.

**Modem:** Short for modulator-demodulator. It is a communication device that translates the electronic signals from a computer into electronic signals that can travel over telephone lines.

**Modulation:** Process of converting digital signals to analog signals.

**Module:** *See* Program module.

**Monitor:** Output device like a television screen that displays data processed by the computer.

**Motherboard:** Also called a system board; the communications medium for the entire system.

**Motion-sensing device:** An input device that controls games with user movements.

**Mouse:** Device that typically rolls on the desktop and directs the cursor on the display screen.

**Mouse pointer:** Typically in the shape of an arrow.

**Multicore chip:** A new type of chip that provides two independent CPUs, allowing two programs to run simultaneously. *Also see* Central processing unit.

**Multidimensional database:** Data can be viewed as a cube having three or more sides consisting of cells. Each side of the cube is considered a dimension of the data; thus, complex relationships between data can be represented and efficiently analyzed. Sometimes called a data cube and designed for analyzing large groups of records.

**Multifunctional devices (MFD):** Devices that typically combine the capabilities of a scanner, printer, fax, and copying machine.

**Multimedia:** Technology that can link all sorts of media into one form of presentation, such as video, music, voice, graphics, and text.

**Multimedia authoring programs:** Programs used to create multimedia presentations bringing together video, audio, graphics, and text elements into an interactive framework. Macromedia Director, Authorware, and Toolbook are examples of multimedia authoring programs.

**Multitasking:** Operating system that allows a single user to run several application programs at the same time.

**Multitouch screen:** Can be touched with more than one finger, which allows for interactions such as rotating graphical objects on the screen with your hand or zooming in and out by pinching and stretching your fingers.

**Musical instrument digital interface (MIDI):** A standard that allows musical instruments to connect to the system using MIDI ports.

**MySpace:** One of the first large-scale social networking sites.

# n

**Naive:** People who underestimate the difficulty of changing computer systems or generating information.

**Natural language:** Language designed to give people a more human connection with computers.

**Netbook:** Similar to notebook system units but smaller, less powerful, and less expensive.

**Network:** The arrangement in which various communications channels are connected through two or more computers. The largest network in the world is the Internet.

**Network adapter card:** Connects the system unit to a cable that connects to other devices on the network.

**Network administrator:** Also known as network manager. Computer professional who ensures that existing information and communication systems are operating effectively and that new ones are implemented as needed. Also responsible for meeting security and privacy requirements.

**Network architecture:** Describes how networks are configured and how the resources are shared.

**Network attached storage (NAS):** Similar to a file server except simpler and less expensive. Widely used for home and small business storage needs.

**Network database:** Database with a hierarchical arrangement of nodes, except that each child node may have more than one parent node. Also called many-to-many relationship.

**Network gateway:** Connection by which a local area network may be linked to other local area networks or to larger networks.

**Network interface card (NIC):** Also known as a network adapter card. Used to connect a computer to one or more computers forming a communication network whereby users can share data, programs, and hardware.

**Network operating system (NOS):** Interactive software between applications and computers coordinating and directing activities between computers on a network. This operating system is located on one of the connected computers' hard disks, making that system the network server.

**Network server:** *See* Network operating system. This computer coordinates all communication between the other computers. Popular network operating systems include NetWare and Windows NT Server.

**Node:** Any device connected to a network. For example, a node is a computer, printer, or data storage device and each device has its own address on the network. Also, within hierarchical databases, fields or records are structured in nodes.

**Notebook:** A small, portable system unit that contains electronic components, selected secondary storage devices, and input devices.

**Notebook computer:** Portable computer, also known as a laptop computer, weighing between 4 and 10 pounds.

**Notebook keyboard:** A keyboard widely used on notebook computers, including netbooks.

**Numbered list:** Sequence of steps or topics on a page organized by numbers.

**Numeric entry:** In a worksheet or spreadsheet, typically used to identify numbers or formulas.

# o

**Object:** An element, such as a text box, that can be added to a workbook can be selected, sized, and moved. For example, if a chart (object) in an Excel workbook file (source file) is linked to a Word document (destination file), the chart appears in the Word document. In this manner, the object contains both data and instructions to manipulate the data.

**Object code:** Machine language code converted by a compiler from source code. Object code can be saved and run later.

**Object-oriented database:** A more flexible type of database that stores data as well as instructions to manipulate data and is able to handle unstructured data such as photographs, audio, and video. Object-oriented databases organize data using objects, classes, entities, attributes, and methods.

**Object-oriented programming (OOP):** Methodology in which a program is organized into self-contained, reusable modules called objects. Each object contains both the data and processing operations necessary to perform a task.

**Object-oriented software development:** Software development approach that focuses less on the tasks and more on defining the relationships between previously defined procedures or objects.

**Objectives:** In programming, it is necessary to make clear the problems you are trying to solve to create a functional program.

**Office automation system (OAS):** System designed primarily to support data workers. It focuses on managing documents, communicating, and scheduling.

**Office software suites:** *See* Productivity suites.

**Office suites:** *See* Productivity suites.

**One-to-many relationship:** In a hierarchical database, each entry has one parent node, and a parent may have several child nodes.

**Online:** Being connected to the Internet is described as being online.

**Online identity:** The information that people voluntarily post about themselves online.

**Online office suite:** Office suite stored online and available anywhere the Internet can be accessed.

**Online processing:** *See* Real-time processing.

**Online shopping:** The buying and selling of a wide range of consumer goods over the Internet.

**Online stock trading:** Allows investors to research, buy, and sell stocks and bonds over the Internet.

**Online storage:** Provides users with storage space that can be accessed from a website.

**Open source:** A free and openly distributed software program intended to allow users to improve upon and further develop the program.

**Operating system (OS):** Software that interacts between application software and the computer, handling such details as running programs, storing and processing data, and coordinating all computer resources, including attached peripheral devices. It is the most important program on the computer. Windows 7, Windows 8, and Mac OS X are examples of operating systems.

**Operational feasibility:** Making sure the design of a new system will be able to function within the existing framework of an organization.

**Operational model:** A decision model that helps lower-level managers accomplish the organization's day-to-day activities, such as evaluating and maintaining quality control.

**Operators:** Operators handle correcting operational errors in any programs. To do that, they need documentation, which lets them understand the program, thus enabling them to fix any errors.

**Optical audio connection:** Port used to integrate computers into high-end audio and home theatre systems.

**Optical carrier (OC):** Provides support for very high speed, all-digital transmission for large corporations.

**Optical-character recognition (OCR):** Scanning device that uses special preprinted characters, such as those printed on utility bills, that can be read by a light source and changed into machine-readable code.

**Optical disc:** Storage device that can hold over 17 gigabytes of data, which is the equivalent of several million typewritten pages. Lasers are used to record and read data on the disc. The three basic types of optical discs are compact discs (CDs), digital versatile or video discs (DVDs), and Blu-ray discs (BDs).

**Optical disc drive:** A disc is read by an optical disc drive using a laser that projects a tiny beam of light. The amount of reflected light determines whether the area represents a 1 or a 0.

**Optical-mark recognition (OMR):** Device that senses the presence or absence of a mark, such as a pencil mark. As an example, an OMR device is used to score multiple-choice tests.

**Optical mouse:** A type of mouse that emits and senses light to detect mouse movement.

**Optical scanner:** Device that identifies images or text on a page and automatically converts it to electronic signals that can be stored in a computer to copy or reproduce.

**Organic light-emitting diode (OLED):** Has the benefits of lower power consumption and longer battery life, as well as possibilities for much thinner displays.

**Organization chart:** Chart showing the levels of management and formal lines of authority in an organization.

**Organizational cloud storage:** High-speed Internet connection to a dedicated remote organizational Internet drive site.

**OS X Lion:** An OS for Mac that introduced several powerful features including Launchpad and Mission Control.

**OS X Mountain Lion:** An OS for Mac that was released in 2012 and designed for desktops and laptops.

**Output:** Processed data or information.

**Output device:** Equipment that translates processed information from the central processing unit into a form that can be understood by humans. The most common output devices are monitors and printers.

# p

**Packet:** Before a message is sent on the Internet, it is broken down into small parts called packets. Each packet is then sent separately over the Internet. At the receiving end, the packets are reassembled into the correct order.

**Page layout program:** *See* Desktop publishing program.

**Pages:** In Microsoft PowerPoint, another name for slides.

**Parallel approach:** Systems implementation in which old and new systems are operated side by side until the new one has shown it is reliable.

**Parallel processing:** Used by supercomputers to run large and complex programs.

**Parent node:** Node one level above the node being considered in a hierarchical database or network. Each entry has one parent node, although a parent may have several child nodes. Also called one-to-many relationship.

**Passive-matrix monitor:** Monitor that creates images by scanning the entire screen. This type requires little energy but clarity of images is not sharp. Also known as dual-scan monitor.

**Password:** Special sequence of numbers or letters that limits access to information, such as electronic mail.

**Patches:** Programming modifications or corrections.

**Payroll:** Activity concerned with calculating employee paychecks.

**PC card:** A small, credit card–sized expansion card developed to meet the size constraints of notebook, tablet, and handheld computers.

**PC card slot:** Also known as Personal Computer Memory Card International Association (PCMCIA) card slot. Credit card–sized expansion cards developed for portable computers.

**PCI Express (PCIe):** New type of bus that is 30 times faster than PCI bus.

**PCMCIA slot:** *See* PC card slot.

**PDA keyboard:** Miniature keyboard for PDAs used to send e-mail, create documents, and more.

**Peer-to-peer (P2P) network:** Network in which nodes can act as both servers and clients. For example, one microcomputer can obtain files located on another microcomputer and also can provide files to other microcomputers.

**People:** End users who use computers to make themselves more productive.

**Perception system robot:** Robot that imitates some of the human senses.

**Periodic report:** Reports for a specific time period as to the health of the company or a particular department of the company.

**Person-to-person auction site:** A type of web auction site where the owner provides a forum for numerous buyers and sellers to gather.

**Personal area network (PAN):** A type of wireless network that works within a very small area—your immediate surroundings.

**Personal digital assistant (PDA):** A device that typically combines pen input, writing recognition, personal organizational tools, and communication capabilities in a very small package. Also called handheld computer.

**Personal laser printer:** Inexpensive laser printer widely used by single users to produce black-and-white documents.

**Personal software:** *See* Integrated package.

**Phased approach:** Systems implementation whereby a new system is implemented gradually over a period of time.

**Phishing:** An attempt to trick Internet users into thinking a fake but official-looking website or e-mail is legitimate.

**Photo editor:** *See* Image editor.

**Photo printer:** A special-purpose inkjet printer designed to print photo-quality images from digital cameras.

**Physical security:** Activity concerned with protecting hardware from possible human and natural disasters.

**Physical view:** This focuses on the actual format and location of the data. *See* Logical view.

**Picture element:** *See* Pixel.

**Pilot approach:** Systems implementation in which a new system is tried out in only one part of the organization. Later it is implemented throughout the rest of the organization.

**Pit:** *See* Lands and pits.

**Pixel (picture element):** Smallest unit on the screen that can be turned on and off or made different shades. Pixels are individual dots that form images on a monitor. The greater the resolution, the more pixels and the better the clarity.

**Pixel pitch:** The distance between each pixel on a monitor.

**Plagiarism:** Representation of some other person's work and ideas as your own without giving credit to the original source.

**Plagiarist:** Someone who engages in plagiarism.

**Platform:** The operating system. Application programs are designed to run with a specific platform. *See* Operating system.

**Platform scanner:** Handheld direct-entry device used to read special characters on price tags. Also known as wand reader.

**Platter:** Rigid metallic disk; multiple platters are stacked one on top of another within a hard disk drive.

**Plotter:** Special-purpose output device for producing bar charts, maps, architectural drawings, and three-dimensional illustrations.

**Plug and Play:** Set of hardware and software standards developed to create operating systems, processing units, expansion cards, and other devices that are able to configure themselves. When the computer starts up, it will search for the Plug and Play device and automatically configure it to the system.

**Plug-in:** Program that is automatically loaded and operates as part of a browser.

**Podcast:** An Internet-based medium for delivering music and movie files from the Internet to a computer.

**Pointer:** For a monitor, a pointer is typically displayed as an arrow and controlled by a mouse. For a database, a pointer is a connection between a parent node and a child node in a hierarchical database.

**Pointers:** Within a network database, pointers are additional connections between parent nodes and child nodes. Thus, a node may be reached through more than one path and can be traced down through different branches.

**Pointing device:** A device that provides an intuitive interface with the system unit by accepting pointing gestures and converting them into machine-readable input.

**Pointing stick:** Device used to control the pointer by directing the stick with your finger.

**Port:** Connecting socket on the outside of the system unit. Used to connect input and output devices to the system unit.

**Portable language:** Language that can be run on more than one type of computer.

**Portable media player:** Also known as digital media player; a specialized device for storing, transferring, and playing audio files.

**Portable printer:** Small and lightweight printers designed to work with notebook computers.

**Portable scanner:**   A handheld device that slides across an image to be scanned, making direct contact.

**Power supply unit:**   Desktop computers have a power supply unit located within the system unit that plugs into a standard wall outlet, converting AC to DC, which becomes the power to drive all of the system unit components.

**Preliminary investigation:**   First phase of the systems life cycle. It involves defining the problem, suggesting alternative systems, and preparing a short report.

**Presentation file:**   A file created by presentation graphics programs to save presentation materials. For example, a file might contain audience handouts, speaker notes, and electronic slides.

**Presentation graphics:**   Graphics used to combine a variety of visual objects to create attractive and interesting presentations.

**Primary key:**   *See* Key field.

**Primary storage:**   Holds data and program instructions for processing data. It also holds processed information before it is output. *See* Memory.

**Printer:**   Device that produces printed paper output.

**Privacy:**   Computer ethics issue concerning the collection and use of data about individuals.

**Privacy mode:**   A browser feature that eliminates history files and blocks most cookies.

**Private Browsing:**   A privacy mode provided by Safari. *See* Privacy mode.

**Proactive:**   Person who looks at technology in a positive, realistic way.

**Procedural language:**   Programming language designed to focus on procedures and how a program will accomplish a specific task. Also known as 3GL or third-generation language.

**Procedures:**   Rules or guidelines to follow when using hardware, software, and data.

**Processing rights:**   Refers to which people have access to what kind of data.

**Processor:**   *See* Central processing unit.

**Production:**   The organizational department that actually creates finished goods and services using raw materials and personnel.

**Productivity suites:**   Also known as office suites; contain professional-grade application programs, including word processing, spreadsheets, and more. A good example is Microsoft Office.

**Program:**   Instructions for the computer to follow to process data. *See* Software.

**Program analysis:**   *See* Program specification.

**Program coder:**   *See* Application generator.

**Program definition:**   *See* Program specification.

**Program design:**   Creating a solution using programming techniques, such as top-down program design, pseudocode, flowcharts, logic structures, object-oriented programming, and CASE tools.

**Program documentation:**   Written description of the purpose and process of a program. Documentation is written within the program itself and in printed documents.

Programmers will find themselves frustrated without adequate documentation, especially when it comes time to update or modify the program.

**Program flowchart:**   Flowchart graphically presents a detailed sequence of steps needed to solve a programming problem.

**Program maintenance:**   Activity of updating software to correct errors, improve usability, standardize, and adjust to organizational changes.

**Program module:**   Each module is made up of logically related program statements. The program must pass in sequence from one module to the next until the computer has processed all modules.

**Program specification:**   Programming step in which objectives, output, input, and processing requirements are determined.

**Programmer:**   Computer professional who creates new software or revises existing software.

**Programming:**   A program is a list of instructions a computer will follow to process data. Programming, also known as software development, is a six-step procedure for creating that list of instructions. The six steps are program specification, program design, program code (or coding), program test, program documentation, and program maintenance.

**Programming language:**   A collection of symbols, words, and phrases that instruct a computer to perform a specific task.

**Project manager:**   Software that enables users to plan, schedule, and control the people, resources, and costs needed to complete a project on time.

**Property:**   Computer ethics issue relating to who owns data and rights to software.

**Protocol:**   Rules for exchanging data between computers. The protocol http:// is the most common.

**Prototyping:**   Building a model or prototype that can be modified before the actual system is installed.

**Proxy server:**   Computer that acts as a gateway or checkpoint in an organization's firewall. *See* Firewall.

**Pseudocode:**   An outline of the logic of the program to be written. It is the steps or the summary of the program before you actually write the program for the computer. Consequently, you can see beforehand what the program is to accomplish.

**Purchase order:**   A form that shows the name of the company supplying the material or service and what is being purchased.

**Purchasing:**   Buying of raw materials and services.

# q

**QR code:**   Graphics that typically appear as black and white boxes that automatically link mobile devices to a variety of different content including games, text, videos, and websites.

**QR code reader:**   An app that allows mobile devices to use their digital cameras to scan QR codes.

**Query:**   A question or request for specific data contained in a database. Used to analyze data.

**Query-by-example:** A specific tool in database management that shows a blank record and lets you specify the information needed, like the fields and values of the topic you are looking to obtain.

**Query language:** Easy-to-use language and understandable to most users. It is used to search and generate reports from a database. An example is the language used on an airline reservation system.

**Quick response code:** *See* QR code.

# r

**Radio frequency (RF):** Uses radio signals to communicate between wireless devices.

**Radio frequency card reader:** A device that reads cards having embedded radio frequency identification (RFID) information.

**RAID system:** Several inexpensive hard-disk drives connected to improve performance and provide reliable storage.

**RAM:** *See* Random-access memory.

**Random-access memory (RAM):** Volatile, temporary storage that holds the program and data the CPU is presently processing. It is called temporary storage because its contents will be lost if electrical power to the computer is disrupted or the computer is turned off.

**Range:** A series of continuous cells in a worksheet.

**Rapid applications development (RAD):** Involves the use of powerful development software and specialized teams as an alternative to the systems development life cycle approach. Time for development is shorter and quality of the completed systems development is better, although cost is greater.

**Raster:** *See* Bitmap.

**Read-only memory (ROM):** Refers to chips that have programs built into them at the factory. The user cannot change the contents of such chips. The CPU can read or retrieve the programs on the chips but cannot write or change information. ROM stores programs that boot the computer, for example. Also called firmware.

**Real-time processing:** Or online processing. Occurs when data is processed at the same time a transaction occurs.

**Recalculation:** If you change one or more numbers in your spreadsheet, all related formulas will automatically recalculate and charts will be recreated.

**Record:** Each row of information in a database is a record. Each record contains fields of data about some specific item, like employee name, address, phone, and so forth. A record represents a collection of attributes describing an entity.

**Redundant arrays of inexpensive disks (RAIDs):** Groups of inexpensive hard-disk drives related or grouped together using networks and special software. They improve performance by expanding external storage.

**Refresh rate:** How often a displayed image is updated or redrawn on the monitor.

**Relation:** A table in a relational database in which data elements are stored in rows and columns.

**Relational database:** A widely used database structure in which data is organized into related tables. Each table is made up of rows called records and columns called fields. Each record contains fields of data about a specific item.

**Repetition structure:** *See* Loop structure.

**Repetitive strain injury (RSI):** Any injury that is caused by fast, repetitive work that can generate neck, wrist, hand, and arm pain.

**Reports:** Can be lists of fields in a table or selected fields based on a query. Typical database reports include sales summaries, phone lists, and mailing labels.

**Research:** The organizational department that identifies, investigates, and develops new products and services.

**Resolution:** A measurement in pixels of a monitor's clarity. For a given monitor, the greater the resolution, the more pixels and the clearer the image.

**Reverse directory:** A special telephone directory listing telephone numbers sequentially, followed by subscriber names.

**RFID (radio-frequency identification) reader:** A device used to read radio-frequency identification information.

**RFID tags:** Microchips that contain electronically stored information and can be embedded in items such as consumer products, driver's licenses, passports, etc.

**Ribbon GUI:** An interface that uses a system of ribbons, tabs, and galleries to make it easier to find and use all the features of an application.

**Ribbons:** Feature of Microsoft Office 2007, 2010, and 2013 that replaces menus and toolbars by organizing commonly used commands into a set of tabs.

**RIM OS:** Mobile operating system originally designed for the BlackBerry handheld computer.

**Ring network:** Network in which each device is connected to two other devices, forming a ring. There is no host computer, and messages are passed around the ring until they reach the correct destination.

**Robot:** Robots are computer-controlled machines that mimic the motor activities of living things, and some robots can solve unstructured problems using artificial intelligence.

**Robot network:** *See* Botnet.

**Robotics:** Field of study concerned with developing and using robots.

**Rogue Wi-Fi hotspot:** Imitation hotspot intended to capture personal information.

**Roller ball:** *See* Trackball.

**ROM:** *See* Read-only memory.

**Router:** A node that forwards or routes data packets from one network to their destination in another network.

**Row:** A horizontal block of cells one cell high all the way across the worksheet.

# s

**Sales order processing:** Activity that records the demands of customers for a company's products or services.

**Satellite:** This type of communication uses satellites orbiting about 22,000 miles above the earth as microwave relay stations.

**Satellite connection services:** Connection services that use satellites and the air to download or send data to users at a rate seven times faster than dial-up connections.

**Scam:** A fraudulent or deceptive act or operation designed to trick individuals into spending their time and money for little or no return.

**Scanner:** *See* Optical scanner.

**Scanning devices:** Convert of scanned text and images into a form that the system unit can process.

**Schema:** *See* Data dictionary.

**Search engine:** Specialized programs assisting in locating information on the web and the Internet.

**Search services:** Organizations that maintain databases relating to information provided on the Internet and also provide search engines to locate information.

**Secondary storage:** Permanent storage used to preserve programs and data that can be retained after the computer is turned off. These devices include hard disks, magnetic tape, CDs, DVDs, and more.

**Secondary storage device:** These devices are used to save, backup, and transport files from one location or computer to another. *See* Secondary storage.

**Sector:** Section shaped like a pie wedge that divides the tracks on a disk.

**Secure file transfer protocol (SFTP):** *See* File transfer protocol.

**Security:** The protection of information, hardware, and software.

**Security suites:** A collection of utility programs designed to protect your privacy and security while you are on the web.

**Selection structure:** Logic structure that determines which of two paths will be followed when a program must make a decision. Also called IF-THEN-ELSE structures. IF something is true, THEN do option one, or ELSE do option two.

**Semiconductor:** Silicon chip through which electricity flows with some resistance.

**Sequential structure:** Logic structure in which one program statement follows another.

**Server:** A host computer with a connection to the Internet that stores document files used to display web pages. Depending on the resources shared, it may be called a file server, printer server, communication server, web server, or database server.

**Shared laser printer:** More expensive laser printer used by a group of users to produce black-and-white documents. These printers can produce over 30 pages a minute.

**Sheet:** A rectangular grid of rows and columns. *See* Spreadsheet or Worksheet.

**Signature:** Provides additional information about a sender of an e-mail message, such as name, address, and telephone number.

**Silicon chip:** Tiny circuit board etched on a small square of sandlike material called silicon. Chips are mounted on carrier packages, which then plug into sockets on the system board.

**Skype:** An audio and video communication service that does not require any dedicated hardware.

**Slide:** A PowerPoint presentation is made up of many slides shown in different views and presentation styles.

**Slot:** Area on a system board that accepts expansion cards to expand a computer system's capabilities.

**Smartphone:** A type of cell phone that offers a variety of advanced functionality, including Internet and e-mail.

**Social networking:** Using the Internet to connect individuals.

**Socket:** Sockets provide connection points on the system board for holding electronic parts.

**Soft copy:** Output from a monitor.

**Software:** Computer program consisting of step-by-step instructions, directing the computer on each task it will perform.

**Software development:** *See* Programming.

**Software development life cycle (SDLC):** A six-step procedure for software development.

**Software engineer:** Programming professional or programmer who analyzes users' needs and creates application software.

**Software environment:** Operating system, also known as software platform, consisting of a collection of programs to handle technical details depending on the type of operating system. For example, software designed to run on an Apple computer is compatible with the Mac OS environment.

**Software piracy:** Unauthorized copying of programs for personal gain.

**Software platform:** *See* Software environment.

**Software suite:** Individual application programs that are sold together as a group.

**Software updates:** Patches in which modifications to the software are typically more extensive and significant.

**Solid-state drive (SSD):** Designed to be connected inside a microcomputer system the same way an internal hard disk would be, but contains solid-state memory instead of magnetic disks to store data.

**Solid-state storage:** A secondary storage device that has no moving parts. Data is stored and retrieved electronically directly from these devices, much as they would be from conventional computer memory.

**Sony/Philips Digital Interconnect Format (S/PDIF):** *See* Optical audio connection.

**Sort:** Tool that rearranges a table's records numerically or alphabetically according to a selected field.

**Sound card:** Device that accepts audio input from a microphone and converts it into a form that can be processed by the computer. Also converts internal electronic signals to audio signals so they can be heard from external speakers.

**Source code:** When a programmer originally writes the code for a program in a particular language. This is called source code until it is translated by a compiler for the computer to execute the program. It then becomes object code.

**Spam:** Unwelcome and unsolicited e-mail that can carry attached viruses.

**Spam blocker:** Also referred to as spam filter. Software that uses a variety of different approaches to identify and eliminate spam or junk mail.

**Spam filter:** *See* Spam blocker.

**Sparks:** A Google Plus service that automatically provides news on selected topics of interest and facilitates sharing this information with others to spark further discussion.

**Speakers:** Audio-output devices connected to a sound card in the system unit. The sound card is used to capture as well as play back recorded sound.

**Specialized applications:** Programs that are narrowly focused on specific disciplines and occupations. Some of the best known are multimedia, web authoring, graphics, virtual reality, and artificial intelligence.

**Specialized search engine:** Search engine that focuses on subject-specific websites.

**Specialized suite:** Programs that focus on specialized applications such as graphics or financial planning.

**Speech recognition:** The ability to accept voice input to select menu options, and to dictate text.

**Spelling checker:** Program used with a word processor to check the spelling of typed text against an electronic dictionary.

**Spider:** Special program that continually looks for new information and updates a search server's databases.

**Spike:** *See* Voltage surge.

**Spotlight:** An advanced search tool on the Mac OS X operating system for locating files, e-mail messages, and more.

**Spreadsheet:** Computer-produced spreadsheet based on the traditional accounting worksheet that has rows and columns used to present and analyze data.

**Spy removal programs:** Programs such as Spybot and Spysweeper, designed to detect web bugs and monitor software.

**Spyware:** Wide range of programs designed to secretly record and report an individual's activities on the Internet.

**Stand-alone operating system:** Also called desktop operating system; a type of operating system that controls a single desktop or notebook computer.

**Star network:** Network of computers or peripheral devices linked to a central computer through which all communications pass. Control is maintained by polling. The configuration of the computers looks like a star surrounding and connected to the central computer in the middle.

**Stock photograph:** Photographs of a variety of subject material from professional models to natural landscapes.

**Storage area network (SAN):** An architecture that links remote computer storage devices such as enterprise storage systems to computers so that the devices are available as locally attached drives.

**Storage device:** Hardware that reads data and programs from storage media. Most also write to storage media.

**Strategic model:** A decision model that assists top managers in long-range planning, such as stating company objectives or planning plant locations.

**Strategy:** A way of coordinating the sharing of information and resources. The most common network strategies are terminal, peer-to-peer, and client/server networks.

**Streaming:** *See* Webcast.

**Structured program:** Program that uses logic structures according to the program design and the language in which you have chosen to write the program. Each language follows techniques like pseudocode, flowcharts, and logic structures.

**Structured programming techniques:** Techniques consisting of top-down program design, pseudocode, flowcharts, and logic structures.

**Structured query language (SQL):** A program control language used to create sophisticated database applications for requesting information from a database.

**Styles:** A feature found in most word processors that quickly applies predefined formats.

**Stylus:** Penlike device used with tablets and PDAs that uses pressure to draw images on a screen. A stylus interacts with the computer through handwriting recognition software.

**Subject:** Located in the header of an e-mail message; a one-line description used to present the topic of the message.

**Subject directory:** Organizes information according to categories or topics.

**Supercomputer:** Fastest calculating device ever invented, processing billions of program instructions per second. Used by very large organizations like NASA.

**Supervisor:** Manager responsible for managing and monitoring workers. Supervisors have responsibility for operational matters.

**Surf:** Move from one website to another.

**Surge protector:** Device separating the computer from the power source of the wall outlet. When a voltage surge occurs, a circuit breaker is activated, protecting the computer system.

**Switch:** The center or central node for other nodes. This device coordinates the flow of data by sending messages directly between sender and receiver nodes.

**Syntax error:** Violation of the rules of a language in which the computer program is written. For example, leaving out a semicolon would stop the entire program from working because it is not the exact form the computer expects for that language.

**System:** Collection of activities and elements designed to accomplish a goal.

**System board:** Flat board that usually contains the CPU and memory chips connecting all system components to one another.

**System bus:** There are two categories of buses. One is the system bus that connects the CPU to the system board. The other is the expansion bus that connects the CPU to slots on the system board.

**System chassis:** *See* System unit.

**System flowchart:** A flowchart that shows the flow of input data to processing and finally to output, or distribution of information.

**System software:** "Background" software that enables the application software to interact with the computer. System software consists of the operating system, utilities, device drivers, and language translators. It works with application software to handle the majority of technical details.

**System unit:** Part of a microcomputer that contains the CPU. Also known as the system cabinet or chassis, it is the container that houses most of the electronic components that make up the computer system.

**Systems analysis:** This second phase of the systems life cycle determines the requirements for a new system.

Data is collected about the present system and analyzed, and new requirements are determined.

**Systems analysis and design:** Six phases of problem-solving procedures for examining information systems and improving them.

**Systems analysis report:** Report prepared for higher management describing the current information system, the requirements for a new system, and a possible development schedule.

**Systems analyst:** Plans and designs information systems.

**Systems audit:** A systems audit compares the performance of a new system to the original design specifications to determine if the new procedures are actually improving productivity.

**Systems design:** Phase three of the systems life cycle, consisting of designing alternative systems, selecting the best system, and writing a systems design report.

**Systems design report:** Report prepared for higher management describing alternative designs, presenting costs versus benefits, and outlining the effects of alternative designs on the organization.

**Systems development:** Phase four of the systems life cycle, consisting of developing software, acquiring hardware, and testing the new system.

**Systems implementation:** Phase five of the systems life cycle is converting the old system to the new one and training people to use the new system. Also known as conversion.

**Systems life cycle:** The six phases of systems analysis and design are called the systems life cycle. The phases are preliminary investigation, systems analysis, systems design, systems development, systems implementation, and systems maintenance.

**Systems maintenance:** Phase six of the systems life cycle consisting of a systems audit and periodic evaluation.

# t

**T1:** High-speed lines that support all digital communications, provide very high capacity, and are very expensive.

**T3:** Copper lines combined to form higher-capacity options.

**Tab:** Used to divide the ribbon into major activity areas, with each tab being organized into groups that contain related items.

**Table (in database):** The list of records in a database. Tables make up the basic structure of a database. Their columns display field data and their rows display records. *See* Field and Record.

**Tablet:** A type of microcomputer that contains a thin system unit, most of which is the monitor. The best-known tablets are Apple's iPad, Motorola's Zoom, and HP's Slate.

**Tactical model:** A decision model that assists middle-level managers to control the work of the organization, such as financial planning and sales promotion planning.

**Tape library:** Device that provides automatic access to data archived on a large collection or library of tapes.

**Task-oriented language:** Programming language that is non-procedural and focuses on specifying what the program is to accomplish. Also known as 4GL or very high level language.

**Technical feasibility:** Making sure hardware, software, and training will be available to facilitate the design of a new system.

**Technical writer:** Prepares instruction manuals, technical reports, and other scientific or technical documents.

**Telephone line:** A transmission medium for both voice and data.

**Telephone modem:** Used to connect a computer directly to a telephone line.

**Telephony:** Communication that uses the Internet rather than traditional communication lines to connect two or more people via telephone.

**Temporary Internet file:** File that has web page content and instructions for displaying this content.

**Text entry:** In a worksheet or spreadsheet, a text entry is typically used to identify or label information entered into a cell as opposed to numbers and formulas. Also known as labels.

**Text messaging (texting):** The process of sending a short electronic message typically less than 160 characters using a wireless network to another person who views the message on a mobile device, such as a smartphone.

**Thermal printer:** Printer that uses heat elements to produce images on heat-sensitive paper.

**Thesaurus:** A word processor feature that provides synonyms, antonyms, and related words for a selected word or phrase.

**Thin-film transistor liquid crystal (TFT-LC):** Type of flat-panel monitor activating each pixel independently.

**Third-generation language (3GL):** *See* Procedural language.

**Third-party cookie:** A cookie generated by an advertising company that is affiliated with the website you are currently visiting. Often also referred to as a tracking cookie.

**Thumb keyboard:** Small thumb-operated keyboard for smartphones and other portable devices. Designed primarily for texting and connecting to the web.

**Toggle key:** These keys turn a feature on or off, like the CAPS LOCK key.

**Toolbar:** Bar located typically below the menu bar containing icons or graphical representations for commonly used commands.

**Top-down analysis method:** Method used to identify top-level components of a system, then break these components down into smaller parts for analysis.

**Top-down program design:** Used to identify the program's processing steps, called program modules. The program must pass in sequence from one module to the next until the computer has processed all modules.

**Top-level domain (TLD):** Last part of an Internet address; identifies the geographical description or organizational identification. For example, using www.aol.com, the .com is the top-level domain code and indicates it is a commercial site. *Also see* Domain name.

**Top management:** Top-level managers are concerned with long-range (strategic) planning. They supervise middle management.

**Topology:** The configuration of a network. The five principal network topologies are *ring, bus, star, tree,* and *mesh.*

**Touch pad:** Used to control the pointer by moving and tapping your finger on the surface of a pad.

**Touch screen:** Monitor screen allowing actions or commands to be entered by the touch of a finger.

**Tower computer:** A desktop system unit placed vertically.

**Track:** Closed, concentric ring on a disk on which data is recorded. Each track is divided into sections called sectors.

**Trackball:** Device used to control the pointer by rotating a ball with your thumb. Also called a roller ball.

**Tracking cookies:** *See* Third-party cookie.

**Traditional keyboard:** Full-sized, rigid, rectangular keyboard that includes function, navigational, and numeric keys.

**Transaction processing system (TPS):** System that records day-to-day transactions, such as customer orders, bills, inventory levels, and production output. The TPS tracks operations and creates databases.

**Transfer rate:** Or transfer speed, is the speed at which modems transmit data, typically measured in bits per second (bps).

**Transition:** Used to animate how a presentation moves from one slide to the next.

**Transmission control protocol/Internet protocol (TCP/IP):** TCP/IP is the standard protocol for the Internet. The essential features of this protocol involve (1) identifying sending and receiving devices and (2) reformatting information for transmission across the Internet.

**Tree network:** Also known as a hierarchical network. A topology in which each device is connected to a central node, either directly or through one or more other devices. The central node is then connected to two or more subordinate nodes that in turn are connected to other subordinate nodes, and so forth, forming a treelike structure.

**Trojan horse:** Program that is not a virus but is a carrier of virus(es). The most common Trojan horses appear as free computer games, screen savers, or antivirus programs. Once downloaded they locate and disable existing virus protection and then deposit the virus.

**Troubleshooting program:** A utility program that recognizes and corrects computer-related problems before they become serious. Also called diagnostic program.

**Twisted-pair cable:** Cable consisting of pairs of copper wire that are twisted together.

**Twitter:** The most popular microblogging site that enables you to add new content from your browser, instant messaging application, or even a mobile phone.

## u

**Unicode:** A 16-bit code designed to support international languages, like Chinese and Japanese.

**Uniform resource locator (URL):** For browsers to connect you to resources on the web, the location or address of the resources must be specified. These addresses are called URLs.

**Uninstall program:** A utility program that safely and completely removes unwanted programs and related files.

**Universal instant messenger:** An instant messaging service that communicates with any other messaging service programs.

**Universal Product Code (UPC):** A bar code system that identifies the product to the computer, which has a description and the latest price for the product.

**Universal serial bus (USB):** Combines with a PCI bus on the system board to support several external devices without inserting cards for each device. USB buses are used to support high-speed scanners, printers, and videocapturing devices.

**Universal serial bus (USB) port:** They have replaced serial and parallel ports. They are faster, and one USB port can be used to connect several devices to the system unit.

**UNIX:** An operating system originally developed for midrange computers. It is now important because it can run on many of the more powerful microcomputers.

**Uplink:** To send data to a satellite.

**Uploading:** Process of transferring information from the computer the user is operating to a remote computer.

**USB drive:** The size of a key chain, these hard drives connect to a computer's USB port enabling a transfer of files.

**User:** Any individual who uses a computer. *See* End user.

**User interface:** Means by which users interact with application programs and hardware. A window is displayed with information for the user to enter or choose, and that is how users communicate with the program.

**Utility:** Performs specific tasks related to managing computer resources or files. Norton Utility for virus control and system maintenance is a good example of a utility. Also known as service programs.

**Utility suite:** A program that combines several utilities in one package to improve system performance.

## V

**Vector:** A common type of graphic file. A vector file contains all the shapes and colors, along with starting and ending points, necessary to recreate the image.

**Vector illustration:** *See* Vector image.

**Vector image:** Graphics file made up of a collection of objects such as lines, rectangles, and ovals. Vector images are more flexible than bitmaps because they are defined by mathematical equations so they can be stretched and resized. Illustration programs create and manipulate vector graphics. Also known as vector illustrations.

**Very high level languages:** Task-oriented languages that require little special training on the part of the user.

**VGA (Video Graphic Adapter) port:** A type of port that provides a connection to an analog monitor.

**Video editing software:** Allows you to reorganize, add effects, and more to your video footage.

**Videoconferencing system:** Computer system that allows people located at various geographic locations to have in-person meetings.

**Virtual environment:** *See* Virtual reality.

**Virtual keyboard:** Displays an image of a keyboard on a touch screen device. The screen functions as the actual input device, which is why the keyboard is considered virtual.

**Virtual machine:** A software implementation of a computer that executes programs like a physical computer.

**Virtual memory:** Feature of an operating system that increases the amount of memory available to run programs. With large programs, parts are stored on a secondary device like your hard disk. Then each part is read in RAM only when needed.

**Virtual private network (VPN):** Creates a secure private connection between a remote user and an organization's internal network. Special VPN protocols create the equivalent of a dedicated line between a user's home or laptop computer and a company server.

**Virtual reality (VR):** Interactive sensory equipment (headgear and gloves) allowing users to experience alternative realities generated in 3-D by a computer, thus imitating the physical world.

**Virtual reality wall:** An immersive experience whereby you are viewing simulations in stereoscopic vision.

**Virtualization:** A process that allows a single physical computer to support multiple operating systems that operate independently.

**Virtualization software:** Software that creates virtual machines.

**Virus:** Hidden instructions that migrate through networks and operating systems and become embedded in different programs. They may be designed to destroy data or simply to display messages.

**Voice over IP (VoIP):** Transmission of telephone calls over networks. *See also* Telephony.

**Voice recognition system:** Using a microphone, sound card, and specialty software, the user can operate a computer and create documents using voice commands.

**Voiceband:** Bandwidth of a standard telephone line. Also known as low bandwidth.

**Voltage surge (spike):** Excess of electricity that may destroy chips or other electronic computer components.

**VR:** *See* Virtual reality.

# W

**WAN:** *See* Wide area network.

**Wand reader:** Special-purpose handheld device used to read OCR characters.

**Warm boot:** Restarting your computer while the computer is already on and the power is not turned off.

**Web:** Introduced in 1992, and prior to the web the Internet was all text. The web made it possible to provide a multimedia interface that includes graphics, animations, sound, and video.

**Web 1.0:** The first generation of the web, which focused on linking existing information.

**Web 2.0:** The second generation of the web, which evolved to support more dynamic content creation and social interaction.

**Web 3.0:** The third generation of the web, which focuses on computer-generated information requiring less human interaction to locate and to integrate information.

**Web auction:** Similar to traditional auctions except that all transactions occur over the web; buyers and sellers seldom meet face-to-face.

**Web authoring:** Creating a website.

**Web authoring program:** Word processing program for generating web pages. Also called HTML editor or web page editor. Widely used web authoring programs include Macromedia Dreamweaver and Microsoft FrontPage.

**Web-based e-mail account:** An e-mail account that does not require an e-mail program to be installed on your computer.

**Web-based e-mail client:** A special program that communicates with the e-mail service provider and must be installed on the computer first.

**Web-based file transfer services:** A type of file transfer service that uses a web browser to upload and download files, allowing you to copy files to and from your computer across the Internet.

**Web bug:** Program hidden in the HTML code for a web page or e-mail message as a graphical image. Web bugs can migrate whenever a user visits a website containing a web bug or opens infected e-mail. They collect information on the users and report back to a predefined server.

**Web log:** A type of personal website where articles are regularly posted.

**Web page:** Browsers interpret HTML documents to display web pages.

**Web page editor:** *See* Web authoring program.

**Web suffix:** Identifies type of organization in a URL.

**Web utilities:** Specialized utility programs making the Internet and the web easier and safer. Some examples are plug-ins that operate as part of a browser and filters that block access and monitor use of selected websites.

**Webcam:** Specialized digital video camera for capturing images and broadcasting to the Internet.

**Webcast:** An Internet delivery medium that uses streaming technology, in which audio and video files are continuously downloaded to a computer while the user is listening to and/or viewing the file content.

**Webmail:** E-mail that uses a webmail client.

**Webmail client:** A special program that runs on an e-mail provider's computer that supports webmail.

**Webmaster:** Develops and maintains websites and web resources.

**WebOS:** A mobile operating system that supports Hewlett-Packard's smartphones and tablets.

**What-if analysis:** Spreadsheet feature in which changing one or more numbers results in the automatic recalculation of all related formulas.

**Wheel button:** Some mice have a wheel button that can be rotated to scroll through information displayed on the monitor.

**Wide area network (WAN):** Countrywide and worldwide networks that use microwave relays and satellites to reach users over long distances.

**Wi-Fi (wireless fidelity):** Wireless standard also known as 802.11, used to connect computers to each other and to the Internet.

**Wiki:** A website that allows people to fill in missing information or correct inaccuracies on it by directly editing the pages.

**Wikipedia:** An online encyclopedia, written and edited by anyone who wants to contribute.

**WiMax (Worldwide Interoperability for Microwave Access):** Technology that extends Wi-Fi networks to operate over greater distances.

**Window:** A rectangular area containing a document or message.

**Windows:** An operating environment extending the capability of DOS.

**Windows 7:** OS from 2009 that has a traditional user interface similar to previous versions of Windows. It provides enhanced features including improved handwriting recognition and advanced searching capabilities for finding files and other content on your computer.

**Windows 8:** OS from 2012 that is designed to better integrate Microsoft's desktop OS with its mobile OS. It provides support for gestures, cloud integration, and apps.

**Windows Phone 8:** Introduced in 2012 by Microsoft to support a variety of mobile devices including smartphones. It has the ability to run many powerful programs designed for desktop and laptop computers.

**Windows RT:** A version of Windows 8 designed to run with tablets using a particular microprocessor from ARM.

**Windows Update:** A utility provided in the Windows platform that allows you to update the device drivers on your computer.

**Wireless access point:** Or base station. The receiver interprets incoming radio frequencies from a wireless LAN and routes communications to the appropriate devices, which could be separate computers, a shared printer, or a modem.

**Wireless keyboard:** Transmits input to the system through the air, providing greater flexibility and convenience.

**Wireless LAN (WLAN):** Uses radio frequencies to connect computers and other devices. All communications pass through the network's centrally located wireless receiver or base station and are routed to the appropriate devices.

**Wireless modem:** Modem that connects to the serial port but does not connect to telephone lines. It receives through the air.

**Wireless mouse:** *See* Cordless mouse.

**Wireless network card:** Allows computers to be connected without cables.

**Wireless network encryption:** Restricts access to authorized users on wireless networks.

**Wireless revolution:** A revolution that is expected to dramatically affect the way we communicate and use computer technology.

**Wireless wide area network (WWAN) modem:** *See* Wireless modem.

**Word:** The number of bits (such as 16, 32, or 64) that can be accessed at one time by the CPU.

**Word processor:** The computer and the program allow you to create, edit, save, and print documents composed of text.

**Word wrap:** Feature of word processing that automatically moves the cursor from the end of one line to the beginning of the next.

**Workbook file:** Contains one or more related worksheets or spreadsheets. *See* Spreadsheet.

**Worksheet:** Also known as a spreadsheet, or sheet; a rectangular grid of rows and columns used in programs like Excel.

**Worksheet file:** Created by electronic spreadsheets to analyze things like budgets and to predict sales.

**Worm:** Virus that doesn't attach itself to programs and databases but fills a computer system with self-replicating information, clogging the system so that its operations are slowed or stopped.

**WPA2 (Wi-Fi Protected Access):** A secure encryption protocol.

**WYSIWYG (what you see is what you get) editors:** Web authoring programs that build a page without requiring direct interaction with the HTML code and then preview the page described by the HTML code.

# Z

**Zombie:** A computer infected by a virus, worm, or Trojan horse that allows it to be remotely controlled for malicious purposes.

# Photo Credits

## Chapter 1

Page 2: © Bettmann/Corbis; opener: Mike Agliolo/Photo Researchers/Getty Images; p. 4(top), 17: Inti St. Clair/Taxi/Getty Images; 1-1(left), p. 19(information systems): © Photodisc/PunchStock RF; 1-1(right), p. 20(software): Used with permission from Microsoft; 1-1(bottom), 1-5, p. 20(software): Microsoft product screen shot(s) and screen captures reprinted with permission from Microsoft Corporation; 1-1(bottom-right): © Royalty-Free/Corbis; 1-1(bottom-left): Courtesy of Dell Inc.; 1-2, p. 19(people): Juice Images/Getty Images RF; 1-7: Courtesy of Lawrence Livermore National Laboratory; 1-8(desktop), 1-9, p. 20(hardware): Courtesy of Dell Inc.; 1-8(screen): Courtesy of Hewlett-Packard; 1-8(notebook): Photo courtesy Fujitsu America, Inc. Fujitsu and the Fujitsu logo are registered trademarks of Fujitsu Limited; 1-8(handheld and tablet): Future Publishing/Getty Images; 1-10, 1-12: © Willis Technology; 1-11: Courtesy of Samsung USA; 1-14(top-left): Copyright © 2012 Research In Motion Limited; 1-14(top-middle and right): Copyright © 2012 HTC Corporation. All rights reserved; 1-14(bottom-right): Courtesy of Hewlett-Packard; 1-14(bottom-left): © maxim .photoshelter.com/Alamy; p. 18: Colin Anderson/Getty Images RF.

## Chapter 2

Page 26: SuperStock/Getty Images; opener: Lois & Bob Schlowsky/Stone/Getty Images; p. 28: © Photosindia/Alamy; p. 30(top): Copyright © 2012 Netflix, Inc. All rights reserved; p. 30(bottom): Copyright © 2012 Hulu. All rights reserved; p. 31(top): Copyright © 2012 Vudu, Inc. All rights reserved; p. 31(bottom): Copyright © 2012 Roku, Inc. Used with permission; 2-6: © Allison Rocks! Photography; 2-7, p. 54(left): Microsoft product screen shot(s) and screen captures reprinted with permission from Microsoft Corporation; 2-9, p. 54(right): Copyright © 2012 Facebook, Inc. All rights reserved; 2-11: Copyright © 2012 WordPress Inc. All rights reserved; p. 40: Copyright © 2012 Twitter, Inc. All rights reserved; 2-13, 2-20, p. 55(left), 56: Copyright © 2012 Google, Inc. Used with permission; 2-17, p. 55(right): Copyright © 2012 PayPal Inc. All rights reserved; 2-23: Copyright © 2012 ContentWatch, Inc. Used with permission; p. 51: © Photosindia/Alamy; p. 52: Reproduced with permission from Antuan Goodwin/CNET.

## Chapter 3

Page 62: Bert Hardy/Hulton Archive/Getty Images; opener: Colin Anderson/Photographer's Choice/Getty Images; p. 64, 76, 82, 87: Comstock Images/Getty Images RF; 3-1, 3-2, 3-5, 3-9, p. 75, 76, 85(left), 91: Microsoft product screen shot(s) and screen captures reprinted with permission from Microsoft Corporation; 3-11, 3-15(top, middle): Copyright © 2012 Adobe, Inc. All rights reserved; p. 76(top): Colin Anderson/Photographer's Choice/Getty Images; 3-20, p. 87: Used with permission from Microsoft; p. 84: © Ocean/Corbis RF.

## Chapter 4

Page 94: Bettmann/Corbis; opener: © Sanford/Agliolo/Corbis; p. 96, 111: Thomas Barwick/Getty Images RF; 4-1(left): © Photodisc/PunchStock RF; 4-1(middle both), p. 113(top): Used with permission

from Microsoft; 4-1(right), 4-4, p. 113(right): Courtesy of Dell Inc.; 4-2, 4-6, 4-7, 4-10, 4-11, p. 105, 106, 4-14, 4-17, p. 114(top-right): Microsoft product screen shot(s) and screen captures reprinted with permission from Microsoft Corporation; 4-3: © Helen Sessions/Alamy; 4-5, p. 114(left): Courtesy of Apple Inc.; 4-10, p. 115(bottom): Copyright © 2012 Canonical Ltd. Ubuntu and Canonical are registered trademarks of Canonical Ltd; 4-15, p. 115(right): Copyright © 2012 Symantec Corporation. All rights reserved; p. 112: Lucas Racasse/Getty Images RF.

## Chapter 5

Page 122: Francis Miller/Time & Life Pictures/Getty Images; opener: Steve Allen/Brand X Pictures RF; p. 124, 141: Pete Stone/Stock This Way/Corbis; 5-1(tower): Courtesy of Dell Inc.; 5-1(all-in-one): Associated Press; 5-2(notebook): Photo by Joseph Branston/MacFormat magazine via Getty Images; 5-2(netbook): Courtesy of Acer Inc. All Rights Reserved; 5-3(tablet), p. 143(system unit): Courtesy of Samsung USA; 5-3, p. 143(screen): Used with permission from Microsoft; 5-4(desktop): © Willis Technology; 5-4(notebook): © Tim Jones/Alamy; 5-4(tablet and smartphone): Reproduced with permission Bill Detweiler/TechRepublic; p. 128(top): © Targus USA. All rights reserved; p. 128(bottom): Courtesy of Arctic Silver, Inc.; 5-5, 5-6, 5-7, 5-10, 5-13, 5-14, 5-15, 5-17, 5-18, 5-19, 5-20, 5-21, p. 143(system board), 144, 145: © Willis Technology; 5-16: Courtesy of USB-IF; p. 138(top): Courtesy of AVerMedia; p. 138(bottom), 149(bottom): Used with permission from Microsoft; p. 142: © E.M. Pasieka/Science Photo Library/Corbis RF.

## Chapter 6

Page 152: Associated Press; opener: BlueMoon Stock/Alamy RF; p. 154, 174: Justin Guariglia/National Geographic/Getty Images RF; 6-1, 6-32, p. 179(ergonomics): © Willis Technology; 6-2(notebook), p. 176(keyboards): Nick Koudis/Getty Images RF; 6-2(virtual): Justin Sullivan/Getty Images; 6-2(thumb), 6-20: Bloomberg via Getty Images; 6-3: © Stock Connection/SuperStock RF; 6-4: PhotoDisc/Getty Images RF; 6-5: LAMB/Alamy RF; 6-6: By Ian Miles-Flashpoint Pictures/Alamy; 6-7, p. 176(pointing devices): Ferran Traite Soler/Getty Images RF; 6-8(top-left): © 2012 Logitech, Inc. All rights reserved; 6-8(top-right): PiaCarrot/GFDL; 6-8(bottom-right): Used with permission from Microsoft; 6-8(bottom-left): Evan-amos/Public Domain; 6-9: Ken Reid/WorkBook Stock/Getty Images; 6-10: Courtesy of Ricoh Electronics, Inc. – USA; 6-11, p. 177(scanning devices): Courtesy of GoodGuide; 6-12: Thomas Cooper/Getty Images; 6-13: Junior Gonzales/Getty Images RF; 6-14, p. 177(image capturing): Travelpix Ltd./Photographer's Choice/Getty Images; 6-15: JGI/Blend Images/Getty Images RF; 6-16, 6-19, 6-22, p. 178(monitors): Used by permission of Sony Electronics Inc.; 6-19, p. 178(screen): © Edward Coyle/Jewel and Associates; p. 164(all): Kindle, Kindle Fire, and the Kindle Fire logo are trademarks of Amazon.com, Inc. or its affiliates; 6-21: © Bob Daemmrich/Alamy; 6-23: From Oxford English Dictionary Online. By permission of Oxford University Press; 6-24, p. 178(printers): Courtesy of Epson America, Inc.; 6-25: Courtesy of Konica Minolta Holdings, Inc.; 6-26: "Wireless Earvolution – Jabra STONE"/GN US, Inc.; 6-27, p. 179(audio and video devices): Courtesy of Apple Inc.; 6-28: Courtesy © Cisco and/or its affiliates. All rights reserved; p. 170,

171: Skype screenshots copyright © 2012. Used with permission; p. 171: Inti St. Clair/Taxi/Getty Images; 6-29: Photo by Koichi Kamoshida/Getty Images; 6-30: Chris Salvo/Getty Images; p. 175: Copyright © 2012 Google, Inc. Used with permission.

## Chapter 7

Page 186: C Squared Studios/Getty Images RF; opener: Sean Gladwell/Alamy RF; p. 188, 200: ColorBlind Images/Getty Images RF; 7-1, p. 202(storage): Nick Koudis/Photodisc/Getty Images RF; 7-5: © Iomega Corporation, eGo Portable Hard Drive; 7-6, p. 203(hard disks): Courtesy of CalDigit, Inc.; 7-8, p. 203(optical discs): Tetra Images/Corbis RF; 7-9: Courtesy of LG Electronics, Inc.; 7-11: MacFormat Magazine/Contributor/Getty Images; 7-12, p. 204(solid-state storage): David Kilpatrick/Alamy; 7-13, p. 204(USB drives): Jim Craigmyle/Corbis; 7-14, p. 204(cloud storage): Copyright © 2012 Google, Inc. Used with permission; p. 201: Courtesy of GE Global Research.

## Chapter 8

Page 210: Jerry Cooke/Corbis; opener: Michel Tcherevkoff/Getty Images; p. 212, 229: Thomas Northcut/Digital Vision/Getty Images RF; 8-1, p. 232(communications): Fuse/Getty Images RF; 8-3, 8-4, 8-5, 8-11(all), p. 233(all): © Willis Technology; 8-7, p. 232(communication channels): Stuart Gregory/Photodisc/Getty Images RF; 8-8: © Oleksiy Maksymenko/Alamy; 8-8: p. 219(all): © 2012 AT&T Intellectual Property. All rights reserved; 8-15: Courtesy of Shenzhen Ogemray Technology Co., Ltd.; p. 230: Copyright © 2012 logmein.com. Used with permission; p. 231: Image Source/Corbis RF.

## Chapter 9

Page 240: Corbis Flirt/Alamy; opener: Lightscapes Photography, Inc./Corbis; p. 242, 265: Peter M. Fisher/Corbis; 9-1: Blend Images/Alamy; 9-2, p. 267(left): Copyright © 2012 phonelookup .com. All rights reserved; 9-3: Copyright © 2012 spokeo.com. Used with permission; 9-4: Copyright © 2012 Google, Inc. Used with permission; 9-5, p. 267(right): Copyright © 2012 Pearlsoftware. Used with permission; 9-6, 9-7, 9-8, p. 257(middle), 9-16, p. 261(bottom): Microsoft product screen shot(s) and screen captures reprinted with permission from Microsoft Corporation; 9-9, 9-11, p. 268(left): Copyright © 2012 Symantec Inc. Used with permission; 9-13: Copyright © 2012 Facebook, Inc. All rights reserved; 9-15(fingerprint): Siemens press picture; 9-15(iris), p. 268(right): Varie/Alt/Corbis; p. 257: Copyright Bitdefender.com. All rights reserved; p. 258: Copyright © 2012 Avast! Used with permission; p. 261(top), 262: Copyright © 2012 Carbonite, Inc. All rights reserved; 9-20, p. 269(right): Copyright © 2012 turnitin.com. Courtesy of www .turnitin.com; p. 266: © Steve Hix/Somos Images/Corbis RF.

## Appendix: The Evolution of the Computer Age

Pages 276(first and fourth generations), 277(top-left and middle), 278(top-right), 279(top-left and bottom): IBM Corporate Archives; p. 276(second generation), 277(bottom), 278(top-left and bottom), 279(top-right), 280(top-left and bottom), 281(top-middle and right): Courtesy of the Computer History Museum; p. 276(fifth generation): © Masahiro Sano/Corbis; p. 277(top-right): © Bettman/ Corbis; p. 280(top-right), 281(bottom), 282(top-left), 284(bottom-left), p. 285(bottom-middle and right): Courtesy of Apple Inc.; p. 281(top-left), 282(bottom-right), 283(top-left), 284(left-middle): Used with permission from Microsoft; p. 282(top-middle and right), 285(bottom-middle): Courtesy Intel; p. 282(bottom-left): © AP Photo/Paul Sakuma; p. 283(top-right): Napster logo; p. 283(bottom): Blogger logo; p. 284(top-left): Amazon.com; p. 284(bottom-right), 286(top-left): Google; p. 285(top-left): MySpace.com; p. 285(bottom-left): YouTube.com; p. 286(top-right): twitter.com.

Privacy, 243–250
    inaccurate information, 245–246
    Internet, 247–250
    large databases, 243–246
    legislation, 250
    online identity, 250
    primary issues, 243
    private networks, 246–247
Privacy mode, 248
Private Browsing, 248
Private network, 246–247
Processing speeds, 131
Processor, 130
Processor temperature, 127
Productivity suite, 81
Professional recovery services, 195
Professional specialized applications, 78
Program, 6
Project Glass, 173
Project management software, 78
Property, 243
Protocol, 220
Proxy server, 228
Public folder, 223

## q

QR code, 80
QR code reader, 80
QuarkXPress, 73
QuiBids, 45
Quick response code, 80
QuickTime, 48, 49
QWXGQ+, 162
QXGA, 162
QXSGA, 162

## r

RAID storage device, 191
RAID system, 199
RAM, 132–133, 188
Random-access memory (RAM), 132–133, 188
Raster, 74
Read-only memory (ROM), 133
Reader, 48, 49
RealPlayer, 48
Record, 72
Recovery/undelete software, 195
Recuva, 195
Recycling, 6
Recycling computer hardware, 130
Redundant arrays of inexpensive disks (RAID), 191
Remote access, 230
ReNaChip, 142
Repetitive strain injury (RSI), 173
Report, 68
Resolution
    monitor, 162
    printer, 166
Restricting access, 255–256
Reverse directory, 243
Rewritable DVD disc drive, 193
RFID reader, 159–160
RFID tags, 159
Ribbon, 65
Ribbon GUI, 65

RIM OS, 100
Ring network, 225
Robot, 169, 231
Robot network, 252
Robotics, 169
Rogue (fake) hotspot, 224
Rogue Wi-Fi hotspots, 254
Roku, 31
ROM, 133
Router, 221, 222
RSI, 173

## s

S/PDIF, 137
Sales forecast, 69
SAN, 200
Satellite, 215
Satellite connection services, 217
Scanner, 158–159
Scanning devices, 158–160
Seagate, 201
Search engine, 43
Search services, 42
Second-generation mobile telecommunications (2G), 218
Secondary storage, 186–209
    cloud storage, 195–196, 197–198
    defined, 188
    future directions, 201
    hard disk, 189–191
    mass storage devices, 199–200
    optical disc, 192–194
    solid-state storage, 194–195
Secondary storage devices, 188
Sector, 108, 189
Secure file transfer protocol (SFTP), 50
Security, 251–260
    anticipating disasters, 260
    careers, 265
    cyberbullying, 253–254
    data manipulation, 254
    DoS attack, 253
    encrypting data, 256–260
    Internet scams, 253
    malicious programs, 251–252
    network, 228–229
    preventing data loss, 260
    restricting access, 255–256
    rogue Wi-Fi hotspots, 254
    social networking risks, 253
Security suite, 256, 257–258
Self-healing computers, 112
Semiconductor, 130
Serve, 46
Server, 11, 221
SFTP, 50
Shared laser printer, 167
Sheet name, 70
Signature, 35
Silicon chip, 130
Silverlight, 49
Skype, 169, 170–171
Slot, 129, 130
Smartphone, 126, 287, 289
Smartphone bar code reader, 159
Smith, David L., 283
Social networking, 37–38

Social networking risks, 253
Socket, 129, 130
Soft copy, 162
Software, 6. See also Application software; System software
Software engineer, 82
Software environment, 99
Software piracy, 192, 263
Software platform, 99
Software suites, 81–82
Software updates, 255
Solaris, 226
Solid-state drives (SSDs), 194
Solid-state storage, 194–195
Sony/Philips digital interconnect format (S/PDIF), 137
Sound card, 134
Spam, 36
Spam blocker, 36
Spam filter, 36
SPAMfighter, 36
Sparks, 37
Speaker, 168
Specialized applications, 73–78
Specialized apps, 80
Specialized ports, 137
Specialized search engine, 43–44
Specialized suites, 82
Specialty processors, 132
Spelling checker, 67
Spider, 42
Spreadsheets, 69, 70
Sprint, 32, 218
Spy removal programs, 249, 250
Spyware, 249
Spyware Doctor, 250
SSDs, 194
Stand-alone operating system, 99
Star network, 225–226
Stock photograph, 77
Storage, 188–189. See also Secondary storage
Storage area network (SAN), 200
Strategy, 226
Streaming, 39
Stuxnet worm, 252
Stylus, 157, 158
Subscription services, 30–31
SugarSync, 196
SUPERAntiSpyware, 250
Supercomputer, 11
Surf, 32
Surface, 84
Switch, 221, 222
Symantec Web Gateway, 50
Sync, 52
System/360 computers, 279
System board, 129–130
System bus, 135
System chassis, 124
System software, 94–121
    defined, 96
    desktop operating systems, 101–103
    device drivers, 109–110
    mobile operating systems, 100
    operating system, 97–100
    utilities, 104–109